Institutions, Resilience, and Dynamic Capabilities of Entrepreneurial Ecosystems in Emerging Economies

Shivani Inder
Chitkara Business School, Chitkara University, India

Amandeep Singh
Chitkara Business School, Chitkara University, India

Sandhir Sharma
Chitkara Business School, Chitkara University, India

A volume in the Advances in Finance, Accounting, and Economics (AFAE) Book Series

IGI Global
PUBLISHER of TIMELY KNOWLEDGE

Published in the United States of America by
IGI Global
Business Science Reference (an imprint of IGI Global)
701 E. Chocolate Avenue
Hershey PA, USA 17033
Tel: 717-533-8845
Fax: 717-533-8661
E-mail: cust@igi-global.com
Web site: http://www.igi-global.com

Library of Congress Cataloging-in-Publication Data

Names: Inder, Shivani, 1984- editor. | Singh, Amandeep, 1982- editor. | Sharma, Sandhir, 1974- editor.
Title: Institutions, resilience, and dynamic capabilities of entrepreneurial ecosystems in emerging economies / Shivani Inder, Amandeep Singh, and Sandhir Sharma, editors.
Description: Hershey, PA : Business Science Reference, [2022] | Includes bibliographical references and index. | Summary: "This book will strengthen the research into the role of entrepreneurship in economic growth in emerging economies and how entrepreneurship is shaping the future of emerging markets"-- Provided by publisher.
Identifiers: LCCN 2022012055 (print) | LCCN 2022012056 (ebook) | ISBN 9781668447451 (hardcover) | ISBN 9781668447468 (paperback) | ISBN 9781668447475 (ebook)
Subjects: LCSH: Entrepreneurship--Developing countries. | Economic development--Developing countries.
Classification: LCC HB615 .I5656 2022 (print) | LCC HB615 (ebook) | DDC 338/.049091724--dc23/eng/20220318
LC record available at https://lccn.loc.gov/2022012055
LC ebook record available at https://lccn.loc.gov/2022012056

This book is published in the IGI Global book series Advances in Finance, Accounting, and Economics (AFAE) (ISSN: 2327-5677; eISSN: 2327-5685)

British Cataloguing in Publication Data
A Cataloguing in Publication record for this book is available from the British Library.

Advances in Finance, Accounting, and Economics (AFAE) Book Series

ISSN:2327-5677
EISSN:2327-5685

Editor-in-Chief: Ahmed Driouchi, Al Akhawayn University, Morocco

MISSION

In our changing economic and business environment, it is important to consider the financial changes occurring internationally as well as within individual organizations and business environments. Understanding these changes as well as the factors that influence them is crucial in preparing for our financial future and ensuring economic sustainability and growth.

The **Advances in Finance, Accounting, and Economics (AFAE)** book series aims to publish comprehensive and informative titles in all areas of economics and economic theory, finance, and accounting to assist in advancing the available knowledge and providing for further research development in these dynamic fields.

COVERAGE

- Internet Banking
- Risk Analysis and Management
- Borrowing and Lending
- Statistical Analysis
- Economic Theory
- Economics of Natural and Environmental Resources
- Finance and Accounting in SMEs
- Entrepreneurship in Accounting and Finance
- Economics of Risks, Uncertainty, Ambiguity, and Insurance
- Theoretical Issues in Economics, Finance, and Accounting

IGI Global is currently accepting manuscripts for publication within this series. To submit a proposal for a volume in this series, please contact our Acquisition Editors at Acquisitions@igi-global.com or visit: http://www.igi-global.com/publish/.

The Advances in Finance, Accounting, and Economics (AFAE) Book Series (ISSN 2327-5677) is published by IGI Global, 701 E. Chocolate Avenue, Hershey, PA 17033-1240, USA, www.igi-global.com. This series is composed of titles available for purchase individually; each title is edited to be contextually exclusive from any other title within the series. For pricing and ordering information please visit http://www.igi-global.com/book-series/advances-finance-accounting-economics/73685. Postmaster: Send all address changes to above address.

Titles in this Series

For a list of additional titles in this series, please visit:
http://www.igi-global.com/book-series/advances-finance-accounting-economics/73685

Modern Regulations and Practices for Social and Environmental Accounting
Teresa Eugénio (Centre of Applied Research in Management and Economics (CARME), School of Technology and Management, Polytechnic Institute of Leiria, Portugal) Graça Azevedo (University of Aveiro, Portugal) and Ana Fialho (CEFAGE, University of Évora, Portugal)
Business Science Reference • © 2022 • 345pp • H/C (ISBN: 9781799894100) • US $215.00

Impact of Open Innovation on the World Economy
Orlando Lima Rua (Polytechnic of Porto, Portugal)
Business Science Reference • © 2022 • 306pp • H/C (ISBN: 9781799886655) • US $225.00

Handbook of Research on Challenges in Public Economics in the Era of Globalization
Şahin Akkaya (Istanbul University, Turkey) and Başak Ergüder (Istanbul University, Turkey)
Business Science Reference • © 2022 • 480pp • H/C (ISBN: 9781799890836) • US $295.00

Handbook of Research on Green, Circular, and Digital Economies as Tools for Recovery and Sustainability
Patricia Ordóñez de Pablos (The University of Oviedo, Spain) Xi Zhang (Tianjin University, China) and Mohammad Nabil Almunawar (Universiti Brunei Darussalam, Brunei)
Business Science Reference • © 2022 • 418pp • H/C (ISBN: 9781799896647) • US $295.00

Handbook of Research on the Significance of Forensic Accounting Techniques in Corporate Governance
Suleman Sherali Kamwani (A'Sharqiyah University, Oman) Elisabete S. Vieira (University of Aveiro, Portugal) Mara Madaleno (University of Aveiro, Portugal) and Graça Azevedo (University of Aveiro, Portugal)
Business Science Reference • © 2022 • 417pp • H/C (ISBN: 9781799887546) • US $265.00

Handbook of Research on Energy and Environmental Finance 4.0
Abdul Rafay (University of Management and Technology, Pakistan)
Business Science Reference • © 2022 • 545pp • H/C (ISBN: 9781799882107) • US $295.00

For an entire list of titles in this series, please visit:
http://www.igi-global.com/book-series/advances-finance-accounting-economics/73685

IGI Global
PUBLISHER of TIMELY KNOWLEDGE

701 East Chocolate Avenue, Hershey, PA 17033, USA
Tel: 717-533-8845 x100 • Fax: 717-533-8661
E-Mail: cust@igi-global.com • www.igi-global.com

Table of Contents

Detailed Table of Contents

This study is based on the generic value proposition concept that was emphasized in business model generation. The generic value propositions offered by international shoe brands such as Geox, Ecco, and five Turkish shoe brands were compared. Mixed approach was chosen as the research method, and a case study was conducted. The texts in the "about us" parts of the websites were analyzed. In addition, the features offered in the product groups were compared. The average product price and the discount ratios throughout the year are compared. As a result of the analysis, it was shown that Geox and Ecco firmly adhered to the generic value propositions of performance (due to the innovation) and design. In comparison, Turkish shoe brands were found to be unable to provide a clear value proposition. Although Turkish shoe firms were founded considerably earlier than their foreign counterparts, it was determined that one of the reasons for their lack of success was their inability to provide a clear value proposition to the consumers.

This chapter details social entrepreneurship. The idea of social entrepreneurship implies various things to various individuals and analysts. A few specialists allude to social businesses as not-revenue-driven businesses and others are of a different viewpoint. Being an emerging concept, social entrepreneurship has certain challenges that are faced by promoters. The chapter enlists the various developments in the

During the COVID-19 pandemic, 41.3% of companies stated they closed temporarily due to the pandemic. In the United Kingdom, 32.5% of entrepreneurs reported they were still able to work during the pandemic, compared to entrepreneurs in Norway (58.5%), Bosnia and Herzegovina (81.6%), North America (55%), and France (55.9%). In a global study for the World Economic Forum, a variety of firms were surveyed, from entrepreneur startups to music festivals, manufacturing companies, and automotive enterprises. Seventy percent of startups stated they had to terminate their full-time employees since the beginning of the COVID-19 pandemic. Only 40% of new enterprises stated they have enough revenue to last for three months of operations. Resilience, financial inclusion, education, and strategic partnerships are needed during crises to protect entrepreneurial ecosystems, especially if firms operate in economies that are emerging, possess institutional voids, institutional forces, or slow economic growth issues.

Entrepreneurial ecosystems have attracted considerable attention from different constituencies. Especially in line with the increasing numbers of start-ups, it is expected that these ecosystems will contribute to entrepreneurial activity and economic growth of a region/nation. However, most of the entrepreneurial ecosystem research and thus developed frameworks focus on advanced economies. On the other hand, ecosystems positioned in emerging economies are exposed different to institutional arrangements that influence resource allocation and entrepreneurial activity. This study argues that context is important in shaping the dynamics of an entrepreneurial ecosystem, the choices of entrepreneurs, and the interactions between the entrepreneurs and other resource providers. To illustrate this, the study focuses on an emerging economy, Turkey, and by utilizing secondary data tries to underpin the institutional voids and resource scarcities that lead to a 'shallow' entrepreneurial ecosystem.

This chapter analyzes entrepreneurship intentions in a medium-size Portuguese university that is in the top 150 of the Times Higher Education ranking for young universities. This higher education institution has grown rapidly over the last decades, has been extremely dynamic in establishing local level partnerships with business and non-business institutions, and is characterized by an environment more multidisciplinary than average with four schools occupying the same buildings (School of Sociology and Public Policy, School of Social Sciences, Business School, and School of Technology and Architecture). Using a sample of 544 students, this group of respondents ranks entrepreneurship as their preferred career choice. Analyzing the factors that influence entrepreneurial intentions, the authors find the relevance of context variables and entrepreneurship-related courses.

Entrepreneurship has long been acknowledged as a means of generating economic rewards for those involved in it. As the notion of sustainable development has emerged as a critical problem impacting the existing system, it has been suggested that it should not be limited to the generation of money alone. The field of sustainable enterprise (SE) has received a lot of academic interest in the previous 10 years. The SE literature is becoming more difficult to explore because of its fast growth and interdisciplinary nature. Because of the growth of research, there is a lack of a theoretical framework; thus, this area must be investigated, structured, and synthesised to offer clarity. The goal of this study is to give a bibliometric analysis of the field's current state. The study is conducted on a sample of 352 articles published during 2002-2022. This study's results may help both novice and experienced sustainable entrepreneurship scholars by providing a comprehensive overview of the field's development and present state.

The manufacturing industry plays a paramount role in the world economy, accounting for almost 16% of the global GDP in 2018. Manufacturing has been identified as the key driver of dynamic growth and development of the country. The COVID-19 pandemic has caused immense devastation around the world. Due to the downturn in the manufacturing industry along with the factory blackout, the coronavirus epidemic reduced the global FDI by 5-15%. This chapter aims to throw light on measures taken by manufacturers to combat the impact of the COVID-19 havoc. It will discuss how internet of things and artificial intelligence will help manufacturing industry to recover effectively and efficiently post pandemic. It would suggest a framework to manufacturing industry on how it can come back in a new normal position post-COVID-19 scenario. Manufacturers, who acknowledge the new standard policies discussed in the present paper and operate on it, will get enough growth opportunities and can have long-term sustainable success in the future.

The Indian Ocean is fundamentally related to the diverse economies, safety, reliability, and availability of jobs of its littoral zones. Notwithstanding, the amelioration in the financial and feasible issues in the edge are especially hard and tough whereas the nations, with varied political frameworks, advancement status, and plans, are home to 33% of the total populace that is widely dependent on marine resources for food. The chapter investigates the momentum administration structure of marine assets of the executives in the Indian Ocean and digs into the difficulties occurring in the blue economy improvement and prescribes approaches to propel blue economy administration to notify pressures and guarantee practical advancement in the locale, and it additionally investigates the flow administration design for blue economy and its substantial potential existing in the Indian Ocean district, especially with regards to fisheries, ecological security, and environmental change impacts.

Preface

Entrepreneurial ecosystems play an instrumental role in pushing the economic engine of an emerging economy. Understanding dynamic capabilities and resilience of entrepreneurial ecosystems in emerging economies can provide meaningful insights to achieve Sustainable Development Goals.

Further, resilient entrepreneurial ventures can play an instrumental role in overcoming institutional voids and barriers. Such insights can extended on theoretical as well as practical dimensions. The capabilities of entrepreneurial ventures offer great opportunity to realize enormous impact on the top as well as bottom line of the business. Every entrepreneurial venture, either big or small, needs valuable understanding and insights.

This book will strengthen the research in the following fields:

- Entrepreneurial perspectives on sustainability
- Organizational cultures in building organizational resilience
- Entrepreneurial intentions among next generations
- Understanding institutional voids to drive economic growth
- Role of institutions in building resilience among entrepreneurial ventures
- Sustainable Entrepreneurship

Entrepreneurial institutions play a dynamic role in understanding valuable insights on building systems to bring in resilience. From every dimension of an entrepreneurial venture, and its response to dynamic environment, we can create resilience organizations that can sustain and survive turbulent times. Entrepreneurs can leverage these insights for improving their strategic response and fetch legitimacy in industry. With these underpinnings, this book is written that will help decision makers and academicians to understand the resilience and dynamic capabilities of entrepreneurial ventures in a better way.

The books contributes to the existing literature on entrepreneurship through following chapters:

INNOVATION AS A FOUNDATION FOR CREATING GENERIC VALUE PROPOSITIONS FOR ENTREPRENEURS

This study is based on generic value proposition concept that was emphasized in "Business Model Generation". The generic value propositions offered by international shoe brands such as Geox, Ecco and five Turkish shoe brands were compared. Mixed approach was chosen as the research method, and a case study was conducted. The texts in the "about us" parts of the websites were analyzed in this section. In addition, the features offered in the product groups were compared. The average product price and the discount ratios throughout the year is compared. As a result of the analysis, it was shown that Geox and Ecco firmly adhered to the generic value propositions of performance (due to the innovation) and design. In comparison, Turkish shoe brands were found to be unable to provide a clear value proposition. Although Turkish shoe firms were founded considerably earlier than their foreign counterparts, it was determined that one of the reasons for their lack of success was their inability to provide a clear value proposition to the consumers.

SOCIAL ENTREPRENEURSHIP: DEVELOPMENTS AND CHALLENGES

This chapter details social entrepreneurship. The idea of Social Entrepreneurship implies various things to various individuals and analysts. Few specialists alludes to social business as not-revenue driven business and others are of different viewpoint. Being an emerging concept, social entrepreneurship has certain challenges which are faced by promoters. The chapter enlists the various developments in the area of social entrepreneurship and also explains the challenges faced by social entrepreneurs while going through the various phases.

SUSTAINABLE DEVELOPMENT OF BIHAR TOURISM: AN ENTREPRENEURIAL OPPORTUNITY

The entrepreneurial opportunity is found in the different segments such as accommodation, recreation and entertainment, transportation and travel services. Hotels, restaurants, tour operators and travel agents have been providing direct business opportunities to people at different levels of the local community. Bihar is a land of enlightenment and salvation. Bihar occupied an important position in the early history of India. The birthplace of Bihar has two religions i.e. Buddhism and Jainism & the birthplace of Guru Govind Singh, the 10th guru of the Sikh religion. There are many holy places for Hindus and important places for the Gandhian movement. Bihar is rich in spiritual, heritage, cultural and recreation places. The total share of tourism is 11.99% of Bihar SGDP and the 11th largest wage earner in revenue with $3.13 billion in 2017. This chapter brings in tourism as an economic area where entrepreneurial sector requires high level of involvement. Further, diversification of tourism products and services is required to meet the rising demand for new sorts of tourism demands.

DEVELOPMENT OF NEW ENERGY VEHICLES IN ENTREPRENEURIAL ECOSYSTEM UNDER THE CARBON NEUTRALITY POLICY IN CHINA

This chapter aims to study how new energy vehicles develop in entrepreneurial ecosystem under the Carbon Neutrality policy in China. This chapter explores the roles of government after the 14th Five-year plan in promoting the sustainability of development of new energy vehicles through policies (i.e. institutions). How do these institutions promote the development of environmental awareness in various industries? How these developments will in turn affect environment in various sectors. This chapter will investigate the impact of China's environmental research and institutional changes of enterprises under the sustainable aims of carbon neutrality. This chapter performs statistical and correlation analysis mainly on the carbon neutrality, carbon trading market, development of new energy vehicles and ESG investment. Cases from China will be used for explanations. This chapter provide suggestions for the development of new energy vehicles and investment under China's environment-based ecosystems.

ASSESSING GOVERNMENT INITIATIVES TOWARDS THE DEVELOPMENT OF ENTREPRENEURSHIP IN INDIA

Entrepreneurs are playing a significant role in economic development. Entrepreneurs create jobs, alleviate poverty, maintain demand supply equilibrium, and solve a number of problems of an economy. It leads to increase in GDP and makes country self-reliant. This makes it possible if participation from all sections of society contribute in self-development and self-employability. Indian government has taken many initiatives to make entrepreneurship a successful model and also to strengthen this innovation ecosystem. The main purpose of such initiatives is to promote entrepreneurship solutions for economic sustainability and growth. This chapter highlights the current innovative ecosystem of entrepreneurship and the challenges it faces. It also highlights the initiatives taken by the Indian government for the promotion of entrepreneurship development in India.

ENTREPRENEURIAL ECOSYSTEMS RESILIENCE AND INSTITUTIONAL VOIDS: SOLUTIONS FOR EMERGING ECONOMIES TO DRIVE ECONOMIC GROWTH

During the COVID-19 pandemic, 41.3% of companies stated they closed temporarily due to pandemic. In the United Kingdom, 32.5% of entrepreneurs reported they were still able to work during the pandemic, compared to entrepreneurs in Norway (58.5%), Bosnia and Herzegovina (81.6%), North America (55%), and France (55.9%) (Stephan et al., 2021). In a global study for the World Economic Forum, a variety of firms were surveyed, from entrepreneur's startups to music festivals, manufacturing companies, and automotive enterprises. Too, 70% of startups stated they had to terminate their full-time employees, since the beginning of the COVID-19 pandemic. Only 40% of new enterprises stated they have enough revenue to last for less than three months of operations. Resilience, financial inclusion, education, and strategic partnerships are needed during crises to protect entrepreneurial ecosystems. Especially if firms operate in economies that are emerging, possess institutional voids, institutional forces, or slow economic growth issues.

ENTREPRENEURSHIP ECOSYSTEMS AND INNOVATION: A STUDY IN AN EMERGING ECONOMY, TURKEY

Entrepreneurial ecosystems have attracted considerable attention from different constituencies. Especially in line with the increasing numbers of start-ups, it is expected that these ecosystems will contribute to entrepreneurial activity and economic growth of a region/nation. However, most of the entrepreneurial ecosystem research and thus developed frameworks focus on advanced economies. On the other hand, ecosystems positioned in emerging economies are exposed different to institutional arrangements that influence resource allocation and entrepreneurial activity. This chapter argues that context is important in shaping the dynamics of an entrepreneurial ecosystem, the choices of entrepreneurs and the interactions between the entrepreneurs and other resource providers. To illustrate this, the study focuses on an emerging economy-Turkey-and by utilizing secondary data tries to underpin the institutional voids and resource scarcities that lead to a 'shallow' entrepreneurial ecosystem.

ENTREPRENEURIAL INTENTIONS OF UNIVERSITY STUDENTS: WHAT ARE THE DIFFERENCES AMONG SCIENTIFIC AREAS?

This chapter analyzes entrepreneurship intentions in a medium-size Portuguese university that is in the top 150 of the Times Higher Education ranking for young universities. This higher education institution has grown rapidly over the last decades, has been extremely dynamic in establishing local level partnerships with business and non-business institutions, and is characterized by an environment more multidisciplinary than average with four schools occupying the same buildings (School of Sociology and Public Policy, School of Social Sciences, Business School, and School of Technology and Architecture). Using a sample of 544 students, this group of respondents ranks entrepreneurship as their preferred career choice. Analyzing the factors that influence entrepreneurial intentions we find the relevance of context variables and entrepreneurship-related courses.

SUSTAINABLE ENTREPRENEURSHIP: A BIBLIOMETRIC ANALYSIS

Entrepreneurship has long been acknowledged as a means of generating economic rewards for those involved in it. As the notion of sustainable development has emerged as a critical problem impacting the existing system, it has been suggested that it should not be limited to the generation of money alone. The SE literature is becoming more difficult to explore because of its fast growth and interdisciplinary nature. Due to growth of research and theoretical framework, this chapter investigates, structures and synthesizes the literature and conduct bibliometric analysis of the field's current state. The chapter present results of 352 articles published during 2002-2022. The chapter would contribute to provide a comprehensive overview of the field's development and present state.

AN INTERROGATION OF ENTREPRENEUR PERSPECTIVES ON THE NEXUS OF SUSTAINABILITY AND ENTREPRENEURSHIP: SUSTAINABLE ENTREPRENEURSHIP

Understanding the effects of entrepreneurs' intentions towards sustainable entrepreneurship can be an initial step in developing sustainable entrepreneurs. Limited research has been conducted on the intention of practicing entrepreneurs, specifically among owners of SMMEs (Small, Medium and Micro Enterprises) towards sustainable entrepreneurship. Previous research focused on a traditional entrepreneurial process, with limited studies having been done to investigate the intentions of entrepreneurs to engage in sustainable entrepreneurship. Studies focusing on intention towards sustainable entrepreneurship are limited, more so in South Africa. To fill this research vacuum, this chapter provides insights on entrepreneurs' perceptions of sustainable entrepreneurship. The chapter reveals that entrepreneurs' intentions to adopt sustainable practices were driven by subjective standards, their views toward sustainability, and their perceived behavioural controls. From a managerial standpoint, this chapter recommends that SMMEs match their business operations with their stakeholders' values.

ANALYTICAL IMPACT OF DIGITAL MARKETING ON SMART WEARABLES IN INDIA

Advancement in innovation and technology has transformed the lifestyle of individuals. Individuals are experiencing, which they would have hardly imagined about years back and was seen as inconceivable, truly. Wearable innovation is an old style case of such insight. Despite the fact that this innovation is common for quite a while, yet the future of wearable development begins when the model of Google Glass was concocted. It helped clients to start thinking past this present reality. Preceding the prototype, customers were uninformed about wearable development. In the 21st century, wearable innovation has purchased new advancements which has helped wearables to take off in the mechanical market. While it is intended to study the awareness of Smart Wearables, it is also synthesized to identify the key perceptions about smart wearables in the study. It is further being analysed to check the influence of digital marketing in purchase decision for Smart wearables with specific focus on all digital platforms.

INSTITUTIONALIZATION OF SPATIAL RESOURCES IN PARTICIPATORY GOVERNANCE SYSTEM

The chapter analyzes the implications of the institutionalization process of spatial resources in participatory governance system. It departs from the assumption that the institutional participatory governance policy as a political option has a chronic neglect despite the omnipresent decision making authority, there is not binding authoritative allocation of values, public support, and the distribution of resources with a growing acceptance among the non-institutional space. The method employed is the analytic reflective thinking based on the theoretical and empirical review of the literature. It is concluded that the allocation of values and spatial resources from the institutional state power to society requires to develop in adequate in spatial form and new modes of participatory governance system in which actors and stakeholders through political actions allocate values and spatial resources to deal legitimately and effectively in the context of unity for the notion of common good for the community.

CONCEPTUAL INSTITUTIONAL ELEMENTS OF PARTICIPATORY GOVERNANCE

This chapter aims to analyze the conceptual elements of institutional participatory governance from an institutional perspective. It is assumed that behind the efforts to increase institutional participation in governance through the inclusion of minority groups may lead to fairer and responsive government. The analysis is also based on the assumption that participation models applied to institutions as legal and political instruments to foster regional mobilization and citizenship participation lead to the merging of the concepts of institutions, participation, and governance. It is concluded that the conceptual framework of institutional participation in governance is related to projects focusing the domains of politics of life issues and concerns.

SMART TECHNOLOGIES: NEW NORMAL MANUFACTURING INDUSTRY 2020

Manufacturing Industry plays a paramount role in the world economy, accounting for almost 16% of the global GDP in 2018. Manufacturing has been identified as the key driver of dynamic growth and development of the country. The COVID-19 pandemic has caused immense devastation around the world. Due to the downturn in the manufacturing industry along with the factory blackout, the Coronavirus epidemic reduced the global FDI by 5 per cent -15 per cent (UNCTAD). This chapter aims to throw light on measures taken by manufacturers to combat the impact of COVID 19 havoc. It discusses how Internet of things and artificial Intelligence help manufacturing industry to recover effectively and efficiently post pandemic. It would suggest a framework to manufacturing industry on how it can come back in a new normal position post-COVID-19 scenario. This chapter suggest standard policies which would provide enough growth opportunities and long term sustainable success in the future.

BLUE ECONOMY: AN EMERGING BUSINESS AND EMPLOYMENT PROSPECTS IN INDIAN OCEAN

The Indian Ocean is fundamentally related to the diverse economies, safety, reliability, and availability of jobs of its littoral zones. Notwithstanding, the amelioration in the financial and feasible issues in the edge are especially hard and tough whereas the nations, with varied political frameworks, advancement status, and plans, are home to 33 percent of the total populace that is widely dependent on marine resources for food. This chapter investigates the momentum administration structure of marine assets the executives in the Indian Ocean digs into the difficulties occurring in the blue economy improvement and prescribes approaches to propel blue economy administration to notify pressures and guarantee practical advancement in the locale and it additionally investigates the flow administration design for Blue Economy and it's substantial potential existing in the Indian Ocean district, especially with regards to fisheries, ecological security, and environmental change impacts.

The chapters in this book would help researchers and academicians to gain insights on entrepreneurship, resilience, dynamic capabilities of organizations and its implications on enterprises. We hope and expect that this book would motivate future research on the same lines.

Shivani Inder
Chitkara Business School, Chitkara University, India

Amandeep Singh
Chitkara Business School, Chitkara University, India

Sandhir Sharma
Chitkara Business School, Chitkara University, India

Chapter 1
Innovation as a Foundation for Creating Generic Value Propositions for Entrepreneurs

Murat Unanoglu
https://orcid.org/0000-0002-5186-885X
İstanbul Aydin University, Turkey

ABSTRACT

This study is based on the generic value proposition concept that was emphasized in business model generation. The generic value propositions offered by international shoe brands such as Geox, Ecco, and five Turkish shoe brands were compared. Mixed approach was chosen as the research method, and a case study was conducted. The texts in the "about us" parts of the websites were analyzed. In addition, the features offered in the product groups were compared. The average product price and the discount ratios throughout the year are compared. As a result of the analysis, it was shown that Geox and Ecco firmly adhered to the generic value propositions of performance (due to the innovation) and design. In comparison, Turkish shoe brands were found to be unable to provide a clear value proposition. Although Turkish shoe firms were founded considerably earlier than their foreign counterparts, it was determined that one of the reasons for their lack of success was their inability to provide a clear value proposition to the consumers.

INTRODUCTION

In recent years, the term value proposition has become one of the most commonly used expressions in business in recent years (Anderson et al., 2006). However, as Lanning (2003) notes, the concept of value proposition is usually used in a very

DOI: 10.4018/978-1-6684-4745-1.ch001

casual and trivial way, rather than being rigorously developed from a strategic standpoint. Most companies do not have clearly articulated value propositions. Frow and Payne (2012) studied more than 200 companies and found that while many companies use the term in their everyday conversations, less than 10 percent formally develop, communicate, and use value propositions. While all companies have some form of value proposition, whether implicit or explicit, they argue that the lack of specifically targeted formal activities involving the development of an overarching value proposition is likely to hinder the market success of many companies. (Frow and Payne, 2014)

Volvo cars can be considered as a traditional example of clearly defined value proposition. Volvo cars have been the first brand that comes to mind when it comes to "safe cars" for years. This is not because their vehicles are safer than other brands in the similar segments. Checking the vehicle safety tests carried out by the Euro NCAP organization will show that different brands are also awarded 5 Star out of 5. (Euro NCAP 2021) It makes sense to ask How come Volvo is the first thing that comes to mind when consumers say safety? Volvo's history has lots of safety related innovations (Volvo, 2021) that eventually builds up a big story with the center theme of "safety".

However, the aim of this study is not to show the importance of innovation. Innovation Value proposition may benefit from innovations so that a company can deliver new kind of solutions to customer problems and needs. In this way they can differentiate themselves much clearly which is a potential of getting better business results. We will try to show you how vital the difference is between an ambiguous value proposition and a clear value proposition developed using innovation.

LITERATURE REVIEW

Value Proposition

Propositions in the context of marketing have been around for about 100 years; prior to the development of the customer value proposition (CVP). From its early beginnings in advertising (Starch 1914; Hopkins 1923; Ogilvy 1947), the concept of the unique selling proposition (USP) was developed (Reeves 1961). Over the next several decades, other variations of selling points emerged, for example, the emotional selling point in the 1960s (Lindstrom 2005). However, it was not until the 1970s and 1980s that this proposition, which refers to consumers' emotional attachment to a product, became more widely recognized. Urban and Hauser (1980) also proposed a core benefits proposition that identifies the product's benefits and "fulfillment of product promises through physical attributes" (p. 155). This statement should be the major aspect on which all elements of the marketing strategy are built. To describe their approach, the authors used a new product design context that involves developing, evaluating, refining, and fulfilling the core benefits proposition. They argued that companies should care about finding breakthrough products. These early offering concepts preceded the development of the CVP concept. The CVP concept originated with strategy consultants (Bower and Garda 1986; Lanning 1998) who sought to solve the problems of a production-oriented organization. Their definition of a CVP goes like this: why customers should buy the company's goods and services. To this end, the CVP was the "precise benefit or utility offered at what price to what group of customers at what cost" (Lanning and Michaels 1988, p. 3). It took a decade for the concept to become common knowledge. A best-selling book on value disciplines (Treacy and Wiersema 1995) increased awareness and interest; examples of value maps (Kambil et al. 1996) also helped reflect alternative representations of value and price in CVPs.

A customer value proposition (CVP) is a strategic tool that an enterprise uses to communicate how it will deliver value to its customers. As one of the most widely used terms in business (Anderson et al. 2006), a value proposition should also be "the company's most important organizing principle" (Webster 2002, p. 61) because it is critical to the value creation process (Payne and Frow 2005) and has significant impact on performance. Harris DeLoach, chief executive officer of Sonoco Products, notes that distinctive value propositions derived from a rigorous assessment of customer value have been a major contributor to Sonoco's business performance (Anderson et al. 2007). This evidence is consistent with the origins of the CVP concept, which was developed by strategy consultants in the early 1980s to implement market orientations in manufacturing-oriented companies (Michaels 2008).

The concept evolved further when Lanning (2000) broadened his original perspective and describes the value proposition as a complete set of experiences, including value for money, that customers get from the organization. Customers may consider this set of experiences to be "better, equal, or worse than counterparts." According to Buttle, A value proposition is a clear promise that a company will deliver a specific package of value-creating benefits to its customers (Buttle, 2009). In other words, "the value proposition is a written statement focusing all the organization's market activities onto customer critical elements that create a significant differential within the customer's decision process, to prefer and/or purchase the organization's offering over a competitor's" (Fifield, 2007). Rintamaki et al. (2007) defined a value proposition as "an encapsulation of a strategic management decision on what the company believes its customers value the most and what it is able to deliver in a way that gives it competitive advantage". Similarly, Frow and Payne (2011) described A value proposition is a product or service that a company offers to customers in exchange for a promise of benefits that the customer would receive both during and after use. Taken together, these ideas suggest that businesses may build, control, and communicate value propositions (Vargo, 2020).

Given that the value proposition is a company's most important organizing principle (Webster, 2002) and that few companies formally develop, communicate, and use value propositions, exploring how leading flagship companies formally develop their value propositions is an important area of management practice to which research should pay attention.

Although the concept is widely used, both scholars and practitioners report a lack of understanding and poor implementation. The lack of a definition of value that everyone agrees on is an important shortcoming (Ballantyne et al. 2011; Skålén et al. 2015), and Lanning (2003, p. 4) defines that the term value proposition ... "unfortunately, is often casually thrown around and trivially applied" rather than "in a much more strategic, rigorous, and actionable way."

In short, a positioning statement represents the key differentiators in the minds of consumers (Ries and Trout 1986) and is usually considered part of an advertising or integrated marketing communications plan. In contrast to the narrower focus of a positioning statement, a business model is a broader concept; many authors consider the value proposition to be a core element of the business model (e.g., Chesbrough and Rosenbloom 2002).

From this perspective Alexander Osterwalder and Yves Pigneur (2010) brings a comprehensive definition to the literature and put the value proposition to the center of the business model. According to their definition generic value propositions in their book as follows:

- Performance
- Newness
- Customization
- "getting the job done"
- Design,
- Brand/status,
- Price
- Cost reduction
- Risk reduction
- Accessibility
- Convenience/usability

The performance value proposition can cover many different themes. Moving on from the Volvo example, embracing a value such as safety in the automobile industry is essentially a kind of performance element. Tesla cars markets their vehicles with two kinds of performance themes. The first is the very fast 0- 100 km/h models (which offer better acceleration than many super sports cars). The second is that it offers long-range vehicles compared to many of its competitors (Model 3 has a range of 415 km with standard batteries, 560 km with optional additional batteries). In addition, the fact that electric motor vehicles are more environmentally friendly compared to internal combustion engine vehicles is also a performance factor (Unanoğlu, 2019).

Newness is always trying to be one step ahead of competitors in relation to the business for which the value proposition is made. The Dyson brand has internalized the newness value proposition. It differentiates itself by incorporating various innovations in every product it offers to the market compared to its equivalent products.

Customization is making special products according to the customer's needs. This can be for individually made products (like the Brioni brand often does a tailor made business), or it can be customizing the products for each customer when mass- producing.

Getting job done is basically trying to do a job that the customer must do. As an example, we can give Do&Co company taking over the catering services of airlines. The design value proposition includes differentiation by offering superior design from similar products. This superiority can focus on ease of use, or it can only focus on being visually different. We can give an example that Braun company designs electrical personal care devices based on the Bauhaus school. Many of the products he designed in this way receive awards in design competitions such as Good Design, IF, and Red Dot. The brand/status value proposition focuses on the belief that owning an existing product will lead to status. In general, most luxury brands are brand/ status based. They achieve this not only by being expensive but also by being rare (by consciously operating at low production capacity). For example, Patek Philippe from Switzerland, one of the most luxurious watch brands, produces around 40,000 watches a year, for most models it takes a few years to wait in line.

The price value proposition is to offer the customer the lowest possible price compared to equivalent products of similar quality. This value proposition can find its way into any business. Ryan Air, BİM, LC Waikiki can be given as examples to companies in our country focused on this value proposition.

The cost reduction value proposition focuses on reducing the customer's high costs for a must-have resource. One of the examples in this area is that Sale Force offers large companies the opportunity to use their own cloud services without purchasing high-cost corporate software.

Firms focusing on risk reduction value proposition offer various guarantees against the negativities that the customer may experience regarding the product they will purchase, with the standard or additional services they offer. For example, we can give 6-month or 1-year limited or extended warranties offered by companies such as Otokoç or DOD, which sell used vehicles.

The easy-to-use value proposition focuses on thinking about user experience and delivering a much better experience than the competition. In this regard, we can give an example that when Instagram first came out, it separated from its competitors in user experience by offering easy photo sharing in three steps and became the application preferred by consumers for sharing photos.

According to the Alexander Osterwalder and Yves Pigneur, a value propostion should be clear and distinctive. Looking at the companies that have achieved great successes, it is seen that they concentrate their work around two or three value propositions that may be related to each other.

The values offered by high end watch brands are brand/status and design. According to the specific preference of the customer, the value proposition of "personality" can be added to these value propositions.

We can count the value propositions offered by the Dyson brand as newness, design and performance. Therefore, we can see these values in every product of Dyson. The reverse is also true. Whoever tries to deliver all generic value propositions at the same time fails to do any of them. Because the distinctive feature disappears. This result seems to complement Porter's warning as well (1980). "To determine how to win, an organization must decide what will enable it to create unique value and sustainably deliver that value to customers in a way that is distinct from the firm's competitors. " "Michael Porter called it competitive advantage—the specific way a firm utilizes its advantages to create superior value for a consumer or a customer and in turn, superior returns for the firm." (Lafley and Martin, 2013) According to Porter, firms should decide to follow one of the two main themes to gain a competitive advantage over competitors. These are: differentiation or low cost. Firms that pursue at least one generic strategy outperformed firms identified as "stuck in the middle." Stuck in the middle means having no clear competitive advantage over competitors. As a result, businesses fail.

In this perspective, the "differentiation" theme is also goes in hand with all generic values but "cost". Porter's low-cost theme goes in line with the "cost" as a generic value. Holding on persistently to the relevant generic value/s may be a key for business success for companies.

Innovation

According to the Oslo Manual, "A business innovation is a new or improved product or business process (or combination thereof) that differs significantly from the firm's previous products or business processes and that has been introduced on the market or brought into use by the firm."

A product innovation is a new or improved good or service that differs significantly from the firm's previous goods or services and that has been introduced on the market. Product can be considered either as a good (tangible objects) or a service (intangible activities). A business process innovation is a new or improved business process for one or more business functions that differs significantly from the firm's previous business processes and that has been brought into use in the firm (OECD, 2018). In this sense, Schumpeter's views on how organizations seek out new opportunities and gain a competitive edge over current or potential competitors have had a significant influence. To describe the disruption of existing economic activity caused by innovations that generate new ways of producing goods or services, or totally new industries, Schumpeter coined the term "creative destruction." This paradigm has been employed in the economic growth literature to explore the drivers of long-term economic growth.

When viewed as an economic activity, innovation necessitates the use of resources that could otherwise be put to better use. The presence of opportunity costs means that the actors involved in an innovation activity are likely to seek some form of value creation (or value preservation). As a result, value is an implicit aim of innovation, but it cannot be guaranteed ex ante due to the uncertainty and heterogeneity of innovation outcomes.

Nevertheless, the enormous number of big successes in business life helped to popularize the innovation concept from the early beginnings of industrial revolution. Josiah Wedgwood began his ceramic innovations with the introduction of creamware tableware, made from refined earthenware with a lead glaze in 1760s. Not only the product innovation but also he made innovation about marketing processes such as: direct mail, money-back guarantees, free delivery, celebrity endorsement, illustrated catalogues and buy one get one free came from Josiah Wedgwood. The company still operates as one of the most luxurious player in the tableware field (Wedgwood, 2020). Similar successes had been achieved by Ford with moving assembly line which was a big innovation for 1910s. McDonalds brothers developed a service system which helped them to deliver hamburgers less than a minute in 1950s as a result initiated for fast-food phenomena.

As can be shown, effective innovations have a significant business counterpart, regardless of whether they are product or process innovations. This phenomena still continues such as the more a company put innovation as a first priority the more they grow (BCG, 2015).

METHODOLOGY

Mixed research method was adopted in this study. Samples chosen from national shoes companies and European shoe companies that are in the same segment by analyzing their product portfolio and average shoe price. Secondary data sources were collected. As a data source, the about sections of the websites where the companies tell their own history were subjected to text analysis. Also the advertisements of these brands evaluated by content analysis lens. In addition, average price of the main product groups were examined through PPP lens to make a viable comparison. The number of sale days throughout the year were compared. The benefits supplied to the user in product features were investigated. This study was conducted from the standpoint of generic value proposition.

CASE ANALYSIS

According to the "about us" section of Geox, they are Italian shoe brand later on added apparel in its product line founded by Mario Polegato. In the following years they opened stores in other countries and became an international brand operating more than thirty countries. The Geox brand states that it produces products for consumers with medium and upper middle economic power. The equivalent brands of Geox in Turkey from economic segmentation perspective are Kemal Tanca, Hotiç, İnci Deri, Desa and Derimod. The last two brands are entered into shoe business after spending more than twenty years in leather clothing and bags. All Turkish brands were founded before Geox. In some, the second or third generation has taken over. ECCO owns and manages practically every aspect of the value chain from tanneries and shoe manufacturing to wholesale and retail activities. ECCO's products are sold in 101 countries from over 2,250 ECCO shops and more than 14,000 sales points. We can refer to the Table 1 to compare basic figures on these initiatives.(Geox; Hotiç; Kemal Tanca; İnci Deri; Derimod; Capital; Desa; 2022). When Geox's corporate page is examined, there is a lot of information about its establishment story and the technologies it produces. Almost all this information, sometimes directly and sometimes indirectly, says: "we provide our customers with tangible additional benefits". The tangible added benefit here is not making or selling shoes. The benefit is the additional things the customer gets when they buy the shoe from Geox. These benefits are always align with Geox's generic value propositions. Looking to the Table 2 will show us the Generic Value Propositons that the brands provides to their consumers. Ecco tells that their work is based on quality craftsmanship, and we challenge convention as we strive for uniqueness. "Innovation is a cornerstone in ECCO. We are constantly seeking to disrupt and provide improvements for the footwear and leather industry. To us, innovation is all about defining new standards, and we acknowledge that we cannot lean back and build the future on experience alone." (Ecco, 2022)

This can be seen in the Table 2, both Geox and Ecco invest in technologies to develop new and innovative materials that helps them to produce products that deliver performance value proposition.

Table 1. Basic figures about the brands

Brand	Foundation	Products	Store No
Geox	1995	Shoes&Apperal	867
Ecco	1963	Shoes	2250
Desa	1972	Shoes&Apperal	290
Derimod	1974	Shoes&Apperal	118
Kemal Tanca	1950	Shoes	130
Hotiç	1938	Shoes	162
İnci Deri	1947	Shoes	108

Table 2. Generic Value Propositions comparison of brands

Brand	Generic Value Proposition	Roots of the Value Proposition
Geox	Performance, Design	Ergonomic, water resistant, thermoregulation breathability
Ecco	Performance, Design	Unique style, quality & sustainable leather
Desa	Not clear	Nothing particular
Derimod	Not clear	Nothing particular
Kemal Tanca	Not clear	Nothing particular
Hotiç	Not clear	Nothing particular
İnci Deri	Not clear	Nothing particular

For each brand there are similar product subgroups for shoes. These are sneakers, classical everyday shoe (casual shoes), formal shoes (moccasins) and boots. We looked for the average price for these groups which usually starts on similar range in the beginning of each season. But the Turkish brands prefers to make discounts without any particular reason such as "end of season" or so. These sale campaigns mentioned in the Table 3 longs throughout the year with an average of % 65 discount on the first price tag. The discount may go up to % 85 if a consumer buy two or three pairs in the same transaction.

Table 3. Average price and discount comparison of brands

Brand	Average First Price (€)	Average Discount	Days with discount in a year
Geox	90	% 40	125
Ecco	120	% 40	110
Desa	80	% 60	180
Derimod	70	% 65	260
Kemal Tanca	100	% 65	270
Hotiç	90	% 70	263
İnci Deri	60	% 75	287

In comparison, it is seen that the "about us" sections of the corporate websites of Turkish shoe brands and the texts describing the history of the brand are written only from a commercial point of view. The story, which starts in a small shop as a theme, reaches hundreds of shops over time. Some brands have opened shops in several different countries. Some brands have emphasized that they use quality products in their stories, but the quality here is a very general statement and cannot be considered as a differentiator from competitors. The main issue here is that while telling the history of Turkish brands, he did not mention what benefit it offers to the consumer. Instead of telling the benefit it offers to the consumer, brands have told their commercial life stories that started from scratch. This point of view reflects the point of view of company executives. It is not enough to explain how much they have grown in revenue instead of the benefit offered to the consumer. The brands that did this tried to survive only with price competition in the next step. This is a major obstacle to their growth.

Looking at the Table 1, it can seen that Geox, and particularly Ecco are the young brands. Despite this, both reached a larger business volume than all other Turkish brands combined. There may be many reasons for this, but when viewed from a generic value proposition point of view, it is necessary to ask: Are these brands any different from Turkish brands? Geox has been giving a clear answer to this since the day it was founded. "Breathing shoes" is Geox's promise to its customers, and they have defined it as the mission of creating people's well-being and absolute comfort since its establishment. Geox shoes offer tangible additional benefits.

These can be listed as breathable and sweatproof shoes, waterproof shoes for wet environments, and comfortable-soled shoes suitable for walking. We are used to seeing these features in boots produced for mountaineering, but Geox offers these features in casual shoes and even in classic leather (loafers) shoes to be worn with a suit. Looking at all this, we can say that Geox focuses on providing performance and design value propositions. Of course, behind these value propositions is investing in R&D. Maybe one sentence will sum it all up. Geox has obtained 55 different patents for its innovations and 11 patent applications are at the approval stage.

Ecco emphasizes about premium leathers, sustainability, technology, and performance materials such as 100% waterproof GORE-TEX membranes, Michelin rubber outsoles and phorene midsoles. With eco-progressive developments such as water-saving DriTan™ technology, they are paving the way for a more sustainable future in the leather tanning industry. In order to create the most comfortable footwear imaginable, they use a wide variety of cutting-edge technological innovations that are exclusive to ECCO shoes. From FLUIDFORM™ to SHOCK THRU, their modern and sophisticated tech provides the most pleasant wearing experience possible.

Considering the product features, the shoe models in Turkish brands do not emphasize any feature such as ergonomic, resistance to harsh weather conditions etc. but only price. And lack of original shoe design was also a shared feature of these brands. The shoes on sale were of very similar design and their prices were very close to each other. From this point of view, it can be concluded that Turkish shoe brands do not have a clear value proposition. Since they could not differentiate otherwise, they have entered the spiral of price competition and as a result faced with low profitability.

According to Banker et al. (2014), both cost leadership and differentiation strategy have a positive impact on contemporaneous performance. However, the differentiation strategy enables a firm to maintain its current performance in the future to a greater extent than the cost leadership strategy.

Nandakumar et al. (2011) also show that companies that pursue one of the strategies, cost leadership or differentiation, perform better than stuck-in-the-middle companies that do not have a dominant strategic orientation. This supports Porter's view that combination strategies are unlikely to be effective in companies. However, cost leadership and differentiation strategies were not strongly correlated with financial performance measures, indicating the limitations of Porter's generic strategies in explaining performance heterogeneity in firms.

CONCLUSION

In this study, we tried to show how shoe companies relate their innovation to generic value propositions. When we look at it in general terms, there is no Turkish shoe brand that constantly strives for innovation. But they also not into the cost leadership strategy due to their nature of operations. This situation makes all brands the same in the eyes of the consumer. As a result, they could not offer a net value proposition. Lack of value proposition makes them fight in the competition with discounts, in other words loose blood in the price war.

In contrast, successfully growing companies are also consistently innovating to support them, consistent with their generic value proposition. We do not intend to attribute business success to this reason alone. However, it seems that there is a correlation. The opposite is also true. Firms that cannot offer a clear value proposition cannot go beyond a certain size, experience economic difficulties, and even go bankrupt.

We thought that this deficiency is one of the main reasons why Turkish shoe brands have not grown as fast as their international competitors and have not been successful in the international arena.

REFERENCES

Anderson, J. C., Kumar, N., & Narus, J. A. (2007). *Value merchants: Demonstrating and documenting superior value in business markets.* Harvard Business Press.

Anderson, J., Narus, J., & Van Rossum, W. (2006). Customer value propositions in business markets. *Harvard Business Review, 84*(3), 91–99. PMID:16515158

Ballantyne, D., Frow, P., Varey, R. J., & Payne, A. (2011). Value propositions as communication practice. *Industrial Marketing Management, 40*(2), 202–210. doi:10.1016/j.indmarman.2010.06.032

Banker, R. D., Mashruwala, R., & Tripathy, A. (2014). Does a differentiation strategy lead to more sustainable financial performance than a cost leadership strategy? *Management Decision.* Advance online publication. doi:10.1108/MD-05-2013-0282

Bower, M., & Garda, R. A. (1986). The role of marketing in management. In V. P. Buell (Ed.), Handbook of Modern Marketing (pp. 1–3–1-15). New York: McGraw-Hill.

Buttle, F. (2009). *Customer relationship management: Concepts and technologies.* Routledge.

Capital. (n.d.). https://www.capital.com.tr/is-dunyasi/soylesiler/umit-beyin-2020-plani?sayfa=6

Chesbrough, H., & Rosenbloom, R. S. (2002). The role of the business model in capturing value from innovation: Evidence from Xerox Corporation's technology spin-off companies. *Industrial and Corporate Change*, *11*(3), 529–555. doi:10.1093/icc/11.3.529

Derimod. (n.d.). https://www.derimod.com.tr/hakkimizda

Desa. (n.d.). https://www.desa.com.tr/hakkimizda

Ecco. (2022). *About Us*. https://group.ecco.com/en/about-us

Euro NCAP. (n.d.). https://www.euroncap.com/en/ratings-rewards/latest- safety- ratings/#?selectedMake=0&selectedMakeName=Select%20a%20make&selectedModel=0&selectedStar=&includeFullSafetyPackage=true&includeStandardSafetyPackage=true&selectedModelName=All&selectedProtocols=417

Euro NCAP. (2021, November 18). *Latest Safety Ratings*. Author.

Fifield, P. (2007). *Marketing Strategy Masterclass: Making Marketing Strategy Happen*. Butterworth-Heinemann.

Frow, P., & Payne, A. (2012). *Diagnosing the value proposition*. Working paper, Discipline of Marketing, University of Sydney.

Hopkins, C. (1923). *Scientific advertising*. Crown Publishers Inc.

Hotiç. (n.d.). *Markamız*. https://www.hotic.com.tr/pages/markamiz

Houston, F. S. (1986). The marketing concept: What it is and what it is not. *Journal of Marketing*, *50*(2), 81–87. doi:10.1177/002224298605000207

İnci Deri. (n.d.). http://kurumsal.incideri.com/

Kambil, A., Ginsberg, A., & Bloch, M. (1996). Re-inventing value propositions. In *Information systems working paper series stern #IS-96-21*. University.

Kemal Tanca. (n.d.). https://www.kemaltanca.com.tr/hakkimizda-sc52ab

Lafley, A. G., & Martin, R. L. (2013). *Playing to win: How strategy really works*. Harvard Business Press.

Lanning, M. (1998). *Delivering profitable value*. Perseus Publishing.

Lanning, M. (2000). *An Introduction to the Market-Focused Philosophy, Framework and Methodology Called Delivering Profitable Value*. Available: http://www.exubrio.com/white-papers/DPVIntro- eXubrio.pdf

Lanning, M. (2003). *An introduction to the market-focused philosophy, framework and methodology called delivering profitable value*. Academic Press.

Lanning, M., & Michaels, E. (1988). *A business is a value delivery system*. McKinsey Staff Paper No. 41.

Lindstrom, M. (2005). *Brand sense: Build powerful brands through touch, taste, smell, sight, and sound*. Free Press.

Martinez, V., & Bititci, U. S. (2006). Aligning value propositions in supply chains. *International Journal of Value Chain Management, 1*(1), 6–18.

Nandakumar, M. K., Ghobadian, A., & O'Regan, N. (2011). Generic strategies and performance–evidence from manufacturing firms. *International Journal of Productivity and Performance Management*.

OECD/Eurostat. (2018). *Oslo Manual 2018: Guidelines for Collecting, Reporting and Using Data on Innovation* (4th ed.). OECD Publishing. doi:10.1787/9789264304604-en

Ogilvy, D. (1947). *Correspondence to Rosser reeves from David Ogilvy. In 1 August 1947. Rosser Reeves Papers*. Wisconsin Historical Society.

Osterwalder, A., & Pigneur, Y. (2010). *Business model generation*. Academic Press.

Frow, P. (2011). A. Payne A stakeholder perspective of the value proposition concept. *European Journal of Marketing*, *45*(1–2), 223–240.

Payne, A., & Frow, P. (2005). A strategic framework for customer relationship management. *Journal of Marketing, 69*(4), 167–176.

Payne, A., & Frow, P. (2014). Developing superior value propositions: A strategic marketing imperative. *Journal of Service Management*.

Porter, M. E. (1980). Competitive strategy. New York: Free Press.

Reeves, R. (1961). *Reality in advertising*. Knopf.

Ries, A., & Trout, J. (1986). *Positioning: The battle for your mind*. McGraw-Hill.

Vargo, S. L. (2020). From promise to perspective: Reconsidering value propositions from a service-dominant logic orientation. *Industrial Marketing Management, 87*, 309–311.

Skålén, P., Gummerus, J., von Koskull, C., & Magnusson, P. R. (2015). Exploring value propositions and service innovation: A service-dominant logic study. *Journal of the Academy of Marketing Science*, *43*(2), 137–158.

Starch, D. (1914). *Advertising: Its principles, practice, and technique*. Scott, Foresman.

Rintamäki, T., Kuusela, H., & Mitronen, L. (2007). Identifying competitive customer value propositions in retailing. *Managing Service Quality*, *17*(6), 621–634.

Treacy, M., & Wiersema, F. (1995). *The discipline of market leaders*. Addison-Wesley.

Unanoğlu, M. (2019). *Girişimcilik, stratejik farkındalık ve inovasyon*. Seçkin Yayınevi.

Urban, G. L., & Hauser, J. R. (1980). *Design and marketing of new products*. Prentice-Hall.

Volvo. (2021, November 18). *A heritage of safety innovations*. Retrieved from Volvo Cars: https://www.volvocars.com/intl/v/car-safety/safety-heritage

Webster, F. E. (2002). *Market-driven management: How to define, develop and deliver customer value* (2nd ed.). John Wiley & Sons.

Chapter 2
Social Entrepreneurship:
Developments and Challenges

Jashandeep Singh
https://orcid.org/0000-0003-0377-811X
Chitkara Business School, Chitkara University, India

Amanjot Kaur
Bhai Gurdas Institute of Management and Technology, Punjab, India

ABSTRACT

This chapter details social entrepreneurship. The idea of social entrepreneurship implies various things to various individuals and analysts. A few specialists allude to social businesses as not-revenue-driven businesses and others are of a different viewpoint. Being an emerging concept, social entrepreneurship has certain challenges that are faced by promoters. The chapter enlists the various developments in the area of social entrepreneurship and also explains the challenges faced by social entrepreneurs while going through the various phases.

INTRODUCTION

Entrepreneurship is multidisciplinary which covers in detail all these disciplines i.e. business administration, economics, economic geography, psychology and sociology (Sternberg, 2014). Therefore, the success of organization is not only beneficial for the entrepreneur- business owners, but it is also equally required for the employees and for the economic growth of the whole society (Van Praag and Versloot, 2007). Entrepreneurship has basically of two types, the first one is the Freelancer and the second one is the Entrepreneur. Presently, both maintain a business, act pioneering

DOI: 10.4018/978-1-6684-4745-1.ch002

and can have workers. However, the primary focal point of their work and their plans of action are completely unique. Since the beginning of the twenty-first century, for the promotion of the economic growth, the importance of the entrepreneurship started to berecognized as an element that's why, the researchers start finding how the contribution of entrepreneurship have become active to the growth. (Park, 2017). The definitions predominantly utilized for the examinations connected with business venture are as following:" Grasp an opportunity notwithstanding accessible assets" (Stevenson and Jarillo, 1986); The approach to deducing, thinking and acting zeroing in on in general methodology and explicit administration in light of the significance of perceiving the valuable open doors" (Dimitratos and Plakoyiannaki, 2003); and "The soul of challenge also experience that markets the potential open doors seized in danger". Meantime, Hisrich and Peters (1998) portrayed business as a perception that an enterpriser thinks about fundamental, rather than characterizing it as his/her mental state. Tune (2011) characterizes the term as an enterpriser's will to make another business through the executives development by showing his/her difficult soul. Park and Ahn (2016) disclosed to the youthful CEOs that business venture is a significant variable in improving their business exhibitions, and they need to use the work to develop their business skill.Although the meaning of business venture differed relying upon the circumstances which individual business, nation or age confronted, the definition chiefly utilized for late examinations is Miller (1983) expresses that business venture is a conduct that re-joins or rearranges assets with imaginativeness, venturesome soul and hazard taking brain to make another worth.

Enterprising Orientation (EO) is a key idea when chiefs are making methodologies with expectations of experimenting and taking advantage of chances that different associations can't take advantage of. EO alludes to the cycles, practices, and dynamic styles of associations that act innovatively. Any association's degree of EO can be perceived by inspecting how it piles up comparative with five aspects:

Autonomy

Autonomy was initially contemplated as a unitary idea (Hackman and Oldham, 1976). Later, different parts of autonomy were perceived, like planning, technique, and rule autonomy. Hence, autonomy alludes to whether an individual or group of people inside an association has the opportunity to foster an innovative thought and afterward own it to the end. In an association that offers high independence, individuals are offered the freedom expected to carry a groundbreaking plan to completion, liberated by the shackles of corporate organization. Whenever people and groups are unhindered by authoritative customs and standards, they can all the more actually research and champion groundbreaking thoughts.

Competitive Aggressiveness

Competitive aggressiveness is the inclination to seriously and straightforwardly challenge contenders rather than attempting to stay away from them. Forceful moves can incorporate cost cutting and expanding spending on advertising, quality, and creation limit. An illustration of serious forcefulness can be found in quite a few "assault advertisements" in the political field. Whenever Justin Trudeau turned into the head of the Liberal Party in Canada, he was dependent upon promotions focusing on his judgment and, explicitly, late remarks on the economy, psychological warfare, and the authorization of maryjane (Nurul, 2018).

At times aggressive moves can blow up. During the 1993 Canadian government political race, the Progressive Conservative Party created a broadcast assault advertisement against Jean Chrétien, the Liberal chief. The advertisement (some of the time alluded to as the "face promotion") was seen by numerous individuals as an emphasis on Chrétien's facial disfigurement, brought about by Bell's paralysis. The subsequent objection is viewed to act as an illustration of elector reaction from negative battling (Hackman and Oldham, 1976).

An excess of forcefulness can subvert an association's prosperity. A little firm that assaults bigger adversaries, for instance, may end up on the losing end of a value war. Laying out a standing for cutthroat forcefulness can harm a company's possibilities being welcome to join cooperative endeavors like joint endeavors and unions. In certain businesses, for example, the biotech business, joint effort is fundamental in light of the fact that no single firm has the information and assets expected to create and convey new items. Leaders accordingly should be careful about making serious moves that obliterate open doors for future teaming up. (Zachary and Mishra, 2011)

Innovativeness

The profile of the social entrepreneur, notwithstanding the regular attributes of the entrepreneur (as far as concerned with innovation, ability and searching for potential chances to make change with added esteem), has the particularity of its main goal to be social (Dees, Emerson and Economy, 2001). Innovativeness is the propensity to seek after imagination and trial and error. A few advancements expand on existing abilities to make steady enhancements, while more extreme developments require pristine abilities and may make existing abilities old. Regardless, ingenuity is pointed toward growing new items, administrations, and cycles. Those associations that are effective in their development endeavors will generally appreciate more grounded execution than those that don't.Known for proficient assistance, FedEx has presented its Smart Package, which permits the two transporters and beneficiaries to screen bundle area, temperature, and dampness. This kind of development is a welcome expansion to FedEx's setup for those occupied with delivery sensitive products, like human organs. Google's two most famous highlights of its Gmail, string arranging and limitless email documenting, were first proposed by an exhausted specialist with his own email misfortunes. The two firms permit representatives to utilize a part of their work time on undertakings fitting their very own preference determined to make new developments for the organization. This last model shows how various EO aspects for this situation, independence and inventiveness can build up each other.

Proactiveness

Proactiveness is the inclination to expect and follow up on future necessities rather than responding to situation after they transpire. A proactive association is one that embraces an open door looking for point of view. Such associations act ahead of moving business sector interest and are frequently either the first to enter new business sectors or "quick adherents" that enhance the underlying endeavors of first movers.Think about Proactive Communications, a suitably named little firm in Killeen, Texas. From its beginnings in 2001, this firm has given interchanges in threatening conditions, for example, Iraq and regions affected by Hurricane Katrina. Being proactive for this situation implies being willing to wear a tactical cap or rest outside exercises frequently stayed away from by different media communications firms. By accepting open doors that others dread, Proactive leaders have cut out a worthwhile specialty in a world that is innovatively, naturally, and politically tempestuous. That's why Entrepreneurs are moderate, dynamic and they address basic sparkplugs for monetary energy (Zachary and Mishra, 2011).

Risk Taking

Risk taking alludes to the propensity to take part in intense rather than careful activities. Starbucks, for instance, took a hazardous action in 2009 when it presented another moment espresso called VIA Ready Brew. Moment espresso has for quite some time been seen by numerous espresso consumers as a boring beverage, yet Starbucks concluded that the chance to disperse its item in various "make-at-home" design merited the danger of partner its image name with moment espresso.Albeit a typical conviction about business visionaries is that they are persistent daring individuals, research recommends that business visionaries don't see their activities as unsafe, and most make a move solely after utilizing arranging and gauging to lessen vulnerability. Yet, vulnerability only from time to time can be completely dispensed with it. Therefore, Risk resistance recommends fearlessness, which has been related with both ideal work results and a hopeful faith in the probability of advantageous results for exhausted endeavors (Ng, Sorensen, and Eby, 2006).

ENTREPRENEURIAL INTENTION

The idea most generally used to comprehend the peculiarities related with the foundationof a business is business venture. Examining the meaning of business viewed as in Morris (1998) studies, it was feasible to see that business has been regularly underlined whenever one intends to lay out an organization. Yoon (2004) considered innovative goal as the initial phase in laying out one's business and an uplifting perspective and experience toward business fire up ought to be gone before preceding really settling on a choice to begin his/her business. Krueger et al. (2000) characterized pioneering expectation as a singular's work to begin his/her business so that without it, one would not have the option to continue further. Taking into account that beginning a business can be satisfied through ascertain and purposeful exercises, the initial step, pioneering expectation, is fundamental for understanding by and large peculiarities associated with business fire up, as it is a critical component in deciding the early attributes of new companies (Bird, 1988). Shapero (1981) guaranteed that the jobs of business visionaries with enterprising aims are significant for the country, district or association to have their force of recovery to brave monetary slumps and self-transforming characteristics. Along these lines, it issignificant for our general public to add to nonstop monetary development by instilling a positive insight in the personalities of understudies with pioneering goals to advance and actuate new companies and let the ones with possibilities to challenge and succeed. The social organizations can be understood in two different dimensions:

1. **Social organizations:** Social organizations endeavor to improve or take care of social causes. These associations might help the destitute, offer free legitimate types of assistance, or assist veterans with tracking down work.A social association's income commonly come from gifts or benefits produced using selling products. Social associations could utilize any benefits to offer types of assistance to those out of luck or to support the association's objectives and activities (e.g., supplies) (Bird, 1988).
2. **Community organizations:** Generally not-revenue driven associations are viewed as local area associations. They could go from little neighborhood gatherings to bigger organizations with branches the nation over.People lay out local area associations to assist with causes around the local area. Certain purposes that local area associations could assist with incorporate tidying up the local area, further developing areas, and advancing reusing locally (Bird, 1988).

Social Entrepreneurship

The term ''social business'' has taken on an assortment of implications (Dees, 1998). Therefore, social entrepreneurship progressively draw in insightful consideration. These are typically seen as people and associations that utilization a business rationale in a novel and innovative manner to advance what is going on of sections of the populace that are prohibited, underestimated, or enduring and are themselves not fit for changing what is happening (Peredo and McLean, 2006). Albeit the thought of social business (SE) has been around since the 1950s (Bowen, 1953), it is just inside the previous ten years that SE research has turned into a significant and compelling writing stream. For instance, SE has been recognized as a strong component to defy destitution (Bloom, 2009), engage ladies (Datta and Gailey, 2012), catalyze social change, encourage comprehensive development in means commercial centers (Ansari, Munir, and Gregg, 2012; Azmat, Ferdous, and Couchman, 2015), and achieve institutional change (Nicholls, 2008). These are plainly very various peculiarities.

The Concept of Social Entrepreneurship

The idea of Social Entrepreneurship implies various things to various individuals and analysts (Dees, 1998). One gathering of specialists alludes to social business as not-revenue driven drives in search of elective subsidizing techniques, or the executives plans to make social worth A second gathering of analysts comprehends it as the socially dependable practice of business organizations occupied with crosssector associations (Sagawa and Segal, 2000). What's more a third gathering sees social business venture as a way to ease social issues and catalyze social change (Alvord et al., 2004).

Social Entrepreneurship and Related Concepts

Social Entrepreneurship and Commercial Entrepreneurship

Like business, social entrepreneurship people take part in pioneering exercises, like open door distinguishing proof, abuse, asset preparation, and development to make "another endeavor or deal with a current association in an imaginative way" to accomplish their social mission (Zahra et al., 2009). Be that as it may, they distinguish and acknowledge potential open doors got from cultural issues, such as neediness and absence of medical services or training (Zahra and Wright, 2016) spaces not generally considered in the business venture writing. The social mission is a critical driver as "for SE to have financial significance, it should address a space in which benefit is considered conceivable however lacking to persuade pioneering activity except if enhanced by moral or social motivators" (McMullen, 2011). Thus, SE is progressively viewed as an extension of the idea of business venture, however it focuses to significant examination questions that compass past the limits of the customary business venture writing.

Social Entrepreneurship and Corporate Social Responsibility

While CSR drives too "seem to additional some friendly great, past the interests of the firm and that which is legally necessary" (McWilliams and Siegel, 2001), these drives actually fall inside the association's benefit amplifying objective and are coordinated toward expanding investor esteem assignment. Besides, "CSR isn't really connected to enterprising activity and advancement however regularly means cultural commitment of associations (e.g., financing a games club or gifts to social associations)" (Shepherd and Patzelt, 2011).

Social Entrepreneurship and Nonprofit/Philanthropic Organizations

Like SE, not-for-profit social associations endeavor to make social worth, comprehensively characterized as "the satisfaction of fundamental and longstanding needs, for example, giving food, water, safe house, training, and clinical benefits to those citizenry who are out of luck" (Certo and Miller, 2008). While these charity associations can participate in pay creating exercises comparative with the association'sby and large financial plan, these incomes are regularly rather little and tiedto the term of a specific program (Doherty et al., 2014).

Social Entrepreneurship and Other Hybrid Ventures

The quest for a double mission isn't novel to SE yet can be found in different types of cross breed adventures, for example, maintainable, institutional, or improvement business (York et al., 2016) or overseeing clashing institutional rationales inside the cross breed adventure (Battilana et al., 2015). Reasonable business has been characterized as the "method involved with finding, assessing, and taking advantage of monetary open doors that are available in market disappointments which diminish manageability, including those that are naturally pertinent" (Dean and McMullen, 2007). Maintainable business venture can along these lines be separated from SE in its quest for a triple rather than a twofold main concern of adjusting "social advantages, monetarily suitable associations, and decrease of natural debasement" (Thompson, Kiefer, and York, 2011). Institutional business visionaries are viewed as "change specialists who start different changes, that is, changes that break the institutional the norm in a field of movement and consequently potentially add to changing existing establishments or on the other hand making new ones," yet where the component of business (e.g., making a new adventure) "is neither fundamental nor adequate to qualify an entertainer as an institutional business person" (Battilana, Leca, and Boxenbaum, 2009). Relatedly, advancement business people look for "to change formal organizations in manners that will improve social government assistance" (McMullen, 2011). Along these lines, the possibility of improvement business venture approaches what Zahra et al. (2009) group as social specialists, social bricoleurs and social constructivists.

SOCIAL ENTRPRENEUR

Social business, Shepherd and Patzelt (2011) people are visionaries who attempt to achieve positive change in the public arena by essentially applying their social business thoughts and methodologies to determine social issues in the general public. These issues are tremendous and different in nature. They are dangers not just restricted to a specific local area or district, however they are worldwide in nature; a portion of the normal social issues and issues are-deficient training and wellbeing offices and framework, ecological dangers, declining and wasteful political frameworks and administration, neediness, joblessness, disparity in view of orientation, rank and statement of faith; expansion in crime percentages, etc (Boschee, 1995).

The Ways of Work Done by A Social Entrepreneur

The term ''social business'' has taken on an assortment of implications (Dees, 1998). Therefore, Social Entrepreneurs initially examine the social issue/issue to be handled. Attempt to discover the hidden causes and foundations of the issue; this is done through exhaustive social business venture research, field investigation discoveries, overviews and perception techniques. Then, at that point, they study and connection them as far as the current cultural examples and arising social business patterns in the public arena. Then, at that point, thoughts and procedures are created to adjust individuals' outlook, acquiring change their way of life and demeanor. They attempt to recognize and foster change-creators from the general public itself; these change-producers fill in as good examples, inspirations and pioneers to achieve positive, moderate changes in the whole framework.These changemakers structure a group, social business organization, and a stage for individuals with comparable objectives and destinations. This stage permits the exchange of thoughts, criticisms and improvement of compelling procedures to determine the issue. This stage likewise relates the funders who need to connect themselves with achieving positive change in the public eye and the change-producers (Ghauri et al., 2014). The social business people team up with social trend-setters, funders, grass-roots pioneers, social specialists, and local area associations to achieve viable, dependable social changes in the public eye.

Development of Social Entrepreneurship

There have been prominent individuals who have filled in to act as an illustration for social business ever. Florence Nightingale, originator of the main nursing school and designer of current nursing rehearses, Robert Owen known for his helpful technique for business were one of few well known social business visionaries from history. The idea of social business venture was first found in exposition in the time of 1960 and 70. Michael Young, advanced thought of Social business people from 1950"s to 90"s. Charge Drayton is advancing them through his Ashoka Foundation from the time of 80"s. he has been elevating and helping to different social business people all around the globe. Michael Young has been pioneer in the field of advancing Social Entrepreneurs everywhere. There have been striking social business visionaries for what it's worth the world (Waddock, 1988).

Importance of Entrepreneurs in The Social Development

For the development of our general public there is need emerges for such business visionary who take well balanced plan of action and make conceivable circumstance to lay out independent society with his energy, development, imagination, drive and change the world. So business person acts like generally dynamic a piece of social change process. An informed business visionary effectively comprehend the issues and he is likewise mindful that how to kill, he is brimming with expertise and insight of all advanced strategies to convert all ineffective things in to useful from (Pache and Santos, 2013). Following are a few focuses which obviously uncovers the significance of a business person in the social turn of events:

- work opportunitis
- improvement of backward areas
- equivalent contibution of wealth
- diminish the gap of rural and urban areas
- works on quality of life
- ideal utilization of resources
- preservation of our heritage
- contribute in the economic growth of nations.
- social satisfaction

Challenges Faced by Social Entrepreneurs

Social entrepreneurs are significantly affecting networks and social relations. Establishing socially mindful new companies, it is critical to realize the difficulties which they are looking at and how to conquer them. (Rawal, 2018). Few of the challenges faced by Social Entrepreneurs are following:

Finding Funding

There isn't a business on the planet that didn't wish it had more cash to put resources into extension and accomplishing its statement of purpose. Sharma. G & Kulshreshtha. K (2014) Sadly, with regards to social undertakings this is typically a lot greater worry than for corporate endeavors.It's not strange to call tracking down subsidizing the main test of an effective social endeavor. An extraordinary thought is useless except if you can completely finish it. What's more that requires subsidizing for activity, however advancement, primary expenses and paying staff.There are two significant difficulties with regards to obtaining financing: persuading financial backers that not seeing a return for 5-7 years merits the venture and captivating everyone of excellent contest all competing for help for their basic issue.One method for beating this issue is through elective subsidizing courses. Crowdfunding, specifically, has altogether filled as of late, turning into a genuine strategy for financing a business that additionally fills in as publicizing for your objective (Thompson, 2002). It permits you to advocate your issue without recounting a tedious pitch.

Overcoming Suspicion

Social endeavors are frequently met with doubt. The general population regularly questions their actual goals. Noble cause can't help thinking about why they aren't non-benefit. A few media give them little inclusion and expect they'll come up short and failure away. This is an extraordinary business obstacle to defeat before you've even truly got everything rolling.Tackling the issue of starting doubts requires demonstrating you're put resources into the reason and moved by the issue. Rawal (2018) One method for doing this is to offer clients the choice to pick where their cash is going. Rather than resembling an almighty business pioneer who thinks they know best, stand by listening to clients and show you have support from specialists. Numerous fruitful social undertakings offer the choice for clients to choose whether the benefit produced using every deal goes to your organization or completely to settling the issue. Assuming your thought is strong, individuals will need to see cash return into your business and you can situate yourself as able to go that additional progression without obliterating your net revenue.To truly conquer doubt you want to demonstrate you're focused on your objective and mindful of different issues on the planet. Coordinating practices that show this into your regular cycles is perhaps the most ideal way to conform to an answer without seeming as though its essential for a showcasing stunt. For instance, assuming that your business works a Shopify store you approach various socially cognizant local area fabricated applications, which can do everything from consequently offset fossil fuel byproduct on each request to make a gift to a foundation each time a buy is made. Being seen settling on moral choices and working your ethos into every last trace of your business, can assist persuading clients and financial backers the same you that you with having the best aims on the most fundamental level with your social endeavor (Seelos and Mair, 2005).

Finding Good Manufacturers

Unaccounted for extra expenses can be a final knockout for a business, closing them down before they get an opportunity to start their main goal. Take online business as an illustration by and by, the expense of creation can be a colossal test in the event that you're selling a quality item with explicit necessities (Katz and Gartner, 1988). Taking into account every one of the extra expenses of running internet business, it very well may be difficult to make it beneficial. This can prompt you searching for a decent maker in a value range they essentially don't exist in. However, try not to hold back on creation. In the event that you stay with anything, ensure its keeping your result of good quality. Assuming the cycle takes longer and costs more, you really want to acknowledge that weight. Rather than bringing down the nature of creation, search for cost-saving choices in different regions. Having the option to separate your pursuit to observe the ideal creation organization in the beginning of your business can assist with staying away from these entanglements.Try not to be discouraged by the difficulties and costs quality brings. The sort of client base you'll draw in is eager to acknowledge longer conveyance times assuming that it implies the undertaking continues onward and they're getting a quality item for a decent objective. McInerney, (2012)

Remaining True to Your Mission

In this way, there's an unmistakable issue that is pestering you and you have an exceptional plan to settle it. It's not unexpected said that the most straightforward business thoughts are awesome, and that is the same for social endeavors. Santhi and Kumar (2011) Creating some distance from the underlying extraordinary thought can kill a business and it's something social business people should be similarly careful about.As your venture develops and gets more external subsidizing it's normal to feel you can accomplish more, or you might feel compelled to extend by your financial backers.However, this is the ideal opportunity to stay consistent with the first mission. Until you've returned on your venture, stay consistent with your unique mission. In any case, you hazard creating openings in your underlying thought and losing significance. Try not to follow the cash into one more issue to acquire subsidizing.

Aligning with Investors

However troublesome as financing seems to be to get for social ventures, there has still been an upswing as of late of effect financial backers searching for amazing open doors. This carries with it the test of keeping the financial backer on-side and drew in with the task. Not exclusively are financial backers cognizant all the time of the reality, but on the other hand they're not reluctant to submit ideas off the mark with your main goal to further develop it.While this varies from one financial backer to another, attempt to engage the side of the business your financial backer inclines most intensely as well (Weick, 1995). On the off chance that they're mission-centered, form your reports around the great you're doing rather than making it benefit centered. Try not to be hesitant to avoid them at all costs if important, and know when and when not to acknowledge their thoughts and information. To keep away from this issue be unquestionably specific with the financial backers you pick. A gleaming pot of cash being tossed at your business might appear to be engaging, however it can accompany added obstruction from individuals not exactly leaned to really assist with accomplishing your social points. Stages, for example, Gust have become well known with social undertaking new companies for this very reason, permitting endeavors to observe believed financial backers who are correct for their business.Social business visionaries are viewed as honorable, inventive, and innocent all simultaneously. Whenever you've begun your undertaking your extraordinary thought turns into an issue generator with a lot more than these six to tackle, however not neglecting to focus on the thinking behind why you began the endeavor is fundamental. Devi (2016)

CONCLUSION

The concept of social entrepreneurship is an emerging concept and there are several developments in the concept so far. It is a sort of entrepreneurship whose foremost objective is to create social value that may be viewed as positive externalities not taken into consideration by government or society. Everyone seems to reach an agreement on the point that social entrepreneurs recognize opportunities to solve the existing social problems. They do it by offering new kinds of services, providing new ideas, by searching for more efficient resources. Therefore, social entrepreneurship is associated with social innovation, although it may not be always the case. Nonetheless, social entrepreneurs face many challenges like finding funding, overcoming suspicion, finding good manufacturers, following the set mission and keeping the investors happy all the time.

REFERENCES

Alvord, S. H., Brown, L. D., & Letts, C. W. (2004). Social entrepreneurship and societal transformation. *The Journal of Applied Behavioral Science*, *40*(3), 260–282.

Ansari, S., Munir, K., & Gregg, T. (2012). Impact at the "bottom of the pyramid": The role of social capital in capability development and community empowerment. *Journal of Management Studies*, (49), 813–842.

Azmat, F., Ferdous, A. S., & Couchman, P. (2015). Understanding the dynamics between social entrepreneurship and inclusive growth in subsistence marketplaces. *Journal of Public Policy & Marketing*, (4), 252–271.

Bacq, S., Hartog, C., & Hoogendoorn, B. (2016). Beyond the moral portrayal of social entrepreneurs: An empirical approach to who they are and what drives them. *Journal of Business Ethics*, (133), 703–718.

Battilana, J., Leca, B., & Boxenbaum, E. (2009). How actors change institutions: Towards a theory of institutional entrepreneurship. *The Academy of Management Annals*, (3), 65–107.

Battilana, J., Sengul, M., Pache, A. C., & Model, J. (2015). Harnessing productive tensions in hybrid organizations: The case of work integration social enterprises. *Academy of Management Journal*, (58), 1658–1685.

Bird, B. (1988). Implementing entrepreneurial ideas: The case for intentions. *Academy of Management Review*, *13*(3), 442–454.

Bloom, P. N. (2009). Overcoming consumption constraints through social entrepreneurship. *Journal of Public Policy & Marketing*, (28), 128–134.

Boschee, J. (1995). Social Entrepreneurship. *Across the Board*, *32*(3), 20–23.

Bowen, H. R. (1953). *The social responsibilities of the businessman*. Harper.

Certo, S. T., & Miller, T. (2008). Social entrepreneurship: Key issues and concepts. *Business Horizons*, (51), 267–271.

Datta, P. B., & Gailey, R. (2012). Empowering women through social entrepreneurship: Case study of a women's cooperative in India. *Entrepreneurship Theory and Practice*, (36), 569–587.

Dean, T. J., & McMullen, J. S. (2007). Toward a theory of sustainable entrepreneurship: Reducing environmental degradation through entrepreneurial action. *Journal of Business Venturing*, (22), 50–76.

Dees, G. (1998). *The meaning of social entrepreneurship*. http:// www.fuqua.duke.edu/centers/case/documents/dees_SE.pdf

Dees, J. G., Emerson, J., & Economy, P. (2001). Enterprising nonprofits: A toolkit for social entrepreneurs. Annual Review of Sociology, (36).

Devi, S. (2016). Social Entrepreneurship: Challenges in Way to rise. *International Journal of Research*, *4*(9), 191–197.

Dimitratos, P., & Plakoyiannaki, E. (2003). Theoretical foundations of an international entrepreneurial culture. *Journal of International Entrepreneurship*, *1*(2), 187–215. doi:10.1023/A:1023804318244

Doherty, B., Haugh, H., & Lyon, F. (2014). Social enterprises as hybrid organizations: A review and research agenda. *International Journal of Management Reviews*, (16), 417–436.

Ghauri, P. N., Tasavori, M., & Zaefarian, R. (2014). Internationalisation of service firms through corporate social entrepreneurship and networking. *International Marketing Review*, (31), 576–600.

Hackman, J. R., & Oldham, G. R. (1976). Motivation through the design of work: Test of a theory. *Organizational Behavior and Human Performance*, *16*(2), 250–279. doi:10.1016/0030-5073(76)90016-7

Hisrich, R. D., & Peters, M. P. (1998). *Entrepreneurship*. Prentice Hall.

Katz, J. A., & Gartner, W. B. (1988). Properties of emerging organizations. *Academy of Management Review*, *13*(3), 429–441.

Krueger, N. F. Jr, Reilly, M. D., & Carsrud, A. L. (2000). Competing models of entrepreneurial intentions. *Journal of Business Venturing*, *15*(5/6), 411–432.

McInerney. (2012). Social Enterprise in Mixed-Form Fields: Challenges and Prospects. In B. Gidron & Y. Hasenfeld (Eds.), *Social Enterprises: An Organizational Perspective* (pp. 162–184). Palgrave Macmillan.

McMullen, J. S. (2011). Delineating the domain of development entrepreneurship: A market-based approach to facilitating inclusive economic growth. *Entrepreneurship Theory and Practice*, (35), 185–215.

McMullen, J. S. (2011). Delineating the domain of development entrepreneurship: A market-based approach to facilitating inclusive economic growth. *Entrepreneurship Theory and Practice*, (35), 185–215.

McWilliams, A., & Siegel, D. (2001). Corporate social responsibility: A theory of firm perspective. *Academy of Management Review*, *26*, 117–127.

Miller, D. (1983). The correlates of entrepreneurship in three types of firm. *Management Science*, *29*(7), 770–791. doi:10.1287/mnsc.29.7.770

Morris, M. H. (1998). *Entrepreneurial Intensity*. Quorum Publishing.

Ng, T., Sorensen, K., & Eby, L. (2006). Locus of control at work: A metaanalysis. *Journal of Organizational Behavior*, *27*(8), 1057–1087.

Nicholls, A. (2008). *Social entrepreneurship: New models of sustainable social change*. Oxford University Press.

Nurul, A. F. (2018). *The role of self-leadership on student's entrepreneurial intention with self-efficacy as mediating variable: a study in Andalas University* (Doctoral dissertation). Universitas Andalas.

Pache, A., & Santos, F. (2013). Inside the hybrid organization: Selective coupling as a response to competing institutional logics. *Academy of Management Journal*, (56), 972–1001.

Park, C. (2017). A study on effect of entrepreneurship on entrepreneurial intention: Focusing on ICT majors. *Asia Pacific Journal of Innovation and Entrepreneurship*, *11*(2), 159–170. doi:10.1108/APJIE-08-2017-024

Park, J. H., & Ahn, T. U. (2016). A Study on the Influence of Young Entrepreneurs' Entrepreneurship and Entrepreneurial preparation upon the Entrepreneurial Performance: Centered on Mediated Effect of Entrepreneurial infra system using. *Asia-Pacific Journal of Business Venturing and Entrepreneurship*, *11*(1), 39–47. doi:10.16972/apjbve.11.1.201602.39

Peredo, A. M., & McLean, M. (2006). Social entrepreneurship: A critical review of the concept. *Journal of World Business*, *41*, 56–65.

Rawal, T. (2018). A study of Social Entrepreneurship in India. *International Research Journal of Engineering and Technology*, *5*(1), 829–837.

Sagawa, S., & Segal, E. (2000). Common interest, common good: Creating value through business and social sector partnership. *California Management Review*, *42*(2), 105–122.

Santhi, N., & Kumar, S. R. (2011). Entrepreneurship Challenges and Opportunities in India International. *Journal of Industrial Engineering and Management Science*, *1*, 14–16.

Seelos, C., & Mair, J. (2005). Social entrepreneurship: Creating new business models to serve the poor. *Business Horizon*, (48), 241-246.

Shapero, A. (1981). Self-renewing economies. *Economic Development Commentary*, *5*(Ap), 19-22.

Sharma, G., & Kulshreshtha, K. (2014). Challenges and Opportunities of Entrepreneurs in Emerging Economies. *International Journal of Public Administration and Management Research*, *2*(3), 1–8.

Shepherd, D. A., & Patzelt, H. (2011). The new field of sustainable entrepreneurship: Studying entrepreneurial action linking "what is to be sustained" with "what is to be developed." *Entrepreneurship Theory and Practice*, *35*, 137–163.

Sternberg, R. (2009). *Regional dimensions of entrepreneurship*. Now Publishers Inc. doi:10.1561/0300000024

Stevenson, H. H., & Jarrillo-Mossi, J. C. (1986). Preserving entrepreneurship as companies grow. *The Journal of Business Strategy*, *7*(1), 10–23. doi:10.1108/eb039138

Thompson, J. (2002). The world of the social entrepreneur. *International Journal of Public Sector Management*, (15), 412–431.

Thompson, N., Kiefer, K., & York, J. G. (2011). Distinctions not dichotomies: Exploring social, sustainable, and environmental entrepreneurship. In G. T. Lumpkin & J. A. Katz (Eds.), *Social and sustainable entrepreneurship: 201-230*. Emerald.

Van Praag, C. M., & Versloot, P. H. (2007). What is the value of entrepreneurship? A review of recent research. *Small Business Economics*, *29*(4), 351–382. doi:10.100711187-007-9074-x

Waddock, S. A. (1988). Building successful partnerships. *Sloan Management Review*, *29*(4), 17–23.

Weick, K. (1995). Definition of theory. In N. Nicholson (Ed.), *Blackwell dictionary of organizational behavior* (pp. 565–567). Blackwell.

Yoon, B. S. (2004). Determinants of entrepreneurial intentions: Individual characteristics and environmental factors. *Korean Academic and Industrial Society of Business Administration*, *17*(2), 89–110.

York, J. G., O'Neil, I., & Sarasvathy, S. D. (2016). Exploring environmental entrepreneurship: Identity coupling, venture goals, and stakeholder incentives. *Journal of Management Studies*, (53), 695–737.

Zachary, R., & Mishra, C. (2011). The future of entrepreneurship research: Calling all researchers. *Entrepreneurship Research Journal*, *1*(1), 1–15. doi:10.2202/2157-5665.1016

Zahra, S. A., Gedajlovic, E., Neubaum, D. O., & Shulman, J. M. (2009). A typology of social entrepreneurs: Motives, search processes and ethical challenges. *Journal of Business Venturing*, (24), 519–532.

Zahra, S. A., Gedajlovic, E., Neubaum, D. O., & Shulman, J. M. (2009). A typology of social entrepreneurs: Motives, search processes and ethical challenges. *Journal of Business Venturing*, (24), 519–532.

Zahra, S. A., & Wright, M. (2016). Understanding the social role of entrepreneurship. *Journal of Management Studies*, (53), 610–629.

Chapter 3
Sustainable Development of Bihar Tourism:
An Entrepreneurial Opportunity

Ankit Dhiraj
Lovely Professional University, India

Sanjeev Kumar
https://orcid.org/0000-0002-7375-7341
Lovely Professional University, India

Divya Rani
Patliputra University, India

ABSTRACT

The entrepreneurial opportunity is found in the different segments such as accommodation, recreation and entertainment, transportation, and travel services. Hotels, restaurants, tour operators, and travel agents have been providing direct business opportunities to people at different levels of the local community. Bihar is a land of enlightenment and salvation. Bihar occupied an important position in the early history of India. Bihar is the birthplace of two religions (i.e., Buddhism and Jainism) and the birthplace of Guru Govind Singh, the 10th guru of the Sikh religion. There are many holy places for Hindus and important places for the Gandhian movement. Bihar is rich in spiritual, heritage, cultural, and recreation places. The total share of tourism is 11.99% of Bihar SGDP and the 11th largest wage earner in revenue with $3.13 billion in 2017. Tourism is one of the economic areas where the entrepreneurial sector requires a high level of involvement: diversification of tourism products and services is required to meet the rising demand for new sorts of tourism demands.

DOI: 10.4018/978-1-6684-4745-1.ch003

INTRODUCTION

Tourism is one of the most important and fastest-growing industries in the world today. Tourism industries are "Smokeless" industries (Prasad, 2004). The tourism industry is one of the most income generator tools for an economy by providing job opportunities and unique business opportunities. Development of Tourism industries means the development of other helping industries like transport; road, and telecommunication, power industries allowing local communities to entrepreneurs. Entrepreneurs can invest in more segments of tourism like travel agencies, tour operators, hotels, restaurants, art and craft, tour operator and many other sectors. It is the fastest growing industry that generates income from tourists" spending on goods and services at various stages of travelling; therefore it is very important for the economic well-being of many countries. Earn foreign exchange directly through tourism without exporting national resources. Some countries' economies depend on tourism. It creates a lot of jobs directly and indirectly. It creates jobs for skilled and non-skilled.

The growth rate of the Travel and Tourism sector is 3.9%. Over the past five years, one in five jobs was created by the sector and generating 10.3% of total world GDP (Shah et al., 2021). WTTC forecasted 1.8 billion international tourists in 2030 (Kushwah & Singh, 2018). In the Indian context Travel and tourism contribute 9.2% of total GDP (USD247.3 billion) and generate 8.1% of total employment in 2018. An international tourist spends USD 28.9 billion in 2018 i.e 5.4% of total Indian exports. India set the target of 20 million overseas tourist arrivals by 2020 & 30.5 million foreign tourist arrivals by 2030. Hence, the study attempted to identify the entrepreneurial opportunity that existed in the tourism industry of Bihar province in India.

The history of Bihar is going back 3000 years. Bihar had a significant role in India's early history. For centuries it was the principal seat of imperial powers and the main focus of Indian culture and civilization (Huntington, 1999). The birthplace of Bihar has two religions i.e. Buddhism and Jainism & the birthplace of Guru Govind Singh, the 10th guru of the Sikh religion (Agrawal et al., 2010). There are many holy places for Hindus and important places for the Gandhian movement (Rahman, 2014). Bihar is rich in spirituality, heritage and culture, rivers, fountains, mountains, hills, abhayaranya, pilgrims, historical sites, and other natural features abound in the state. There are many religious and non-religious tourist places in Bihar; these are the Buddhist circuit, Jain Circuit, Sikh Circuit, Ramayana circuit, Sufi circuit, Shiv Shakti circuit, Gandhi circuit, Eco circuit (Tourism, 2022). Bihar has found a place in the top 10 list of foreign tourist arrivals in the country.

Table 1. State wise domestic and foreign tourist visits during 2019

		NO OF TOURIST		RANK	
SI No	**STATE NAME**	**FOREIGN**	**DOMESTIC**	**FOREIGN**	**DOMESTIC**
1	Tamil Nadu	6866327	494865257	1	2
2	Maharashtra #	5528704	149294703	2	5
3	Uttar Pradesh	4745181	535855162	3	1
4	Delhi #	2983436	36467598	4	13
5	West Bengal	1656145	92366025	5	6
6	Rajasthan	1605560	52220431	6	10
7	Kerala	1189771	18384233	7	16
8	Punjab	1101343	47385387	8	11
9	**Bihar**	**1093141**	**33990038**	**9**	**15**
10	Goa	937113	7127287	10	21

(Source: India Tourism Statistics 2019)

Sustainable tourism development means managing all resources as a need of the social community to fulfil cultural heritage and life support system. Tourists demanded local and small scale goods. Tourism is one of the economic sectors in which a great degree of involvement is needed by the entrepreneurial sector due to its rapid international market growth (Harvey, 2012). The necessary characteristic of small entrepreneurs is that they are gap fillers. They can spot market opportunities and develop new products or services in response to market demands, as well as provide a new source of employment for people (Burnet, 2000). They do not have to change big entities or organizations to develop a new strategic direction. Together with job creation, such small enterprises are recognized as major players in innovation. Moreover, these entrepreneurs are seen as a major link in the product and service supply (Perera, 2007).

Concept of Entrepreneurship

"Entrepreneur" is a French loanword. The word first appeared in the Dictionnaire Universel de Commerce, a French dictionary compiled by Jacques des Bruslons and published in 1723 (Navale, 2013). The term "adventurer" was frequently used to imply the same idea, particularly in the United Kingdom (Wengenroth, 2010). The study of entrepreneurship can be traced back to the work of Irish-French economist Richard Cantillon in the late 17th and early 18th centuries, which was foundational to classical economics (AE Murphy, 1986) .

An entrepreneur is a person who starts a new firm and bears most of the risks while reaping the majority of the benefits (Zoltan.j.acs, 2010). Entrepreneurship refers to the process of starting a business. The entrepreneur is frequently portrayed as a pioneer, a provider of novel ideas, products, services, and/or business processes. The root of the word 'entrepreneur' comes from the French verb 'entreprendre', which means 'to undertake' (J. Couger, L. F. Higgins, 1990) (Lordkipanidze et al., 2005).

Features of an Entrepreneur

- An entrepreneur is a person who takes the risk of beginning a new business enterprise.
- Entrepreneurship is the process of bringing a business idea to life by combining capital and labour to generate goods or services for profit.
- Entrepreneurship is highly risky but also can be highly rewarding, as it serves to generate economic wealth, growth, and innovation.
- Ensuring funding is key for entrepreneurs: Financing resources include SBA loans and crowdfunding.
- The way entrepreneurs file and pay taxes will depend on how the business is set up in terms of structure.

As a result, an entrepreneur is defined as a person who either generates new production combinations or is prepared to take chances in the organisation and reorganization of social and economic mechanisms or as a person who, by exploiting market opportunities, eliminates disequilibrium between supply and demand, or as one who owns and operates a business (Hébert & Link, 2009). Despite the fact that tourism appears to be a lucrative market for investors and entrepreneurs, the notion of tourist entrepreneurship is little understood. The scant literature in the field of tourism entrepreneurship reveals that the sector has little entrepreneurial activity. The truth, on the other hand, demonstrates the contrary. The hospitality and tourist industry has always been a rich ground for start-ups.

The Opportunity for Entrepreneurship

The Bihar government is working hard to promote tourism in the state and is supporting it just like any other industry, according to Santosh Kumar Mall, the state's IT and Tourism Secretary. "Tourism and hospitality are a part of the industrial promotion policy of the state. So the state government is providing all the facilities like interest subvention, electricity duty subvention, and support in registration duties to the tourism sector as well," Mall told Business Today (Rajat Mishra, 2021). These are the following important factors to start a new tourism venture in Bihar.

Motivational Support

Motivation to start a business venture rests on various aspects such as the desire to achieve, a surplus of money, previous experiences, more demand in the area, family business, availability of loan assistance and professionally qualified person, need to achievement, desire for independence, job satisfaction from work (Lordkipanidze et al., 2005).

Wide Destination Range

Bihar's antiquity is evident from its name, which is derived from the ancient word "VIHARA" (monastery) (Geary, 2008). It is indeed a land of monasteries. In this historic land where India's first major empires grew and collapsed, Hindu, Buddhist, Jain, Muslim, and Sikh shrines abound. In the abyss of time, the remains of the world's first university sleep. Where the ruins of the worlds' earliest university slumber in the void of time. Bihar is a versatile destination that meets expectations of varied interests be it religious, art & culture, heritage or even ecological (BiharTourism, 2022). There are the following tourism categories in Bihar.

Figure 1. Tourism

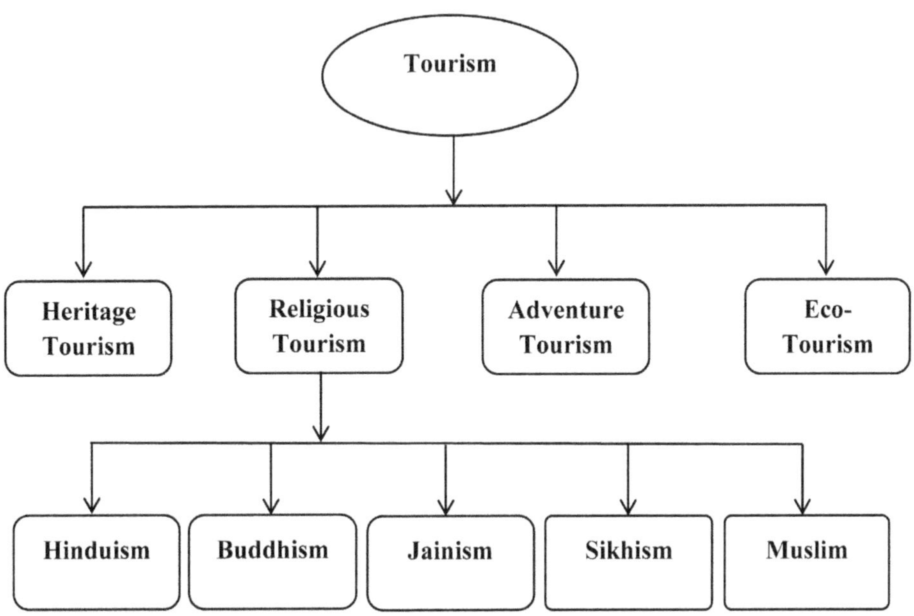

Table 2. Destination category by circuit

Circuit	Destination
Buddhist Circuit	Bodhgaya, Patna, Vaishali, Rajgir, Nalanda
Jain Circuit	Pawapuri, Rajgir, Jamui, Nalanda
Ramayana Circuit	Bhojpur, Buxur, Gaya, Jamui, Jehanabad, Madhepura, Madhubani, Munger, Vaishali, Darbhanga, Sitamarhi, West Champaran
Sikh Circuit	Patna
Sufi Circuit	Sasaram, Patna, Vaishali, Siwan, Jehanabad, Nalanda
Gandhi Circuit	East Champaran, West Champaran, Patna
Shiv Shakti Circuit	Kaimur,Gaya, Lakhisarai, Sultanganj, Darbhanga, Madhepura, Dighwara,Thawe, Chhapra, Patna, Chandi, Saharsa, Mahisi, Deoria
Eco Circuit	Valmiki nagar, Bhimbandh, Kakolat (Nawada), Rajgir

(Source: Bihar State Tourism Development Corporation)

Bihar has a wide range of tourism destinations of different segments like religious, eco-tourism, heritage tourism and adventure tourism with different circuits. More than 50 main famous tourism destinations with two world heritage site 1. Mahabodhi temple, Bodhgaya (RPB Singh & Kumar, 2011) and 2. Ruins of Nalanda University (Kulshreshtha, 2018). It means a big opportunity for an entrepreneur to operate different services for tourists.

Security

Security is an important factor for tourists and entrepreneurs who provide tourism services. The crime rate of Bihar was slung down in 2020 by 12.7% i.e crime rate in 2019 was 224.0 and 2020 was 211.3, the low crime rate National crime rate i.e 2019 was 385.5 and 2020 was 487.8 (NCRB, 2020). The safety and security of the tourists is one of the essential prerequisites for the sustainable long-term growth of this sector. Bihar government introduced tourist police. Tourist Police for the security and safety of the tourists from their existing Police set up. This is high-tech police who speak foreign language. The responsibility of tourist police is to do the safety of the tourist. Bihar State Tourism Development Corporation (BSTDC) launched a 24X7 helpline number.

Table 3. Crime against foreigners (top ten foreign tourist arrival states) –2019

State	Total Crime in 2019	% of State Share to Total Crimes - 2019
Bihar	**1**	**0.2**
West Bengal	6	1.5
Punjab	10	2.4
Kerala	15	3.7
Rajasthan	16	3.9
Uttar Pradesh	21	5.1
Goa	21	5.1
Tamil Nadu	23	5.3
Maharashtra #	48	11.7
Delhi #	123	30.1

(Source: National Crime Records Bureau, 2019)

Table 3 shows crime records against foreign tourists in the top 10 states where foreign tourists visited more. Bihar has less crime rather than Tamilnadu, Maharastra, and Uttar Pradesh secured first and second positions for foreign tourist arrivals in 2019 and Goa. Bihar has reported only 1 crime report with foreign tourists. The opportunity to invest tourism segment in Bihar is safe. An entrepreneur should invest in Bihar without any fear.

Government Policy

Government policy is a very important factor to invest any entrepreneur in any location. In 1980, the Bihar government established BSTDC (RU Singh, 2017) for the development of tourism in Bihar. The government of Bihar introduced New Tourism Policy-2019. The main motto of this policy is to accelerate the growth of tourism in Bihar.

The Bihar government provides a special incentive for the entrepreneur. These are

1. 100% stamp duty and registration fee exemption if set up tourism project
2. 7 years Luxury tax exempted for a new project
3. 100% electricity duty-free for seven years
4. 100% conversion charges exemption
5. Financial support for preparing project reports by tourism units up to 50% maximum Rs75000

6. Development of Food Park/ Agri Export Zone offering subsidy up to 25% maximum Rs 15.00 lakh
7. Seven years of entertainment tax exempted for a new unit

Requirement of Support Infrastructure

The hotel accommodation in Bihar is grossly inadequate for a tourist inflow of 3.5 crores. There are very less no opportunities for an entrepreneur to invest in these segments. Budget Hotels for Domestic Tourists and 3 Star and 2 Star Hotels of international standards for foreign tourists are required. Keeping in view this factor, new accommodation facilities have been proposed at Star categories of hotels.

Table 4. Tourism service provider list

Category	Total
Hotel	80
Guide	100
Travel Agency	36

(Source: Bihar tourism)

The opportunities are waiting to invest in the following category

1. Hotel, Motel/ Road Side Facilities, Resort, Guest/Tourist Rest House
2. Dharamshala, Ashrams
3. Health-Spa Resort
4. Tent Colony
5. Timeshare Apartment
6. Motor Caravan
7. River/Lake Cruise and/or House Boats
8. Travel Agent, Domestic Tour Operator, Excursion Agents
9. Restaurant / Fast Food Centre/food Plaza/Food Court, etc
10. Adventure Tour Operators dealing with water sports
11. Adventure Tour Operators dealing with aero-sports
12. Adventure Tour Operators dealing with safaris of various types
13. Adventure Tour Operators dealing with mountaineering and trekking
14. Yoga Kendra
15. Wildlife Photography
16. Wedding Points

17. Para Gliding
18. River Rafting
19. Amusement Park
20. Operators dealing with ATB, Mountain Bikes, Cycles, Snow Scooters, Performance Bikes, Fat Bikes
21. Tour Operators dealing with Buddhism
22. Tour Operators dealing with Jain
23. Tour Operators dealing with Sikh
24. Tour Operators dealing with Muslim

CONCLUSION

To operate, entrepreneurs require some driving forces, such as motives and precise conditions for success. But the most important is the enabling environment that provides comfort and support to the entrepreneur. Bihar tourism has a lot of potential for producing revenue and developing business opportunities. Bihar offers a lot of room for new product creation, some of which are currently popular in the Western world. Bihar has an abundance of religious places, historical places, archaeological sites, and entertainment complexes such as amusement parks, water parks, cable car rides, aquariums, casinos, and sound and light shows which can be an increase tourist inflow and Waterfront Tourism. Bihar has a diverse cultural legacy that is celebrated through fairs, festivals, and dances.

REFERENCES

Agrawal, M., Choudhary, H., & Tripathi, G. (2010). Enhancing Buddhist tourism in India: An exploratory study. *Worldwide Hospitality and Tourism Themes*, *2*(5), 477–493. doi:10.1108/17554211011090102

BiharTourism. (2022). *About Us*. https://state.bihar.gov.in/bihartourism/CitizenAboutUs.html

Burnet, D. (2000). *The Supply of Entrepreneurship and Economic Development*. Academic Press.

Couger, J., & Higgins, L. F., S. M. (1990). Differentiating creativity, innovation, entrepreneurship, intrapreneurship, copyright and patenting for I.S. products/processes. *Twenty-Third Annual Hawaii International Conference on System Sciences*, *4*, 370-379. 10.1109/HICSS.1990.205281

Geary, D. (2008). Destination enlightenment: Branding Buddhism and spiritual tourism in Bodhgaya, Bihar. *Anthropology Today*, *24*(3), 11–14. doi:10.1111/j.1467-8322.2008.00584.x

Harvey, P. (2012). *An introduction to Buddhism: Teachings, history and practices*. Academic Press.

Hébert, R. F., & Link, A. N. (2009). *A History of Entrepreneurship*. Academic Press.

Huntington, S. (1999). The lonely superpower. *The Lonely Superpower. Foreign Affairs*, *78*(2), 35–50. doi:10.2307/20049207

Kulshreshtha, S. (2018). Removable heritage: Nalanda beyond the Mahavihara In Decolonising Heritage in South Asia. Routledge.

Kushwah, R., & Singh, P. (2018). Application of Public-Private Partnership Approach in Marketing Mix of Buddhist Tourism. *Amity Research Journal of Tourism, Aviation and Hospitality*, *3*(1), 39–49.

Lordkipanidze, M., Brezet, H., & Backman, M. (2005). The entrepreneurship factor in sustainable tourism development. *Journal of Cleaner Production*, *13*(8), 787–798. doi:10.1016/j.jclepro.2004.02.043

Murphy, A. E. F. M. (1986). Richard Cantillon: Entrepreneur and economist. Oxford University Press.

Navale, A. (2013). Developing entrepreneur skills for corporate work. *Research Directions, 4*(1).

NCRB. (2020). *Crime in India 2020*. NCRB.

Perera, O. (2007). *State of play in sustainable public procurement*. International Institute for Sustainable Development.

Prasad, S. (2004). *Tourism of the Buddhist shrines in UP and Bihar.* Shodhganga. inflibnet.ac.in

Rahman, M. (2014). Marketing of Bihar Tourism–A Buddhist Destination Transforming to Leisure Destination. *Prestige E-Journal of Management & Reserach*, *1*(1), 69–88.

Rajat Mishra. (2021, November 15). *Supporting tourism like any other industry; will promote state's cultural heritage: Bihar Tourism Secy*. Academic Press.

Shah, C., Chowdhury, A., & Gupta, V. (2021). Impact of COVID-19 on tourism and hospitality students' perceptions of career opportunities and future prospects in India. *Journal of Teaching in Travel & Tourism*, *21*(4), 359–379. doi:10.1080/15313220.2021.1924921

Singh, R. (2017). Operational Performance Analysis of Bihar State Tourism Development Corporation. *Indian Journal of Commerce.*, *70*(1), 132–152.

Singh, R., & Kumar, D. (2011). Bodh Gaya, a World Heritage Site: Tourists' and Natives' Perceptions of Heritage and its Value. *Heritagescapes and Cultural Landscapes,* 255–286.

Tourism, B. (2022). *Bihar tourism.* https://tourism.bihar.gov.in/

Wengenroth, U. (2010). History of Entrepreneurship. *Innovation and Entrepreneurship*, 273.

Zoltan.j.acs. (2010). High-Impact Entrepreneurship. *Handbook of Entrepreneurship Research, 5*, 165–182.

Chapter 4
Assessing Government Initiatives Towards the Development of Entrepreneurship in India

Jyoti Verma
https://orcid.org/0000-0002-7559-4312
Chitkara Business School, Chitkara University, India

ABSTRACT

Entrepreneurs are playing a significant role in economic development. It helps in creating jobs, reducing poverty, maintaining demand-supply equilibrium, and solving a number of problems of any country. It will thus automatically increase the GDP of the country and make the country self-reliant. This can only be possible if, and only if, equal participation from all sections of the society should come forward and join hands for self-development and self-employability. Now there is a strong need to change youth mindsets. The Indian government has taken many initiatives to make entrepreneurship a successful model and also to strengthen this innovation ecosystem. The main purpose of such initiatives is to promote entrepreneurship solutions for economic sustainability and growth. This chapter highlights the current innovative ecosystem of entrepreneurship and the challenges it faces. It also highlights the initiatives taken by the Indian government for the promotion of entrepreneurship development in India.

DOI: 10.4018/978-1-6684-4745-1.ch004

INTRODUCTION

Entrepreneurship is a very crucial term for the development of the economy (Urbano, 2016; Aribaba et al., 2019). Entrepreneurs are significantly playing a crucial role in the economic development and solving the problem of unemployment of any country. Over the decades, India has been facing problems of unemployment, poverty, financial distress, uneven income distribution etc. When entrepreneur starts a business, it will provide jobs to many people that helps in boosting the economy (Tambunan, 2009). Despite having an education base and a huge technology-oriented infrastructure, India has not utilized its innovation and creativity potential fully. For this purpose, government of India has decided to take some initiatives and established various departments and policies. The establishment of the Technology and Innovation Policy, National Innovation Council, Introduction of Science, and coordination with educational institutions are some examples of such initiatives. There are many councils and structures under various ministries, whose prime objective is to serve the needs of entire research areas. In order to achieve the goals of sustainable economy, equal participation from all sections of society should be indulge for entrepreneurship (Verma and Gagandeep;2020). During budget speech[1] on 28th February 2015, finance minister said that "If we want to create job, then we need to make India as an investment destination, which allows them to start a business by abiding rules and regulations". In India, educated youth is a job-seeker and they wish to join as labour workforce in any public or private sector. It has been assumed by them that they will be getting job after study and it will be the easiest option for them. Here, there is a strong need to make their minds for entrepreneurship and aligned them to be a job creator rather than job-seeker. Entrepreneurs are equipped with wide range of skills and possess various traits. Many researchers found traits like- immediate response to upgrade themselves as well as their the business surroundings (Tehseen et al, 2015), having passion about entrepreneurial activities (Korunka et al, 2003; Lee and Wong, 2004; Agarwal et al, 2016; Aggarwal 2019), better understanding in good interpersonal skills (Agarwal and Lenka, 2017), always ready to assume risks (Boermans et al, 2017), desire for new innovations and learning (Lenka et al, 2017), huge amount of confidence (Ferreira et al. 2017), etc. In the past time, the term entrepreneurship was recognized by the male dominant factor, which has resulted in huge gap for women entrepreneurship. Now the perspective of society has been changed towards women (Alam et.al., 2011) as it has been found that they are managing their personal life and work life together and are being considered as proficient in their work. This can be only possible with the continuous support of self-help groups (SHG), help from Non-Government Organization (NGOs), education level and liberalization policies (Mathew & Panchanatham, 2011) and due to which women got upgraded platforms and status quo. On the basis of gender, both factors are considered as two important poles which exhibits variations of behavior but they have resemblance too on many aspects like motivation level, risk-aversion behavior, self-fulfillment, startup activities, internal locus of control (Alsos et al, 2006; Ajzen, 2002; Bird,1988; Verma et al 2021). According to Birley (1989), the major difference between male and female entrepreneurs is the selection of their market-entry choices. According to Zeithaml and Rice (1987), Gorman et al (1997), and Ronstadt (1987) recommended that entrepreneurial programs should be outlined in such a way so that the potential entrepreneurs have fundamental knowledge of entrepreneurship so that they are capable of removing all hurdles for initiating their entrepreneurial careers. Brush (1992) has concluded that the similarities between male and female entrepreneurs are based upon some demographic features, business skill set and psychological trait; whereas dissimilarities have been found on the basis of occupation, educational background, motivational forces to start a new business and strategic approach for creation and growth of business. Prabha (2019) concluded that entrepreneurship education is quite significant for female students who are inclined towards entrepreneurship goal and found in her study that the innovativeness and attitude come only from entrepreneurial education. According to Souitaris et al, 2007, there are ample implications for entrepreneurial intentions and the outcomes are inclined with the results of past studies that showed that educational programmes upraise the entrepreneurial attitudes and intentions. V.V et al (1998) have designed a new research scale for entrepreneurial motivation and identified five core motivations like entrepreneurial core, individual core, social core, economic core and work core motivation. Gundry et al. (2002) examined the impact of factors like family, culture, industry on women originated enterprises. Hughes et al. (2012) concluded that there needs to be a strong inclusion of diverse voices in entrepreneurship field. Neneh (2017) found in his study that different types of family support are positively associated with the firm performance for any startups and also concluded that this is most crucial factor of entrepreneurship. Jennings et al (2013) in their research study recommended that entrepreneurship can only result from opportunity and strong need that will persuade entrepreneurs to achieve their goals. Goyal and Yadav (2014) found that there are immense challenges faced by women entrepreneurs in the developing countries. It may include socio-cultural bias, less infrastructural support, raising of funds, low levels of entrepreneurial education and low self-esteem. Hence, there is a strong need to overcome these issues and help women entrepreneurs by some assistance policy. Jantje (2020) contributed the new dimensions in the literature review by exploring on the key topic- social entrepreneurship orientation (SEO) and concluded how SEO affects social entrepreneurial performance for both novel start-ups and established industrial firms. Review of literature work is quite significant in research as it identifies the possible research gaps. After this critical literature review, new areas are identified for further research which demands for the new perspective of looking for various initiatives done so far by the government for exceling entrepreneurship. This chapter highlights the current innovative ecosystem of entrepreneurship and the challenges it faces. It also highlights the initiatives taken by the Indian government for the promotion of entrepreneurship development in India.

Government Initiatives for Entrepreneurship

India is gradually enhancing its robust startup ecosystem and in order to encourage and support entrepreneurs, the government has established a government ministry whose task is to assist emerging startups financially and assisting new businesses. Here are some prominent schemes[2] launched by government to develop and encourage entrepreneurship in India- ATAL Innovation Mission, MUDRA Bank, Credit Linked Capital Subsidy for Technology Upgradation, NewGen Innovation and Entrepreneurship Development Centre (NewGen IEDC), Startup India Initiative, etc. In India, enterprises owned by women entrepreneurs are of the range between 13.5 million to 15.7 million. Due to Government intervention in entrepreneurship sector, this status has been improved and the numbers have been increased from 14% to 20% in the last decade[3]. The Indian government is making full effort to promote women entrepreneurship. National Commission for Women (NCW) is the statutory organization that enables women to attain the status of equality in life. To make women empowerment in the country. Its objective is to create a lasting impact of women across the nation by assisting them with knowledge and skills which is essential for their entrepreneurial ventures. The ultimate motive is to encourage innovation and employment across various industries. New Age Technology and Government initiatives are also helping to nurture the entrepreneurship culture in India. Some initiatives are mentioned below-

- **Atal Innovation Mission/ Atal Incubation Centres:** Atal Incubation Centres (AIC) are being headed by Atal Innovation Mission. Its aim is to promote entrepreneurship and innovation in India. The startups projects, which are approved under this scheme, can easily get funding for operational expenses up to INR 10 crore for a maximum period of five years. For example: - Goa Institute of Management (GIM) has been setup as a joint venture under the Atal Innovation Mission by NITI Aayog and Goa Institute of Management. Here, the industries which are applicable under this mission are- AI, AR/ VR, Automobiles, Aeronautics, Aviation, Animals, Chemicals, Computers, Design, Healthcare, IT, Nano-Tech, Non-Renewable Energy, Pets, Social Impact, Telecom, Food Sector. In the year 2015, government[4] allocated funds around 150 crores (Indian currency) for this mission.

- **Bridge Loan:** This scheme was launched by Indian Renewable Energy Development Agency (IREDA) and the objective of this scheme is to promote startups which are engaged in renewable energy projects like biomass power, small hydropower projects etc. Here, the industries which are applicable under this mission are- Renewable Energy startups and related companies.
- **Credit Linked Capital Subsidies for Technology Upgradation:** MSME has introduced this scheme to help small manufacturers, agri-startups, and SMEs to update their existing technologies, plants with state of art technology. Those units can easily apply for this grant facility and receive funds for their expenses. Here, the industries which are applicable under this scheme are- Khadi, Village, Coir industry, Manufacturing, Small Scale Industry, SMEs.
- **MSME Market Development Assistance:** This scheme was launched by MSME and its aim is to help the units which are registered with Directorate of Industries/District Industries Centre. It is not specific to any kind of industry and is applicable to retailers, startups, and SMEs. It is related with organizing Workshops, Seminars, Awareness Campaigns, Vendor Development Programmes etc.
- **Infrastructure Development Scheme:** This scheme was launched by National Small Industries Corporation (NSIC) for helping the fresh startups establishments and related infrastructure. This scheme has zero lock-in period. It is applicable to those companies only which are fulfilling the criteria as per rules and regulations of Ministry of Micro, Small and Medium Enterprises. For instance: - The Smart Cities Mission which is a major urban renewal program.
- **Raw Material Assistance Scheme:** This scheme has been introduced by National Small Industries Corporation (NSIC) which assist MSMEs and manufacturers for procuring raw materials, both indigenous & imported level. It helps them to focus more on the quality of their finished products, as they can avail financial help at low-interest rates and purchase raw materials.
- **Credit Guarantee Scheme**: This scheme has been launched by Credit Guarantee Fund Trust for Micro and Small Enterprises (CGTMSE) and the prime goal of this scheme is to run credit delivery system effectively and to assist educational institutes, retailers, self-help groups (SHGs), SMEs and farmers.
- **Make in India**: This scheme has been introduced in 2014 by Indian Government. The main aim of this initiative is to boost the Indian domestic manufacturing sector. By reviving the existing manufacturing sector, this scheme put much emphasis on making India as a global manufacturing hub. It also aims to boost both domestic and foreign investments in the country.

- **SAMRIDH Scheme:** This initiative is designed to facilitate funding support to new start-ups and it will help them to bring skill sets together so as to grow successfully in the market. This scheme aims to focus on speedy growth of start-ups and by extending its scope further with customers, investors, and other international opportunities for expansion in the future. Indian government also announced the launch of the 'Startup India Seed Fund' worth 1,000 crores INR for assisting start-ups and support ideas from young aspiring entrepreneurs.
- **Mudra Yojana:** The government has introduced Pradhan Mantri Mudra Yojana (PMMY) to support small businesses in India and revive the growth of small-scale business in rural areas. MUDRA stands for Micro Units Development Refinance Agency and the financial institutions under this scheme is helpful for enhancing credit facility. These banks provide startup loans to small enterprises, which are non-corporate. Under this scheme, three types of loans have been categorized namely Shishu, Tarun, and Kishore. There is no collateral security required for this purpose.
- **Ministry of Skill Development and Entrepreneurship:** Earlier, entrepreneurship was promoted and taken care of by different government agencies. After 2014, Indian government recognized that the skill development field require greater support from government's end and decided to dedicate a special ministry to build this sector.
- **The Venture Capital Assistance Scheme (VCA):** Agriculture Sector is the primary sector of Indian economy and contributes towards Indian GDP. Therefore, it is necessary to take necessary measures for its growth and development. It has been introduced by Small Farmer's Agri-Business Consortium (SFAC) for the betterment of farmers entrepreneurs and to further develop their agribusiness. It intends to provide financial assistance to farmers so that their capital requirements for project's implementation can be achieved. It further promotes training and nurturing of Agri sector entrepreneurs and orient them towards Agri business.

CONCLUSION

India is a country of diversity, which consists of many young people with innovative minds, but still who are seeking employment. The country is on the right way to further development and growth. The government has identified this root cause problem and made appropriate reforms to strategically work upon these issues. There has been a substantial upheave toward creativity, science, technology, and innovation in past years, and many initiatives have been attempted in that direction. But despite that, the investments in creativity, science, technology, and innovation are not yet rendering into desirable outcomes. For this government has taken various initiatives and this entrepreneurship development holds assurance for sustainable growth. The successful implementation of these initiatives will lead to the progressive growth of the economy.

REFERENCES

Agarwal, S., & Lenka, U. (2016). An exploratory study on the development of women entrepreneurs: Indian cases. *Journal of Research in Marketing and Entrepreneurship, 18*(2), 232–247. doi:10.1108/JRME-04-2015-0024

Agarwal, S., & Lenka, U. (2017). *Does growth of ventures depend on competencies? Selected cases from India*. Academic Press.

Aggarwal, A. (2019). Journey of Women Entrepreneurs for Two Decades: A Meta-Analytical Review. *Advancing Women in Leadership, 39*, 3-20. Available online at https://awl-ojs-tamu.tdl.org/awl/index.php/awl/article/view/343

Ajzen, I. (2002). Perceived Behavioral Control, Self-Efficacy, Locus of Control, and the Theory of Planned Behavior[1]. *Journal of Applied Social Psychology, 32*(4), 665–683. doi:10.1111/j.1559-1816.2002.tb00236.x

Alam, S. S., Jani, M. F. M., & Omar, N. A. (2011). An empirical study of success factors of women entrepreneurs in southern region in Malaysia. *International Journal of Economics and Finance, 3*(2), 166.

Alsos, G. A., Isaksen, E. J., & Ljunggren, E. (2006). New venture financing and subsequent business growth in men–and women–Led businesses. *Entrepreneurship Theory and Practice, 30*(5), 667–686. doi:10.1111/j.1540-6520.2006.00141.x

Aribaba, F. O., Oladele, R., Ahmodu, A. O., & Yusuff, S. A. (2019). Tax policies and entrepreneurship sustainability in Ondo State, Nigeria. *Journal of Global Entrepreneurship Research, 9*(53), 1–13. doi:10.118640497-019-0168-0

Bird, B. (1988). Implementing entrepreneurial ideas: The case for intention. *Academy of Management Review, 13*(3), 442–453. doi:10.5465/amr.1988.4306970

Birley, S. (1989). Female entrepreneurs: Are they really different? *Journal of Small Business Management, 27*, 32–37.

Boermans, M. A., & Willebrands, D. (2017). Entrepreneurship, risk perception and firm Performance. *International Journal of Entrepreneurship and Small Business*, *31*(4), 557–569. doi:10.1504/IJESB.2017.085426

Brush, C. G. (1992). Research on Women Business Owners: Past Trends, a New Perspective and Future Directions. *Entrepreneurship Theory and Practice*, *16*(4), 4, 5–30. doi:10.1177/104225879201600401

Ferreira, J. J. M., Fernandes, C. I., Peris–Ortiz, M., & Ratten, V. (2017). Female entrepreneurship: A co–citation analysis. *International Journal of Entrepreneurship and Small Business*, *31*(2), 325–340. doi:10.1504/IJESB.2017.10004863

Gorman, G., Hanlon, D., & King, W. (1997). Some Research Perspectives on Entrepreneurship Education, Enterprise Education and Education for Small Business Management: A Ten-Year Literature Review. *International Small Business Journal*, *15*(3), 56–77. doi:10.1177/0266242697153004

Goyal, P., & Yadav, V. (2014). To be or not to be a woman entrepreneur in a developing country? *Psychosociological Issues in Human Resource Management*, *2*(2), 68–78.

Gundry, L. K., Ben-Yoseph, M., & Posig, M. (2002). Contemporary perspectives on women's entrepreneurship: A review and strategic recommendations. *Journal of Enterprising Culture*, *10*(01), 67–86. doi:10.1142/S0218495802000141

Halberstadt, J., Niemand, T., Kraus, S., Rexhepi, G., Jones, P., & Kailer, N. (2021, April). Social entrepreneurship orientation: Drivers of success for start-ups and established industrial firms. *Industrial Marketing Management*, *94*, 137–149. Advance online publication. doi:10.1016/j.indmarman.2020.06.012

Hughes, K. D., Jennings, J. E., Brush, C. G., Carter, S., & Welter, F. (2012). Extending women's entrepreneurship research in new directions. *Entrepreneurship Theory and Practice*, *36*(3), 429–442. doi:10.1111/j.1540-6520.2012.00504.x

Jennings, J. E., & Brush, C. G. (2013). Research on women entrepreneurs: Challenges to (and from) the broader entrepreneurship literature? *The Academy of Management Annals*, *7*(1), 663–715. doi:10.5465/19416520.2013.782190

Jennings, J. E., & McDougald, M. S. (2007). Work-Family Interface Experiences and Coping Strategies: Implications for Entrepreneurship Research and Practice. *Academy of Management Review*, *32*(3), 747–760. doi:10.5465/amr.2007.25275510

Jyoti, Verma, Gagandeep. (2020). A Holistic Approach of Quality in Higher Education System vis-a-vis Sustainable Development. *International Journal of Management*, *11*, 10,433–440.

Korunka, C., Frank, H., Lueger, M., & Mugler, J. (2003). The Entrepreneurial Personality in the Context of Resources, Environment, and the Start- up Process -A Configurational Approach. *Entrepreneurship Theory and Practice*, *28*(1), 23–42. doi:10.1111/1540-8520.00030

Lee, S. H., & Wong, P. K. (2004). An exploratory study of technopreneurial intentions: A career anchor perspective. *Journal of Business Venturing*, *19*(1), 7–28. doi:10.1016/S0883-9026(02)00112-X

Lenka, U., & Agarwal, S. (2017). Role of women entrepreneurs and NGOs in promoting entrepreneurship: Case studies from Uttarakhand, India. *Journal of Asia Business Studies*, *11*(4), 451–465. doi:10.1108/JABS-07-2015-0088

Mathew, R. V., & Panchanatham, N. (2011, July 1). An exploratory study on the work-life balance of women entrepreneurs in South India. *Asian Academy of Management Journal*, *16*(2), 77–105.

Neneh, B. N. (2017, September 01). Family Support and Performance of Women-owned Enterprises: The Mediating Effect of Family-to-Work Enrichment. *The Journal of Entrepreneurship*, *26*(2), 196–219. doi:10.1177/0971355717716762

Prabha, D. T., Panigrahi, S. K., Maisnam, C., Alyani, W. A., & Bino, E. (2019). The Female Entrepreneurs' attitude towards Entrepreneurship: How Entrepreneurial Orientation and Desirability Influence Intention of Entrepreneurial Students? *Delhi Business Review, 20*(2), 11-24.

Ronstadt, R. (1987). The educated entrepreneurs: A new era of entrepreneurial education is beginning. *American Journal of Small Business*, *11*(4), 37–53. doi:10.1177/104225878701100403

Souitaris, V., Zerbinati, S., & Al-Laham, A. (2007). Do entrepreneurship programmes raise entrepreneurial intention of science and engineering students? The effect of learning, inspiration and resources. *Journal of Business Venturing, 22*(4), 566.

Tambunan, T. (2009). Women entrepreneurship in Asian developing countries: Their development and main constraints. *Journal of Development and Agricultural Economics, 1*(2), 27-40.

Tehseen, S., & Ramayah, T. (2015). Entrepreneurial competencies and SMEs business success: The contingent role of external integration. *Mediterranean Journal of Social Sciences*, *6*(1), 50–61. doi:10.5901/mjss.2015.v6n1p50

Urbano, D., & Aparicio, S. (2016). Technological forecasting & social change entrepreneurship capital types and economic growth: International evidence. *Technological Forecasting and Social Change*, *102*, 34–44. doi:10.1016/j.techfore.2015.02.018

V, V., & T.J, K. (1998). A Scale to Assess Entrepreneurial Motivation. *Journal of Entrepreneurship, 7*(2), 183-198.

Verma, J., Sood, K., & Grima, S. (2021). Factors affecting Indian parents' adoption of online learning applications for their children. *Review of International Geographical Education Online*, *11*(9), 1328–1338.

Zeithaml, C. P., & Rice, G. H. (1987). Entrepreneurship/Small business education in American universities. *Journal of Small Business Management*, *25*(1), 44–50.

ENDNOTES

1 https://www.edelweiss.in/insight/today-s-perspective-1/sme-business-loans-powering-growth-across-india-b8891a
2 https://startuptalky.com/list-of-government-initiatives-for-startups/
3 https://economictimes.indiatimes.com/small-biz/startups/newsbuzz/why-women-are-less-likely-to-start-new-ventures-than-men/articleshow/74503787.cms?from=mdr
4 https://startuptalky.com/list-of-government-initiatives-for-startups/

Chapter 5
Entrepreneurial Ecosystems Resilience and Institutional Voids:
Solutions for Emerging Economies to Drive Economic Growth

Kyla L. Tennin
https://orcid.org/0000-0002-9849-1316
Forbes School of Business, USA & Lady Mirage Global, Inc., USA

ABSTRACT

During the COVID-19 pandemic, 41.3% of companies stated they closed temporarily due to the pandemic. In the United Kingdom, 32.5% of entrepreneurs reported they were still able to work during the pandemic, compared to entrepreneurs in Norway (58.5%), Bosnia and Herzegovina (81.6%), North America (55%), and France (55.9%). In a global study for the World Economic Forum, a variety of firms were surveyed, from entrepreneur startups to music festivals, manufacturing companies, and automotive enterprises. Seventy percent of startups stated they had to terminate their full-time employees since the beginning of the COVID-19 pandemic. Only 40% of new enterprises stated they have enough revenue to last for three months of operations. Resilience, financial inclusion, education, and strategic partnerships are needed during crises to protect entrepreneurial ecosystems, especially if firms operate in economies that are emerging, possess institutional voids, institutional forces, or slow economic growth issues.

DOI: 10.4018/978-1-6684-4745-1.ch005

INTRODUCTION

Crises in economies, not just institutional voids, possess the ability to cause hardships to both businesses and markets, including creating additional institutional voids. For example, Bartik et al. (2020) conducted a quantitative study on the North American small business ecosystem within the Alignable Business Network of 4.6 million companies. Bartik et al. (2020) reported out of the entire sample, 7500 businesses responded to taking the resilience, *per se*, survey, where 41.3% of companies stated they closed temporarily due to the COVID-19 pandemic. From the same sample, 1.8% reported they closed permanently due to the pandemic, but approximately 55.5% advised they were still able to operate; found a way to operate (Bartik et al., 2020). Comparably, in the United Kingdom, 32.5% of entrepreneurs reported they were still able to work during the pandemic, compared to entrepreneurs in Norway (58.5%), Bosnia and Herzegovina (81.6%), and France (55.9%) (Stephan et al., 2021).

On the other hand, distinct from Stephan et al. (2021) and Bartik et al. (2020), Cuyper et al. (2020) conducted a global study for the World Economic Forum, surveying a variety of industries and firms, from entrepreneur's startups to music festivals, manufacturing companies, and automotive enterprises. Cuyper et al. (2020) reported over 70% of startups stated they *had to* terminate their full-time employees, since the beginning of the COVID-19 pandemic. Likewise, only 40% of new enterprises only have enough revenue to last for less than three months of operations. With consultation clients in nearly 50 nations, working with investment forums, various world leaders, president's of nations, and business owners, Cuyper et al.'s (2020) claims are closely related to what may entrepreneurs stated, although Bartik et al. (2020) and Stephan et al.'s (2021) claims seem appropriate too.

Nevertheless, for many years small businesses have been claimed to be the driving force behind economies existence and stability. Gargi (2019) postulated entrepreneurship regards contributing to economies by employing people and is connected to new technologies and innovations that have the potential to create additional employment for markets. The new innovations and technologies also possess the ability to be profitable (Gargi, 2019). Somewhat similar to Gargi (2019), Fotache and Bucsa (2020) stated The European Commission defined entrepreneurship as the formalization of ideas and opportunities, and then transforming those ideas and opportunities into something that will bring value to people. The value developed can be within the context of social, cultural, or financial value (Fotache & Bucsa, 2020).

Entrepreneurs and Entrepreneurship

Venugopalan et al.'s (2021) argued entrepreneurship can be exercised to empower women. The same is can be true for empowering entrepreneurs in general. For example, Gargi (2019) warranted women who own small businesses actually work in their careers, as entrepreneurs, and employ other workers. The same is true for entrepreneurs in general, who employ personnel. Entrepreneurs work for themselves. Also, Gargi (2019) argued entrepreneurship is not just about employing people, which contributes to economies, but regards launching new innovations, even with technology linked so additional workers can be employed and the innovations and business become profitable. Profitability allows organizations to hire more workers and ultimately profits economies too (Gargi, 2019). What Gargi (2019) exemplified is economic development and growth.

Gargi (2019) also contended innovation is the primitive reason for increased investments in societies and innovations are usually connected to businesses. Comparably, Abril et al. (2021) reported women's empowerment using entrepreneurship and even innovation as an economic growth strategy. To point out again, entrepreneurship and innovation in general can be empowering, for individuals (the owner and employees) and economies because jobs can be created and profits earned, to circulate markets. Both used as an economic growth strategy.

In comparison to Gargi (2019) and Abril et al. (2021), but mostly to Tiba and Frikha (2020), Alrubaishi et al. (2021) conducted a qualitative interpretive case study on 10 Saudi Arabian family-owned businesses and argued entrepreneurship and new business creation activities are the way to build legacies, future generations. Specifically for family businesses, this is appropriate and to build wealth to pass down businesses to future generations for economic well-being and job creation. However, using entrepreneurship to build legacies, for future generations is appropriate, and traditional, for economies too. Businesses are needed for economies to operate.

Mair (2005) claimed entrepreneurial behaviors means to apply innovative resources to recognize and then pursue opportunities. Alrubaishi et al. (2021) advised entrepreneurship helps families with brining in income. Income as capital can be utilized for personal and professional needs. In considering the definitions of entrepreneur, entrepreneurship, and even economic development, whether from an economic development, pandemic recovery, or family business context, as examples, each are necessary to empower entrepreneurs and construct legacies societies can continue. Jain-Chandra et al. (2017) did state obtaining credit and opening and controlling bank accounts are empowerment actions. Comparably, Dalal (2011) and Simbar et al. (2017) defined economic empowerment as owning investments, property, finances, obtaining an education.

Economic Development (Growth)

Economic development does not just mean you are *creating or developing* something, like an economy, but you are also *growing* the economy. With this in mind and within the context of economies, economic growth, and sustainable development, empowerment somewhat has the same definition, but within distinct environments depending upon the situation, organization and/or economy.

However, still remaining within the boundaries of *conducting business*, as the final outcome. To exemplify, globally and contemporarily, the definition of economic *development* means to grow or improve an economy. Traditionally by harnessing prosperity, a variety of resources, finances (e.g. investments), and wealth. Likewise, improving an economy usually involves increasing access to jobs for people and their quality of life. Increasing access to employment is particularly important during times of crisis, like in recession, pandemic, or epidemic, to pull economies out of constant downward situations. Founders of organizations who are entrepreneurs can also create jobs for other people. Obeidat et al. (2018) claimed human capital is critical for economic *development*, and is the most significant resource for businesses since globalization is taking place. Alike, Obeidat et al. (2021) reported the association between human capital and empowerment is statistically significant and is allows knowledge sharing.

Henceforth, economic empowerment, economic development, and even women's empowerment can be linked because of decision-making. Generally, decision-making involves leadership, finances, and resources allocation to enhance the quality of life or well-being of a group of individual's lives or one person's life. A group of individuals can be a municipality or even a family, a household. To compare, Rao et al. (2014) reported when people are empowered economically, economic development is directly influenced and vice versa. When economic developed increases it is because people are being empowered economically. Duflo (2012) mentioned a great point worth noting, similar findings to Rao et al. (2014), but the *empowerment-development linkage*, although connected, is too weak for self-sustainment after an extensive review of research. The result of this is equality policy commitments need to be reviewed and revised on a regular basis (Duflo, 2012).

Institutional Voids in Emerging Economies

Generally, the term void means the absence of something. Traditionally, an institutional void is the absence of institutional infrastructure in a nation. Institutional voids are a term created by leading Harvard professor Tarun Khanna in his book *Winning in Emerging Markets* (Singapore Management University, 2013). Examples of institutional infrastructure can be capital providers, employment agencies, as well as legal systems or arbitration mechanisms (van Dijk, 2018). Meanwhile, SMU (2013) proclaimed institutional voids in emerging markets is where intermediaries like credit card systems, market research firms, and other institutions significant for building the structure of economies and to efficiently link sellers and buyers are absent. The absence of the connection (intermediaries) causes major barriers for organizations attempting to operate or even expand in emerging economies (SMU, 2013).

Moreover, certain countries contain specific institutional voids. First, Onsongo (2019) completed a case study on Vodafone Group PLC and its partner Safaricom Kenya Ltd and the institutional voids they encountered as multinational corporations when expanding into the market (Onsongo, 2019). Institutional voids faced were policy, social, and market voids. Particularly social innovation voids (Onsongo, 2019). Social innovation regards a product or service and company appealing to the needs of the target audience (Onsongo, 2019). Likewise, Onsongo (2019) argued continuous engagement with policy-makers needs to occur and institutional voids are actually market opportunities for new innovations to be birthed. What actually is an institutional void can be seen as a seemingly institutional void because the void is a complexity and complexities can be disguised opportunities for entrepreneurial ventures.

Onsongo (2019) warranted the multinational corporations of Vodafone Group PLC and Safaricom Kenya Ltd partnered to launch M-Pesa (a commercial banking service) in Kenya in 2007. The purpose of the launch was to connect with local market customers by providing mobile money services, hence mobile phone-based money transfers between commercial banking populations who weren't currently using a bank to exchange finances (Onsongo, 2019). Such a population were called the *non-banking population*, yet allowed the two multinationals to come together to enter the market in a new way, connect with and gain local commercial business customers, and close a gap to financial inclusion (Onsongo, 2019).

In comparison to Africa (Kenya), Gao et al. (2015) explicated, China has three particular institutional voids, which are lack of a (1) developed economy, (2) specialized market intermediaries, and (3) contract enforcing tools that are already matured (Gao et al., 2015). The lack of the three aspects prohibits institutions from acquiring not only knowledge to expand, launch, survive, and thrive, but resources and information to conduct transactions in the market (Gao et al., 2015). Comparably, in India, institutional voids include the weakness, essentially the absence of both informal and formal institutions (Kumar, 2018). Such voids are detrimental and greatly affect the formation of an economy and both the economic growth and development of that market (Kumar, 2018; Khanna & Palepu, 1997).

Meanwhile, in Africa and somewhat similar to the voids in China Gao et al. (2015) highlighted, institutional voids include lack of contract enforcing tools, regulatory systems, and specialized intermediaries, each Khanna et al. (2005) and White and Kitimbo (2018) claimed. Comparably, van Dijk (2018) defined institutional voids in Dutch markets, particularly where small-medium-sized enterprises attempt to enter, as the underdevelopment or absence of quality certification firms, vendors (database vendors), and regulatory organizations. Alike how Khanna and Palepu

(2010) defined. Distinct from van Dijk (2018) and Khanna and Palepu (2011) stating regulatory systems can be institutional voids, Valente (2018) argued regulatory systems can be institutional forces, something organizations have no choice, but to conform to, or else be fined. In addition to this, debarments, suspensions, and even dissolution can occur when firms do not conform.

Institutional Forces in Entrepreneurship and Institutional Theory

Briefly, institutional theory regards how external pressures to an organization or system causes impact or some sort of change (Davidsson et al., 2006). Comparably, Newenham-Kahindi (2015) performed a qualitative study on multinational companies' sustainability efforts within 18 communities in Tanzania exercising institutional theory. Data collection tools were of archival documents and semi-structured interviews. Newenham-Kahindi (2015) explicated institutional theory, in general, is about organizations behaviors, culture, and setting. Hence, environmental surrounding, both societal and social (Newenham-Kahindi, 2015).

Institutional theory is about how leaders in companies make decisions (Newenham-Kahindi, 2015). Too, based on deep practitioner knowledge and experience of institutional theory, the theory regards companies obtain methods and even form from similar enterprises. As a result, companies become a part of an organizational field (Kostova et al., 2008). The establishment of shared values, rules, expectations, and regulations for *members* to adhere to, is an organizational field (Greenwald, 2008). Similarly, DiMaggio and Powell (1983) claimed businesses that sell services and products similar to one another belong to the same organizational field, just like regulatory agencies and suppliers. Companies might even tailor leadership teams or departments within the institution like other enterprises in their organizational field.

Overall, institutional theory provides a logical account for comprehending how institutions within the same industry develop and operate businesses. Specifically, the chapter herein regards institutional theorist Roy Suddaby's (2013) and (2015) institutional theories. Developed in 2013 and refined in 2015. Suddaby (2015) and Greenwald (2008) argued institutional theory arose between the 20th and 21st centuries, to provide understanding on phenomena that happen in *large firms*. In comparison to Kostova et al. (2008), institutional theory also regards businesses are created and operate according to how similar institutions in the same industry are constructed and operate (Suddaby, 2015; Greenwald, 2008). Leading to becoming a part of an organizational field (Greenwald, 20008; Suddaby, 2015).

From the 2013 Roy Suddaby institutional theory, Suddaby et al. (2013) contended norms and social structures are equivalent and are expected in companies. Plus, institutionalization happens in companies. To compare, Selznick (1996) argued a business is composed of norms, values, and rules with norms coming from norms and social architectures external to the company. As a result, Selznick (1996) argued companies rules and structure are institutionalized, but not the firms themselves.

Moreover, Davidsson et al. (2006) performed a qualitative study using structured telephone interviews on 321 new (young) knowledge-intensive companies that participated in a training program at Linköping University in Sweden, to study institutional forces (external pressures). Particularly regarding young firms in economies, when launching a venture idea and how pressures sometimes cause startups to change the venture idea because of the external market pressures (Davidsson et al., 2006). Data from 167 enterprise were collected (Davidsson et al., 2006).

DiMaggio and Powell (1983) stated institutional forces can be coercive, normative, and or mimetic (mimic) forces. DiMaggio and Powell (1983) advised all three forces can cause organizations to struggle when looking for ways to combat uncertainty and even gain legitimacy in a market. To compare, and to report the outcomes of the examination, Davidsson et al. (2006) claimed coercive forces can be informal or formal and are derived from regulated expectations societies place on the organization, and from pressures other companies that provide legal or other resources exert on institutions receiving the aid or resources. Davidsson et al. (2006) argued that coercive forces examples can be when firms are in the start-up phase and must follow incorporation procedures local or federal governments require. For example, filing specific tax forms and other paperwork (Davidsson et al., 2006).

Normative forces which are also called normative pressures come about because of professionalization (Davidsson et al., 2006). For example, moving from abilities to formal titles, like in professional associations that harness, improve, and defend organizational members skills (Davidsson et al., 2006). Hence, when working in an institution, internal pressures can arise and become a part of how the firm operates and portrays itself to external constituents. In considering both DiMaggio and Powell (1983) and Davidsson's et al. (2006) perspectives, Oliver (1991) advised both perspectives are examples of institutional theory. However, enterprises can be active or passive and institutional theory is probability and prediction based, at a *population level* (Oliver, 1991).

Yet, regarding *individual enterprises*, they can be active, passive, conforming, or resistant, showing institutional theory to be predictive instead of predefined, truly theoretically (Oliver, 1991). Hence, theoretically predefined results of institutions procedures, internally and within markets (Oliver, 1991). Overall, Oliver (1991) is basically asserting businesses possess options in markets, and do not have to conform to institutional theory elucidating certain institutional forces provoke conformity. Institutions can either conform, resist, avoid, comprise, or even manipulate or be manipulated when external market pressures arise. Something worth exploring is if Oliver's (1991) argument is true for both established and developing economies, and for startups versus multinational corporations. Start-ups typically start small and grow, so their general behaviors and reactions to internal or external pressures that arise because of being in an emerging market will likely vary.

However, organizational fields also exist, as DiMaggio and Powell (1983) discussed. Firstly, to quickly touch on mimetic forces, Davidsson et al. (2006) claimed mimetic in markets means for an institution to copy what is thought to be best practice, due to uncertainty in the economy or environment. Davidsson et al. (2006) seemed to imply organizations practice this, whether large or small, to protect the company. Davidsson et al. (2006) did state this towards the end of the study, organizations practice mimetic behaviors for survival, but also for success. What is of concern, in emerging markets, is if startups copy other startups, because multinationals operate on a different dimension? What is needed to be successful (scale) from level zero to level five, *per se*, is not necessarily a technique a firm can use to survive or scale from level 10 to 20, open regional offices, subsidiaries, and bring on 20 new teams' members for the expansion while also considering financial status.

Last, institutional theory regards companies obtain methods and even their form from similar enterprises. As a result, companies that acquire such form and methods become a part of an organizational field (Kostova et al., 2008). The establishment of share values, rules, expectations, and regulations for *members* to adhere to, is an organizational field (Greenwald, 2008). Similarly, DiMaggio and Powell (1983) claimed businesses that sell services and products similar to one another belong to the same organizational field, just like regulatory agencies and suppliers. Businesses might even tailor leadership teams or departments within the institution like other enterprises in their organizational field.

Nevertheless, institutional theory is not always seen as negative. DiMaggio & Powell (1983) argued institutions are *assumed* to create leadership structures, for instance, similar to firms in their industry. Yet, Greenwald (2008) and Jones (2013) claimed such design appropriateness depends on the firm's purpose, and even capabilities, not on mimicking other organizations. Plus, markets, industries, organizational fields, and even societies are distinct.

However, what is still unsettled amongst institutional scholars is, what part of markets, societies, industries, and even organizational fields make them different from one another. As an example, Suddaby and Greenwood (2001) and Greenwald (2008) advised an organizational field contains shared rules, expectations, values, and companies, as abovementioned. Furthermore, Hotho and Saka-Helmhout (2017) and Zheng (2012) argued elements of organizational fields are educational, political, financial, and other systems, necessary for the operation of the field and can impact the company's *individual* entry and exit modes, and operations. This is paramount when considering entrepreneurial ecosystem resilience, during crises, and when seeking institutional void solutions in emerging economies. The speculations of Hotho et al. (2017) and Zheng's (2012) definition of an organizational field seems to imply *institutionalization* exists, as previously discussed.

DiMaggio and Powell (1983) contended some organizational fields are already homogenous. Particularly, more homogenous in behaviors, procedures, and design. Therefore, one entity might copy another business if (1) the copying of the first company depends on the other company for resources, (2) if the firm to copy appears to be successful, and/or (3) if market risk or uncertainty exists (DiMaggio & Powell, 1983; de la luz Fernandez-Alles & Valle-Cabrera, 2006). For example, if the company that seems successful displays certain goals and seems to be accomplishing the goals and/or is a part of specific trade or professional association (DiMaggio & Powell, 1983; de la luz Fernandez-Alles & Valle-Cabrera, 2006). Nevertheless, leaders of companies should be familiar with the structure of their enterprises, including the purpose, mission, and leadership hierarchy. Unless *institutionalism* is being exercised by the organization, causing the company to become a part of an organizational field, which Suddaby and Greenwood (2001) explained, and makes institutional theory relevant.

Past and Current Behavioral Responses to Institutional Forces

Germinal and current research, in abundance, on behavioral responses to institutional forces is scarce. Most research covers companies' responses to institutional voids. Within the *institutional forces in entrepreneurship and institutional theory, and institutional voids in emerging economies sections* of this chapter, Oliver (1991) argued businesses typically conform to institutional forces or be fined because many institutional forces are regulatory or a part of an organizational field. Arum (2000) provided the example of neighborhoods, zones, or other entities shaping or regulating school-level practices. For example, school discipline, resources, and even curriculum (Arum, 2000).

Rules, norms, routines, and embeddedness is about associations being subject to environmental constraints to conform to, so they can become legitimate enterprises in their field (Hinings & Greenwood, 2015; Kostova et al., 2008) and survive in their fields, or industries. Shaw et al. (2017) posited legitimacy is needed for businesses to become embedded within the firm's context. Yet, embeddedness seems associated with or is institutionalization. Historically, DiMaggio and Powell (1983) argued some of the pressures discussed herein are only about mimicking other companies. This can be intimidating for organizations, causing internal and external pressures to become structured, operate at a certain level, and even perform, in emerging markets. DiMaggio and Powell (1983) stated the same, but from a standpoint of companies imitating one another. For example, concerning firms imitating one another, DiMaggio and Powell (1983) seemed to imply institutional theory regards pressures in companies arise from societal expectations the firm operates within. This causes those firms to adopt similar or exactly the same economic behaviors, responses, and events. To explain, *nations* themselves are discrete institutional environments with different social standards, like rules and customs (Love & Roper, 2004), which can be seen as *external institutional forces*.

Comparable to DiMaggio and Powell (1983) and Love and Roper (2004), Wang (2014) conducted a longitudinal study to explore the association between the innovation competence and quality management practices of 607 high technology companies exercising the resource-based view of firms in contemporary literature and institutional theory. Wang (2014) argued institutional theory is about enterprises functions in social settings. Also, the social pressures of company's external surroundings and public's viewpoint of the company are capable of shaping the entities behaviors (Wang, 2014). In present day circumstances, such settings can be what's called *paternalistic or bureaucratic nations*, which ties into what Love and Roper (2004) highlighted.

BACKGROUND

In discussing the background of emerging markets or economies and what they are, to lay foundation, emerging simply means emerging or getting started and developed means established. A developed economy is a feature of a developed market with a high level of economic security, capital (financial market), and growth. Plus, emerging economies have some features of a developed market, but do not fully meet developed market standards. Developed market standards range, but are the core characteristics of a developed market.

In comparison, Gao et al. (2017) explicated emerging markets are recognized by the features of constant environmental changes and underdeveloped institutions. However, sometimes such economies contain organizations that were established a long time ago, but survived over generations and are still in existence (Gao et al., 2017). Gao et al. (2017) proclaimed although the environments of the emerging economies the long-term firms have survived are weak the institutions have been able to survive because of the strength of the company's local reputation and branding, for example, by utilizing a family business and name. Yet, emerging economies do contain transaction uncertainty which makes firms considering entering the market not want to commit resources to entering, like in Argentina (Gao et al., 2017).

Gao et al. (2017) argued some countries consider transaction uncertainty to be equivalent to environmental uncertainty, like in Mexico. Too, in Mexico, corruption exists, and laws are not enforced, legal consequences are included in contracts and business agreements if laws are not followed (Gao et al., 2017). Telecommunications company AT&T experienced this when attempting to partner and work with smaller organizations looking to enter the Mexican market, via AT&T (Gao et al., 2017). AT&T eventually advised they would no longer financially contribute to such contract in an uncertain, emerging market (Gao et al., 2017). Nevertheless, Gao et al. (2017) explicated environmental uncertainty means frequent environmental shocks of some kind, like chaos, political and/or regulatory shocks, *and even wars.* Recall, Khanna et al. (2005) and White and Kitimbo (2018) explained institutional voids in Africa regard the lack of specialized intermediaries, regulatory systems, and contract enforcing instruments.

As demonstrated in Table 1, the International Monetary Fund (IMF) (2021) highlighted there are 19 emerging economies in the world. In other reports, prior to 2021, the IMF outlined 40 emerging economies. Comparable to IMF (2021), as shown in Table 2, Golden Gate University (2021) delineated 22 markets as the top emerging markets in the world and advised emerging markets are also termed emerging economies and developing countries. Golden Gate University (2021) depicted 12 nations as general top emerging economies, four countries as BRIC (Brazil, Russia, India, and China acronym) countries and six nations as CIVETS (Colombia, Indonesia, Vietnam, Egypt, Turkey, and South Africa acronym). The BRIC economies represent nations currently under consideration for being the top four emerging economies and the CIVETS are nations predicted to be the next emerging economies to rapidly gain economic prominence (Golden Gate University, 2021).

Table 1. International Monetary Fund (IMF) emerging economies of the world

Countries	Countries Continued
Argentina	Mexico
Brazil	Philippines
Chile	Poland
Colombia	Russia
Egypt	Saudi Arabia
Hungary	South Africa
India	Thailand
Indonesia	Turkey
Iran	United Arab Emirates
Malaysia	

Source: (International Monetary Fund, 2021)

Table 2. Golden Gate University top emerging economies of the world

Country	Top Emerging Country, BRIC, or CIVETS Country
Brazil	BRIC
Russia	BRIC
India	BRIC
China	BRIC
Columbia	CIVETS
Indonesia	CIVETS
Vietnam	CIVETS
Egypt	CIVETS
Turkey	CIVETS
South Africa	CIVETS
Chile	Top emerging country
Czech Republic	Top emerging country
Hungary	Top emerging country
Indonesia	Top emerging country
Malaysia	Top emerging country
Mexico	Top emerging country
Morocco	Top emerging country
Philippines	Top emerging country
Poland	Top emerging country
South Korea	Top emerging country
Taiwan	Top emerging country
Thailand	Top emerging country

Source: (Golden Gate University, 2021)

What are Entrepreneurial Ecosystems?

Entrepreneurial ecosystems are distinctive systems of interdependent relations and actors that indirectly or directly support the development and growth of new ventures (Tech Startup School, 2015a). Clearer, entrepreneurial ecosystems are a source of innovation, growth, productivity, and even employment for organizations, to improve economies (Tech Startup School, 2015a). In addition, entrepreneurial ecosystems possess nine key components that are interdependent actors of one another, but operate in a way to where they activate productive entrepreneurship within a specific territory (Tech Startup School, 2015b). Regarding ecosystems,

ecosystems are a specific social and economic environment that impact the local or regional entrepreneurship (Tech Startup School, 2015b). Henceforth, the nine main elements of entrepreneurial ecosystems are (1) entrepreneurial finance, (2) culture and social norms, (3) government programs, (4) legal and commercial infrastructure, (5) government policy, (6) physical infrastructure, (7) entrepreneurship education, (8) market openness, and (9) research and development transfer (Tech Startup School, 2015b).

What is Resilience? Community, Institutional, and Entrepreneurship Resilience

Masik and Grabkowska (2020) claimed economic, social, and natural dilemmas are becoming more and more frequent in societies and people's lives, and are intense. So, resilience strategies serve as a response to such challenges (Masik & Grabkowska, 2020).

Moreover, a variety of resilience frameworks and definitions exist. For example, within Google searches. Listings that display are psychological, community, physical, emotional, mental, social, natural, adaptive, restored, and even stress resilience. Masten (2013) proclaimed psychological resilience is where a system possesses the ability to successfully adapt to difficulties that threaten the survival, function, or future development of that particular system. When searching for types of resilience within peer-reviewed scholarship databases, including among double-blind reviewed research, resilience can be institutional, entrepreneurship, cognitive, psychological, behavioral, and even ecosystem related. Pearson et al. (2021) argued the type of disturbance, especially when considering the spread of disease, determines how ecosystems will respond to pressure, with the objective to conserve the ecosystem. Likewise, what should always be taken into account is ecosystems can have multiple stressors (Pearson et al., 2021) at the same time that need to be addressed to conserve the ecosystem.

Henley et al. (2011) wrote a report about resilience, the outcomes, and applying the lessons learned from creating and implementing a New York City project called "Project Liberty" based on the September 11, 2001 attack in the United States of America. Project Liberty regards integrating *structured mental health services* in conjunction with community-based social service programs large-scale humanitarian relief response entities offer (Henley et al., 2011). From the perspective of practicing resilience in organizations, specifically relief or disaster response entities programs, Henley et al. (2011) argued resilience-enhanced methods focus on offering support, structure, stability, community cohesion, and screening. Screening to identify individuals with suffering from traumatic or mental health conditions due to resilience issues; not applying resilience strategies in difficult circumstances (Henley et al.,

2011). Support is likely mentioned to help individuals with coping and developing internal resilience, to respond positively to external circumstances. Since traditionally negative responses to crises are usually trauma, stress, more violence, psychological issues, substance abuse or alcoholism, and other inappropriate coping mechanisms. Support can help establish positive mental well-being.

Comparable to Henley et al. (2011), Nuwayhid et al. (2011) conducted a qualitative study on the July 2006 Lebanon war and who are termed internally displaced persons (IDPs). Nuwayhid et al. (2011) advised community resilience exists based on completing the study and what public health personnel and relief agencies stated about the war and IDPs. Community resilience is a process and not an outcome (Nuwayhid et al., 2011) like Henley et al. (2011) seemingly described. Nuwayhid et al. (2011) stated, alike Henley et al. (2011), being resilient or practicing resilience involves being connected to social support networks, public health intervention programs, associated political leadership to sustain programs to help IDPs, social solidarity, and community cohesiveness. Henley et al. (2011) also mentioned resilience should be built in a person over time, especially IDPs whom have experienced wars and now possess a collective identity. As a result disaster relief practices must continually be reviewed and shifted to accommodate individuals who have experienced wars (Henley et al., 2011).

The same is true concerning other traumatic community and economic events, including those that cause businesses to suffer, which help the economy operate financially. Other traditional crises or disturbances to communities, societies, economies, and businesses are earthquakes, epidemics, floods, tornadoes, tsunamis, and occurring more frequently, community movement led riots or community violence where businesses are broken into and destroyed. To place in a context, as an example, entrepreneurs who are farmers and even live in rural areas or emerging economies can severely suffer economically from such catastrophes. Including entire regions of economies who depend on growers and fisheries from international territories to supply food or produce, at ports, whether shipped in by air, water, or land.

Last, comparable to Nuwayhid et al. (2011) and Henley et al. (2011), Riess (2021) explicated when crises occur, employees of organizations are most likely to operate in resilience when institutions or institutional leaders show workers empathy. Empathy is important because since the COVID-19 pandemic, for example, a global crises, the wellness and resilience of workers, particularly healthcare workers have become a national concern. The same can be said about any *nation*, including firms of entrepreneurs. Similarly, Riess (2021) argued institutions values play a vital and active role in both the institution and personnel of the institution operating in resilience when crises arise, to help them be resilient. To help employees be resilient, institutional values must be inherent and revolve around access to caring and correct information, safety, human connections, and employee wellbeing, specifically mental health assistance (Riess, 2021).

Mental health, which is linked with wellbeing, assistance can occur via the use of Employee Assistance Programs (EAPs) programs in organizations and is typically provided by a third party EAP firm. When considering startups and operating in emerging economies these costs, compared to overhead, would need to be weighed and carefully planned. Also, the human connections piece Riess (2021) highlighted is equivalent to the social solidarity, social support networks, and public health intervention programs Henley et al. (2011) mentioned. Health invention programs can be private, like through an EAP because public programs are likely to benefit the public holistically. For example, through a community effort under the community resilience uses community cohesiveness Henley et al. (2011) discussed. And recall, support can help establish positive mental well-being.

As well, entrepreneurship resilience regards a broad topic. Fatoki (2018) expounded resilience itself is a broad topic, but essentially means to bounce back from something. Yet, entrepreneurial resilience is an adaption process that allows entrepreneurs to continue moving forward despite adversities they face in marketplaces (Fatoki, 2018). Fatoki (2018) conducted a study on male and female entrepreneur's resilience who possess varying education, are ages 20-50, and have owned a firm one to 10 plus years with zero to nine employees. Ten resilience variables were used. For example, focused under pressure, able to adapt to change, and can achieve goals despite obstacles (Fatoki, 2018). Likewise, as a reference, Fatoki (2018) illustrated the Connor-Davidson Resilience Scale can be used to measure entrepreneurial resilience. Other scales that can be employed are the Connor-Davidson Resilience Scale-10, the Brief Resilience Scale (BRS), and the Resilience Scale for Adults (RSA) (Fatoki, 2018).

Furthermore, Fatoki (2018) reported there is a positive association between organizations success and entrepreneurial resilience. Additionally, businesses (entrepreneurs) can increase resilience by attending entrepreneurship seminars and trainings on change, coping strategies, pressure, and managing failure (Fatoki, 2018).

Improving Business Resilience for Entrepreneurial Ventures

Typically, when people think of entrepreneurial ecosystems and emerging economies they only consider startups, farmers, technology driven companies, and even multinationals here and there. Usually, other organizations that are needed for an emerging economy to function in times of calamities like private practices, are forgotten about. For example, private practice physicians and various kinds of nurses, although large hospitals are given consideration. Private practice owners are entrepreneurs too. To insert private practices into the conversation of resilience,

Gogo et al. (2019) claimed individual resilience strategies exist. For example, physicians, as individuals, can use self-awareness, self-reflection, connection and communication, flexibility, spirituality, time for oneself, and even self-compassion as coping tools (Gogo et al., 2019).

Still, not a lot of research is listed on how businesses or entrepreneurs can practice resilience, to protect the business. For instance, from a structural, behavioral, systems, operations, or even processes standpoint. Consider automations, like automating products, services, and even customers. Most organizations nowadays only focus on cyber security, threats to technological systems. However, in comparison to Gogo et al. (2019), Jamal et al. (2020) conducted a qualitative case study exercising semi-structured interviews to study how victims of the Syrian war navigated threat and applied resilience strategies. Jamal et al. (2020) divided resilience into three categories, with individual and business resilience strategies noted.

Jamal et al. (2020) explicated individuals or organizations have the capacity to be *adaptive, absorptive, or transformative* in resilience during crises, with particular emphasis on organizations. Adaptive capabilities allow a business to be flexible, collaborative, and sustain service delivery by revising logistics in response to a crisis (Jamal et al., 2020). With harnessing organizational and human resources, absorptive abilities allow an immediate response to crises and possessing transformative ability allows an enterprise to develop new services as a response to shifting needs within the local community impacted (Jamal et al., 2020). The same can be true for developing products as a response to a crises, to keep the business from dissolving, but brining products to market with a shorter launch to market plan. After data analysis and considering all interviews completed and recognizing patterns within the data, Jamal et al. (2020) reported organizational resilience within the context of crises can be sustained by three top resilience strategies. The three top useful resilience strategies for institutions identified were: (1) gaining staff commitment, (2) implementing collaborative strategies to maintain service quality and delivery to clients/customers, and (3) organizational flexibility during crises. During the pandemic many companies switched from customer's shopping in-store to ordering online and then in-store pick up or delivery. Last, collaborative strategies can be realized within the context of strategic partnerships, collaborations external to the organization.

MAIN FOCUS OF THE CHAPTER

The aim of the chapter herein is to emphasize (1) resilience and (2) strategic partnerships are needed to address entrepreneurial ecosystems, while also filling institutional voids in emerging economies, driving economic development. Schuler et al. (2010) contended the same. Entrepreneurial ecosystems with entrepreneurs considering resilience and digital business transformation as tools to guard against not only unprecedented times, but for crises in general and to grow and be sustained while operating in an emerging market.

Entrepreneurial Ecosystems Used to Grow Economies

Gao et al. (2017) explicated institutional voids can be resolved by organizations creating and maintaining favorable reputations and reducing any transaction uncertainty. Institutional voids are threats to emerging economies growth and long-term existence and must be mitigated. Gao et al. (2017) advised resolutions to practice to overcome institutional voids are defense mechanisms against the threats. At the same time, institutional voids should be used to create new opportunities and emerging markets, as an offensive strategy. The suggestion is aligned with what Gargi (2019) defined entrepreneurship to mean, as mentioned earlier.

Gargi (2019) argued entrepreneurship is not just about employing people, which contributes to economies, but regards launching new innovations, even with technology linked so additional workers can be employed and the innovations and business become profitable. The argument is kind of contradictory because additional workers can be hired when new innovations (products and services) that create supply, demand, customers, and even contracts are launched. For example, at the 2021 World Business Angel Investors Week (WBAW) United States of America (USA) summit, the general partner and co-founder of the Artemis Fund (venture capital fund for women) advised only 1-2% of women owned firms in the USA were funded in 2013 and the same amount in 2021 so far, nearly a decade later (L. Goldman, personal communication, October 22, 2021), which is a very big problem. Achi et al. (1998) argued conglomerates can be utilized to grow economies because their size allows them to leverage various types of opportunities presented depending on business-specific capabilities, which is where conglomerates have strength and because they possess the size to accomplish the minimum required economy of scale. Overall, the business-specific capabilities of conglomerates allows them to adapt to environments they operate in that continuously change (Achi et al., 1998).

Institutional Voids in Emerging Economies Dilemmas

Within a Harvard business school article, originally published in Forbes, the term institutional voids created by Harvard business school faculty Tarun Khanna and Krishna Palepu, was coined to help explain market ecosystems companies (Khanna & Palepu, 2011). Particularly, how the enterprises that depend on and make up the market ecosystems are not functioning as expected or they do not exist at all in emerging economies (Harvard Business School & Forbes, 2011). Nevertheless, alike Gao et al. (2015) and White and Kitimbo (2018), in a Harvard Business Review article, Khanna et al. (2005) deemed institutional voids as ecosystems that lack regulatory systems specialized intermediaries and contract enforcing strategies in emerging economies. Comparable to Gao et al. (2015) and White and Kitimbo (2018), Khanna and Palepu (2011) explicated, due to institutional voids, a variety of multinational corporations perform poorly in developing economies.

SOLUTIONS AND RECOMMENDATIONS

Solutions and recommendations can be idealized and implemented to respond to entrepreneurial ecosystems resilience issues and institutional voids. Providing economic empowerment and financial inclusion to entrepreneurs and entrepreneurial ecosystems via strategic partnerships.

Solutions to Respond to Entrepreneurial Ecosystems Resilience Dilemmas and Institutional Voids

Schrammel (2013) argued an interesting position about institutional voids being a theory and a competitive disadvantage to enterprises, but creates opportunities for such companies *to pay for services they need to operate*, expand, or advance. Bernardino et al. (2016) stated the same about institutional void being a theory, where social organizations too can be created to fill the voids left by existing formal organizations. Schrammel (2013) explicated, as a result of companies paying for services they need to operate, *participation incentives* can also be birthed (Schrammel, 2013).

The claims seem appropriate because entrepreneurial ecosystems and businesses in general within emerging economies or areas where institutional voids exist, need services, partners, resources, and all of the systems that are missing in emerging markets that scholars, practitioners, firm leaders, and consumers term institutional voids. However, during times of crises, where will entrepreneurs and non-multinational corporations without revenue to do so, find revenue to stay in operation, obtain resources, and even pay for services they need? Revenue needs to circulate economies, so partnerships are a must in emerging markets where institutional voids exist. As one solution to increase resilience, fill present institutional voids, and drive business and economic growth.

Economic Empowerment and Financial Inclusion for Entrepreneurs

Kara et al. (2021) performed a systematic review on how finances are dealt with at lending institutions across borders. To evaluate individuals access to credit and if not having access negatively impacts accomplishing or gaining access to other things (Kara et al., 2021). For example, gaining access to education. More specifically, do individuals socio-economic (income and education level) and demographic (race and gender) status prevent them from receiving financing (Kara et al., 2021)? Kara et al. (2021) reported both entrepreneurs *and* individual's demographic and socio-economic characteristics directly impact their ability to secure credit.

Too, the dilemma of obtaining credit, owning property (which counts as collateral), and opening and controlling a bank account are gender-based obstacles that occur throughout various countries, particularly in North Africa, South Asia, the Middle East, and sub-Saharan Africa, mostly posing a challenge for women entrepreneurs (Jain-Chandra et al., 2017). Also, Jain-Chandra et al. (2017) advised some nations enforce laws that prohibit women from working in certain professions in the workforce. Similar to Jain-Chandra et al., (2017) the Global Partnership for Financial Inclusion (GPFI) (2021) argued, when dealing with financial inclusion, women are the most disadvantaged group, especially with being approved to opening a bank account and obtaining credit. As an exemplary, GPFI (2021) argued 58% of women compared to 65% of men in emerging economies are able to open a bank account at a *formal* financial institution. Sawaneh and Badjie (2021) and Kara et al. (2021) reported similar findings.

Henceforth, *non-formal* financial institutions can be *moneylenders*. Such lenders have high credit rates and require collateral to secure credit (GPFI, 2021). Collateral like gold saved as savings, livestock, or pawned assets (GPFI, 2021). Also, risks such as falling ill from time to time, uneven cash flow, and seasonal income occur in the lives of adults and entrepreneurs in emerging markets and cause them to seek and secure *informal* strategies for gaining access to credit, savings, and loans. Nevertheless, access to capital will allow entrepreneurs in developing nations the opportunity to start businesses and improve the overall quality of life of people in respective societies economic development is claimed to do.

Application of Strategic Partnerships to Fill Institutional Voids (Opportunities to Establishing Strategic Partnerships in Emerging Economies)

Business Standard (2013) provided an example of how Blue River Capital, a private equity firm, capitalized on the emerging market of India, back in the 2000s. To stand out from the competition of financial services companies and foreign investors flocking to the nation to gain some of the competitive advantage of the institutional voids in the market, Blue River Capital tapped middle market enterprises and family-owned and operated businesses and entrepreneurs to work with (Business Standard 2013). Business Standard (2013) claimed these as big businesses, other global companies, and research analysts weren't tapping and knew nothing about because the firms weren't widely talked about nor actively [publicly] traded. Although the absence of intermediaries like background check companies complicated Blue River's efforts, Blue River Capital partnered with the firms *they identified*, to recognize and execute investment deals (Business Standard, 2013).

Application of Strategic Partnerships to Build Entrepreneurial Ecosystems

Blue River Capital sought to provide financial capital to high-potential, low risk, high-growth emerging market companies and entrepreneurs (Business Standard, 2013). Although they might not be seen as high growth in markets like the United States (Business Standard, 2013). Products and services Blue River Capital provided to such organizations, aside from direct finances, were through microfinance programs, as one example. Too, sitting on the enterprise's boards of directors, appointing board members to companies in their portfolios, and even engaging in strategic partnerships with local middle-market focused investment banks (Business Standard, 2013). Like with Edelweiss Capital, as long as Edelweiss Capital was willing to invest resources, time, and capital into the local ventures that were outside of the investment banks comfort zone in terms of corporate governance (Business Standard, 2013).

Additionally, Business Standard (2013) advised out of comfort zone also meant service-oriented firms lacked the hard assets needed as collateral to obtain bank loans in emerging markets lacking established cash-flow lending institutions. As management consultancy KPMG slowly entered the market, Blue River Capital utilized KPMG to conduct background checks and other due diligence on local businesses and entrepreneurs to work with (Business Standard, 2013). Still, the firm also relied on their own firm for market research and other institutions like deal brokers, accountants, various local investment banks, and law firms to conduct due diligence research (Business Standard, 2013). The Blue River Capital example is a great illustration on how strategic partnerships can be exercised to build entrepreneurial ecosystems.

Financial Inclusion Strategic Partnerships: Challenges and Opportunities

The Blue River Capital illustration provides a roadmap for organizations to follow. Not only to provide finances, but the framework exercises financial inclusion, to close institutional voids for a variety of parties involved in emerging markets, for entrepreneurial ecosystem resilience and economic development. Challenges of course are lack of established business structure with board members for entrepreneurs, collateral to acquire bank loans, and even due diligence intermediaries.

Education Strategic Partnerships: Challenges and Opportunities

The approach of Blue River Capital to have some of their board members sit on the boards of companies they were investing in was an interesting idea. Inclusive of sourcing external board members for their portfolio companies. What is of concern is ethical and regulatory compliance. Blue River Capital and the local firms involved do not want to be seen as forming strategic partnerships for the purpose of a corrupt benefit. Especially since emerging markets lack regulatory intermediaries, which implies no formal business oversight. No formal oversight is a problem, especially in economies where bribery, corruption, and gifts are given to gain finances, resources, competitive advantage, and to scale. Utilizing external board members to Blue River Capital is a *wiser* approach and long-term strategy suggestion.

However, an outside board search firm should be used from another nation with a global footprint, and perhaps hybrid work included. For example, board members being appointed locally and from other countries, to meet remotely online and visit the firm in-person for due diligence checks.

Either way, board members provide oversight, education, support, and access to external resources and networks. Similar to how The Smart Financing Model for entrepreneurs helps business startup and even scale using investors or capital firm's personal networks, finances, resources, and mentorship. Mentorship, which is an opportunity, to get educated on all things concerning the business under operation, in a specific industry with certain products and/or services the investor as mentor is highly familiar with. Education strategic partnerships can also occur directly with banks, government organizations, NGOs, and private enterprises. For instance, to provide entrepreneurship education to women entrepreneurs.

Recommendations to Implement Strategic Partnerships *and* Entrepreneurial Ecosystems

Most companies accomplishing sustainable development goals (SDGs), as an example, utilize partnership registration databases, called The Partnership Platform. See here: https://sdgs.un.org. Inclusive for sustainable transport conferences, to accomplish business and economic objectives. Additionally, match-making events occur within government and NGOs programs and events. Each approach can be applied to the entrepreneurial ecosystems of emerging economies. So companies are not tasked with locating their own partnerships and going the long route, per se, Blue River Capital took.

FUTURE RESEARCH DIRECTIONS

A variety of scholarly writings exist on institutional theory and emerging economies. However, practitioner research, resources, educational materials, and actionable items like trainings and seminars on the topic and its components herein are scarce. Further, a variety of quantitative studies were completed on the topic of resilience in entrepreneurship and institutional voids. Still, more qualitative research is needed and in general longitudinal and mixed methods studies.

Researchers tend to shy away from mixed methods and longitudinal studies because of personal time, resources, and data collection methods, methodology, and analysis skills inadequacy. Such research does not have to take years, but can be studied over a certain timeframe of weeks, months, or within a series. Researchers, scholars, practitioners, and leaders can also collaborate or sponsor on projects. Explaining quantitative and qualitative threats to reliability are also necessary in final reports. Particularly, regarding population, theoretical, ecological, and temporal transferability.

Last, *organizational theory* and *institutional void theory* need to be considered to extend the research presented here, scholarship in the field of organizational studies and on institutional theory. Provoking new qualitative propositions and/or research questions and hypotheses to ask and test. To provide more insight on the institutional voids, even in conjunction with entrepreneurial ecosystems resilience and institutional forces phenomena. For example, institutional void theory, although scarce in research, was stumbled upon and identified towards the end of peer-reviewed and market research performed for this chapter.

CONCLUSION

To conclude, entrepreneurship is a vehicle to help economies grow and even recover from crises. Similar to how financial inclusion, education, and strategic partnerships can help maintain and scale enterprises. Driving economic empowerment and growth.

Moreover, entrepreneurs face a variety of entrepreneurial and emerging market challenges when operating in emerging economies. Entrepreneurship in emerging markets burdens can be reduced and tackled easier if financial inclusion, education, and strategic partnership issues are addressed. Like using partnerships to resolve financial inclusion (which Blue River Capital did) and education dilemmas. Hence, women entrepreneurs have only received 1-2% of venture capital funds, ever year, for many decades. The same amount.

Too, findings writers report from future research can provoke interventions in entrepreneurial leadership and ecosystems, and emerging economies. To be implemented to help both entrepreneurs and large-scale corporations interested in strategic partnerships with small businesses and SME enterprises in emerging markets. To address institutional voids, entrepreneurial ecosystems resilience, and drive economic growth.

ACKNOWLEDGMENT

This research received no specific grant from any funding agency in the public, commercial, or not-for-profit sectors.

REFERENCES

Abril, D. Y. O., Lopez, A. M. C., & Bravo, I. M. R. (2021). Empowerment of women in entrepreneurship and innovation. *Poblacion y Desarrollo*, *27*(52), 69–91. doi:10.18004/pdfce/2076-054x/2021.027.52.069

Achi, Z., Boulas, C., Buchanan, I., Forteza, J. H., & Zappei, L. (1998). *Conglomerates in emerging markets: Tigers or dinosaurs?* https://www.strategy-business.com/article/16137

Alrubaishi, D., McAdam, M., & Harrison, R. (2021). Culture, Islamic capital and the entrepreneurial behavior of family firms in Saudi Arabia. *International Journal of Entrepreneurial Behaviour & Research*, *27*(6), 1476–1501. doi:10.1108/IJEBR-09-2020-0575

Arum, R. (2000). Schools and communities: Ecological and institutional dimensions. *Annual Review of Sociology*, *26*(1), 395–418. doi:10.1146/annurev.soc.26.1.395

Ballon, P. (2018). A structural equation model for female empowerment. *The Journal of Development Studies*, *54*(8), 1303–1320. doi:10.1080/00220388.2017.1414189

Bartik, A. W., Bertrand, M., Cullen, Z., Glaeser, E. L., Luca, M., & Stanton, C. (2020). The impact of COVID-19 on small business outcomes and expectations. *Proceedings of the National Academy of Sciences of the United States of America*, *117*(30), 17656–17666. doi:10.1073/pnas.2006991117 PMID:32651281

Bernardino, S., Santos, J. F., & Ribeiro, J. C. (2016). Social entrepreneurship: Does institutional environment make a difference? In L. Carvalho (Ed.), *Handbook of research on entrepreneurial success and its impact on regional development* (p. 26). IGI Global. doi:10.4018/978-1-4666-9567-2.ch022

Business Standard. (2013). *Exploiting institutional voids*. https://business-standard.com/article/management/exploiting-institutional-voids-110052400034_1.html

Civera, C., de Colle, S., & Casalegno, C. (2019). Stakeholder engagement through empowerment: The case of coffee farmers. *Journal of Business Ethics. European Review (Chichester, England), 28*(2), 156–174. doi:10.1111/beer.12208

Cuyper, L. D., Kucukkeles, B., & Reuben, R. (2020). *Discovering the real impact of COVID-19 on entrepreneurship*. World Economic Forum. https://www.weforum.org/agenda/2020/06/how-covid-19-will-change-entrepreneurial-business/

Dalal, K. (2011). Does economic empowerment protect women from intimate partner violence? *Journal of Injury & Violence Research, 3*(1), 35–44. doi:10.5249/jivr.v3i1.76 PMID:21483213

Davidsson, P., Hunter, E., & Klofsten, M. (2006). Institutional forces: The invisible hand that shapes venture ideas? *International Small Business Journal, 24*(2), 115–131. doi:10.1177/0266242606061834

de la luz Fernandez-Alles, M., & Valle-Cabrera, R. (2006). Reconciling institutional theory with organizational theories: How neoinstitutionalism resolves five paradoxes. *Journal of Organizational Change Management, 19*(4), 503-517.

DiMaggio, P., & Powell, W. (1983). The iron cage revisited: Institutional isomorphism and collective rationality in organizational fields. *American Sociological Review, 48*(2), 147–160.

Duflo, E. (2012). Women empowerment and economic development. *Journal of Economic Literature, 50*(4), 1051–1079.

Fatoki, O. (2018). The impact of entrepreneurial resilience on the success of small and medium enterprises in South Africa. *Sustainability, 10*, 2527–2539. https://doi.org/10.3390/su10072527

Fotache, G., & Bucsa, R.-C. (2020). Aspects regarding entrepreneurship education in Europe. *Economy Transdisciplinarity Cognition, 23*(2), 1–12.

Gao, C., Zuzul, T., Jones, G., & Khanna, T. (2017). Overcoming institutional voids: A reputation-based view of long run survival. *Strategic Management Journal, 38*(11), 2147–2167. https://doi.org/10.1002/smj.2649

Gao, Y., Gao, S., Zhou, Y., & Huang, K.-F. (2015). Picturing firms' institutional capital-based radical innovation under China's institutional voids. *Journal of Business Research, 68*(6), 1166–1175.

Gargi, B. (2019). Financial inclusion, women empowerment, and entrepreneurship: A special emphasis to India. *Malaysian E-commerce Journal, 3*(3), 18–21.

Global Partnership for Financial Inclusion (GPFI). (2021). *Why financial inclusion?* Global findex. https://gpfi.org/why-financial-inclusion

Gogo, A., Osta, A., McClafferty, H., & Rana, D. T. (2019). Cultivating a way of being and doing: Individual strategies for physician well-being and resilience. *Problems in Pediatric and Adolescent Health Care, 49*(12). doi:10.1016/j.cppeds.2019.100663

Golden Gate University. (2021, December). *Country research: Emerging markets.* https://ggu.libguides.com/country

Greenwald, H. P. (2008). *Organizations: Management without control.* Sage Publications.

Henley, R., Marshall, R., Vetter, S., & Vetter, S. (2011). Integrating mental health services into humanitarian relief responses to social emergencies, disasters, and conflicts: A case study. *The Journal of Behavioral Health Services & Research, 38*(1), 132–141.

Hinings, C. R., & Greenwood, R. (2015). Missing in action: The further contribution of Philip Selznick to contemporary institutional theory. *Research in the Sociology of Organizations, 44*, 121–148. https://doi.org/10.1108/S0733-558X20150000044006

Hotho, J., & Saka-Helmhout, A. (2017). In and between societies: Reconnecting comparative institutionalism and organizational theory. *Organization Studies, 38*(5), 647–666.

International Monetary Fund (IMF). (2021). *Miles to go: The future of emerging markets.* https://www.imf.org/external/pubs/ft/fandd/2021/06/the-future-of-emerging-markets-duttagupta-and-pazarbasioglu.htm

Jain-Chandra, S., Kochhar, K., Newiak, M., Zeinullayev, T., & Zhuang, L. (2017). Gender inequality around the world. In K. Kochhar, S. Jain-Chandra, & M. Newiak (Eds.), *Women, work, and economic growth: Leveling the playing field* (1st ed., pp. 13–27).

Jamal, Z., Alameddine, M., Diaconu, K., Lough, G., Witter, S., Ager, A., & Fouad, F. M. (2020). Health system resilience in the face of crisis: Analysing the challenges, strategies and capacities for UNRWA in Syria. *Health Policy and Planning, 35*, 26–35. https://doi.org/10.1093/heapol/czz129

Jones, G. R. (2013). *Organizational theory, design, and change* (7th ed.). Prentice Hall.

Kara, A., Zhou, H., & Zhou, Y. (2021). Achieving the United Nations' sustainable development goals through financial inclusion: A systematic literature review of access to finance across the globe. *International Review of Financial Analysis, 77*, 12–23. https://doi.org/10.1016/j.irfa.2021.101833

Khanna, T., & Palepu, K. (1997). Why focused strategies. *Harvard Business Review, 75*(4), 41–51.

Khanna, T., & Palepu, K. G. (2011). *Filling "institutional voids" in emerging markets*. https://www.hbs.edu/news/Pages/item.aspx?num=1524

Khanna, T., Palepu, K. G., & Sinha, J. (2005). *Strategies that fit emerging markets*. https://www.hbr.org/2005/06/strategies-that-fit-emerging-markets

Kostova, T., Roth, K., & Dacin, M. T. (2008). Institutional theory in the study of multinational corporations: A critique and new directions. *Academy of Management Review, 33*(4), 994–1006.

Kumar, M. (2018). Institutional voids and Indian automotive industry: Challenges and reflection. In Emerging markets from a multidisciplinary perspective: Advances in theory and practice of emerging markets (1st ed., pp. 405–414). Springer. https://doi.org/10.1007/978-3-319-75013-2_30.

Love, J. H., & Roper, S. (2004). The organisation of innovation: Collaboration, cooperation and multifunctional groups in UK and German manufacturing. *Cambridge Journal of Economics, 28*(3), 379–395.

Mair, J. (2005). Entrepreneurial behavior in a large traditional firm: Exploring key drivers. In T. Elfring (Ed.), *Corporate entrepreneurship and venturing* (pp. 49–72). Springer.

Masik, G., & Grabkowska, M. (2020). Practical dimension of urban and regional resilience concepts: A proposal of resilience strategy model. *Regional Studies on Development, 24*(1), 30–34.

Mohyuddin, A., Chaudhry, H., & Ambreen, M. (2012). Economic empowerment of women in the rural areas of Balochistan. *Pakistan Journal of Women's Studies, 19*(2), 239-257.

Newenham-Kahindi, A. (2015). Managing sustainable development through people: Implications for multinational enterprises in developing countries. *Personnel Review, 44*(3), 388–407.

Nuwayhid, I., Zurayk, H., Yamout, R., & Cortas, C. S. (2011). Summer 2006 war on Lebanon: A lesson in community resilience. *Global Public Health: An International Journal for Research, Policy and Practice, 6*(5), 505–519.

Obeidat, A. M., Abualoush, S. H., Irtaimeh, H. J., Khaddam, A. A., & Bataineh, K. A. (2018). The role of organizational culture in enhancing the human capital applied study on the social security corporation. *International Journal of Learning and Intellectual Capital, 15*(3), 258–276.

Obeidat, A. M., Atef Wahiby, H., Alshammari, D. M., Alzu'bi, S. K., Hadrab, A. F., & Samarah, M. A. (2021). The moderate role of knowledge sharing on the effect of human capital in job empowerment. *Ilkogretim Online – Elementary Education, 20*(5), 163-172. doi:10.17051/ilkonline.2021.05.15

Oliver, C. (1991). Strategic responses to institutional processes. *Academy of Management Review, 16*(1), 145–179.

Onsongo, E. (2019). Institutional entrepreneurship and social innovation at the base of the pyramid: The case of M-Pesa in Kenya. *Industry and Innovation, 26*(4), 369–390. https://doi.org/10.1080/13662716.2017.1409104

Pearson, R. M., Schlacheer, T. A., Jinks, K. I., Olds, A. D., Brown, C. J., & Connolly, R. M. (2021). Disturbance type determines how connectivity shapes ecosystem resilience. *Scientific Reports, 11*(1), 1–8. https://doi.org/10.1038/s41598-021-80987-1

Rao, S., Vlassoff, C., & Sarode, J. (2014). Economic development, women's social and economic empowerment and reproductive health in rural India. *Asian Population Studies, 10*(1), 4–22.

Riess, H. (2021). Institutional resilience: The foundation for individual resilience, especially during COVID-19. *Global Advances in Health and Medicine: Improving Healthcare Outcomes Worldwide, 10*, 1–3. https://doi.org/10.1177/21649561211006728

Sawaneh, K., & Badjie, F. (2021). Empowering women in the Agricultural Value Chain through Islamic blended products to attain the agenda 2030 in The Gambia. *European Journal of Islamic Finance*, *17*, 1–11.

Schrammel, T. (2013). Bridging the institutional void: An analytical concept to develop valuable cluster services. *Management Revenue, 24*(2), 114-132. doi:10.1688/1861-9908_mrev_2013_02_Schrammel

Shaw, E., Wilson, J., & Pret, T. (2017). The process of embedding a small firm in its industrial context. *International Small Business Journal: Researching Entrepreneurship, 35*(3), 219-243. doi:10.1177/0266242616671170

Simbar, M., Alizadeh, S., Hajifoghaha, M., & Dabiri, F. (2017). Comparison of social, economic, and familial empowerment in married women in three cities of Iran. *International Journal of Community Based Nursing and Midwifery*, *5*(3), 248–255.

Singapore Management University (SMU). (2013). *Institutional voids: Black hole or opportunities?* https://ink.library.smu.edu.sg/pers/21

Stephan, U., Zbierowski, P., Perez-Luno, A., & Klausen, A. (2021). *Entrepreneurship during the COVID-19 pandemic: A global study of entrepreneurs challenges, resilience, and well-being*. King's Business School. https://www.kcl.ac.uk/business/assets/pdf/research-papers/global-report-entrepreneurship-during-the-covid-19-pandemic-a-global-study-of-entrepreneurs'-challenges-resilience-and-well-being.pdf

Suddaby, R. (2013). Institutional theory. In E. Kessler (Ed.), *Encyclopedia of management theory* (pp. 379–384). Sage.

Suddaby, R. (2015). Can institutional theory be critical? *Journal of Management Inquiry*, *24*(1), 93–95.

Suddaby, R., & Greenwood, R. (2001). Colonizing knowledge: Commodification as a dynamic of jurisdictional expansion in professional service firms. *Human Relations*, *54*(7), 933–953.

Tech Startup School. (2015a). *Entrepreneurship ecosystem and its elements: Business accelerator*. https://techstartupschool.com/news/entrepreneurship-ecosystem-and-its-elements.html

Tech Startup School. (2015b). *Entrepreneurship ecosystem nine elements*. https://techstartupschool.com/news/img/

Tiba, S., & Frikha, M. (2020). Sustainability challenge in the agenda of African countries: Evidence from simultaneous equation models. *Journal of the Knowledge Economy*, *11*, 1270–1294. https://doi.org/10.1007/s13132-019-00605-4

Valente, M. (2018). *Organizing for sustainability*. https://www.organizingforsustainability.com

van Dijk, P. (2018). *Dealing with institutional voids in emerging markets: A small and medium sized enterprise perspective* [Master's Thesis]. Radboud Universiteit Nijmegen Digital Archive. https://theses.ubn.ru.nl/bitstream/handle/123456789/6823/Dijk%2C_Philip_van_1.pdf?sequence=1

Venugopalan, M., Bastian, B. L., & Viswanathan, P. K. (2021). The role of multi-actor engagement for women's empowerment and entrepreneurship in Kerala, India. *Administrative Sciences*, *11*(1), 31. https://doi.org/10.3390/admsci11010031

Wang, C.-H. (2014). A longitudinal study of innovation competence and quality management on firm performance. *Innovation (North Sydney, N.S.W.)*, *16*(3), 392–403.

White, L., & Kitimbo, A. (2018). Institutions and the location strategies of South African firms in Africa. *The Internationalization of African Firms*, *61*(1), 61-73. doi:10.1002/tie.21965

Zheng, C. (2012). Isomorph isomorphic influences and aspiration: Reference group choice in entry mode decisions. *Journal of International Business Research*, *11*(2), 129–141.

ADDITIONAL READING

Gupta, M. (2021). Role of NGOs in women empowerment: Case studies from Uttarakhand, India. *Journal of Enterprising Communities: People and Places in the Global Economy*, *15*(1), 25–41. doi:10.1108/JEC-04-2020-0066

Masten, A. S. (2013). Global perspectives on resilience in children and youth. *Child Development*, *85*(1), 6–20. doi:10.1111/cdev.12205 PMID:24341286

Selznick, P. (1996). Institutionalism "old" and "new". *Administrative Science Quarterly*, *41*(2), 270–277. doi:10.2307/2393719

Shikha, K. (2019). Entrepreneurship for economic and social empowerment of women: A case study of a self-help credit program in Nithari Village, Noida, India. *Australasian Accounting, Business, and Finance Journal, 13*(2), 123–142. doi:10.14453/aabfj.v13i2.8

Singapore Management University. (2013). *Institutional voids: Black hole or opportunities?* https://ink.library.smu.edu.sg/pers/21

Stromquist, N. P. (2015). Women's empowerment and education: Linking knowledge to transformative action. *European Journal of Education, 50*(3), 308–324. doi:10.1111/ejed.12137

Suddaby, R. (2010). Challenges for Institutional Theory. *Journal of Management Inquiry, 19*(1), 14–20. doi:10.1177/1056492609347564

Suddaby, R., & Greenwood, R. (2005). Rhetorical strategies of legitimacy. *Administrative Science Quarterly, 50*(1), 35–67. doi:10.2189/asqu.2005.50.1.35

Suddaby, R., Seidl, D., & Le, J. K. (2013). Strategy-as-practice meets neo-institutional theory. *Strategic Organization, 11*(3), 329–344. doi:10.1177/1476127013497618

Tahir, M. W., Kauser, R., Bury, M., & Bhatti, J. S. (2018). "Individually-led" or "female-male partnership" models for entrepreneurship with the BISP support: The story of women's financial and social empowerment from Pakistan. *Women's Studies International Forum, 68*, 1–10. doi:10.1016/j.wsif.2018.01.011

KEY TERMS AND DEFINITIONS

Economic Development: To enhance or grow an economy, traditionally with utilizing various resources, wealth, job creation, prosperity, and/or finances (e.g., investments) to improve the overall well-being or quality of life of people in the society.

Economic Empowerment: Economic empowerment is the ownership of finances, investments, property, and gaining education (Dalal, 2011). Economic empowerment directly impacts economic development and vice versa (Rao et al., 2014). Within the context of *economic empowerment of women*, economic empowerment involves being in a position to make decisions (Mohyuddin et al., 2012). When women are economically empowered, they participate in decision-making (Mohyuddin et al., 2012; Ballon, 2018). Similarly, when women are empowered, they make leadership, income, time, and resources decisions (Aziz et al., 2021).

Empowerment: Empowerment can be socially, economically, or even ecologically structured. Generally, empowerment encompasses empowerment *areas, benefits, and actions*. *Empowerment areas* frequently studied and reported on were (1) sustaining income and productivity, including through knowledge transfer and technological tools, (2) developing business skills and industry specific know-how and skills, (3) supporting business creation and entrepreneurial innovation, (4) developing collaborative partnerships for collaborative solutions, and (5) favoring gender equality (Civera et al., 2018).

Entrepreneurship: The use various innovative resources to identify and then pursue opportunities (Mair, 2005). Also, entrepreneurship regards employing others, contributing to societies, and is connected to technology and new innovations that eventually produce additional employment and profit opportunities for economies (Gargi, 2019).

Financial Inclusion: When certain groups of disadvantaged are included or regarded to obtain credit and gain access to opening a bank account or receiving other finances services for personal, professional, or commercial use.

Sustainable Development: Sustainable development is where economic development, social development, and environmental development, and governance interact, work cohesively (Tiba & Frikha, 2020). An institutional pillar can also be added (Tiba & Frikha, 2020).

Women's Empowerment: Women's empowerment is connected to economic empowerment. Women being capable of achieving things, free to collaborate on tasks with others at will, possessing resources, and having control in their personal, financial, social, and economical lives for independence, which increases self-esteem and self-confidence. Economic empowerment is also the ownership of property, investments, and finances (Simbar et al., 2017), and gaining education (Dalal, 2011).

Chapter 6
Entrepreneurship Ecosystems and Innovation:
A Study in an Emerging Economy, Turkey

Beyza Oba
Istanbul Bilgi University, Turkey

ABSTRACT

Entrepreneurial ecosystems have attracted considerable attention from different constituencies. Especially in line with the increasing numbers of start-ups, it is expected that these ecosystems will contribute to entrepreneurial activity and economic growth of a region/nation. However, most of the entrepreneurial ecosystem research and thus developed frameworks focus on advanced economies. On the other hand, ecosystems positioned in emerging economies are exposed different to institutional arrangements that influence resource allocation and entrepreneurial activity. This study argues that context is important in shaping the dynamics of an entrepreneurial ecosystem, the choices of entrepreneurs, and the interactions between the entrepreneurs and other resource providers. To illustrate this, the study focuses on an emerging economy, Turkey, and by utilizing secondary data tries to underpin the institutional voids and resource scarcities that lead to a 'shallow' entrepreneurial ecosystem.

INTRODUCTION

During the last decade, the concept of entrepreneurial ecosystems (EE) has been popular among business practitioners, academia, and policy makers. The rise of the concept coincides with the increase in the number of start-ups, the worldwide

DOI: 10.4018/978-1-6684-4745-1.ch006

diffusion of the practices, business models employed by them and emergence of knowledge-based economy. This increase in start-ups and its consequences in terms of economic development, creating new job opportunities and increasing opportunities for innovation has attracted the attention of various constituencies. It is expected that entrepreneurial ecosystems will be instrumental in developing a milieu where the problems faced by start-ups would be weakened, they would function more efficiently and improve their innovation capacity. Although in other fields the concept of ecosystems was used much earlier (for example Joseph Schumpeter and his explanation on the business life cycles) in other disciplines (Colombo, 2019), the earliest mention of this phenomenon in business and management literature was made by Moore (1993) in relation to business ecosystems where interrelated actors (such as firms, universities, government offices) in a given setting co-existed in the provision of products/services. In later years, academic work following Moore developed the concept of "ecosystem" that replaced "environment" (Isenberg, 2010, 2014; Adner et al., 2013). The underlying idea was that competitive advantage of firms could be enhanced by utilizing shared resources, knowledge spillovers and government supports (Audredsch et al., 2018). By conducting a bibliometric study Malecki (2017) shows that the term "entrepreneurial ecosystem" appeared in scholarly studies in early 2000s and became dominant only after 2006. In their 2004 article Iansiti and Levien (2004) used the ecosystem metaphor that was originally mentioned by Moore (1993) and since than "ecosystem" replaced "environment" in most of the academic work. Another study by Audredsch et al., (2018) shows how the studies on "entrepreneurship ecosystem" exploded after 2004.

Leading work mainly focused on the relation between entrepreneurial activity and EEs. The extant research argues that the features of a specific EE will have positive or negative contributions to the entrepreneurship activity and thus to economic growth (Stam, 2018; Malecki, 2018; Spigel, 2017). The relation between EEs and entrepreneurship is not unidirectional, i.e., a high-quality EE leads to productive entrepreneurship. However, as stressed by Stam (2015, 2018), although the qualities of a specific EE influence the entrepreneurial activity, the role of the entrepreneurs in the making of the EE should not be neglected. This study aims to develop a conceptual framework (Figure 1) in line with the above-mentioned explanations of EEs and entrepreneurship. The proposed framework is based on the extant literature on EEs and data collected from secondary sources (academic papers, government statistics etc.) in an emerging economy – Turkey. Furthermore, this study adopts an approach similar to the emergence of EEs and claims that the emergence of entrepreneurial activity, and the EEs dependent on the institutional voids related to changes in technology (for example availability and usage of digital technologies), and government policies (for example, subsidies, legislation). Such an approach is close to the natural systems and bottom-up approaches. However, given the context specific conditions, the dominant state tradition in Turkey and focusing on power configurations among the government and firms, it has similarities to the top-down approach in explaining the evolution of EEs. In other words, the framework developed for the Turkish case – an emerging economy – is structured around a third form of evolution i.e., hybrid evolution model. Basically, the dominant institution is government and voids are shaped by the very actions and policies of the government. Given this background on the Turkish system, the paper aims to develop an argument about the role of institutional voids and arrangements (formal and informal) in a hybrid model in promoting productive entrepreneurial activity.

The paper is structured as such; after introduction part two will cover the concepts of EEs and entrepreneurship. In relation to EEs their differences from clusters, triple helix and industrial districts and their major components as well as outcomes will be studied. Then in the third part the framework components i.e., institutional voids, formal and informal institutions and enabling inputs will be studied with a reference to the Turkish context. The paper will conclude with a discussion on the interaction between framework components and the outcomes of the EEs in Turkish context.

Entrepreneurial Ecosystem

The concept of entrepreneurial ecosystem has similarities to "clusters", "innovation clusters", "triple helix" and "industrial districts" that has been previously developed and studied. Autio et al., (2018) study, provides a detailed comparison of innovation clusters, industrial districts, and entrepreneurial ecosystems (EEs) in terms of aims, economic benefits offered, roles attributed to entrepreneurs, locus of opportunities and structural elements. Accordingly, EEs are systems of entrepreneurial opportunity discovery, pursuit and scale-up" (pp.15) that facilitate experimentation, development and diffusion of new business models and experience sharing. Different than other cluster types, the major and central actor in EEs are the entrepreneurs – entrepreneurs in discovery and pursuit of an opportunity. Similarly, the other actors (for example, state, incumbent firms, universities) are organized around entrepreneurs for promoting entrepreneurial discovery. The structural elements of the EEs (for example, co-working spaces, venture capital networks) are organized for developing new types of ventures and business models. In other words, the major outputs of EEs, different than clusters, are the creation of new ventures and business models. Or to put it differently, EEs are spaces that facilitate entrepreneurial activity by shared knowledge and experience for opportunities outside the ecosystem. They enable the development and utilization of a shared knowledge base (Asheim et al., 2011) for a generic business model where participants voluntarily share their experiences. Such a conceptualization of an EE requires the study of actors and processes that enable their cooperation and consensus in knowledge sharing as well as the institutions that host them.

A stream of academic work on EEs is related to their evolution. One strand of arguments about the emergence and evolution of EEs stress that they are natural systems and develop in a bottom-up fashion (Isenberg 2010, 2014). Inspired by the neoclassical economics this approach supports the view that different actors (venture capitalists, investors, public offices, entrepreneurs etc.) driven by self-interest will be coordinated by an invisible hand and benefit from path dependencies. Culture as a set of shared assumptions, rules, and behavior patterns, acts as the invisible hand (Colombo, 2019) and contributes to the self-directing qualification of an EE. Taking EEs as self-regulating natural systems driven by self-interest of the constituents and governed by an invisible hand, disregards their governance, the way resources are distributed and redistributed, power configurations within the system and the role(s) played by the powerful members of the ecosystem. On the other hand, top-down, planned EEs are created by the deliberate actions of the governments in line with the policies pursued. In such EEs in terms of power configurations, the government has a more dominant position and usually feeds the system with resources (Stam, 2015; Colombo, 2019) and the EEs is instrumentalized for a political goal. However, as indicated by Lehmann and Seitz (2017), this type of EEs is less innovative.

Another strand of research on EEs focusses on the relation between EEs and the entrepreneurial activity and provide evidence how 'good quality' EEs are instrumental in promoting a productive entrepreneurial activity (Stam, 2017; Malecki, 2018; Spigel, 2017). These studies also incorporate the role of entrepreneurs as actors in the development and perseverance of good quality EEs. In order to have a better understanding of the contextual conditions that enable the emergence of EEs conducive to a vigorous entrepreneurial activity, a framework need to be developed. In this study based on the studies of Stam (2015), and Spigel (2015) a framework that constitutes the basic components of an EE and the relation among these components is developed. Accordingly, the study takes EEs as spaces that promote entrepreneurial activity, for the creation of new business models and ventures that is shaped by the collaboration of governments, incumbent firms, public authorities, and universities that facilitate the involvement of enabling inputs. As seen in Figure 1, besides facilitating formal and informal institutional arrangements, the 'enabling inputs', i.e., availability of skillful labor, financial resources, provision of support services and opportunity networks foster entrepreneurial activity. Furthermore, the framework developed in this study, accentuates the role of exogenous factors under the title 'context specific voids' in an effort to elaborate the role of context and further discuss that EEs situated in different regions/countries have different performance outputs.

Figure 1. A framework for the EEs in an Emerging Economy

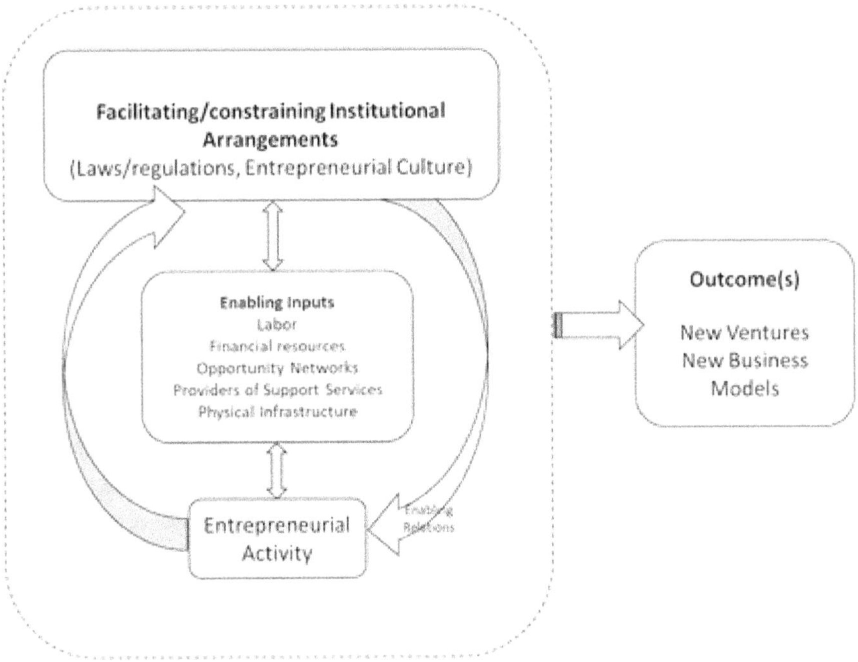

Facilitating/Constraining Institutional Arrangements

Institutions can be defined as human constructed formal and informal arrangements that regulate, shape, and stabilize the economic, political, and social realms. They are devised by humans through time and structure human interaction by imposing constraints. Institutions are made up of formal (codified, written rules, laws, constitutions) and informal constraints (i.e., culturally specified norms, belief systems, conventions, and codes of conduct) (North, 1990). In other words, institutions can be taken as the "rules of the game". Thus, institutions comprise an area of operation, legitimate rules (formal and informal) and actors (individuals/groups/firms) with a legitimate interest in the application of these rules while pursuing their goals. Institutions bring continuity and stability to a social/political/economic system, as well as an agreement of the form and content of legitimate rules. And finally, institutions are accepted and shared by the actors involved, they are habitualized and taken for granted. Actors in an effort to be legitimate accept and implement the formal and informal institutional constraints prevalent in a system. Thus, we can claim that entrepreneurs in an EE develop institutional arrangements, practice them, through time as arrangements become habitualized the same arrangements turn out to be constraints for the same EE and the same entrepreneurs. In other words, EEs are arenas of interaction between actors (entrepreneurs) and institutions that influence the level and content of entrepreneurial innovation (new venture and business model creation). As discussed by Autio et. al., (2014), although the institutional context is influential in regulating the entrepreneurial innovation process most of the existing literature on innovation and entrepreneurship focuses on the entrepreneur rather than the context. Similarly, Spigel (2017) proposes that the interaction between cultural, social, and material attributes reproduces an EE; institutional context can facilitate or impede interfirm cooperation and knowledge sharing. Governments, incumbent firms, entrepreneurs, and universities collectively through their interactions construct and persevere formal and informal institutional arrangements in an ecosystem. Thus, in different countries/regions specified by a different institutional context we can expect to have different types of new ventures and business models.

The extant research on emerging economies in relation to the institutional context mainly specifies institutional voids as a barrier for entrepreneurial creativity and activity (Cao & Shi, 2021). In these studies, inconsistency of government policies, lack of cooperation between different actors (universities and firms), limited funding opportunities, cultural constrains in developing and sharing knowledge, inadequate physical infrastructure are discussed as institutional voids (For example, Manimala & Wasdani, 2015). Institutional voids are the outcomes of scarcities in the number and quality of intermediaries, regulations, rule of law and contract enforcing mechanisms financial, labor and product markets (Khanna & Palepu, 2000). Institutional voids can differ across countries and their outcomes can be mitigated differently (for example, different types of intermediary organizations).

Studies on the role of formal and informal institutions in emerging economies focus on voids that constrain entrepreneurial activities and innovation (Cao & Shi, 2021). For example, Arruda et al., (2013) study mentions regulatory framework as a constraint in the Brazilian entrepreneurial ecosystem and Guerrero and Urbano (2017) pinpoints how taxation schemes and red tape restrained entrepreneurial activity in Mexico. One of the consequences of institutional voids is the increase in the number of informal entrepreneurial activity. Autio and Fu, (2015) study show that the quality of economic and political institutions within a country influence the rate of formal and informal entrepreneurial activity, i.e., as the quality of the institutions increase the rates of formal institutions increase as well. The same study identifies, regulation of entry, of financial markets, legislation on bankruptcy as formal economic institutions. Political institutions such as rule of law, protection of property, legislation for intellectual property and equality in front of the law also promote formal entrepreneurship. In the same study it is stated that formal entrepreneurship rate in Turkey is 0.10 as compared to 1.03 informal entrepreneurship. Thus, we can claim that one of the reasons for high informality in Turkey is the lack of deepening in the formal institutional arrangements. In this study, with reference to the Turkish context, wo constraints-the regulating role assumed by the governments and the entrepreneurial culture-will be studied as facilitating/constraining institutional arrangements.

Government and Regulations

As stated by Autio et al., (2014), policy decisions and the decisions of the governments can hinder or promote entrepreneurial activity. Governments by legislations and regulations (for example, taxation, easing procedures for the formation of new businesses, intellectual property laws), by the provision of physical infrastructure and through various financing mechanisms (such as taking the role of venture capitalist, subsidizing research and development of firms) can contribute to the development of a positive/negative milieu for entrepreneurial activity. Governments by taking various roles–regulator, resource provider–can facilitate the growth of entrepreneurial ecosystems. Extant research in different context shows that for promoting entrepreneurial activity governments introduce reduced tax schemes (for example, Mack & Meyer, 2016), reduce legal barriers for establishing firms, provide public funds for supporting networking and incubation services (Spiegel, 2017), decrease red tape for licenses (Cohen, 2006) and develop legislation for protecting intellectual property (Autio et al., 2014). Furthermore, governments by utilizing various tools can facilitate the development of networks that enable access to social capital, qualified labor, and professional services (Lux et. al., 2020).

World Economic Forum (WEF) indicates that taxation policies of governments can both have a facilitating and inhibiting role on the formation of new firms (2014). For example, according to OECD data tax on corporate net profits levied in Turkey is lower (2.08) than the OECD average (2.98). This can be taken as a stimulating factor for the establishment of new ventures. However, the tax wedge, the ratio of tax paid by a single worker to the total labor costs of an employer is higher (39.66) than the OECD average (34.62). Tax wedge reflects labor costs and is a factor that discourages employment. Taxes can also influence the formation of new businesses; Djankov et al., (2002) study on the regulation of entry across 75 countries, provides information about the number of tax procedures (for example, registration for VAT, validation of accounting books) that is to be completed by a start-up (2002). In the same study, Turkey ranks 42nd, with 11 procedures of which 2 are on tax and on the average, it takes 55 business days for becoming operational. Similarly, the 2019 World Bank Enterprise Survey indicates that 66.6 per cent of the firms in Turkey see tax rates as a major constraint for their operations. As compared with the ratio of the other countries (30.5 per cent) it is a very high perceived obstacle. Given this data, we can claim that in Turkey, government regulations in relation to taxation, bureaucratic procedures for firm formation constrain the formation of new ventures. Furthermore, governments through various regulative policies can also implement pro-market reforms that enables the enlargement of a specific industry by promoting local and international new entrants. Pro-market reforms, by reducing the entry barriers can open opportunities for new ventures as well as incumbent firms (Singh et al., 2019). For example, Çeviker (2021) study in Turkish traffic insurance industry provides a detailed explanation on the role of pro-market reforms in increasing the number of firms in a specific industry.

According to WEF study (2014) on EEs, an efficient regulatory framework is considered as a precondition for the growth of firms. However, in the same study and Global Innovation Index (2021) prepared by World Intellectual Property Organization (WIPO), the regulatory environment of Turkey is given as a weakness. One of the major problems in this realm is the lack of transparency regarding the policy decisions of the government. According to OECD data (2021), in Turkey, public is never informed about an approaching planned public consultation and stakeholders are not involved in the evaluations of the existing regulations. Moreover, ongoing consultations, views of the participants, the evaluations are not publicly announced, and policy makers do not provide a public response to the made public evaluations. In other words, the regulations and legislation are drafted singlehandedly by the government, the stakeholders and practitioners are left out of the process which in turn leads to inefficiencies in the implementation process.

Turkish Management Culture

Culture is comprised of patterns of thinking, feeling, and acting, it is "the collective programming of the human mind which distinguishes one group of people from another" (Hofstede, 1991, pp.5). Culture is shared, learned, transferred, and is manifested in symbols, heroes, rituals, and values. Cultural beliefs and attitudes about entrepreneurship in a society shapes the career choices of individuals. In case entrepreneurship is taken as a normal, standard career path a positive milieu for entrepreneurship activity will be created and individuals will be encouraged to be entrepreneurs. Cultural attitudes towards entrepreneurship and risk-taking shapes the way things are done in an EE and the creation of new ventures, business models. Also, stories of the prominent successful entrepreneurs (heroes) that reflect the values and behavior patterns of an 'ideal' entrepreneur inspire others, guide them in their career choices and practices.

Extant studies in emerging economies take culture as an institutional void (for example, Arruda et al., 2013; Manimala & Wasdani, 2015). As stated in these studies fear of failure, avoiding uncertainty restrain engagement in new ventures and influence the choice of a career as a paid employee in well-paid secure jobs.

According to Hofstede study (2020), the Turkish management culture is characterized as high in power distance and uncertainty avoidance and low in individualism and masculinity. Accordingly, it is claimed that in the workplace "the ideal boss is a father figure" with centralized power. Employees rather than using their discretion "expect to be told what to do". High score on uncertainty avoidance hints that there is need for laws and regulations and less room for risk taking. People seek consensus, avoid open conflict and belonging to a group/network, being loyal to the in-group members are important. And nepotism is practiced frequently.

According to 2020 Global Entrepreneurship Monitor (GEM), Turkey has a lower score in its group (Group B) in social and cultural norms, i.e., culture does not encourage and praise entrepreneurship. In a culture characterized with high uncertainty avoidance, like Turkey, it is expected that fear of failure will be high, and willingness to take risks will be less. Doğan study (2016) on Turkish national culture and entrepreneurship, identify that, Turkish entrepreneurs fear failure, they are not risk takers and entrepreneurship is not considered as a valid career path. The GEM report (2020) states that motivations of early-stage entrepreneurs are "to build great wealth or very high income" and the underlying reason for the choice of entrepreneurship is "to earn a living because jobs are scarce". The outcome of low individualism score in Turkey can be related to the low degree of creativeness and innovativeness as entrepreneurial activities. As explained by Doğan (2016), in Turkey creativeness and innovation are not important in explaining the entrepreneurial activity. This assertion is accentuated by the GEM report that identifies "to earn a living" as the mostly mentioned motivation for entrepreneurial motivation and "to make a difference" as the least mentioned. Given these explanations about Turkish management culture we can claim that choice of entrepreneurship as a career path is necessity-driven, potential and existing entrepreneurs are reluctant to take risks and innovativeness is not taken as an act of entrepreneurship. Thus, we can argue that in such a milieu, there will be less innovations in terms of new ventures and business models.

Enabling Inputs

Financial Resources

Governments can facilitate the founding of new ventures by providing inputs such as human resources, financial resources, and physical infrastructure. The major sources of equity for a new venture, besides bootstrapping are state funds, venture capital, angel investors and bank loans. The availability of such financial tools in an economy and the efficiency in their operations will have a positive impact in promoting entrepreneurial activity and thus formation of new business ventures. One of the mostly cited problems of small business entrepreneurs in Turkey is related to the provision of financial resources and the availability of effective funding mechanisms. Major sources of funding for entrepreneurs consist of funds provided by TUBITAK (The Scientific and Technological Research Council of Turkey), and KOSGEB (Organization for the Development of Small and Medium Enterprises). TUBITAK supports projects for research and development, entrepreneurship support (BIGG) and venture capital funding. Tech-InvestTr is a venture capital support program that provides funds to early-stage companies for R&D. The program is run in cooperation with the Ministry of Finance and Treasury. Another program-Capacity Building-for developing and improving the quality of entrepreneurial ecosystem provides financial resources for support firms, universities and NGOs that are involved in mentorship, training, and fundraising events. Also, small, and medium sized companies are supported by grants to improve their competitiveness in research capability. Finally, entrepreneurship support program-BIGG- provides training and support to entrepreneurs in all stages of the lifecycle of a venture - namely idea generation, seeding, growth and maturity. As the data provided by TUBİTAK shows these programs, both in quantity and the amount of financial resources granted are more utilized by SMEs; 66 per cent of the projects supported are proposed by small firms. However, the project approval rates are low. For example, only 6.2 percent of the projects (business idea and business plan) submitted to the BIGG program were funded. Another problem in the distribution TUBİTAK funds is the uneven representation of different cities/regions. Most of the funds (36 per cent) are captured by firms located in İstanbul (TUBİTAK, 2017). On the other hand, financial supports of KOSGEB are in the form of loans; loans for SME development (up to 1.000. 000 TL, approximately 70.000 US dollars) and SME finance support (up to 500.000 TL). Only in some cases some portions of the loans are interest free and paid as a grant. These financing mechanisms falls short in meeting needs of firms (Belitski & Büyükbalcı, 2020). Furthermore, there seems to be problems in the allocation of these funds: the appointment of referees for project evaluation and selection should be based on meritocracy and the process, the criteria on which decisions are based, the evaluation process must be transparent.

Labor

Availability of educated, talented human resources have a positive effect on the entrepreneurial activity and as well improve the quality of a specific EE. Extant studies identify availability of a talented (for example, management and technical talent) workforce either local or immigrant, as an important enabling input of an EE (Isenberg, 2011; WEF, 2013; Stam, 2015; Spigel, 2015). In emerging economies, it has been argued that labor gaps exist in finding high-quality entrepreneurs and specialized employees. Most of the entrepreneurs in these economies are necessity driven and choose entrepreneurial career because of unemployment (Cao & Shi, 2021). In contrast to advanced economies, university graduates in Turkey prefer an employment in a well-paid secure job. According to 2021 GEM Report, in Turkey more non-graduates than graduates opt for being an entrepreneur and the motivations for choosing this career path are given as scarcity of jobs, earning a living, and having a high income. This situation somehow is contrary to the common expectation that people with higher levels of education will be more for entrepreneurship since they will see themselves having skills to do so. The same Report also indicates that there is a gender gap, that is more men consider being an entrepreneur than women. Although universities in Turkey offer courses on entrepreneurship, provide opportunities to start-ups by offering their services at technoparks, incubation centers located within the boundaries of the universities and organize university club meetings so that success stories are shared (Belitski & Büyükbalcı, 2020), students still prefer employment in a well-established firm. This can be explained in relation to the Turkish management culture (especially uncertainty avoidance dimension), scarcity of and difficulty in finding financial resources and inefficiency of governmental supports. Government supports for the betterment of secondary education, making vocational education attractive to younger generations by providing job opportunities, for drafting legislation that will lessen informal employment can be influential in improving the choice of entrepreneurship as a career path. Also, governments can improve the conditions for women (such as availability of childcare centers in the workplaces) who would like to have an entrepreneurial career.

The role of governments on the labor as a critical input can be studied in two areas: education and legislation. Governments by increasing expenditure on education, and funding students can improve the quantity and quality of labor. Although Turkey has a comparable strength on tertiary education, especially in terms of enrollment (WIPO Report, 2021), secondary school education falls far beyond the OECD average. According to OECD PISA test results the quality of education is significantly behind the average. Governments can also influence labor conditions by various legislation. In Turkey, labor participation, especially women, to formal economy is low, legal employment costs are high, severance system is expensive (OECD Country Report, 2021). Especially, after the adoption of the Labour Law (4857) in 2003, flexible work, temporary work and subcontracting is legalized, working conditions worsened and formal labor is enfeebled. Number of unions declined. Consequently, informality and brain drain increased. According to data provided by state agencies as of 2020 informal employment rate in Turkey is 30.59 percent, of which 64.3 per cent is for self-employed. According to OECD data, emigration of Turkish citizens to OECD countries exhibits an increasing trend and mainly educated, professional groups due to poor working and living conditions prefer to seek jobs in developed economies.

Entrepreneurial labor market in Turkey is characterized by a gap: entrepreneurs and specialized employees equipped with skills and competencies prefer well-paid jobs in established big firms either at home or abroad. This can be explained in relation to the uncertainties in economic conditions and loss of confidence in the decisions of the government for a stable economic and political milieu conducive for new investments. Furthermore, due to the dire working conditions endorsed by the prevailing Labor Law, competent professionals prefer to work in other countries and consequently Turkey faces a brain drain in its educated, competent workforce.

Physical Infrastructure

One of the major components of an EE is the tangible physical assets such as office/ factory space, telecommunication facilities, transportation means (roads, bridges, railways, airports), energy supplies that enable the creation and perseverance of new ventures (Theodorakiet al., 2017, Spiegel, 2015, Neck et al., 2004, Lux et al., 2020). Availability or scarcity of such infrastructure is influential on the decisions of the potential entrepreneurs to launch their business in a specific country, region, or city. Governments through various subsidies and tax concessions can make some cities/regions attractive for the agglomerations of start-ups. Such agglomerations by providing geographical proximity are also instrumental in developing a milieu where entrepreneurs can meet each other and share information and knowledge. On the other hand, as these cities/regions become more attractive for entrepreneurial activity, it is highly probable that cost of living, rents and land prices will increase. This increase in the cost of physical infrastructure can eventually limit the growth of the EE (Theodoraki et. al., 2017) and put a pressure on the profitability of the existing ventures.

In case of emerging economies one of the major problems related to physical infrastructure so far reported, are related to the scarcity of such facilities (Cho and Shi, 2021). In Turkey, the problem is unreliability and expensiveness of such infrastructural elements. For example, electricity supply and price has been one of the most common debates currently raised by citizens and firms. Frequent electricity outages, sometimes up to four days, had been one of the major obstacles for many of the firms of all sizes. Furthermore, after the privatization of electricity supply and distribution, energy prices drastically increased; according to data provided by the Chamber of Electrical Engineers the increase in electricity bills between 2007 and 2022 has been 816 times (EMO, 2022). Similarly, in Turkey, the transportation means are available but expensive; most of the industrial regions/cities are connected by paid highways and bridges that are constructed by privately owned conglomerates. These conglomerates operate on a 'public-private partnership' and their revenues are guaranteed by the government. Continuous increases on the prices of such transportation means increases the input costs of the producers and thus have a negative effect on the entrepreneurial activity. According to the 2019 World Bank Enterprise Survey, 15 per cent of the business owners in Turkey, state transportation as a major constraint, as compared to 11 percent in Europe and Central Asia. Another constraint in relation to the physical infrastructure is the availability of office/factory space and the rents. In Turkey, especially in big cities where EEs are located land is scarce and rents are high. One alternative for SMEs to leverage this problem is the availability of science and technology parks (technoparks) located at the campuses of some universities. These Parks are also attractive for the entrepreneurs of SMEs due to the taxation policies implemented by the government; according to the legislation (Law 4691), firms located in one of these Parks can benefit from tax incentives such as exemption from corporate tax for R&D activities, income tax exemption for R&D personnel and VAT exemption for software products (ODTU, 2022). During the last couple of years another alternative for the provision of office space has been the founding of public (owned by universities and municipalities) and private co-working spaces. Besides providing an office space at a reasonable rent they are instrumental in providing a milieu that foster professional interaction, knowledge sharing, networking opportunities and socializing through recreational events (Belitski & Büyükbalcı, 2020). In sum, we can say that physical infrastructure (transportation, energy, and facilities) is expensive and given the limited availability of financial resources, physical infrastructure is a constraint on the efficient functioning of an EE.

Digital Infrastructure

Digital infrastructures are the "information technologies and organizational structures, along with the related services and facilities necessary for an enterprise or industry to function" (Tilson et. al., 2010, pp. 748). In EEs the major outcome in terms of innovation is the creation of new ventures and new business models. In other words, entrepreneurs in search of opportunity outside the ecosystem, scaling-up and developing new business models rely on shared knowledge which is facilitated by digital technologies (Autio et al., 2017). Digital technologies can contribute to the innovation (new ventures and business models) capacity of an EE by providing direct interactions with the users and facilitating creative inputs from a diverse range of audiences. As stated by Nambisan et al., (2018), digitalization supports the development and maintenance of business model innovations. Due to generativity, digital technologies allow a variety of distributed actors (individuals and organizations) to participate in the innovation process. The efficient usage of digital technologies is dependent on information communication technologies. In other words, the availability of and access to Internet, communication services (such as international cables, towers, and spectrum) and communication networks is an important element for fostering entrepreneurial innovations. Digital technologies (for example, cloud computing, 4G/5G networks and platforms) can enable collaboration and knowledge sharing among entrepreneurs and mentors for experimenting new business models. Furthermore, digital technologies delocalize knowledge creation and sharing and promote a milieu where entrepreneurial culture(s) are shared and transferred. In emerging economies digital infrastructure turns out to be an important enabler for knowledge transfer, collaboration and learning for creating and capturing value (Cao & Shi, 2021). We can claim that two issues in relation to digital infrastructure are important for promoting entrepreneurial activity: the availability of efficient, low-cost digital technologies and a culture for their utilization for business creation purposes. As stated by the 2021 World Economic Forum (WEF) Report, digital culture is built on collaboration for the co-creation of innovative solutions, habitualizing data-driven decision-making process, a positive attitude for trying novel models and risk taking.

In Turkey one of the biggest problems in relation to digital infrastructure is the cost of access to Internet. According to 2021 Inclusive Internet Index, on the overall Turkey is ranked at the bottom of all EU countries, affordability of Internet services is a weakness and in terms of relevance (existence and extent of local language content) a significantly poor performance is reported. Although there is a capacity to access Internet in terms of cultural acceptance and skills due to low level of competition in the Internet market cost of access is very high. Consequently, a high rate of people does not use Internet and inequality in Internet usage is high (OECD, 2019). This can be explained in relation to the industry structure: a single firm that is privatized in 2005 is the provider of Internet and the service provider segment of the industry is highly concentrated. Although due to COVID-19 there has been an expansion on e-retailing, e-education, e-government services, and more and more firms opt for including Internet mediated services, due to access and affordability problems it is expected that digitalization in the Turkish entrepreneurial landscape will be limited in terms of usage and investments.

Support Services

Availability of mentorship and support systems are indicated as one of the major enabling inputs of an efficient EE (Isenberg, 2011; WEF, 2013; Stam, 2015; Spigel, 2015). As discussed by Cao and Shi (2021), in emerging economies a knowledge gap develops due to lack of mentoring. Since EEs are relatively new in these countries, knowledge accumulation for establishing and maintaining a start-up lack deepening and there are limited number of mentors specialized on start-ups. In Turkey, the first incubator was established in 2004, currently most of them are located in the three big cities-İstanbul, Ankara and İzmir (Kepenek and Eser, 2018) and are categorized in four groups; business-based, university-based, university-private collaboration and municipality-based (Birden et. al., 2020). However, most of these incubation centers are university-based and located within the technoparks of the universities. They offer mentorship, training, and support for writing projects. As indicated by Kepenek and Eser (2018) in relation to pre-incubators, these services are offered free of charge, and nearly all incubation centers work with a small number of staff. Due to limitations of available staff and red tape they cannot offer individualized services for each entrepreneur. And especially university-based centers from time to time are unable to find mentors that will match the requirements of the incubatees. Most of the incubation centers have their own mentor pool and if requested by the entrepreneurs' mentors are assigned and interviews with mentors are organized by the center. We can conclude that in Turkey, mentorship activities are weak, accelerator programs and incubation centers usually focus on technology-based firms that operate in information communication technologies and electronics (Belitski & Büyükbalcı 2020: Kepenek & Eser, 2018).

CONCLUSION

In the last decade the concept of entrepreneurial ecosystems has attracted the attention of policy makers, academicians, and practitioners. It is expected that an efficient EE will improve entrepreneurial activity that will lead to innovations in new ventures and business models and thus to the economic betterment of a region/city/nation. In Turkey, the concept initially was promoted by the various strategies and tools adopted by the government and later academic circles were drawn in for the efficient running of such a system. However, only by looking at the outcomes of such initiatives, Turkey scores low on Global Innovation Index, an entrepreneurial landscape where number of successful start-ups are less and experimenting with new ventures/business models is risky. This can be explained in relation to institutional voids and scarcities of the enabling resources and support services. In this study government regulations and entrepreneurial culture are identified as institutional voids. Government regulations in relation to taxation, bureaucratic procedures for firm formation acts as a constraint in the formation of new ventures. Furthermore, since the regulations and legislation are drafted in a top-down manner, single handedly by the government without consulting the opinions of stakeholders, their implementation poses some problems. A dialogue between different actors such as incumbent firms, government offices and universities does not exist; for example, universities when drafting their curriculum on entrepreneurship do not consult and listen to the needs of the entrepreneurs. Similarly, government regulations are prepared on an ad hoc fashion for solving immediate problems rather than with a long-term orientation. Thus, frequent changes, updates, amendments do not provide stability, induce uncertainty, risk and are short of building confidence. The other void identified in relation to Turkish entrepreneurial ecosystem is related to culture; a culture characterized by high uncertainty avoidance and collectivism. The implications of these cultural dimensions on entrepreneurial activity are reflected in low risk taking and disregarding innovativeness as an entrepreneurial capacity. Furthermore, in such a culture, people with university degrees and equipped with skills and competencies prefer to be employed in secure and well-paid jobs rather than taking risks and being self-employed. This leads to a gap, i.e., less numbers of people choose entrepreneurship as a career path, those who choose to be entrepreneurs are usually non-graduates, and their choice is motivated to raise an income. This gap is exacerbated with the decisions and implementations of government that leads to uncertainties in the economic realm. Finally, resource scarcities pose a serious problem for the efficiency of EE in Turkey. Scarcity of financial resources, high cost of physical and digital infrastructures, inefficiencies in support services, lack of qualified, creative entrepreneurs and specialized labor, absence of training focused on entrepreneurship are identified as the drivers of low entrepreneurial activity and EE performance in Turkey.

REFERENCES

Adner, R., Oxley, J. E., & Silverman, B. S. (2013). Introduction: Collaboration and Competition in Business Ecosystems. In Collaboration and Competition in Business Ecosystems. Emerald Books.

Arruda, C., Nogueira, V. S., & Costa, V. (2013). The Brazilian entrepreneurial ecosystem of startups: An analysis of entrepreneurship determinants in Brazil as seen from the OECD pillars. *Journal of Entrepreneurship and Innovation Management*, *2*(3), 17–57.

Asheim, B. T., Smith, H. L., & Oughton, C. (2011). Regional innovation systems: Theory, empirics, and policy. *Regional Studies*, *45*(7), 875–891. doi:10.1080/00343404.2011.596701

Audretsch, D. B., Cunningham, J. A., Kuratko, D. F., Lehmann, E. E., & Menter, M. (2019). Entrepreneurial ecosystems: Economic, technological, and societal impacts. *The Journal of Technology Transfer*, *44*(2), 313–325. doi:10.100710961-018-9690-4 PMID:30956392

Autio, E., & Fu, K. (2015). Economic and political institutions and entry into formal and informal entrepreneurship. *Asia Pacific Journal of Management, 32*(1), 67–94. doi:10.100710490-014-9381-0

Autio, E., Kenney, M., Mustar, P., Siegel, D., & Wright, M. (2014). Entrepreneurial innovation: The importance of context. *Research Policy, 43*(7), 1097–1108. doi:10.1016/j.respol.2014.01.015

Autio, E., Nambisan, S., Thomas, L. D., & Wright, M. (2018). Digital affordances, spatial affordances, and the genesis of entrepreneurial ecosystems. *Strategic Entrepreneurship Journal, 12*(1), 72–95. doi:10.1002ej.1266

Belitski, M., & Büyükbalci, P. (2021). Uncharted waters of the entrepreneurial ecosystems research: Comparing Greater Istanbul and Reading ecosystems. *Growth and Change, 52*(2), 727–750. doi:10.1111/grow.12457

Birden, M., Bastug, M., & Yazici, S. (2020). The Impact of Incubators on Entrepreneurial Process in Turkey: A Guide For Startups. *Journal of Business Economics and Finance, 9*(2), 132–142. doi:10.17261/Pressacademia.2020.1219

Cao, Z., & Shi, X. (2021). A systematic literature review of entrepreneurial ecosystems in advanced and emerging economies. *Small Business Economics, 57*(1), 75–110. doi:10.100711187-020-00326-y

Çeviker, E. (2021). *Strategic Actions in Response to Pro-market Reforms: A Study on Turkish Traffic Insurance Industry* (PhD thesis). İstanbul Bilgi University.

Cohen, B. (2006). Sustainable valley entrepreneurial ecosystems. *Business Strategy and the Environment, 15*(1), 1–14. doi:10.1002/bse.428

Colombo, M. G., Dagnino, G. B., Lehmann, E. E., & Salmador, M. (2019). The governance of entrepreneurial ecosystems. *Small Business Economics, 52*(2), 419–428. doi:10.100711187-017-9952-9

Djankov, S., La Porta, R., Lopez-de-Silanes, F., & Shleifer, A. (2002). The regulation of entry. *The Quarterly Journal of Economics, 117*(1), 1–37. doi:10.1162/003355302753399436

Doğan, E. (2016). The role of national culture on entrepreneurship: An assessment on the entrepreneurial culture of Turkey. *Sosyal Bilimler Araştırma Dergisi, 5*(1), 98–110.

Electrical Engineers Chambre (EMO). (2022). www.emo.org

Global Entrepreneurship Monitor. (2020). https://www.gemconsortium.org/report/gem-2019-2020-global-report

Guerrero, M., & Urbano, D. (2017). The dark side of entrepreneurial ecosystems in emerging economies: Exploring the case of Mexico. In Academy of Management Proceedings (Vol. 2017, No. 1, p. 12941). Academy of Management.

Hofstede, G. (1991). *Cultures and Organizations: Software of the Mind.* McGraw-Hill.

Hofstede Insights. (2022). https://www.hofstede-insights.com/product/compare-countries/

Iansiti, M., & Levien, R. (2004). *The keystone advantage: what the new dynamics of business ecosystems mean for strategy, innovation, and sustainability*. Harvard Business School Press.

Inclusive Internet Index. (2021). https://theinclusiveinternet.eiu.com/

Isenberg, D. (2014). What an entrepreneurship ecosystem actually is. *Harvard Business Review*, *5*(1), 7.

Isenberg, D. J. (2010). How to start an entrepreneurial revolution. *Harvard Business Review*, *88*(6), 40–50.

Kepenek, E. B., & Eser, Z. (2018). Impact of pre-incubators on entrepreneurial activities in Turkey: Problems, successes, and policy recommendations. In *Innovation and the Entrepreneurial University* (pp. 57–82). Springer. doi:10.1007/978-3-319-62649-9_4

Khanna, T., & Palepu, K. (2000). The future of business groups in emerging markets: Long-run evidence from Chile. *Academy of Management Journal*, *43*(3), 268–285.

KOSGEB. (2022). https://en.kosgeb.gov.tr/site/tr/genel/destekler/6311/sme-finance-supports

Lehmann, E. E., & Seitz, N. (2017). Freedom and innovation: A country and state level analysis. *The Journal of Technology Transfer*, *42*(5), 1009–1029. doi:10.100710961-016-9478-3

Lux, A. A., Macau, F. R., & Brown, K. A. (2020). Putting the entrepreneur back into entrepreneurial ecosystems. *International Journal of Entrepreneurial Behaviour & Research*, *26*(5), 1011–1041. doi:10.1108/IJEBR-01-2020-0031

Mack, E., & Mayer, H. (2016). The evolutionary dynamics of entrepreneurial ecosystems. *Urban Studies (Edinburgh, Scotland)*, *53*(10), 2118–2133. doi:10.1177/0042098015586547

Malecki, E. J. (2018). Entrepreneurship and entrepreneurial ecosystems. *Geography Compass*, *12*(3), e12359. doi:10.1111/gec3.12359

Manimala, M. J., & Wasdani, K. P. (2015). Emerging Economies: muddling through to development. In M. Manimala & K. Wasdani (Eds.), *Entrepreneurial Ecosystem*. Springer. doi:10.1007/978-81-322-2086-2_1

Moore, J. F. (1993). Predators and prey: A new ecology of competition. *Harvard Business Review*, *71*(3), 75–86. PMID:10126156

Nambisan, S., Siegel, D., & Kenney, M. (2018). On Open Innovation, Platforms, and Entrepreneurship. *Strategic Entrepreneurship Journal*, *12*(3), 354–368. doi:10.1002ej.1300

Neck, H. M., Meyer, G. D., Cohen, B., & Corbett, A. C. (2004). An entrepreneurial system view of new venture creation. *Journal of Small Business Management*, *42*(2), 190–208. doi:10.1111/j.1540-627X.2004.00105.x

North, D. C. (1991). Institutions. *The Journal of Economic Perspectives*, *5*(1), 97–112. doi:10.1257/jep.5.1.97

ODTU Technokent. (2022). http://odtuteknokent.com.tr/en/information/why-odtu-teknokent

OECD. (2021a). https://data.oecd.org/tax/tax-on-corporate-profits.htm#indicator-chart

OECD. (2021b). https://data.oecd.org/tax/tax-wedge.htm#indicator-chart

OECD. (2021c). Key figures on immigration and emigration – Turkey. In *International Migration Outlook 2021*. OECD Publishing. doi:10.1787/7b896aa0-en

OECD. (2022). *Labour: Labour market statistics. Main Economic Indicators* (database). OECD.

OECD Country Report. (2021). https://data.oecd.org/turkey.htm

Republic of Turkey, Social Security Institution. (2022). http://www.sgk.gov.tr/wps/portal/sgk/tr/calisan/kayitdisi_istihdam/kayitdisi_istihdam_oranlari

Singh, D., Pattnaik, C., Gaur, A. S., & Ketencioglu, E. (2018). Corporate expansion during pro-market reforms in emerging markets: The contingent value of group affiliation and diversification. *Journal of Business Research*, *82*, 220–229.

Stam, E. (2015). Entrepreneurial ecosystems and regional policy: A sympathetic critique. *European Planning Studies*, *23*(9), 1759–1769.

Stam, E. (2018). Measuring Entrepreneurial Ecosystems. In A. O'Connor, E. Stam, F. Sussan, & D. Audretsch (Eds.), Entrepreneurial Ecosystems. International Studies in Entrepreneurship (Vol. 38). Springer. https://doi.org/10.1007/978-3-319-63531-6_9.

The Scientific And Technological Research Council of Turkey (TUBITAK). (n.d.). https://www.tubitak.gov.tr/en/funds/industry/national-support-programmes

Theodoraki, C., Messeghem, K., & Rice, M. P. (2018). A social capital approach to the development of sustainable entrepreneurial ecosystems: An explorative study. *Small Business Economics*, *51*(1), 153–170.

Tilson, D., Lyytinen, K., & Sørensen, C. (2010). Research commentary—Digital infrastructures: The missing IS research agenda. *Information Systems Research*, *21*(4), 748–759.

WIPO. (2021a). https://www.wipo.int/global_innovation_index/en/

WIPO. (2021b). https://gpseducation.oecd.org/CountryProfile?plotter=h5&primaryCountry=TUR&treshold=5&topic=PI

World Bank Enterprise Survey. (2019). https://www.enterprisesurveys.org/en/data/exploreeconomies/2019/turkey#firm-characteristics

World Economic Forum. (2014). *Entrepreneurial ecosystems around the globe and early-stage company growth dynamics: the entrepreneur's perspective*. Author.

Chapter 7
Entrepreneurial Intentions of University Students:
What Are the Differences Among Scientific Areas?

Nadia Simoes
https://orcid.org/0000-0002-4334-4482
ISCTE, Instituto Universitário de Lisboa, Portugal

Nuno Crespo
https://orcid.org/0000-0002-6546-6325
ISCTE, Instituto Universitário de Lisboa, Portugal

ABSTRACT

This chapter analyzes entrepreneurship intentions in a medium-size Portuguese university that is in the top 150 of the Times Higher Education ranking for young universities. This higher education institution has grown rapidly over the last decades, has been extremely dynamic in establishing local level partnerships with business and non-business institutions, and is characterized by an environment more multidisciplinary than average with four schools occupying the same buildings (School of Sociology and Public Policy, School of Social Sciences, Business School, and School of Technology and Architecture). Using a sample of 544 students, this group of respondents ranks entrepreneurship as their preferred career choice. Analyzing the factors that influence entrepreneurial intentions, the authors find the relevance of context variables and entrepreneurship-related courses.

DOI: 10.4018/978-1-6684-4745-1.ch007

INTRODUCTION

The influence of higher education on entrepreneurial intentions of young students has received considerable attention over the past years (Krueger et al., 2000; Autio et al., 2001; Fayolle & Gailly, 2015). The attention given to these issues is accompanied by a strong increase in the number of universities offering programs focusing on or, at least, including entrepreneurial education (Katz, 2003; Martin et al., 2013).

Several topics are addressed in these studies, including: (i) the role of entrepreneurial education on students' motivation and career choices (Fayolle et al., 2006; Souitaris et al., 2007; Oosterbeek et al., 2010; Jabeen et al., 2017); (ii) the study of the contours of entrepreneurial education (Nabi et al., 2018); (iii) the impact of this type of education on the definition of the skills of the entrepreneur and on entrepreneurial success (van der Sluis et al., 2008; Premand et al., 2016); (iv) the channels that potentiate the contents taught in universities (Acs et al., 2005); and (v) the impact of this investment on economic growth (Shane, 2004). Concerning many of these issues, we are far from a consensus in terms of evidence. Arranz et al. (2017, p. 1980) summarize the current state-of-the-art affirming that "the results of such research have produced numerous studies on education and entrepreneurship but these tend to be limited and contradictory". Given the obvious importance of this issue as both field of research and as support for the definition of adequate policies, we clearly need additional research, providing more definitive conclusions regarding some of the key aspects under scrutiny.

In this book chapter we follow this objective taking a Portuguese university in the region of Lisbon as reference. This topic is critical for Portugal because it has long been considered that the country needs better educated entrepreneurs. For many years, the educational attainment was below the average of the European Union. In 1997, 78% of the population aged between 25 and 64 had less than upper secondary education, which compares with 42.6% for the European Union – EU15, in that year. For this reason, since the 1990s, consecutive governments have considered education as a top priority.

Several measures have been introduced to increase the educational attainment, such as establishing secondary education as mandatory. As a consequence, the overall picture today is significantly better: in 2017, 52.2% of the Portuguese population aged 25 to 64 had less than upper secondary education and 24.1% had tertiary education, which compares to 25.3% and 32.6%, respectively, for the EU15. For the entire period considered, self-employed persons had education levels below the average of the working population. In 1997, 85.5% had less than upper secondary education. In 2015, despite some improvement, this number was at 59.8%. The size and composition of the human capital of the self-employed persons has consequences in the size-class and volume of business of the firms they own. For that reason, in

2016, 88.2% of the Portuguese firms from the non-financial sector employed fewer than 10 workers (Statistics Portugal, 2018).

As stressed by Egerová et al. (2017, p. 320) "universities are expected to play a central role in their regions as entrepreneurship promoters and regional development facilitators". In the present study we analyze the case of a Portuguese university (Lisbon University Institute - ISCTE-IUL) located in Lisbon, characterized by some degree of diversity, in the sense that ISCTE-IUL has four schools and students from all schools take classes in the same buildings. As a consequence, the environment in the university is more multidisciplinary than average. Information about the initiatives in different scientific areas is shared in the halls, email or through social media. Our research explores the differences between preferred employment options (entrepreneurship vs. organizational jobs) and the motivations for these preferences. In this analysis we assess if students' perceptions vary between schools. Finally, key determinants of entrepreneurial intentions are identified.

The remainder of this book chapter is as follows. Section 2 characterizes ISCTE-IUL. Section 3 presents the data and methods. Results are discussed in Section 4 and Section 5 concludes.

BACKGROUND

ISCTE-IUL is one of Portugal's 13 public universities. Located in the center of Lisbon, it is a specialized university composed of four schools: (i) Business School; (ii) School of Technology and Architecture; (iii) School of Social Sciences; (iv) School of Sociology and Public Policy. ISCTE-IUL has around 9300 students (7th position in Portugal) with international students representing 22% of total. The university has 301 full-time professors, 360 researchers, and 263 staff members.

ISCTE-IUL appears in the top 150 of the Times Higher Education ranking for young universities (less than 50 years old). The Business School is accredited by AACSB and AMBA and is now preparing EQUIS accreditation in order to obtain the "triple crown". Additionally, it is ranked among the top 80 European business schools and some master programs are included in the Financial Times rankings. In turn, the engineering programs of the School of Technology and Architecture are accredited by EUR-ACE.

In the last Strategic Plan (ISCTE-IUL, 2014), three main objectives were defined: (i) promote high-quality teaching; (ii) increase research performance; (iii) promote the transfer of knowledge and entrepreneurship. The development of entrepreneurship is a cultural characteristic of the institution, supported not only by teaching and research but also by AUDAX-ISCTE, an entity devoted to its promotion. Founded in 2005, its action is focused on: (i) supporting social and local entrepreneurship; (ii) promoting technological innovation; (iii) managing activities for entrepreneurial incubation; and (iv) promoting youth entrepreneurship. Several initiatives are developed in partnership with the municipalities of the region, including Lisboa, Torres Vedras, Alenquer, Torres Novas and Loures, among others, increasing therefore the impact on local development and endogenous capacity of the region.

DATA AND METHODS

Data

Our data are obtained from a convenience sample based on ISCTE-IUL, gathered by distributing a questionnaire to students from different courses and degrees during class. We obtain a total number of 544 valid questionnaires. Our sample can be characterized as follows: *Gender*: male (41.36%), female (58.64%); *Age* (58.64% between 18-23 years of age); *Education level*: undergraduate students (41.36%), master students (58.64%); *School*: Business School (44.85%), School of Technology and Architecture (16.73%), School of Social Sciences (19.49%), and School of Sociology and Public Policy (18.93%).

Research Questions

The questionnaire was developed to provide answers to the following research questions:

- Research question 1: What are the main motivations of young people to pursue a career as employee or as an employer with his/her own business?
- Research question 2: What are students' perceptions about the extent to which the degrees they are completing help them to have the interest and skills to start their businesses?
- Research question 3: Do students from the Business School and the School of Technology and Architecture show a higher propensity toward entrepreneurship than others?
- Research question 4: What is the role of entrepreneurial courses in the development of entrepreneurial intentions?

Research Methods

In order to answer our research questions, we combine descriptive evidence (research questions 1 and 2) with results from an econometric model (research questions 3 and 4). Concerning the model, we assume entrepreneurial intentions as dependent variable and apply a probit regression (see Greene, 2017, for additional details).

Aiming to capture entrepreneurial intentions, each student was asked "whether he/she would like to start a business within a period of 5 years". The dependent variable of the model is a dummy variable coded "1" when the student indicates preference toward entrepreneurship.

We consider three types of variables. First, variables related to the higher education pathway namely the educational level (1: master level; 0: undergraduate level) and the school in which the student is enrolled (Business School, School of Technology and Architecture, School of Social Sciences, and School of Sociology and Public Policy). Second, we account for the acquisition of skills through entrepreneurship-related courses (1: yes; 0: no). Third, control variables that include a set of individual characteristics: gender (1: female; 0: male), race (1: Caucasian; 0: other), and risk attitude (1: risk preference; 0: other). The dummy variable to capture risk attitude is coded "1" if the student reports to disagree or strongly disagree with the following statement "One should not start a business if there is a risk it might fail". Aiming to capture the influence of role models, we consider a dummy variable to see whether the student has relatives or friends who are entrepreneurs (1: yes; 0: no). We also account for financial constraints through a dummy variable coded "1" if the student reports to agree or strongly agree with the following statement "It is difficult to start one's own business due to lack of available financial support". Finally, we include a dummy variable coded "1" if the respondent has previous experience working as employer.

RESULTS

Research Question 1: What Are the Main Motivations of Young People to Pursue a Career as Employee or As an Employer with His/Her Own Business?

According with the evidence provided in Table 1, 57.17% of the students reveal a preference for entrepreneurship while 36.03% prefer organizational jobs. This preference is in line with the results obtained by Fayolle and Gailly (2015) and Jabeen et al. (2017).

Table 1. Preferred career choices of students

Preferred career choice	Number of answers	Percent
Employee	196	36.03
Employer	311	57.17
Don't know	37	6.80

Tables 2 and 3 show evidence regarding the main reasons for the preferred choice. Concerning the choice for wage employment, most respondents justify their option through differences in working conditions. Preference toward wage employment is explained by the perception of higher stability in terms of job duration and access to a wage with lower variance. Intrinsic lack of ideas, skills, and capital represent the key reason for 32.13% of the students preferring to work as employee. In turn, Table 3 shows that preference for entrepreneurship is to a great extent driven by the intrinsic wish for self-fulfillment (55.95%), followed by the perspective of access to higher wages (19.61%) and more autonomy (10.61%).

Table 2. Main reasons for the preferred career choice as employee

Main reason for the preferred career choice as employee	Number	Percent
Reasons related to working conditions		
Job stability	60	30.61
More stable working hours	14	7.14
More stable and regular wage	59	30.10
Reasons related to lack of critical assets for starting a business		
Lack of financial capital	20	10.20
Lack of knowledge or skills	24	12.24
Lack of business ideas	19	9.69

Table 3. Main reasons for the preferred career choice as employer

Main reason for the preferred career choice as employer	Number	Percent
Reasons related to working conditions		
Higher income perspective	61	19.61
Autonomy in choosing time and place to work	33	10.61
Reasons related to intrinsic rewards		
Self-fulfillment	174	55.95
Bigger contribution to society	15	4.82
Other reasons		
Having skills and knowledge to identify business opportunities	20	6.43
Having family or friends with business background	3	0.96
Lack of job opportunities	5	1.61

Research Question 2: What Are Students' Perceptions About the Extent to Which the Degrees They Are Completing Help Them to Have the Interest and Skills to Start Their Businesses?

For this question we analyze the level of agreement to three statements: (i) "My school education helped me to develop my sense of initiative"; (ii) "My school education made me interested to become an entrepreneur"; and (iii) "My school education gave me skills and know-how that enable me to run a business".

Table 4. Students' perceptions about their courses developed their sense of initiative, interest for entrepreneurship, and skills for starting a new business

	School				
	Sociology and Public Policy	**Social Sciences**	**Business School**	**Technology and Architecture**	**Total**
"My school education helped me to develop my sense of initiative"					
Strongly agree	13.46%	21.70%	22.54%	14.29%	19.27%
Agree	51.92%	51.89%	44.67%	60.44%	50.09%
Neither agree nor disagree	19.23%	17.92%	22.54%	1.10%	17.43%
Disagree	13.46%	7.55%	8.61%	24.18%	11.93%
Strongly disagree	1.92%	0.94%	1.64%	0.00%	1.28%
"My school education made me interested to become an entrepreneur"					
Strongly agree	6.73%	7.55%	18.85%	8.79%	12.66%
Agree	21.15%	26.42%	28.69%	39.56%	28.62%
Neither agree nor disagree	30.77%	18.87%	33.20%	4.40%	25.14%
Disagree	32.69%	35.85%	15.98%	34.07%	26.06%
Strongly disagree	8.65%	11.32%	3.28%	13.19%	7.52%
"My school education gave me skills and know-how that enable me to run a business"					
Strongly agree	7.69%	4.72%	18.85%	5.49%	11.74%
Agree	20.19%	32.08%	34.84%	20.88%	29.17%
Neither agree nor disagree	21.15%	15.09%	27.46%	2.20%	19.63%
Disagree	41.35%	30.19%	15.57%	52.75%	29.54%
Strongly disagree	9.62%	17.92%	3.28%	18.68%	9.91%

Most students from all the schools agree or strongly agree that their courses stimulate initiative (with the lowest value reaching 65.38%, in the case of the School of Sociology and Public Policy), thus confirming the existence of a strong entrepreneurship culture in the university.

The students from the Business School and the School of Technology and Architecture agree or strongly agree that their courses stimulate the interest for entrepreneurial activities (around 48% of total answers). The corresponding evidence for both schools in the area of social sciences is much lower – 27.88% in the School of Sociology and Public Policy and 33.97% in the School of Social Sciences. Only

19.26% of the students from the Business School disagree or strongly disagree with the idea that their course stimulates the interest in entrepreneurship, while for the remaining schools the values are higher than 41%. As expected, almost 54% of the students from the Business School agree or strongly agree that their course allows the development of skills related to entrepreneurship.

Research Question 3: Do Students from The Business School and The School of Technology and Architecture Show a Higher Propensity Toward Entrepreneurship Than Others?

Table 5 presents the results from the econometric model. One of the most important determinants of entrepreneurial intentions is the school in which the student is enrolled. This can be interpreted as signaling the influence of environmental factors in entrepreneurial intentions (Sieger et al., 2014; Arranz et al., 2017; Jabeen et al., 2017). Students from the two schools offering courses in Social Sciences have a lower propensity to entrepreneurship. Interestingly, it is among students from Technology and Architecture that entrepreneurial intentions are higher. This evidence corroborates previous results obtained by Souitaris et al. (2007) and Arranz et al. (2017). The explanation usually offered for this pattern is related to the technological skills and level of creativity that favor the development of new products. Another feature emerging from this evidence is that entrepreneurial intentions are not mainly driven by necessity, which could more easily emerge among students from social sciences (more likely to work outside their area of specialization and finding organizational jobs characterized by lower than average wages).

Table 5. Determinants of entrepreneurial intentions

Variables	Entrepreneurial intention		
	Coef.	**Odd's ratios**	**s.e**
Independent variables			
Educational level (1: master level; 0: undergraduate level)	0.332	1.394	(0.375)
School of Sociology and Public Policy		Ref	
School of Social Sciences	0.130	1.139	(0.513)
Business School	0.700*	2.013*	(0.780)
School of Technology and Architecture	1.191**	3.291**	(1.458)
Entrepreneurial courses (1: yes; 0: no)	0.924***	2.519***	(0.600)
Control variables			
Female	-0.453**	0.635**	(0.145)
Age	0.109***	1.116***	(0.030)
Race (1: Caucasian; 0: Other)	0.070	1.073	(0.362)
Risk preference	0.674**	1.963**	(0.605)
Having family/friends with business background	0.922***	2.515***	(0.609)
Having professional experience in entrepreneurship	1.280***	3.595***	(1.337)
Financial constraints	-0.716**	0.488**	(0.138)
Constant	-5.724***	0.003***	(0.003)
Number of observations		544	
Log-likelihood		-245.12482	
Pseudo-R^2		0.2178	

Note: *, **, *** Significant at 10, 5, and 1%, respectively

Research Question 4: What Is the Role of Entrepreneurship-Related Courses in The Development of Entrepreneurial Intentions?

The influence and effectiveness of entrepreneurship-related programs and courses on the entrepreneurial intentions is one of the most researched topics in this area since it goes to the core of the university's mission: the learning process. Evidence on the impact of entrepreneurship education on entrepreneurial intentions is mixed as documented in some systematic reviews and meta-analysis on this topic (Pittaway & Cope, 2007; Martin et al., 2013; Bae et al., 2014). Our results show that the link between the two variables is positive and that this is one of the most important explanatory variables. This confirms the conclusions obtained by Souitaris et al. (2007), Maresch et al. (2016), and Herman and Stefanescu (2017).

The general results deriving from our control variables are in line with evidence from previous empirical studies. Gender, age, risk preference, absence of perceived financial constraints, having family or friends with a business background, and experience in entrepreneurship influence entrepreneurial intentions. Among these factors, exposure to role models emerges as one of the most important determinants of this intentions (for comparable evidence see Schjoedt & Shaver, 2007; Zellweger et al., 2011; Egerová et al., 2017; Herman & Stefanescu, 2017).

CONCLUSION

Research on entrepreneurship intentions among young people emerges due to the perception that previously most attention was directed to adults. This book chapter contributes to this line of research by studying the impact of degrees in different scientific areas and entrepreneurship-related courses on the disposition of university students to start their own business. Our findings suggest two main ideas for future discussion. First, universities can develop an environment and a culture favorable to entrepreneurial intentions, can contribute to the learning process by giving students the skills relevant for entrepreneurship, and can help them engage in these activities (for example, through incubator centers or interaction with the experience of role models). Second, given that the entrepreneurial intentions can be developed, this opens the debate about how universities and outside partners such as local business and non-business institutions, and regional and central governments can strengthen their collaboration to seize this potential, remove barriers to entry in entrepreneurship, and create the platform to help young people to develop successful business, minimizing the risk of failure that, in these age groups, can have negative effects in both the short and long terms. The university from which we develop this study is a very interesting case study since it has grown consistently over the last decades and has developed a considerable effort to establish arrangements with a wide variety of local partners, amplifying in this way the regional impact of the entrepreneurial initiatives.

REFERENCES

Acs, Z., Arenius, P., Hay, M., & Minniti, M. (2005). Global Entrepreneurship Monitor 2004. Executive Report. Academic Press.

Arranz, N., Ubierna, F., Arroyabe, M. F., Perez, C., & Fdez. de Arroyabe, J. C. (2017). The effect of curricular and extracurricular activities on university students' entrepreneurial intention and competences. *Studies in Higher Education*, *42*(11), 1979–2008. doi:10.1080/03075079.2015.1130030

Autio, E., Keeley, R., Klofsten, M., Parker, G., & Hay, M. (2001). Entrepreneurial intent among students in Scandinavia and in the USA. *Enterprise and Innovation Management Studies*, *2*(2), 145–160. doi:10.1080/14632440110094632

Bae, T., Qian, S., Miao, C., & Fiet, J. (2014). The relationship between entrepreneurship education and entrepreneurial intentions: A meta-analytic review. *Entrepreneurship Theory and Practice*, *38*(2), 217–254. doi:10.1111/etap.12095

Egerová, D., Eger, L., & Mičík, M. (2017). Does entrepreneurship education matter? Business students' perspectives. *Tertiary Education and Management*, *23*(4), 319–333. doi:10.1080/13583883.2017.1299205

Fayolle, A., & Gailly, B. (2015). The impact of entrepreneurship education on entrepreneurial attitudes and intention: Hysteresis and persistence. *Journal of Small Business Management*, *53*(1), 75–93. doi:10.1111/jsbm.12065

Fayolle, A., Gailly, B., & Lassas-Clerc, N. (2006). Assessing the impact of entrepreneurship education programmes: A new methodology. *Journal of European Industrial Training*, *30*(9), 701–720. doi:10.1108/03090590610715022

Greene, W. (2017). *Econometric analysis* (8th ed.). Pearson.

Herman, E., & Stefanescu, D. (2017). Can higher education stimulate entrepreneurial intentions among engineering and business students? *Educational Studies*, *43*(3), 312–327. doi:10.1080/03055698.2016.1277134

ISCTE-IUL. (2014). *Plano Estratégico 2014-2017*. ISCTE-IUL.

Jabeen, F., Faisal, M., & Katsioloudes, M. (2017). Entrepreneurial mindset and the role of universities as strategic drivers of entrepreneurship: Evidence from the United Arab Emirates. *Journal of Small Business and Enterprise Development*, *24*(1), 136–157. doi:10.1108/JSBED-07-2016-0117

Katz, J. (2003). The chronology and intellectual trajectory of American entrepreneurship education: 1876–1999. *Journal of Business Venturing*, *18*(2), 283–300. doi:10.1016/S0883-9026(02)00098-8

Krueger, N. Jr, Reilly, M., & Carsrud, A. (2000). Competing models of entrepreneurial intentions. *Journal of Business Venturing*, *15*(5-6), 411–432. doi:10.1016/S0883-9026(98)00033-0

Maresch, D., Harms, R., Kailer, N., & Wimmer-Wurm, B. (2016). The impact of entrepreneurship education on the entrepreneurial intention of students in science and engineering versus business studies university programs. *Technological Forecasting and Social Change, 104*, 172–179. doi:10.1016/j.techfore.2015.11.006

Martin, B., McNally, J., & Kay, M. (2013). Examining the formation of human capital in entrepreneurship: A meta-analysis of entrepreneurship education outcomes. *Journal of Business Venturing, 28*(2), 211–224. doi:10.1016/j.jbusvent.2012.03.002

Nabi, G., Walmsley, A., Liñán, F., Akhtar, I., & Neame, C. (2018). Does entrepreneurship education in the first year of higher education develop entrepreneurial intentions? The role of learning and inspiration. *Studies in Higher Education, 43*(3), 452–467. doi:10.1080/03075079.2016.1177716

Oosterbeek, H., Van Praag, M., & Ijsselstein, A. (2010). The impact of entrepreneurship education on entrepreneurship skills and motivation. *European Economic Review, 54*(3), 442–454. doi:10.1016/j.euroecorev.2009.08.002

Pittaway, L., & Cope, J. (2007). Entrepreneurship education: A systematic review of the evidence. *International Small Business Journal, 25*(5), 479–510. doi:10.1177/0266242607080656

Premand, P., Brodmann, S., Almeida, R., Grun, R., & Barouni, M. (2016). Entrepreneurship education and entry into self-employment among university graduates. *World Development, 77*, 311–327. doi:10.1016/j.worlddev.2015.08.028

Schjoedt, L., & Shaver, K. G. (2007). Deciding on an entrepreneurial career: A test of the pull and push hypotheses using the panel study of entrepreneurial dynamics data. *Entrepreneurship Theory and Practice, 31*(5), 733–752. doi:10.1111/j.1540-6520.2007.00197.x

Shane, S. (2004). *Academic entrepreneurship: University spinoffs and wealth creation*. Edward Elgar Publishing. doi:10.4337/9781843769828

Sieger, P., Fueglistaller, U., & Zellweger, T. (2014). *Student entrepreneurship across the globe: A look at intentions and activities. International Report of the GUESSS Project 2014*. Swiss Research Institute of Small Business and Entrepreneurship at the University of St. Gallen.

Souitaris, V., Zerbinati, S., & Al-Laham, A. (2007). Do entrepreneurship programmes raise entrepreneurial intention of science and engineering students? The effect of learning, inspiration and resources. *Journal of Business Venturing, 22*(4), 566–591. doi:10.1016/j.jbusvent.2006.05.002

Statistics Portugal. (2018). *Estatísticas das Empresas – 2016*. National Statistics.

van der Sluis, J., Van Praag, M., & Vijverberg, W. (2008). Education and entrepreneurship selection and performance: A review of the empirical literature. *Journal of Economic Surveys*, *22*(5), 795–841. doi:10.1111/j.1467-6419.2008.00550.x

Zellweger, T., Sieger, P., & Halter, F. (2011). Should I stay or should I go? Career choice intentions of students with family business background. *Journal of Business Venturing*, *26*(5), 521–536. doi:10.1016/j.jbusvent.2010.04.001

Chapter 8
Sustainable Entrepreneurship: A Bibliometric Analysis

Renuka Sharma
https://orcid.org/0000-0002-6514-3411
Chitkara Business School, Chitkara University, India

Kiran Mehta
Chitkara Business School, Chitkara University, India

ABSTRACT

Entrepreneurship has long been acknowledged as a means of generating economic rewards for those involved in it. As the notion of sustainable development has emerged as a critical problem impacting the existing system, it has been suggested that it should not be limited to the generation of money alone. The field of sustainable enterprise (SE) has received a lot of academic interest in the previous 10 years. The SE literature is becoming more difficult to explore because of its fast growth and interdisciplinary nature. Because of the growth of research, there is a lack of a theoretical framework; thus, this area must be investigated, structured, and synthesised to offer clarity. The goal of this study is to give a bibliometric analysis of the field's current state. The study is conducted on a sample of 352 articles published during 2002-2022. This study's results may help both novice and experienced sustainable entrepreneurship scholars by providing a comprehensive overview of the field's development and present state.

DOI: 10.4018/978-1-6684-4745-1.ch008

INTRODUCTION

Economists and policymakers have always supported the promotion of entrepreneurship to boost economic growth. Past research has also proved a significant impact of entrepreneurship on the performance of macroeconomic indicators of a country (Atems and Shand 2018). However, past researchers also documented some contradictory findings where entrepreneurship is detrimental to macroeconomic indicators under given economic scenarios (Andersson and Noseleit 2011). The intricate link between entrepreneurship and economic development may provide a rationale for these contradicting findings. In the first published findings of entrepreneurship's macroeconomic effect, characteristics such as industry affiliation (Fritsch 1996), nation development level (Carree et al. 2002), and the density of local firm owners were shown to be relevant. On the other hand, some new businesses, like those that are very innovative or have high growth expectations, only make money and start the "creative destruction" process defined by Schumpeter (Szerb et al. 2018).

Traditionally, entrepreneurship has been examined, evaluated, and applied to develop a kind of self-employment that can generate economic advantages (Segal et al., 2005) or as one of the means to create job opportunities (Sarango-Lalangui et al., 2018). It means that entrepreneurial activity has been studied from an economic development perspective (Kirzner, 1973), but societal and environmental concerns have been neglected (Sarango-Lalangui et al., 2018). With more entrepreneurship datasets available, researchers found that this is true. However, over the last decade, scientists have explored a wide range of pertinent indicators (e.g., new firm longevity rates, structural and institutional contexts, and the entrepreneur's possible motives and academic credentials), resulting in an increasingly complex web of interconnected determinants surrounding the macroeconomic impact of entrepreneurship.

However, the increasing attention being paid to environmental issues by governments, non-governmental organisations, researchers, and businesses (Aghelie et al., 2016), as well as the emergence of the concept of sustainable development (Kerlin, 2006), have led several academics to assert that entrepreneurship should not be based solely on the generation of profits. According to the findings of this research, entrepreneurship should be focused on activities that have commercial, social, and environmental goals and that are responsive to the demands and requirements of today's economic environment (Schaltegger and Wagner, 2011). Additionally, according to the second study results (Shepherd and Patzelt, 2011), entrepreneurs who want to construct a profitable company that also contributes to development must include and adopt sustainable practices or non-economic advantages into their business strategy (Urbaniec, 2018). According to some analysts, entrepreneurship may also guide economic sectors toward long-term development (Shepherd and Patzelt, 2011).

In recent years the interlinkages between entrepreneurship and economic development have become significantly important to various stakeholders (Cohen and Winn, 2007; O'Neill Jr. et al., 2006) to generate the concept of sustainable entrepreneurship (Muoz and Cohen, 2018). Also, interest among businesses and entrepreneurs in understanding the actual effect of their operations on the environment and society has intensified over the previous decade, and the new term is emerged known as sustainopreneurship (Sustainable Development Entrepreneurship) (Aghelie et al., 2016). SE is based on and linked to the TBL (triple bottom line), which includes (1) environmental factors, which include long-term safeguarding and minimisation of side effects, (2) social aspects, where workers, customers, partners, stakeholders, and the community are given due attention, and (3) economic factors, which are based on economic performance (Urbaniec, 2018, Aghelie et al., 2016). As a result, sustainable entrepreneurs are increasingly believed to be transformational leaders devoted to finding the right balance between economic viability, social welfare, and environmental preservation (Belz and Binder, 2017).

As sustainable development has emerged as a severe concern for the current global economy, it has been emphasised that entrepreneurship should not be centred exclusively on money generation. It led to the development of the sustainable entrepreneurship concept (StbEtp.), which has gained much attention in the recent decade. Sustainable entrepreneurship research has emerged as one of the most vibrant subdomains in the last decade, reflecting the surge of entrepreneurship solutions to social and environmental problems. Until now, most theories and normative frameworks proposed have been derived from well-established domains, such as social entrepreneurship and environmental economics. As is the case with numerous new subjects, SE is burdened by a profusion of competing definitions, resulting in a scarcity of a theoretical framework emphasised in the literature (Sarango-Lalangui et al., 2018).

The basic tenet of StbEtp is that entrepreneurs' operations in pursuit of opportunities must not endanger the ecological, social and environments in which they conduct business (Shepherd and Patzelt, 2011) and that they should strive to revive or foster such ecosystems whenever feasible to rebalance nature, society, and economic activities (Parrish, 2010). These emerging activities are framed under the concept of 'sustainable prospering', where the potential for StbEtp to generate revolutionary rather than incremental change (Schaefer et al. 2015). These are the kinds of activities and processes that sustainable entrepreneurs are interested in launching, which are both lucrative and contribute to sustainable development at the same time (Lans et al., 2014). Ultimately, StbEtp is the only model capable of integrating various dimensions essential for the well being of future generations. These dimensions include value for the environment aligned with economic and social goals. As a result, StbEtp starts with identifying environmental or social concerns before moving on to the development of potential solutions through innovation (Eller et al., 2020).

Given that the first SE publication appeared in the "Journal of Organizational Change Management" twenty-two years ago, it is now appropriate to assess the field's progress, identify the key players like- countries, institutions, and authors, and reflect on the past while identifying potential future research directions. It is necessary to conduct ongoing review studies (e.g. bibliometric analysis, meta-analysis and systematic analysis) to emphasise achievement and restrictions, encourage discussion about future research, and drive more remarkable advancement. There are some review-based studies, too, which have been conducted earlier too. Levinsohn (2013) conducted a systematic evaluation of SE publications published in the first decade of the twenty-first century. Gast et al. (2017) conducted a comprehensive review of 114 papers published between 1996 and 2015 and identified and advised future research directions. They accomplished this by repeatedly discovering broad patterns and clusters of repeating issues, which resulted in identifying six critical research streams. Munoz and Cohan (2017) also examined eighty-one articles of StbEtp and established a conceptual framework for motivating academic discussion and enhancing knowledge on the subdomain of StbEtp in the entrepreneurship research area. They restricted their research to the two leading journals named "Journal of Cleaner Production and Greener Management International". Sarango-Lalangui et al. (2018) lack a map to evaluate geographical representations of how authors, nations, organisations, and keywords link. This study is the only bibliometric study that focuses entirely on author and journal citations, ignoring additional bibliometric performance indicators like the h-Index. Also, it is vital to study nations, affiliated institutions, and most significantly, the most often used keywords and research directions in this sector. Since StbEtp research has earned interest from scholars across a growing number of disciplines, we are seeing a surge of new studies that challenge the notion that StbEtp is merely a subset of social or environmental entrepreneurship. However, as more research is conducted, a lack of a theoretical framework necessitates that this field is examined, organised, and synthesised to provide clarity.

This study aims to offer a bibliometric analysis of sustainable entrepreneurship to have a more comprehensive approach to this issue and to highlight the most influential authors, nations, and journals that are currently investigating this topic in more depth. Co-citation, bibliographic coupling, and co-authoring are all visual components that maps may represent in the same way. In the same way, the display of the citation structure by years helps us comprehend the historical development of both the number of publications and the number of citations in the literature. For this analysis, we have used VOSviewer software.

METHODOLOGY

The researchers used bibliometric analysis to accomplish the objective of the study. Earlier studies have frequently employed this analysis approach (Cobo et al., 2011; Ansari and Kant, 2017) to demonstrate and identify essential aspects (country, institutes/institutions, researchers/authors, publications etc.) in various academic topics. The present study follows the following steps of bibliometric analysis (Capobianco-Uriarte et al., 2019). These steps are defining the field of the study, selecting a database, selecting the search string, applying codes to the selected material, and the last step is examining the information collected so far. A variety of measures may be used to assess an author's academic output; the most often used are the overall number of papers published and the overall number of articles published in a given period. There are metrics to assess the extent of papers published. It includes the total number of citations, the average number of citations per paper, and the impact of the journals in which the manuscripts are published. These all should be considered while undertaking a bibliometric analysis of the manuscripts. A few of the most important studies include bibliographic coupling, co-citation, and co-occurrence of key terms, among other things. Following that, each of the following is discussed in depth (Boyack and Klavans, 2010; Merigó et al., 2018; Zupic and Ater, 2015): Bibliographic coupling sources 'a common reference between two papers'; for example, if paper A is mentioned in papers B and C, indicates that the papers are connected bibliographically. Kessler (1963) found that the bigger the number of shared references, the greater the strength of this link. When two papers are referenced in the same paper, this is referred to as co-citation. For example, when papers A and C are mentioned in the same paper, this is called co-citation (Small, 1973). Co-authorship is a term that refers to publications that include more than one author, which allows for the identification of scientific cooperation (Merigó et al., 2018). The researchers have used bibliometric analysis based on a topic, author, country/region, institution etc. (Liao et al., 2018; Bonilla et al., 2015; Cancino et al., 2018).

Before discussing it in detail, we want to mention how we started our search. After establishing the boundaries of sustainable entrepreneurship based on key research, we built on Doherty et al. (2014) 's review of hybrid enterprising research and Ansari and Kant's (2017) recent review framework. We began our review using the term 'sustainable entrepreneurship' of pre-defined keywords drawn from the titles, abstracts, and keywords of papers between 2002 and 2022. After writing this keyword, we get 382 papers from the database. Then we selected 'articles', 'English language' and from the web of science index, we selected 'Social Sciences Citation Index (SSCI) and Science Citation Index Expanded'. Finally, we excluded the conference proceedings etc, from our research.

Papers that specifically address StbEtp and reference the existence of people seeking entrepreneurial possibilities while concurrently pursuing social, environmental and economic value creation were hand-selected for inclusion in this collection (Hall et al., 2010). Researching eco-entrepreneurship is not at the heart of our work since such research focuses on making money in ecologically sensitive regions. This collection does not include papers on corporate sustainability, corporate social responsibility, environmental management, or similar works aimed at mature firms or large organisations (e.g. Provasnek et al., 2016). Even while both young entrepreneurs and multinational organisations are committed to long-term sustainability, their approaches to explaining their sustainable strategic goals, which impact business operations and how they react to competitive pressures, vary significantly.

Finally, we shortlisted 352 articles for further analysis. The detailed information about these papers is downloaded in text format to be linked to the VOSviewer for further analysis based on different criteria (Eck and Waltman, 2017). VOSviewer is a sophisticated tool for illustrating, visualising and discovering research maps. Maps illustrating the links between nations, organisations, journals, contributors, and words may also be displayed to facilitate analysis and comprehension (Castillo-Vergara et al., 2018).

Figure 1. Outline of the research

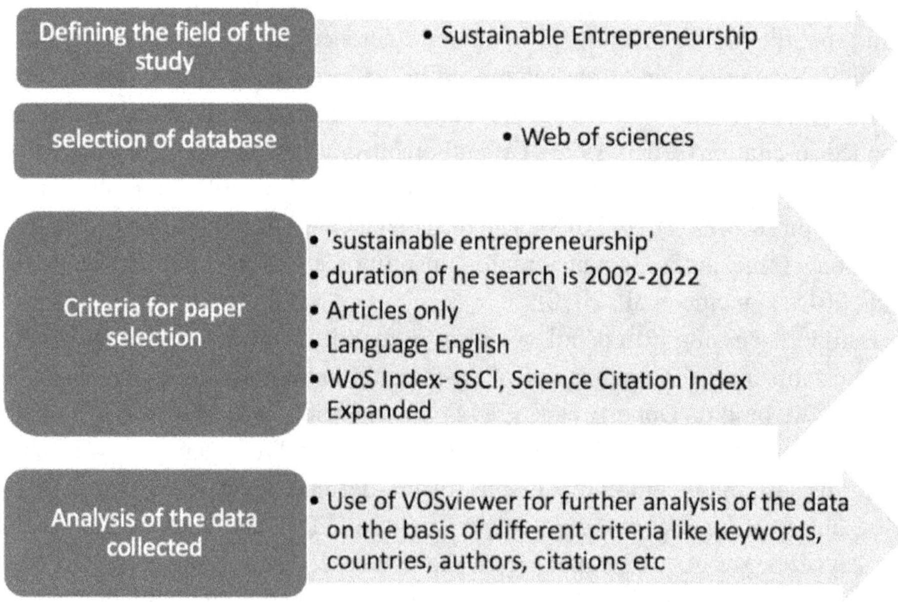

Over the previous five years, StbEtp has received much attention (see Figure 2). In 2002, just one piece of work was made available for public consumption. Since then, the publishing has been in the tens of thousands. Every year since 2016, this subject has gained traction, increasing the number of papers published. It can be because many other disciplines have grown their interest in the subject, and there is an increasing relevance to the concept of sustainability. Ninety-five articles were published in 2021, followed by 60 in 2020, 45 in 2018 and 44 in 2019. As can be seen from Figure 2, a whopping 91.5% of the papers (322) from 2015 to 2022.

Figure 2. Yearly publication of selected articles

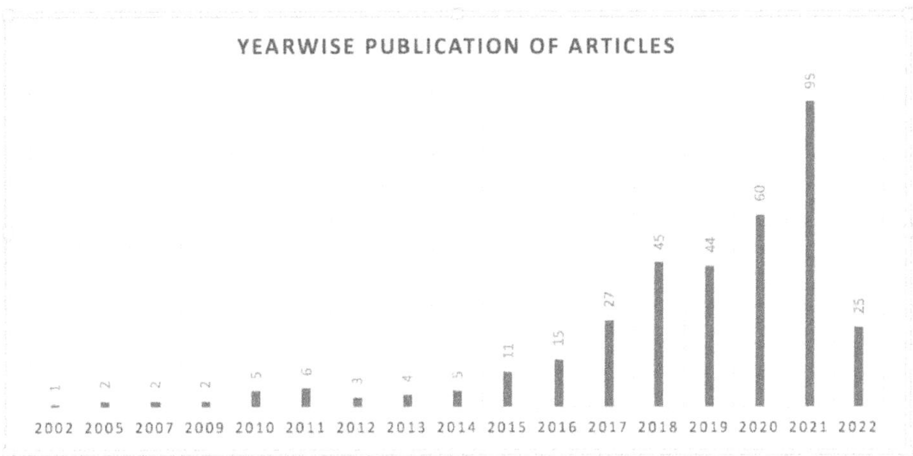

The following table (Table 1) summarises the WoS categories assigned to the topics of the chosen articles. The bulk of papers picked are in the environmental sciences (145) and green sustainable science and technology (142) categories, followed by business (127) and environmental studies (127). In addition, there are over one hundred articles in the category of Management.

Table 1. Web of science categories of subjects

Environmental Sciences	145
Green Sustainable Science Technology	142
Business	127
Environmental Studies	127
Management	110

Following that, Table 2 describes the journal titles that published more than ten papers throughout the study period relevant to the topic of research. Only five journals with more than ten publications published during the research period were discovered. The International Journal of Entrepreneurial Behavior Research published precisely ten publications during the research period. Five more journals are shown in Table 2, having published more than five but less than ten publications during the research period. Additional interesting facts were discovered due to the findings reported in Table 2. Although the Sustainability journal published the most articles (83) and had the most citations, the Journal of Business Venturing had the greatest total link strength (TLS) and citations (2398). Similarly, the Journal of Cleaner Production's total citations (1401) is far more than the Sustainability journal, even though the Journal of Cleaner Production publishes significantly fewer pieces. These results are also shown in the map given in Figure 3.

Table 2. Journal titles having more than 10 articles over the study period

	Title	No of articles	Citations	TLS
1	Journal of Business Venturing	11	2398	365
2	Sustainability	83	810	327
3	Business Strategy and the Environment	23	1169	249
4	Journal of Cleaner Production	47	1401	232
5	Small Business Economics	12	338	86
6	Organisation & environment	9	386	68
7	Journal of Business Ethics	7	283	57
8	International Journal of Entrepreneurial Behavior Research	10	103	41
9	International Entrepreneurship and	6	17	35
10	Journal of Business Research	6	27	31
11	Journal of Small Business Management	6	96	29

TLS- total link strength

Figure 3. Top journals and their citation strength

Table 3 similarly lists the top five publications. Elsevier and Mdpi have 84 and 83 articles in this list, followed by 'Wiley, Springer Nature, and Emerald Group Publishing, which have 39, 36, and 34 published papers, respectively, from a sample of 39, 36, and 34 articles.

Table 3. Top five publishers

Elsevier	84
Mdpi	83
Wiley	39
Springer Nature	36
Emerald Group Publishing	34
Others like sage, taylor & Francis, Vilnius Gediminas Tech Univ, Walter De Gruyter, IEEE, etc.	76
Total	352

During the period under consideration, seventeen publications got more than 100 citations. From 2002-to 2022, the most cited study was conducted by Schaltegger and Wagner (2011), which received 674 citations. Dean and McMullen (2007) received 617 citations during the same period, and Cohen and Winn (2007) received 600 citations during the same period (study period). Table 4 and Figure 4 show the most cited papers in the study's sample, as determined by the number of citations they received. More than forty publications have received citations above 50 times. In addition, 87 publications have received more than 20 citations altogether. The articles with more than ten citations number 162, while the papers with one or more citations amount to 293 in total. The Web of Science database has reported an increasing number of papers published in the field of StbEtp. Schaltegger and Wagner (2011) are determined to have received the most number of citations during the course of the investigation, with 674 citations in total (see Table 4 and Figure 4).

Table 4. Top studies as per the citation count

Author Full Names	Publication Year	Times Cited	Link strength
Dean, Thomas J.; McMullen, Jeffery S.	2007	617	161
Schaltegger, Stefan; Wagner, Marcus	2011	674	145
Cohen, Boyd; Winn, Monika I.	2007	600	138
Hockerts, Kai; Wuestenhagen, Rolf	2010	512	106
Pacheco, Desiree F.; Dean, Thomas J.; Payne, David S.	2010	238	79
Munoz, Pablo; Cohen, Boyd	2018	103	69
Belz, Frank Martin; Binder, Julia Katharina	2017	169	61
Kuckertz, Andreas; Wagner, Marcus	2010	308	58
Pinkse, Jonatan; Groot, Koen	2015	82	41
York, Jeffrey G.; O'Neil, Isobel; Sarasvathy, Saras D.	2016	130	37
Vuorio, Anna Maija; Puumalainen, Kaisu; Fellnhofer, Katharina	2018	71	34
Lans, Thomas; Blok, Vincent; Wesselink, Renate	2014	164	33
Sarango-Lalangui, Paul; Santos, Jane Lucia S.; Hormiga, Esther	2018	40	32
Dai, Shengli; Xue, Hongyan; Jiang, Yuan; Zhang, Wei; Zhang, Xin	2018	5	31
Spence, Martine; Gherib, Jouhaina Ben Boubaker; Biwole, Viviane Ondoua	2011	97	30
Argade, Padmaja; Salignac, Fanny; Barkemeyer, Ralf	2021	3	30
Choongo, Progress; Van Burg, Elco; Paas, Leo J.; Masurel, Enno	2016	39	29

Figure 4. Above figure is based on "citations and document"

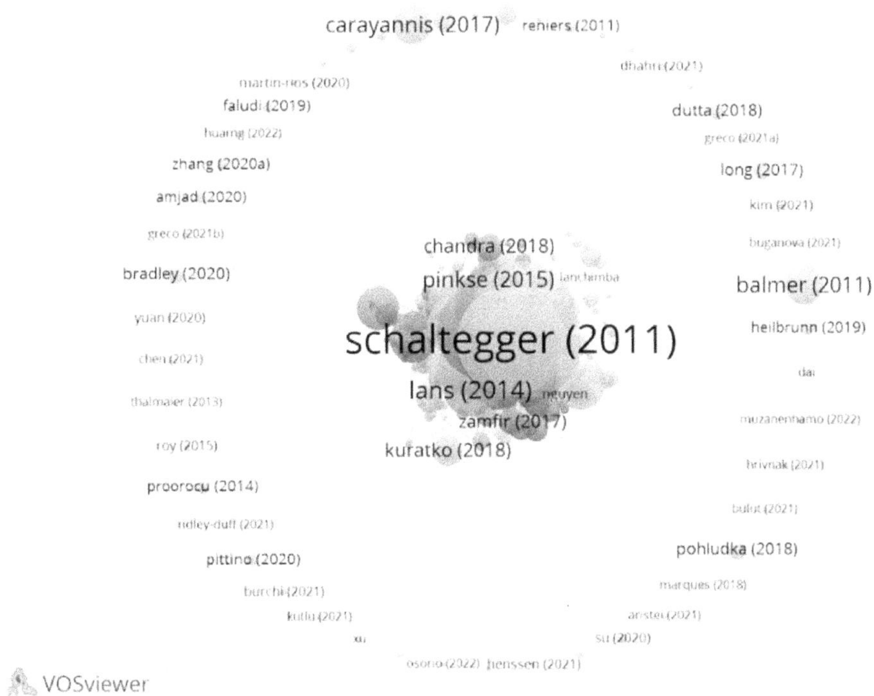

The following bibliometric analysis is based on bibliographic coupling. Table 5 shows the results of bibliographic coupling and authors. As given in Table 5, seven documents by Blok and Vincent have been cited together 307 times. Similarly, another bibliographic coupling of authors is found in the case of Long and Thomas b. (6 documents with 47 citations) and Ozeren and Emir (5 documents with five citations). It can be observed through bibliographic coupling and the authors' map in Figure 5.

Table 5. Bibliographic coupling and authors

	No of documents	Citations
Blok, Vincent	7	307
Long, Thomas b.	6	47
Ozeren, Emir	5	5

Figure 5.

Further, Table 6 shows the bibliometric analysis based on university. The analysis is done based on the number of documents, citations and total link strength of the publication by each university. As mentioned in the table below, Univ Utrecht, Univ Groningen, Wageningen Univ, and Univ Southampton were found with the highest number of publications in the field of study. While based on citations, Wageningen Univ reported 314 citations and led the list, followed by Leuphana Univ Luneburg (287) and Indiana University (278). The link strength of the publication was found highest for Univ Utrecht, followed by Vrije Univ Amsterdam (1787) and Leuphana Univ Luneburg (1635). These results are shown with the help of the map given in Figure 6 too.

Table 6. Analysis based on documents published by a university

Organisations	Documents	Citations	Link Strength
Univ Utrecht	8	169	1988
Vrije Univ Amsterdam	7	120	1787
Leuphana Univ Luneburg	7	287	1635
Univ Politecn Calencia	6	56	1564
University Hamburg	5	242	1528
Univ Valencia	7	98	1508
Carl Von Ossietzky univ oldendurg	5	108	1426
Indiana University	5	278	1098
Univ Groningen	8	23	913
Wageningen Univ	8	314	888
Bucharest Univ Econ Studies	5	62	858
George Washington Univ	5	158	844
Ryerson Univ	5	98	842
Univ Southampton	8	75	782
Dokuz Eylul Univ.	5	5	351

Figure 6.

However, when the nations with the most publications are examined, it is discovered that Germany has the most papers published on the subject of StbEtp, followed by the Netherland, England, Spain, and Italy. (see Table 7 and Figure 7).

Table 7. Citations and countries

		Documents	Citations	Link Strength
1	Germany	44	2144	722
2	USA	35	1837	536
3	Netherland	44	1056	430
4	England	44	1066	409
5	Spain	34	458	389
6	Canada	14	855	305
7	Peoples R China	39	378	282
8	Denmak	11	587	240
9	Italy	30	540	227
10	France	16	409	199
11	Switzerland	6	594	190
12	Poland	11	71	141
13	Sweden	17	316	131
14	Pakistan	13	68	120
15	Finland	12	171	118
16	Austria	11	302	116
17	Ecuador	6	56	93
18	Belgium	13	178	85

Continued on following page

Table 7. Continued

		Documents	Citations	Link Strength
19	Iran	8	83	84
20	New Zealand	5	161	72
21	Romania	9	129	69
22	South Korea	6	88	68
23	Australia	11	232	63
24	Norway	5	249	63
25	Portugal	7	133	59

Figure 7.

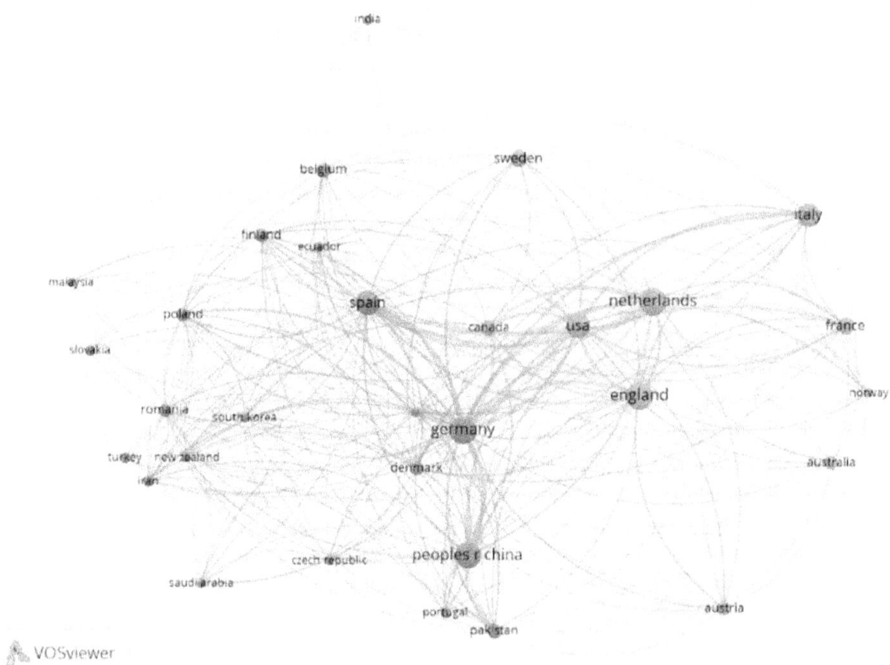

DISCUSSION AND FUTURE RESEARCH AGENDA

The bibliometric methodologies used in this work enable us to expose the connected character of knowledge generation in the SE sector, which is critical. One of the hallmarks of SE research is its ability to traverse the borders of different academic disciplines. This is to be expected. The increasing interest among researchers to continue research on StbEtp since 2015 has happened due to several reasons (with publication numbers in the double digits). The first is that the issue of sustainability is rapidly growing, and the second is that more publications on the subject can be observed as a result of increased access to databases and the internet. Furthermore, beginning in 2010, the terms "entrepreneur" and "sustainable" have shown a tremendous increase, and this growth has continued today. According to this approach, sustainability as a business strategy says that StbEtp is becoming more relevant to individuals across various disciplines of study, entrepreneurs, the government, and other professions and enterprises. Early StbEtp researchers spent a significant amount of time figuring out who sustainable entrepreneurs are and what distinguishes them from more traditional enterprises should come as no surprise. Similarly Gartner (1988) characterises the development of entrepreneurship theory and practice as following a similar path, with a primary focus on personality traits that ultimately led the field to embrace cognition theories anchored in cognitive psychology (Mitchell et al., 2002). Researchers profited from improvements in entrepreneurial studies and were quick to incorporate cognition as a method of investigation. Because ethics and moral cognition in the context of sustainable businesses have not been well-studied in the literature, we now know a great deal more about how these individuals think. An positive discovery is that, based on the SE research organising framework, there are clusters of research that may be found to occupy each area of the framework. Quantitative, qualitative, and conceptual research are all equally represented in SE. Within a short period of time, significant progress has been accomplished, and an excellent collection of contributions has emerged at all levels of analysis. Despite the fact that certain regions have been extensively studied, there are still a number of blind spots. Both the SE procedure and the adoption of SE continue to be an important issue in the area.

Humans and other life forms face considerable risks in the following decades due to deforestation, environmental degradation, land-use changes, water scarcity, and other sustainable development practices. In order to be successful in addressing these challenges, any activity must make decisions based on two aspects that are, at times, conflicting with one another: scientific facts and moral principles (Garvey, 2008). Committing to sustainability seems to include more than just using the appropriate formulae and procedures to raise our existing levels of prosperity. As a result, it also entails accepting the responsibility of distributing well-being between the affluent and the poor, between humans and non-humans, and between current and future generations.

Researchers have discovered that the moral importance of a sustainability problem substantially influences how people see the issue and what they are ready to do to address it positively. Because of the high level of moral intensity, the relationship between past knowledge and opportunity intention becomes apparent. Encouragement of entrepreneurs to act in the interests of sustainable development requires a high level of moral intensity on their part. According to Muoz and Dimov (2017), persons who are already aware of the importance of sustainability would only search for an opportunity if they are confronted with a high degree of moral intensity.

Though the study of sustainability ethics and conduct is still in its infancy, the most recent studies have revealed that these entrepreneurs place a greater emphasis on moral principles than their conventional counterparts, suggesting that ethical and moral values may be of greater relevance to those who start sustainable ventures. According to Shepherd (2015), the expansion of the entrepreneurial sector will result in a more compassionate and pro-social environment and the ability to express a kind of activity that will have the potential to relieve others' pain. Therefore, it is vital to take a deeper look at the moral cognitive underpinnings of such a mental proclivity. In contrast to a sustainable entrepreneur whose aims include social equality and environmental conservation, commercial entrepreneurs have a more significant opportunity to renounce ethical and moral principles in their pursuit of wealth, according to this viewpoint.

Researchers have focused their attention on various topics, including innovation issues, sustainable innovation, and sustainable business models, among others. There is a push to define StbEtp in a similar vein, although there is no agreement on what that term means. There are many different definitions of StbEtp. It is critical to recognise how these trends have contributed to the resolution of environmental and social problems and how sustainable business contributes to the resolution of these challenges. The researchers also found out how market inefficiencies encourage long-term entrepreneurship.

CONCLUSION

This research contributes to the field of inquiry by offering the most significant authors and resources on the subject and the most important countries and publications from now until 2019. Finally, according to the study, Germany, the United States, the Netherlands, England, and Spain are the countries with the largest concentration of publications on the issue under investigation. According to authors with links to major newspapers, the Journal of Business Venturing is the most applicable phrase to use in this context. According to authors with connections to major publications, "sustainability" is the most crucial concept to consider. Dean, Schaltegger, Cohen, Hockerts, and Pacheco are the authors who have had the most work published in a variety of venues. Academic output and co-authorship are meagre in many countries, making it imperative to increase academic productivity in various jurisdictions.

Given that our study encompassed business/management, the environment, and engineering, we feel that it will be advantageous for academics to understand better what is being explored and where it is heading in the future. Finally, it was determined that there was an unanswered research obstacle, namely the absence of an index that could assess StbEtp. It might be a highly productive research avenue to follow in the future.

REFERENCES

Aghelie, A., Sorooshian, S., & Azizan, N. A. (2016). Research gap in sustainopreneurship. *Indian J. Sci. Technol., 9*. doi:10.17485/ijst/2016/v9i12/77648

Andersson, M., & Noseleit, F. (2011). Start-ups and employment dynamics within and across sectors. *Small Business Economics, 36*(4), 483. doi:10.100711187-009-9252-0

Ansari, Z. N., & Kant, R. (2017). Exploring the framework development status for sustainability in supply chain management: a systematic literature synthesis and future research directions. *Business Strategy and the Environment*. doi:10.1002/bse.1945

Atems, B., & Shand, G. (2018). An empirical analysis of the relationship between entrepreneurship and income inequality. *Small Business Economics, 51*(4), 905–922. doi:10.100711187-017-9984-1

Belz, F. M., & Binder, J. K. (2017). Sustainable entrepreneurship: A convergent process model. *Bus. Strateg. Environ., 26*, 1–17. doi:10.1002/bse.1887

Bonilla, C. A., Merigó, J. M., & Torres-Abad, C. (2015). Economics in Latin America: A bibliometric analysis. *Scientometrics, 105*(2), 1239–1252. https://doi.org/10.1007/s11192-015-1747-7

Boyack, K. W., & Klavans, R. (2010). Co-Citation Analysis, Bibliographic Coupling, and Direct Citation: Which Citation Approach Represents the Research Front Most Accurately? *Journal of the American Society for Information Science and Technology, 12*(61), 2389–2404.

Cancino, C. A., Merigó, J. M., Torres, J. P., & Diaz, D. (2018). A bibliometric analysis of venture capital research. *Journal of Economics, Finance and Administrative Science, 23*(45), 182–195. https://doi.org/10.1108/JEFAS-01-2018-0016

Capobianco-Uriarte, M. de las M., Casado-Belmonte, M. del P., Marín-Carrillo, G. M., & Terán-Yépez, E. (2019). A Bibliometric Analysis of International Competitiveness (1983–2017). *Sustain., 11*, 1877. doi:10.3390/su11071877

Carree, M., van Stel, A., Thurik, R., & Wennekers, S. (2002). Economic development and business ownership: An analysis using data of 23 OECD countries in the period 1976–1996. *Small Business Economics, 19*(3), 271–290. doi:10.1023/A:1019604426387

Castillo-Vergara, M., Alvarez-Marin, A., & Placencio-Hidalgo, D. (2018). A bibliometric analysis of creativity in the field of business economics. *Journal of Business Research, 85*, 1–9. https://doi.org/10.1016/j.jbusres.2017.12.011

Cobo, M. J., López-Herrera, A. G., Herrera-Viedma, E., & Herrera, F. (2011). Science mapping software tools: Review, analysis, and cooperative study among tools. *Journal of the American Society for Information Science and Technology, 62*, 1382–1402. https://doi.org/10.1002/asi.21525

Cohen, B., & Winn, M. I. (2007). Market imperfections, opportunity and sustainable entrepreneurship. *Journal of Business Venturing, 22*, 29–49. https://doi.org/10.1016/j.jbusvent.2004.12.001

Doherty, B., Haugh, H., & Lyon, F. (2014). Social enterprises as hybrid organizations: A review and research agenda. *International Journal of Management Reviews, 16*(4), 417–436.

Eller, F. J., Gielnik, M. M., Wimmer, H., Thölke, C., Holzapfel, S., Tegtmeier, S., & Halberstadt, J. (2020). Identifying business opportunities for sustainable development: Longitudinal and experimental evidence contributing to the field of sustainable entrepreneurship. *Business Strategy and the Environment, 29*(3), 1387–1403. https://doi.org/10.1002/bse.2439

Fritsch, M. (1997). New firms and regional employment change. *Small Business Economics, 9*(5), 437–448. doi:10.1023/A:1007942918390

Gast, J., Gundolf, K., & Cesinger, B. (2017). Doing business in a green way: A systematic review of the ecological sustainability entrepreneurship literature and future research directions. *Journal of Cleaner Production, 147*, 44–56. https://doi.org/10.1016/j.jclepro.2017.01.065

Hall, J., Daneke, G., & Lenox, M. (2010). Sustainable development and entrepreneurship: Past contributions and future directions. *Journal of Business Venturing, 25*(5), 439–448.

Kerlin, J. A. (2006). *Social enterprise in the United States and Europe: Understanding and learning from the differences*. doi:10.1007/s11266-006-9016-2

Kessler, M. M. (1963). Bibliographic coupling between scientific articles. *American Documentation*, *24*, 123–131.

Kirzner, I. M. (1973). *Competition and entrepreneurship*. University of Chicago Press.

Lans, T., Blok, V., & Wesselink, R. (2014). Learning apart and together: Towards an integrated competence framework for sustainable entrepreneurship in higher education. *Journal of Cleaner Production*, *62*(C), 37–47.

Levinsohn, D. (2013). Disembedded and beheaded? - a critical review of the emerging field of sustainability entrepreneurship. *International Journal of Entrepreneurship and Small Business*, *19*, 190–211. https://doi.org/10.1504/IJESB.2013.054963

Liao, H., Tang, M., Luo, L., Li, C., Chiclana, F., & Zeng, X. J. (2018). A bibliometric analysis and visualization of medical big data research. *Sustainability*, *10*(1), 1–18. https://doi.org/10.3390/su10010166

Merigó, J. M., Pedrycz, W., Weber, R., & de la Sotta, C. (2018). Fifty years of Information Sciences: A bibliometric overview. *Information Sciences*, *432*, 245–268. https://doi.org/10.1016/j.ins.2017.11.054

Muñoz, P., & Cohen, B. (2018). Sustainable entrepreneurship research: Taking stock and looking ahead. *Bus. Strateg. Environ.*, *27*, 300–322. doi:10.1002/bse.2000

O'Neill, G. D., Jr., Hershauer, J. C., & Golden, J. S. (2006). The cultural context of sustainability entrepreneurship. *Greener Manag. Int.*, 33–46. doi:10.9774/GLEAF.3062.2006.au.00005

Parrish, B. D. (2010). Sustainability-driven entrepreneurship: Principles of organization design. *Journal of Business Venturing*, *25*(5), 510–523.

Provasnek, A. K., Schmid, E., Geissler, B., & Steiner, G. (2017). Sustainable corporate entrepreneurship: Performance and strategies toward innovation. *Business Strategy and the Environment*, *26*(4), 521–535.

Sarango-Lalangui, P., Santos, J. L. S., & Hormiga, E. (2018). The development of sustainable entrepreneurship research field. *Sustain.*, *10*(6), 2005. Advance online publication. doi:10.3390u10062005

Schaefer, K., Corner, P. D., & Kearins, K. (2015). Social, environmental and sustainable entrepreneurship research. *Organization & Environment*, *28*(4), 394–413.

Schaltegger, S., & Wagner, M. (2011). Sustainable entrepreneurship and sustainability innovation: Categories and interactions. *Bus. Strateg. Environ., 20*, 222–237. doi:10.1002/bse.682

Segal, G., Borgia, D., & Schoenfeld, J. (2005). The motivation to become an entrepreneur. *International Journal of Entrepreneurial Behaviour & Research, 11*(1), 42–57. doi:10.1108/13552550510580834

Shepherd, D. A., & Patzelt, H. (2011). The new field of sustainable entrepreneurship: Studying entrepreneurial action linking "what is to be sustained" with "what is to be developed." *Entrepreneurship Theory and Practice, 35*, 137–163. https://doi.org/10.1111/j.1540-6520.2010.00426.x

Small, H. (1973). Co-citation in the scientific literature: A new measure of the relationship between two documents. *Journal of the American Society for Information Science, 24*(4), 265–269. https://doi.org/10.1002/asi.4630240406

Szerb, L., Lafuente, E., Krisztina Horvath, K., & Páger, B. (2019). The relevance of quantity and quality entrepreneurship for regional performance: The moderating role of the entrepreneurial ecosystem. *Regional Studies, 53*(9), 1308–1320. doi:10.1080/00343404.2018.1510481

Urbaniec, M. (2018). Sustainable entrepreneurship: Innovation-related activities in European enterprises. *Polish Journal of Environmental Studies, 27*, 1773–1779. https://doi.org/10.15244/pjoes/78155

Van Eck, N. J., & Waltman, L. (2010). Software survey: VOSviewer, a computer program for bibliometric mapping. *Scientometrics, 84*(2), 523–538.

Zupic, I., & Čater, T. (2015). Bibliometric methods in management and organization. *Organizational Research Methods, 18*(3), 429–472. https://doi.org/10.1177/1094428114562629

Chapter 9
An Interrogation of Entrepreneur Perspectives on the Nexus of Sustainability and Entrepreneurship:
Sustainable Entrepreneurship

Naisha Ramlal
University of KwaZulu-Natal, South Africa

Nigel Chiweshe
https://orcid.org/0000-0001-7757-211X
University of KwaZulu-Natal, South Africa

ABSTRACT

Understanding the effects of entrepreneurs' intentions towards sustainable entrepreneurship can be an initial step in developing sustainable entrepreneurs. Limited research has been conducted on the intention of practicing entrepreneurs, specifically among owners of SMMEs (small, medium, and micro enterprises) towards sustainable entrepreneurship. Previous research focused on a traditional entrepreneurial process, with limited studies having been done to investigate the intentions of entrepreneurs to engage in sustainable entrepreneurship. Studies focusing on intention towards sustainable entrepreneurship are limited, more so in South Africa. To fill this research vacuum, this chapter provides insights on entrepreneurs' perceptions of sustainable entrepreneurship. The chapter reveals that entrepreneurs' intentions to adopt sustainable practices were driven by subjective standards, their views toward sustainability, and their perceived behavioural controls. From a managerial standpoint, this chapter recommends that SMMEs match their business operations with their stakeholders' values.

DOI: 10.4018/978-1-6684-4745-1.ch009

INTRODUCTION

Small and medium-sized enterprises (SMEs) are self-contained, non-affiliated businesses with few employees (Cantele, Vernizzi, & Campedelli, 2020). The number of employees, however, varies according to the national statistical system. These enterprises contribute significantly to economic growth in all countries; they account for around 90% of all corporations globally and employ approximately 50%–60% of the global workforce (Cantele et al., 2020).

Over the last decade, issues such as ecological degradation and social sustainability have piqued the interest of a sizable segment of society, including consumers, non-governmental organisations, and elected officials (Cantele et al., 2020). Now, consumers are increasingly concerned about the environmental and social impacts of businesses and are exerting tremendous pressure on them to change their business practices in favour of a more sustainable model (Cantele et al., 2020).

Among scholars, sustainability policies of large corporations were frequently addressed, owing to their high visibility in the society and also to the ease with which their effects may be observed. Cantele et al. (2020) opine that while a single SME has a negligible impact on environmental issues in comparison to a single large business, when aggregated, SMEs account for a sizable portion of resource consumption, air and water pollution, and waste generation. They are believed to contribute between 60 and 70% of industrial pollution in Europe.

According to Cantele et al. (2020), entrepreneurs are increasingly addressing the issue of sustainable development. While firms are held accountable for social and environmental impacts, they are also viewed as social actors capable of successfully integrating sustainability solutions into market transactions.

Despite the growing field of sustainable entrepreneurship, most of the available literature has been mainly theoretical and qualitative, or has focused on developed countries, and very little has been done in developing countries such as South Africa (Nhemachena, 2017). Therefore, to address this research gap, the objective of this chapter was to investigate what motivates entrepreneurs to engage in sustainable entrepreneurship.

BACKGROUND

According to Bajdor, Pawełoszek, and Fidlerova (2021), sustainable entrepreneurship" is a concept that combines several aspects of traditional entrepreneurship, combining the terms "sustainable development" with "entrepreneurship." The fundamentals of sustainable activity are less concerned with management systems and more concerned with an entrepreneur's initiative and ability to succeed in the market and effect (good) changes in society and the natural environment. Sustainable entrepreneurship is built on two distinct pillars: social entrepreneurship and eco entrepreneurship. While eco-entrepreneurship is concerned with the environment, social entrepreneurship is concerned with social well-being (Bajdor et al., 2021)

Sustainable entrepreneurship, on the other hand, “goes farther” by incorporating social, environmental, and economic factors (Bajdor et al., 2021). Based on the preceding, Bajdor et al. (2021) assume the foundation was traditionally defined as entrepreneurship, upon which social and eco-entrepreneurship were founded, hence creating the foundation for sustainable entrepreneurship (Bajdor et al., 2021).

According to Bajdor et al. (2021), The phrase “sustainable enterprise” evolved as a result of the introduction of a new paradigm known as “sustainability,” which can be informally translated as “renewable,” “sustainable,” or a continuous process of achieving balance in specific areas. In terms of the enterprise, this paradigm has two interpretations:

It stresses the organisation’s ability to sustain business continuity in a highly dynamic and variable environment, and secondly, it helps the organisation to capitalise on the opportunities created by the changes. The notion of “sustainable enterprise” answers to the constant changes occurring in the contemporary reality in which businesses function (Bajdor et al., 2021).

Additionally, they must overcome obstacles in order to continue developing and strengthening their market position. Sustainable firms create jobs that are adequate and decent, are productive and competitive, and contribute to social inclusion. Environmentally sustainable production can make a major contribution to the SDGs’ attainment (Sustainable Development Goals) (Bajdor et al., 2021).

As a result, the objective of a sustainable firm is constant growth and development. This involves continuous access to vital resources and redefining the core business to fulfill the needs of both customers and shareholders. As a comprehensive and all-encompassing concept, sustainable development has spawned a plethora of fields that, to varying degrees, execute its central ideas (Bajdor et al., 2021). In other words, the term “sustainable” is frequently used as an adjectival phrase to refer to activities that adhere to the principles of sustainable development. Due to their size, contribution to economic and sustainable growth, and adaptability in tackling environmental and social challenges, SMEs are critical to sustainable entrepreneurship (Bajdor et al., 2021).

The unifying denominator between sustainable entrepreneurship and sustainable enterprise is the commercial success of ecologically and socially responsible products (Bajdor et al., 2021). However, sustainable entrepreneurship can also refer to an enterprise with a well-established market position and a long history of operation that, in addition to pursuing financial profits, initiates, for example, social changes or engages in activities aimed at improving the state of the natural environment (Bajdor et al., 2021).

Crals and Vereeck (2005) emphasized the importance of the connection between sustainable entrepreneurship and sustainable enterprise. They asserted that it is a business's ongoing commitment to ethical behaviour and economic development while improving the quality of life of employees, their families, local communities, society, and, ultimately, the entire globe and its future generations.

Apart from institutional pressures and internal resources, managers' attitudes, beliefs, and perceptions may also be predictors of proactive environmental solutions (Testa et al., 2016). Testa et al. (2016) assert that a manager's personal attitude toward the natural environment has a significant impact on how he or she responds to (or ignores) environmental challenges.

The Value Belief Norm (VBN) paradigm emphasises the importance of individuals' attitudes and moral standards as predictors of pro-environmental conduct in businesses (Testa et al., 2016). Individual attitudes toward pro-environmental actions, this theory contends, might be motivated by a proper feeling of need to act according to moral standards. Moral standards influence individual views, and when a moral standard is violated, an individual should bear responsibility for the resulting negative consequences (Testa et al., 2016). Testa et al. (2016) have shown that organisations with managers who have strong environmental values execute a set of measures aimed at improving environmental management. Testa et al. (2016) have shown a strong influence of senior management commitment to environmental issues and the implementation of environmental management methods.

While some previous research has established a direct relationship between managerial attitudes and performance in large organisations, other research on small firms has claimed that this relationship is not obvious. Testa et al. (2016) found a positive correlation between entrepreneurs' attitudes and environmental management practices, but not between entrepreneurs' attitudes and waste management practices, or between entrepreneurs' attitudes and the design of environmental and operational practices for the environment. Previous research has emphasised the relevance of examining the influence of small enterprises' personal attitudes toward the environment and the implementation of proactive environmental initiatives (Testa et al., 2016).

Bahena-Álvarez et al. (2019) state that business organisations appear to agree on the notion that their activities cannot ignore the expectations of diverse interest groups pushing for ethical business practices that encompass novel concepts of risk and opportunity.

Sustainable entrepreneurship is a term that refers to the study of the relationship between innovation and societal values (Bahena-Álvarez et al., 2019). It calls for a more nuanced understanding of the effects of human actions and the ramifications of the multi-level innovation system on society as a whole (Bahena-Álvarez et al., 2019).

In the majority of industrialised countries, the notion has been promoted and regulated legally, with a total budget of 91 million euros dedicated to study and implementation of responsible innovation (Bahena-Álvarez et al., 2019).

According to Bajdor et al. (2021) sustainable entrepreneurship" is a concept that combines several aspects of traditional entrepreneurship, combining the terms "sustainable development" with "entrepreneurship." The fundamentals of sustainable activity are less concerned with management systems and more concerned with an entrepreneur's initiative and ability to succeed in the market and effect (good) changes in society and the natural environment. Sustainable entrepreneurship is built on two distinct pillars: social entrepreneurship and eco-entrepreneurship.

According to Mathew (2009), sustainable entrepreneurship can be defined as the enhancement and commitment to the business that incorporates ethical issues, community commitment, social responsibility, and other issues such as economic development. A sustainable business, in terms of the product and services given by the company, takes into account factors such as quality, continuous improvement, and innovation. As a company's shareholder, the notion refers to the long-term development of business families, local communities, society, and the globe at large.

MAIN FOCUS OF THE CHAPTER

According to Hall and Wagner (2012), while the notion of innovation and entrepreneurship as a solution to our sustainability problems is theoretically appealing, the literature on the relationship between sustainable development and entrepreneurship is more prescriptive than descriptive and rather optimistic, and it remains to be seen whether entrepreneurs are indeed more capable of creating sustainable economies.

Indeed, for a variety of reasons, small businesses may have intrinsic disadvantages over their larger counterparts. To begin, smaller enterprises are frequently buried in the supply chain and are not subject to the same kind of demand to improve their sustainability performance as large, high-profile firms are (Hall & Wagner, 2012). Second, there has been significantly more research on the impact of sustainable development on large firms in mainstream management journals, with numerous university endowed chairs and courses on business strategy and sustainable development, providing legitimacy and increased awareness for large firms (Hall & Wagner, 2012). This legitimacy may enable huge corporations to overcome their rigorous decision-making criteria, heuristics, and evaluation techniques. Third, larger organisations with the capacity to comprehend varied stakeholder concerns may be better equipped to manage the enormous complexity of sustainability requirements, but smaller firms may simply lack the financial and managerial resources necessary to manage in such an environment (Hall & Wagner, 2012). Thus, while interest and progress continue to grow, there are still significant research opportunities in the sustainable development – innovation – entrepreneurship nexus (Hall & Wagner, 2012).

Issues, Controversies, Problems

As increasing global expansion and international competition unfold, both in the industrial and commercial sectors, it is imperative for large corporates as well as Small, Micro and Medium Sized Enterprises (SMMEs) to develop sustainability plans for present and future developments. Researchers have agreed on the importance of entrepreneurs for the economic development of a country. Despite their constructive contributions on economic development, entrepreneurial activities have also led to environmental degradation. Thus, it is believed that entrepreneurs should solve environmental issues themselves.

In recent years, linking entrepreneurial activity and sustainable development has become an essential practice for all businesses nowadays (Koe & Majid, 2014). Dean and McMullen (2007) suggest that entrepreneurs should help resolve environmental problems. Linking economic and environmental interests to create benefit for the whole society has become a vital practice among businesses nowadays (Palazzi & Starcher, 2006). Businesses are required to perform in an equal footing between economic gains and sustainable practices. Being "green" and being "economically successful" should be at the central attention of all business leaders today (Schaltegger et al., 2001). Economic gain is no longer the only objective of entrepreneurship.

Due to the increasing awareness and rapid development of concepts related to Corporate Social Responsibility (CSR), ecological modernization and sustainability development, many businesses have re-examined their roles on social-economic issues. In many cases, the term "corporate sustainability" is a synonym for "CSR" (Hall et al., 2010). As such, adopting sustainable practices is not only a trend but also a must, for most current entrepreneurs. In South Africa, entrepreneurs of large corporates and SMMEs are striving to develop new ideas and processes for their ventures in order to sustain their current position in the future (Belz & Binder, 2017; Sarango-Lalangui et al., 2018).

Limited research has been conducted on the intention of practicing entrepreneurs, specifically among owners of SMMEs towards sustainable entrepreneurship (Koe & Majid, 2014). Previous studies focused on a traditional entrepreneurial process, with limited studies having been done to investigate the intentions of entrepreneurs to engage in sustainable entrepreneurship. To date, studies by Moriano et al. (2012),

Shook and Bratianu (2010) and Schwarz et al. (2009) on entrepreneurship intention have captured the attention of multiple researchers in the entrepreneurship field. However, studies focusing on intention towards sustainable entrepreneurship are still lacking, especially in the local setting (Koe & Majid, 2014). Not much has been known regarding the antecedents of intention towards sustainable entrepreneurship in South Africa (Belz & Binder, 2017; Koe & Majid, 2014; Nhemachena, 2017).

According to the Theory of Planned Behavior (TPB), attitude, subjective norms, and perceived behavioral control all contribute to the explanation of entrepreneurial purpose (Moriano et al. 2012; Shook and Bratianu, 2010). These key features are depicted and described in further detail in Figure 1 below.

Figure 1. Theory of planned behaviour
Source: (Ajzen, 1991)

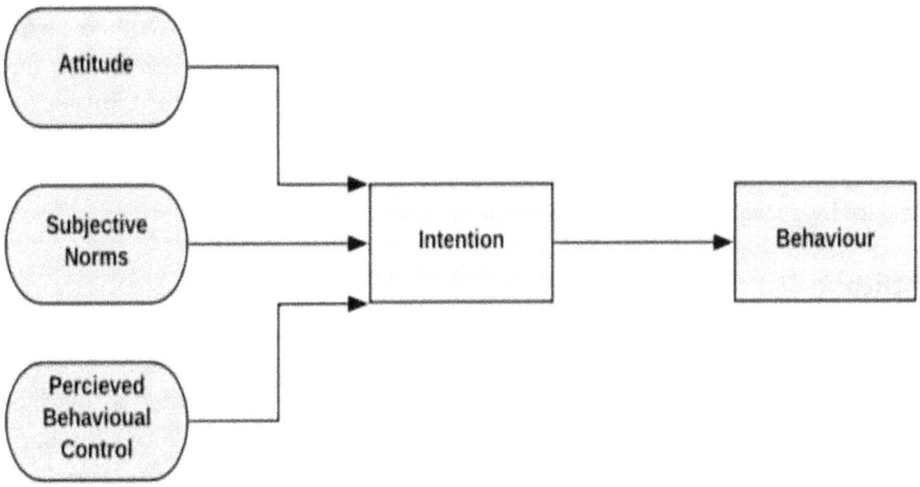

The theory of planned behaviour (TPB) is made up of four elements: "attitude, subjective norms, perceived behavioral control, and intention" (Ajzen, 1991). TPB is frequently used in a variety of fields to analyze human behavior (Ajzen, 1991). It is presupposed that intention can predict people's behavior, and that intention is influenced by a variety of elements, including personal attitude, others' perceptions of the behavior (subjective norm), and self-efficacy (perceived behavioural control).

To far, the TPB has been widely used in research of entrepreneurial intention, owing to its capacity to accurately predict intention (Moriano et al. 2012; Shook and Bratianu, 2010). Additionally, it has been used in investigations predicting individual pro-environmental intention behaviour (Kaiser & Gutscher, 2003; Kaiser et al., 2005). Kaiser et al. (2005) argued that the TPB's theoretically significant section appears to be correct since it accurately defines the relationships between its ideas. However, Conner and Armitage (1998); Oreg and Katz-Gerro (2006), and Fielding et al. (2008) have proposed that additional factors be included to improve the model's predictive utility.

According to the paradigm of theory of planned behaviour indicated above this chapter investigated three independent variables: attitude, subjective norm, and perceived behavioral control. The dependent variable is an indicator of an individual's intention to engage in sustainable entrepreneurship.

Intention

Ajzen (1991) asserts that intention captures the motivating component affecting behavior. Ajzen (1991:181) defined this idea as "an indication of how far people are willing to go or how much effort they intend to exert to complete the behavior." In short, the stronger the purpose, the more probable the behavior will be carried out. Similarly, businesspeople adopt sustainable methods for a cause, i.e., they do it consciously. Most importantly, anyone can have an aim toward Sustainable Entrepreneurship, regardless of whether the individual is a practicing entrepreneur or not. However, the aim for Sustainable Entrepreneurship among SMME owners has not been evaluated yet (Majid et al. 2017).

Attitude

Attitude is described as a person's opinion or appraisal of another person's behavior, whether favorable or unfavorable (Ajzen, 1991). It is often regarded as the most significant predictor of pro-environmental intention (Tonglet et al., 2004). Similarly, (Chen et al., 2011) Chen, Gregoire, Arendt, and Shelly (2011) discovered that attention may be used to predict behavioral intent to adopt sustainable activities. Stern (2000), Bamberg and Möser (2007), and Vermeir and Verbeke (2008) all found that attitude did influence behavioral intention positively.

Subjective Norms

Subjective norms are defined as "felt social pressure to perform or refrain from performing a behavior" (Solesvik, Westhead, Kolvereid and Matlay, 2012). It is regarded as a component that influences persons' ability to behave sustainably (Majid et al. 2017). Additionally, Van Birgelen, Semeijn, and Keicher (2009) discovered a substantial correlation between ecological, behavioral aim and the opinion of reference persons such as family and friends, teachers, successful entrepreneurs, and business consultants. Fielding et al. (2008) and Chen et al. (2010) both discover a substantial association between subjective norm and sustainability intention (2011). Subjective norms are defined in these research as the degree to which others or an individual exert influence over Sustainable Entrepreneurship.

Perceived Behavioral Control

Ajzen (1991:188) proposed a third factor of intention: perceived behavioral control, which he characterized as "perceived ease or difficulty in doing the behavior." However, in recent years, numerous researchers, including Bandura (1997), have substituted self-efficacy for perceived behavioral control, for example, Shook and Bratianu (2010), Moriano et al. (2011), and Schwarz et al (2009). Self-efficacy and perceived behavioral control are interchangeable terms. Kaiser and Gutscher (2003) demonstrated convincingly that perceived behavioral control is a strong predictor of ecological behavior intention. Additionally, Tonglet et al. (2004), Oreg and Katz-Gerro (2006), and Bamberg and Möser (2007) all demonstrated that perceived behavioral control was a predictor of pro-environmental behavioral intention in their investigations. The interaction of the TPB components and entrepreneurial intention has sparked a great deal of research (Solesvik et al., 2012). There is, however, a dearth of study on perceived behavioral control as a motivator for entrepreneurs to engage in sustainable entrepreneurship. As a result, this study addressed this gap by examining eight factors that influence perceived behavioral control: core business, competitive advantage, resources, confidence, status of the environment, consumption, budget, and lack of information.

Studies conducted by Wahga et al. (2018), Gasbarro et al. (2018), Dhahri and Omri (2018), Kraus et al. (2018) and Hörisch (2018) have successfully explained how entrepreneurs practice sustainable entrepreneurship and what their contributions are. Unfortunately, the psychological aspects, such as intention and motivation that drive people towards sustainable entrepreneurship, have not been adequately addressed in the current literature. Despite the growing field of sustainable entrepreneurship, most of the available literature has been mainly theoretical and qualitative, or has focused on developed countries, and very little has been done in developing countries such as South Africa (Nhemachena, 2017). Therefore, to address this research gap, the objective of this study was to investigate what motivates entrepreneurs to engage in sustainable entrepreneurship.

Exploratory studies are used to perform early study in areas of inquiry that are relatively unexplored. Researchers pursue research with an open, adaptable, and inductive mindset in order to discover novel insights on things. Exploratory research designs indicate how the researcher wants to collect data and where he or she intends to look for it (Creswell & Creswell, 2017). According to Sekaran and Bougie (2016) "an exploratory study is conducted when little is known about a scenario or when there is no information accessible on how similar difficulties or research issues have been resolved in the past." In such circumstances, exploratory research are done to better grasp the nature of the problem, as very few studies have been conducted in that field.

To accomplish the study's objectives, an exploratory research design was employed to ascertain entrepreneurs' perceptions on sustainable entrepreneurship. The researcher adopted an exploratory research design due to the scarcity of data on the subject under examination. As a result, this approach will reveal details if there is insufficient information. This research design collects data and elucidates the phenomenon's complexities. The primary aim for conducting exploratory research is to gain a more in-depth understanding of entrepreneurs' perceptions of sustainable entrepreneurship This technique enabled the researchers to diagnose a condition and formulate hypotheses in order to address the research topic. The argument for using an exploratory research strategy is that it focuses on a topic that is under-researched. Therefore, this strategy was explored.

According to Knabe (2012), the majority of TPB research studies used a survey instrument to assess the theory's efficacy. Recent research utilizing the TPB bolster this decision to apply the idea to sustainability through quantitative analysis (Ajzen, 2006). Quantification facilitates data aggregation, comparison, and summarization, as well as statistical analysis. All of these are necessary results when putting Ajzen's theory to the test. Additionally, a quantitative approach enables additional verification of the model's theoretical sufficiency (Knabe, 2012). The findings presented in this chapter were extracted from a questionnaire disseminated to entrepreneurs across various sectors.

Figure 2. Respondent profiles

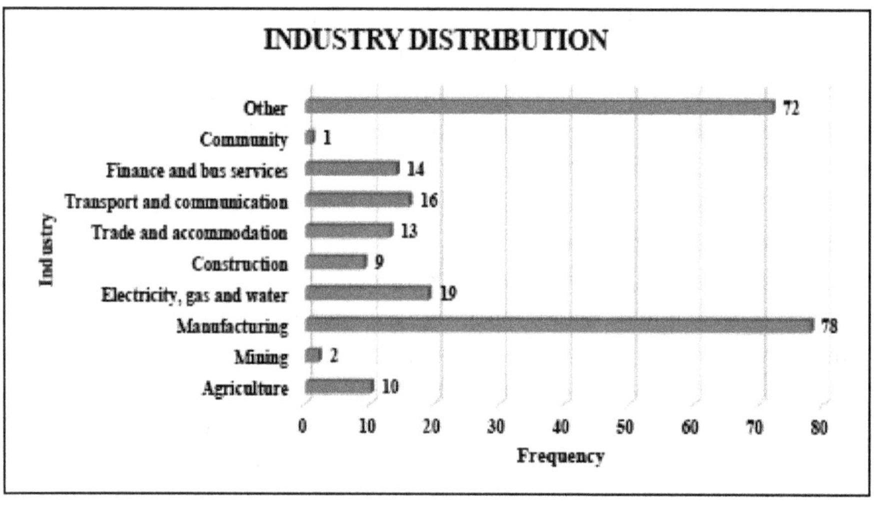

To evaluate the validity of the results and whether comparable results would be achieved if the sample size was increased, Cronbach's Alpha was used as a reliability test. Cronbach's alpha was calculated for attitude, subjective norms, and perceived behavioural controls. The results are displayed below

Table 1. Reliability analysis: Cronbach's Alpha

Item	Number of Items	Cronbach's Alpha (%)
Overall questionnaire (B1-D9)	234	94.9
Attitude variables (B1-B16)	234	91.9
Subjective Norm variables (C1-C5)	234	83.5
Perceived Behavioural Control variables (D1-D8)	234	86.2

The reliability of the whole questionnaire had a Cronbach Alpha of 94.9%. This shows very high internal consistency from the questionnaire items. When an item was deleted, the scale did not show an increase in Cronbach Alpha except for PBC8, which had been earlier found to have negative correlations with other questions. Its increase was only 0.05%; hence, the item was not deleted from the questionnaire. Therefore, it can then be established that the researcher would get similar results if the questionnaire were administered on a larger sample of respondents.

Table 2. Sustainable entrepreneurship intentions

Sustainable Entrepreneurial Intentions			Frequency Distribution				
			Strongly Disagree	Disagree	Neutral	Agree	Strongly Agree
Q1.	My company engages in Sustainable Entrepreneurship as part of its business case	Freq	9	7	35	95	88
		%	3.8	3.0	15.0	40.6	37.6
Q2.	My company engages in Sustainable Entrepreneurship as part of its moral case	Freq	8	5	36	93	92
		%	3.4	2.1	15.4	39.7	39.3
Q3.	My company engages in Sustainable Entrepreneurship to improve society	Freq	8	6	25	95	100
		%	3.4	2.6	10.7	40.6	42.7
Q4.	My company engages in Sustainable Entrepreneurship to create happiness amongst all its stakeholders	Freq	10	8	29	83	104
		%	4.3	3.4	12.4	35.5	44.4
Q5.	My company thinks manufacturing green products is a good idea	Freq	7	3	17	88	119
		%	3.0	1.3	7.3	37.6	50.9
Q6.	My company believes that sustainable practices will reduce pollution	Freq	5	8	20	73	128
		%	2.1	3.4	8.5	31.2	54.7
Q7.	My company derives pleasure in environmentally sustainable products	Freq	9	5	29	92	99
		%	3.8	2.1	12.4	39.3	42.3
Q8.	My company is willing to reduce its consumption to help protect the environment	Freq	3	7	20	82	122
		%	1.3	3.0	8.5	35.0	52.1

Table 3. Sustainable entrepreneurship norms

Sustainable Entrepreneurial Norm Distribution			Frequency Distribution				
			Strongly Disagree	Disagree	Neutral	Agree	Strongly Agree
Q1.	My company engages in Sustainable Entrepreneurship to meet the growing demand of sustainable consumption from our customers	Freq	7	8	23	123	73
		%	3.0	3.4	9.8	52.6	31.2
Q2.	My company engages in Sustainable Entrepreneurship because our competitors are leading by a moral case	Freq	24	27	39	85	59
		%	10.3	11.5	16.7	36.3	25.2
Q3.	My company engages in Sustainable Entrepreneurship to satisfy the needs of our Investors	Freq	23	15	41	89	66
		%	9.8	6.4	17.5	38.0	28.2

Table 4. Sustainable entrepreneurship behavioral controls

Sustainable Entrepreneurial Behavioural Control			Frequency Distribution				
			Strongly Disagree	Disagree	Neutral	Agree	Strongly Agree
Q1.	We engage in Sustainable Entrepreneurship because it forms part of our core business	Freq	11	11	31	104	77
		%	4.7	4.7	13.2	44.4	32.9
Q2.	We engage in Sustainable Entrepreneurship because it is our source of competitive advantage	Freq	15	13	28	99	79
		%	6.4	5.6	12.0	42.3	33.8
Q3.	We have all required resources to engage in Sustainable Entrepreneurship	Freq	12	15	41	102	64
		%	5.1	6.4	17.5	43.6	27.4
Q4.	Our company's confidence lies in manufacturing green products	Freq	12	23	65	73	61
		%	5.1	9.8	27.8	31.2	26.1
Q5.	Our company is concerned about the state of our environment	Freq	4	2	18	80	130
		%	1.7	0.9	7.7	34.2	55.6
Q6.	Our company is willing to reduce its consumption to help protect the environment	Freq	2	3	24	90	115
		%	0.9	1.3	10.3	38.5	49.1

SOLUTIONS AND RECOMMENDATIONS

The chapter revealed that the more committed entrepreneurs are to sustainable practices, the more likely they are to engage in them. As a result, this chapter recommends that efforts to promote and strengthen sustainable entrepreneurship should focus on entrepreneurs who demonstrate appropriate intentions to start sustainable businesses, rather than on those who want to start businesses solely because some financial assistance is available for start-ups in that sector. External stakeholders were revealed to have a substantial impact on entrepreneurs' aspirations to embrace sustainable business practices. As a result of this study, SMMEs are advised to match their business operations with the values of their external stakeholders.

The study revealed that both extrinsic and intrinsic rewards are critical drivers of entrepreneurial ambitions that are sustainable. As a result of this, government, government agencies and entrepreneurs should prioritize initiatives aimed at building and enhancing intrinsic and extrinsic motives for sustainability among entrepreneurs.

The study also revealed that there is a dearth of information on how to begin implementing sustainable practices. As a result, the chapter proposes that government agencies responsible for economic development and environmental affairs strengthen efforts to promote sustainable entrepreneurship through the provision of suitable support to both existing and prospective sustainable businesses. The chapter further proposes that efforts to foster sustainable entrepreneurial activity should focus on building adequate business management skills to ensure the success of start-ups and established SMMEs.

FUTURE RESEARCH DIRECTIONS

The chapter insights serve as a lens for future research on entrepreneurial perceptions of sustainable entrepreneurship. Future researchers could consider conducting a similar study on a larger sample in a metropolitan environment, where there is greater economic activity. Furthermore, to allow for generalizability of the results, the study could be broadened by undertaking a national wide study to better understand the drivers of entrepreneurial behaviour related to Sustainable Entrepreneurship across the country. Alternatively, a comparative study could be conducted to investigate whether the levels of education affect entrepreneurs' intentions towards Sustainable Entrepreneurship

CONCLUSION

The aim of this chapter was to provide insights on the perceptions of entrepreneurs on sustainable entrepreneurship. The findings from chapter were that entrepreneurs of SMMEs showed a significant level of intention towards sustainable entrepreneurship. It can be concluded that there is a statistically significant relationship between sustainable entrepreneurial intentions and all identified constructs. The findings further illustrated that entrepreneurs are motivated by the strong obligation they have towards incorporating sustainable practices into their company. The incorporation of sustainable practices into SMMEs creates a long-term value for the company and promotes the longevity of the SMMEs. Further to this, the findings revealed the willingness of entrepreneurs to put extra effort regularly into sustainable practices in their companies. Entrepreneurs are striving to create new ideas and processes for their ventures to sustain their current position.

The pressures placed by the demands of customers, society, and employees or colleagues directly influenced the decisions of entrepreneurs to engage in Sustainable Entrepreneurship. Furthermore, it can be concluded that for an SMME to truly thrive and have real sustainability, it is critical to achieve a positive company culture where all employees "buy-in" and everyone is on board.

Another insight from this chapter is that SMMEs are taking large steps in terms of reducing their environmental impact. A company's performance is dependent on the availability of unique resources that enables a competitive advantage for the SMME. There has been an increasing number of SMMEs that are committed to reducing their negative impact on the environment and are working towards having a positive influence on the environment.

REFERENCES

Aykol, B., & Leonidou, L. C. (2015). Researching the Green Practices of Smaller Service Firms: A Theoretical, Methodological, and Empirical Assessment. *Journal of Small Business Management*, *53*(4), 1264–1288. doi:10.1111/jsbm.12118

Bahena-Álvarez, I. L., Cordón-Pozo, E., & Delgado-Cruz, A. (2019). Social Entrepreneurship in the Conduct of Responsible Innovation: Analysis Cluster in Mexican SMEs. *Sustainability*, *11*(13), 3714. doi:10.3390u11133714

Bajdor, P., Pawełoszek, I., & Fidlerova, H. (2021). Analysis and Assessment of Sustainable Entrepreneurship Practices in Polish Small and Medium Enterprises. *Sustainability*, *13*(7), 3595. doi:10.3390u13073595

Belz, F. M., & Binder, J. K. (2017). Sustainable entrepreneurship: A convergent process model. *Business Strategy and the Environment*, *26*(1), 1–17. doi:10.1002/bse.1887

Cantele, S., Vernizzi, S., & Campedelli, B. (2020). Untangling the Origins of Sustainable Commitment: New Insights on the Small vs. Large Firms' Debate. *Sustainability*, *12*(2), 671. doi:10.3390u12020671

Crals, E., & Vereeck, L. (2005). The affordability of sustainable entrepreneurship certification for SMEs. *International Journal of Sustainable Development and World Ecology*, *12*(2), 173–183. doi:10.1080/13504500509469628

Dean, T. J., & McMullen, J. S. (2007). Toward a theory of sustainable entrepreneurship: Reducing environmental degradation through entrepreneurial action. *Journal of Business Venturing*, *22*(1), 50–76. doi:10.1016/j.jbusvent.2005.09.003

Dhahri, S., & Omri, A. (2018). Entrepreneurship contribution to the three pillars of sustainable development: What does the evidence really say? *World Development*, *106*, 64–77. doi:10.1016/j.worlddev.2018.01.008

Gasbarro, F., Rizzi, F., & Frey, M. (2018). Sustainable institutional entrepreneurship in practice: Insights from SMEs in the clean energy sector in Tuscany (Italy). *International Journal of Entrepreneurial Behaviour & Research*, *24*(2), 476–498. doi:10.1108/IJEBR-11-2015-0259

Hall, J., Daneke, G., & Lenox, M. (2010). Sustainable development and entrepreneurship: Past contributions and future directions. *Journal of Business Venturing*, *25*(5), 439–448. doi:10.1016/j.jbusvent.2010.01.002

Hall, J., & Wagner, M. (2012). Editorial: The Challenges and Opportunities of Sustainable Development for Entrepreneurship and Small Business. *Journal of Small Business and Entrepreneurship*, *25*(4), 409–416. doi:10.1080/08276331.2012.10593581

Hörisch, J. (2018). 'Think big'or'small is beautiful'? An empirical analysis of characteristics and determinants of success of sustainable crowdfunding projects. *International Journal of Entrepreneurial Venturing*, *10*(1), 111–129. doi:10.1504/IJEV.2018.090982

Koe, W.-L., & Majid, I. A. (2014). Intention towards Sustainable Entrepreneurship: A Conceptual Framework. *The Journal of Technology Management and Technopreneurship*, *1*(1).

Kraus, S., Burtscher, J., Vallaster, C., & Angerer, M. (2018). Sustainable entrepreneurship orientation: A reflection on status-quo research on factors facilitating responsible managerial practices. *Sustainability*, *10*(2), 444. doi:10.3390u10020444

Mathew, V. (2009). Sustainable Entrepreneurship in Small-Scale Business: Application, Concepts and Cases. *ICFAI Journal of Entrepreneurship Development*, *6*(1), 41–61.

Moriano, J. A., Gorgievski, M., Laguna, M., Stephan, U., & Zarafshani, K. (2012). A cross-cultural approach to understanding entrepreneurial intention. *Journal of Career Development*, *39*(2), 162–185. doi:10.1177/0894845310384481

Nhemachena, C. (2017). *Motivations of sustainable entrepreneurship in Gauteng province, South Africa* (Doctoral dissertation).

Palazzi, M., & Starcher, G. (2006). *Corporate Social Responsibility and Business Success*. Retrieved from http://centreonphilanthropy.com/files/kb_articles/1269270655EBBF%20Corporate%20Responsibility%20and%20Business%20Success.pdf

Reyes-Rodríguez, J. F., Ulhøi, J. P., & Madsen, H. (2016). Corporate Environmental Sustainability in Danish SMEs: A Longitudinal Study of Motivators, Initiatives, and Strategic Effects. *Corporate Social Responsibility and Environmental Management*, *23*(4), 193–212. doi:10.1002/csr.1359

Sarango-Lalangui, P., Santos, J., & Hormiga, E. (2018). The development of sustainable entrepreneurship research field. *Sustainability, 10*(6), 2005. doi:10.3390u10062005

Schaltegger, S., Synnestvedt, T., & Vei, E. S. (2001). *The Forgotten Link Between" Green" and Economic Success.* Center for Sustainability Management.

Schwarz, E. J., Wdowiak, M. A., Almer-Jarz, D. A., & Breitenecker, R. J. (2009). The effects of attitudes and perceived environment conditions on students' entrepreneurial intent: An Austrian perspective. *Education + Training, 51*(4), 272–291. doi:10.1108/00400910910964566

Shook, C. L., & Bratianu, C. (2010). Entrepreneurial intent in a transitional economy: An application of the theory of planned behavior to Romanian students. *The International Entrepreneurship and Management Journal, 6*(3), 231–247. doi:10.100711365-008-0091-2

Testa, F., Gusmerottia, N. M., Corsini, F., Passetti, E., & Iraldo, F. (2016). Factors Affecting Environmental Management by Small and Micro Firms: The Importance of Entrepreneurs' Attitudes and Environmental Investment. *Corporate Social Responsibility and Environmental Management, 23*(6), 373–385. doi:10.1002/csr.1382

Wahga, A. I., Blundel, R., & Schaefer, A. (2018). Understanding the drivers of sustainable entrepreneurial practices in Pakistan's leather industry: A multi-level approach. *International Journal of Entrepreneurial Behaviour & Research, 24*(2), 382–407. doi:10.1108/IJEBR-11-2015-0263

ADDITIONAL READING

Ali, M. (2021). A systematic literature review of sustainable entrepreneurship with thematic analysis. *World Journal of Entrepreneurship, Management and Sustainable Development, 17*(4), 742–764. doi:10.1108/WJEMSD-11-2020-0150

Barrera Verdugo, G., & Villarroel Villarroel, A. (2021). Measuring the association between students' exposure to social media and their valuation of sustainability in entrepreneurship. *Heliyon, 7*(6), e07272. doi:10.1016/j.heliyon.2021.e07272 PMID:34189315

Chhabra, S., Raghunathan, R., & Rao, N. V. M. (2020). The antecedents of entrepreneurial intention among women entrepreneurs in India. *Asia Pacific Journal of Innovation and Entrepreneurship, 14*(1), 76–92. doi:10.1108/APJIE-06-2019-0034

Crnogaj, K., Rebernik, M., Bradac Hojnik, B., & Omerzel Gomezelj, D. (2014). Building a model of researching the sustainable entrepreneurship in the tourism sector. *Kybernetes*, *43*(3/4), 377–393. doi:10.1108/K-07-2013-0155

Hoogendoorn, B., van der Zwan, P., & Thurik, R. (2019). Sustainable Entrepreneurship: The Role of Perceived Barriers and Risk. *Journal of Business Ethics*, *157*(4), 1133–1154. doi:10.100710551-017-3646-8

Kimuli, S. N. L., Orobia, L., Sabi, H. M., & Tsuma, C. K. (2020). Sustainability intention: Mediator of sustainability behavioral control and sustainable entrepreneurship. *World Journal of Entrepreneurship, Management and Sustainable Development*, *16*(2), 81–95. doi:10.1108/WJEMSD-12-2019-0096

Nguyen, H. T. T., Costanzo, L. A., & Karatas-Özkan, M. (2020). Stakeholders' perceptions of sustainable entrepreneurship within the context of a developing economy. *Journal of Small Business Management*, 1–40. doi:10.1080/00472778.2020.1796465

Sharma, S., Goyal, D. P., & Singh, A. (2021). Systematic review on sustainable entrepreneurship education (SEE): A framework and analysis. *World Journal of Entrepreneurship, Management and Sustainable Development*, *17*(3), 372–395.

Soomro, B. A. K., Almahdi, H., & Shah, N. (2021). Perceptions of young entrepreneurial aspirants towards sustainable entrepreneurship in Pakistan. *Kybernetes*, *50*(7), 2134–2154. doi:10.1108/K-07-2019-0504

Vuorio, A. M., Puumalainen, K., & Fellnhofer, K. (2018). Drivers of entrepreneurial intentions in sustainable entrepreneurship. *International Journal of Entrepreneurial Behaviour & Research*, *24*(2), 359–381. doi:10.1108/IJEBR-03-2016-0097

KEY TERMS AND DEFINITIONS

Economic Sustainability: Concentrates on the economic value that is provided by the organisation to the surrounding environment in a manner that prospers and promotes it for its ability to sustain future generations.

Entrepreneurship: Is the method of developing a fresh and useful product or service, while taking into consideration all the factors needed to make the product or service accessible to the market.

Environmental Sustainability: Refers to engaging in practices that do not compromise the environmental resources for future generations.

Social Sustainability: Social sustainability happens when formal and informal processes, systems, structures, and relationships, actively support the capacity of current and future generations to create healthy and liveable communities.

Sustainability: The capability of continuously providing conditions conducive to a longer life for a group of people and their descendants in a specific ecosystem.

Sustainable Development: Is regarded as the development that meets the needs of the present without compromising the ability of future generations to meet their own needs.

Sustainable Entrepreneurship: The emphasis on maintaining nature, life support, and community in pursuit of perceived chances to create new products, processes, and services for gain, where gain is generally defined to include economic and non-economic benefits to individuals, the economy, and society.

Triple Bottom Line: Is a method used in business accounting to expand stakeholders' knowledge of the company further. It goes beyond the traditional and financial aspects and reveals the company's impact on the world around it.

Chapter 10
Analytical Impact of Digital Marketing on Smart Wearables in India

Devesh Bathla
https://orcid.org/0000-0003-3990-5934
Chitkara Business School, Chitkara University, India

Raina Ahuja
Kurukshetra University, India

Shraddha Awasthi
Chitkara Business School, Chitkara University, India

Amrith Santhosh
University of Prince Edward Island, Canada

ABSTRACT

Advancement in innovation and technology has transformed the lifestyle of individuals. Wearable innovation is an old-style case of such insight. Despite the fact that this innovation has been common for quite a while, the furor of wearable development began when the model of Google Glass was concocted. It helped clients to start thinking past this present reality. Preceding the prototype, customers were uninformed about wearable development. In the 21st century, wearable innovation has purchased new advancements which have helped wearables to take off in the mechanical market. While it is intended to study the awareness of smart wearables, it is also synthesized to identify the key perceptions about smart wearables in the study. It is further being analysed to check the influence of digital marketing in purchase decision for smart wearables with specific focus on all digital platforms.

DOI: 10.4018/978-1-6684-4745-1.ch010

INTRODUCTION

In the 21st century, wearable innovation has purchased new advancements which has helped wearables to take off in the mechanical market. The Bluetooth headset, with the assistance of new Bluetooth innovation was introduced in the year 2002, by Nokia. The headset permitted clients to get calls without utilizing their hands. This headset accomplished extraordinary prevalence in that time and still numerous clients are utilizing it. Further in 2007, sportswear brands like Nike and technology giants like Apple group have made a wellness following unit which is utilized to follow the development of the clients. With the assistance of shoe installed tracker, clients can see the ongoing, separation secured, calories and speed expended through exercise on the Nano screen of iPod. While it is intended to study the awareness of Smart Wearables, it is also synthesized to identify the key perceptions about smart wearables in the study. It is further being analysed to check the influence of digital marketing in purchase decision for Smart wearables with specific focus on all digital platforms.

Purpose

The purpose of this paper is to analyse the impact of other influencing factors in purchase decision. A simultaneous purpose lies to evaluate if digital marketing indirectly impacts the influencing factors. Cohort of the learnings from marketing analytics theories spreading over VALS Framework, Pareto Principle etc. may be drawn with the optimised industry models leveraging machine learning techniques that propose the most appropriate offer or user interaction among a range of probable offerings.

Methodology and Design

This work builds up a feasible system alongside recommendations by incorporating the set of scholastic as well as professional written works, in the very sphere of smart wearables pertinent to Antecedents of Consumer Buying behaviour towards Smart Wearables.

Research Constraints and Implications

The paper aims to give suggestions to the organisations in the exhibition of consumer analytics for improving the consumer buying behaviour experience by the application of purchase analytics as a key instrument in the smart wearable industry. It also aims to provide a view of customers which is essentially dynamic in nature and other key data points observed during the life cycle of a customer. The user profile, buying behaviours and the potential to pre-empt user preferences and future behaviours at an individual user level with an highly satisfactory level of accuracy towards the smartwearbles.

In previous decades, circumstances have been difficult for regular people to examine the principal physical prosperity properties without any other person. They expected to visit clinical centers and offices to research cholesterol, circulatory strain, sugar, and other physical activities. Nevertheless, with help of wearable innovation nowadays, people can check all these principal prosperity related nuances and screen health works out, all finished and at whatever point. As of now specialists were using unmistakable contraption for the enlistment of the patient, yet nowadays one splendid wearable mechanical get together can be used for meeting various targets.

Further, this imaginative innovation of wearable nature might be viewed as coordination of advancement with customary ornament which make customer's life less complex. Nowadays, if someone thinks about the latest mobile phones, they are in like manner unmistakable of the smartwatch that uncovers that wearable contraptions are ending up being standard bit by bit. The inspiration driving the wearable development is to give snappier access on advancement by saving time and effort of the customers. Despite the fact that wearable innovation has a lot of potential, yet at the same time there are a few issues in it. Security, correspondence limit, power utilization, protection are a few difficulties which may looked by innovative wearable. These types of gadgets have a little processor subsequently it has less safety efforts with respect to the other figuring gadgets. Along these lines, wellbeing and security of the clients are in danger, which may diminish the interest of wearable gadgets later on. A principle challenge in the wearables may be defined as that these gadgets are not independent gadgets, they need to touch base with different devices to conduct the vast majority of the capacities, for example, advanced cells. These sorts of intricacies are purpose behind security issues in wearable gadgets.

Marketing system is the central objective of expanding deals and accomplishing a supportable upper hand. Computerized showcasing system is the manner by which we connect with clients through web-based media to make mindfulness and create leads. The technique comprises of different key boundaries that need to consider at the hour of procedure plan. The great structure squares will guarantee a productive chain of distinguishing targets to observing lead transformation. They key boundaries are commitment and reaction to the privilege the client. The quickness of reaction will make a positive electronic verbal which is as yet the best type of showcasing procedure. Wearable have gotten hugely well known in the previous one year with more players expected to dispatch items in coming years. Ventures are being made for the nonstop improvement of items to give better an incentive to clients and the market is required to develop on all boundaries, for example, value, item highlights and target portions. Notwithstanding, the main part in the wearable gadgets market for Q4 2016 happens to be a Health fire up firm GOQii with a 15.5% piece of the pie as far as shipments, firmly followed by Xiaomi with a 13.2% piece of the pie, while Fitbit represented 7.9% piece of the overall industry during a similar quarter. The admittance to a fitness coach has been the extraordinary selling purpose of the GOQii.

The Indian market is prevalently an essential wearable market with wellness trackers and less expensive savvy watches. In spite of the fact that brands like Samsung and Apple do offer premium keen watches to the clients who are eager to dish out a heavy aggregate. Despite the fact that the overall wearables market is required to almost twofold by 2021 and India's purchasers purchased another 2.7 million units a year ago, the subcontinent's device purchasers are giving indications of exhaustion. They're done hurrying out to purchase wearables at a similar sweltering movement as from before. Furthermore, exacerbating the situation is the way that new brands are bouncing into an undeniably packed field of contenders. Apparently unflinching by the headwinds, Fitbit is planning to catch a more noteworthy portion of the wearables class in India. What's more, it expects to do this by giving customers there an extended setup of wellness trackers and smartwatches.

Specifically, Fitbit sees a lot of undiscovered potential for smartwatches that exploit its overall qualities in wellbeing and wellness following despite the fact that that class actually presently can't seem to increase a lot of footing among India's purchasers. Statistical surveying firm IDC said deals of smartwatches still just made up about 10% of the complete market for wearable gadgets a year ago. IDC orders keen wearables as those that can run outsider applications, similar to Apple Watch and Fitbit Versa, versus fundamental wearables which can't run the equivalent applications, for example, Xiaomi's Mi Band and Fitbit Alta. With the most recent adaptation of the Fitbit OS, for instance, the gadget producer offers a few interesting advantages like female wellbeing following to assist ladies with following their monthly cycle and assessed ripe window, on-screen exercises and savvy highlights like snappy answers and on-gadget music, all with more than four days of battery life.

In the past various researches have been done in the area of smart wearables consumer behaviour and their acceptance. Independent studies have been done in the area of digital marketing strategy for smart wearables devices but no research has been done to find exact correlation between Digital Marketing & purchase and how does Digital Marketing impact other influencing factors also. Through this work, it is intended to identify impact of digital marketing, if any on the consumer behaviour and if there are any more other influencing factors which impacts consumer decision making.

Objectives

These objectives characterize what wearable gadget organizations need to achieve through web-based media promoting exercises. There are numerous significant elements should be considered before setting up the commitment with clients. The choice of boundaries is noteworthy to guarantee that targets are; explicit, quantifiable, attainable, and sensible and time explicit. The SMART methodology can decide the good outcome and territories required location.

- **Specific** – Exact objective with focus on better comprehension of Achievement. Most recent inclination in wearable medical services gadgets and keen watches that augments income.
- **Measurable** – Substantial or immaterial nature of the objective. The association should clear about subjective and measurables nature of objectives.
- **Achievable** – Objectives are expected to be sensible with respect to accomplishment. The objective must be lined up with the mission and vision of the association. The transient attainable objective may help to dynamic the drawn out objective.
- **Realistic** – Realistic objective relies upon the emotionally supportive network to make the wave in online media. The association ought to have enough asset and time to accomplish the target. At times change rate relies upon the brand mindfulness and infiltration in the market.
- **Time specific** – Objects ought to be time-bound, and quantifiable. Development gauges for the wearable gadget ought to have a timetable. Normal advancement update on an occasional premise can assist with following the degree of achievement

Segmentation

Kotler et al. (2005, p. 391) characterizes division as "partitioning a market into particular gatherings of purchasers with various necessities, qualities or conduct, who may require separate items or showcasing blends". The motivation behind market division is to focus promoting assets on one or a few market sections to increase upper hand (Thomas, 1980). Web-based media is tied in with sharing data in the networks having a common intrigue. The bigger the rundown of individuals in the network, the better method to arrive at the mass. Notwithstanding, at times organizations decide to focus in general market however focusing to the whole market isn't proficient in all cases. The taste, conduct, and brain science of buyers are unique, and an organization focusing on all clients is regularly not extremely compelling in its correspondence since all clients are extraordinary. In this way, to isolate a market into a few fragments encourages the correspondence more effective and correspondence scopes to the correct client. The segment division dependent on sexual orientation, age, geographic area is less applicable today in wording long range informal communication. These days the critical factor that makes the network is shopper's feelings and enthusiasm towards wearable gadgets. Psychographic division is more fitting to draw in clients towards new item or administrations. Purchasers purchase in or select themselves in the circles or social affairs where they would like to be instructed about sound lifestyle, shared and drew in about the new focal points and features. Zeroing in on those social occasions to make care and pull them to grow the change from opportunity to lead is significantly less difficult than zeroing in on the more broad group. It's basic for the relationship to keep up the summary of online media influencers to have the Doppler effect in electronic media about the brand. Online media influencers are the brand advocates and have a significant part in affecting the organization. It's critical to pick the online media influencers during electronic media mission to make the vibe. It's furthermore basic to wipe out the overview of spoilers from division to decrease negative casual. Over the long haul, the intellectuals will offer negative remarks, yet that furthermore gives another information to appreciate the snares of the organization or thing. Association need to see all the negative comments anyway need not connect with those are not considerable.

Segmentation Antecedents

- Demographic division which centers around attributes of a client. For instance, sexual orientation, age, level of pay, training, position, and social foundation.
- Purchase inclination significantly impacted by Lifestyle, for example, social class, solid way of life, assessments towards new contraptions, brave character, and perspectives to control food diet.
- Consumer conduct assumes a noteworthy part to decide on the wearable gadget like wellness Behavior, online wellbeing tips endorser and wellbeing gear inclination and furthermore dependent on earlier buys.
- A topographical area, for example, nation and landmasses additionally assumes the significant job. The decision of activity likewise relies upon nation and territory.

DIGITAL CHANNEL SELECTION

The customary method of channel choice relies upon the item and administrations which can be accomplished by immediate or circuitous channels. The mission or advancement can be viral and spread out to the bigger crowd than anticipated or the other way around. A wide web-based media system is presently an absolute necessity for any wearable gadget organization that desires to enter or stay related in the present serious market. Each organization has made a huge move to promote their item in online media to raise network commitment. Pretty much every organization has expanded their statistical surveying to upgrade their image and notoriety. Presumably item include that drives change and steady deals however right channel gives the fuel to teach clients about separation. Besides, an online media methodology is needed to fulfill other desire also like message perusing and going to the call from gadget. These advantages are extra highlights separated from wellbeing checking.

The present purchasers are keen and complex online media clients. They tune in and investigations the survey before purchasing any item. Consequently, the association must choose which correspondence stages to receive, to get their best preferred position. Leading studies and surveying through online media have likewise become a way to straightforwardly draw in clients and to gather helpful information to upgrade the item life cycle.

Content

Content expects a urgent capacity in online media elevating and it's critical to have an inside and out portrayed framework to help the thing vision. Customer division and capacity isn't everything to promote the thing or to construct the brand detectable quality. The connecting with story is must to attract the probable buyer and make a circumstance in customer's mind. The better substance has a constructive outcome in peruser's mind. Huge substance makes a promotion and restricted time practices more observable in the upheaval of unessential business. Content is the specialty of correspondence with the group without clearly selling things or plans. Content fill is to give significant prosperity related information to general society and awaken to keeping watch on gave prosperity tips by the association. The mindful information makes more brand immovability and pulls in the customer to associate more. The substance should organize the DNA of affiliations' middle competency. The significant pillars of practical substance publicizing are to give appropriate, mindful, solid and genuine information to customers.

Engagement

Online media rose as a business wonder from singular duty. There are an enormous number of associations from additional opportunity and existing customers about the thing and organizations. It has become the client contact network for various sorts questions and organizations. Settled prosperity related requests make gigantic opportunity to drive more imperative business regard for an undertaking. It also helps with understanding the circumstance of thing and their organizations in the market. Hanna et al. (2011) demonstrated that electronic media could be seen as experience and accepted that experience would rise when promoters had the alternative to meld reach, closeness, and duty into the affiliation's overall consolidated displaying method, which she proposed would incite a positive outcome (Hanna et al., 2011). Points of interest of responsibility with customers through electronic media.

1. Brand promoters to make swell in network
2. Familiarity with new wearable industry or product
3. Brand notoriety management
4. Lead creation options
5. Resolve client issues/worries to pick up brand devotion
6. Issues with current item/arrangement
7. Supporting clients to be more social and dynamic
8. Optimization of cost

We see the change in outlook in specialized technique from one-to-numerous correspondence to one-to - one conversation to comprehend the client in a superior manner. Coordinated correspondence can possibly move message the correct way. It assists with making faithful client when we go into a discourse to comprehend their concern or give significant data to comprehend the correct item. There is no restriction of web-based media commitment and levels of commitment. Investment, as per Brodie et al. (2011a), is another essential for client commitment, as it decides clients affinity to partake on online web-based media stages.

Monitor Results

The results can be seen in two unmistakable habits for instance Progressing assessment and mission express assessment. Advancing examination is the standard assessment to understand the prosperity status of existing framework. There is no surprising confirmation of assessment of online media exhibiting endeavors through electronic media channels yet there are different frameworks to evaluate the chief layer of the relational association. It's hard to control the spread of message and the accomplishment assessment for the accompanying level of layers. It might get viral in light of right mission to the right customer or may evaporate in the accompanying layer of online media network. It's unavoidable to make a strategy to contact all the brand allies and right section of customers on the essential level of the casual network. This may have Doppler effect in next level of layers to spread the mission. We can make a powerful mission with right online media procedure yet can't guess the headway in next level of association layers.

Key components to consider for assessment of online media presentation First layer traffic-The system must focus to contact the chief layer of customers with the right message. The methodology must fuse the amount of visits, sees, fans, allies and endorsers. Target Metrics-Every mission must have a goal to evaluate and focus to give direction.

1. Measuring care can be cultivated by focusing in on reach, presentation, and volume estimations. This helps with understanding the spreading of message over the association layers.
2. Measuring responsibility can be cultivated by focusing in on retweets, comments, and individuals in duty.
3. Measuring snaps, offers and changes are useful estimations to understand the traffic to the site.

Campaign Effectiveness Measurement

The effect can be assessed with customer duty volumes, care, find advertisers and traffic to the site. Customer responsibility could be positive or negative reliant on the response to the mission. The best way to deal with check reasonability is to make a trial bunch from the summary of target customers before the mission. The mission must abrupt spike sought after for with or without target customers from test get-together to fathom the post-campaign sway. The modifications in duty or lead change can be followed the attracted customers to measure the lift of effect due to the mission. An assessment concentrate with test social occasion can help with understanding the mission adequacy.

DIGITAL STRATEGY IN SMART WEARABLES SEGMENT

Review of Techniques at Present Utilized in Conventional Marketing

It has been seen by standard publicists that a buyer followed a six phases decision methodology before buying Rani, Gupta (2017). Unmistakably, this method doesn't commonly provoke a purchase and these stages can be followed self-governing and depending the purchase unconventionality. At the point when everything is said in done, the six phases are:

- Acknowledgment of Problem
- Pursuit of Information
- Option Evaluation
- Choice of Purchase
- Purchase
- After purchase direct and appraisal result

Purchasers are also influenced by four essential elements in their decision buying measure. These elements can be social, individual, social, and additionally mental. Further bifurcating as:

- **Correspondence or Communication:** The crucial inspiration driving the correspondence work is to engage the collaboration to happen. Information regarding the thing or the organizations should be passed on the customer.
- **Procedural or Process:** The fundamental explanation behind the technique work is to manage the strategy related with the trade, the computerizations the frameworks organization of the two PCs drew in with the trade.
- **Organization or Support:** Improvement in the organization provided for the customer is what really attaches the customer to the association. To manage the organization provided for the customer is the inspiration driving the organization work.
- **Trade or Transaction:** To enable the trading of buying and offering to encounter is one the essential inspiration driving the trade work.

Utilization of Digital Marketing Levers

In April 2016, Ranjith and Mahalaxmi proposed: A Purchase Decision Study on Impact of Digital Marketing in Customer Buying in Trichy, to find answers about the veritable impact of cutting edge promoting in purchase decision. They made a composed survey and accumulate the fitting reactions from 50 people. The examination revealed that by far most were by then aware of electronic channels paying little regard to their level of preparing or ability. Customers moreover preferred progressed channels when they planned to buy something. 72% bought things from locales or composes and 60% said that destinations/online diaries were the most impressive progressed channel for them. Whether or not this assessment just addresses a bit of mechanized customers arranged in Delhi and NCR, it shows that cutting-edge exhibiting is affecting a consistently expanding number of people to buy.

How might we be able to utilize wearables to blend both?

As shown by Matt Goddard publicists could use IoT, like the wearables section, in order to make progressed advancing strategies following a two-advance method. First thing, their guideline target will be to accumulate data from their customers' thing use. This movement will allow to make or improve existing customer organizations as shown by customer's needs and essentials. The idea will be to improve "things and organizations to make them logically accommodating and alluring". Goddard incorporated a second step which includes in making available to advertisers, the sponsors as of late created structures. Along these lines, this advancing framework will make focal points balanced notice frameworks for IoT (Max V. Maier, The Internet of Things (IoT) (Goddard 2015).

For Accenture (2014), associations need first to show customers the extra advantage of offering their data to "unequivocal, quantifiable results" in order to convince them to keep using wearable devices and to keep sharing the data they produce. To get the best preferred position of the new wellspring of customer coordinated effort wearables are, Accenture appeal associations to execute "a solid framework, stunning development, powerful change in the chiefs, and a cutting edge progressed proximity". Wearables change advancing into "development based responsibility", which was from the outset a substance web exhibiting KPI (Koo 2017).

It enables a correspondence between customary publicizing (detached advancing) and progressed exhibiting. Sponsors have now the opportunity to follow a client in a store, have information about its preferred position, it's running outing, standard penchants, to handle this data by virtue of gigantic data examination and to push messages, triggers purchase movement, through comparative wearables.

CONCLUSION

This current century is foreseen to be a period of advances at the time everyone, every association, every affiliation apply them to make their endeavors end up being significantly less difficult and continuously convincing. The pervasiveness of using the Internet, alongside the improvement of computerized gear and programming endeavors, thoroughly uphold the headway of e-promoting in the whole system of buying from before-arrangement to arrangement to after-bargain and further improvement of customer relationship. New comers around there need to consider carefully the use of these front line channels. The two orders are correct, yet do exclude one basic viewpoint that various experts find noteworthy in describing a wearable, the part that makes it have a spot with the IoT class: the sensors. Without a doubt, if we can wear inventive contraptions for basically 50 years, the wearable progressions we will consider in this paper prepared to associate with us, either freely or through other handling devices, for instance, PCs or phones.

Advanced Marketing is the essential goal of extending bargains and achieving an acceptable advantage. Computerized Marketing methodology is the way we attract customers through online media to make care and make leads. The framework contains different key limits that need to consider at the hour of method itemizing. The incredible structure squares will ensure a successful chain of recognizing focuses to watching lead change. They key limits are responsibility and response to the benefit the customer. The briskness of response will make a positive electronic verbal which is up 'til now the best kind of advancing approach.

RECOMMENDATION

Digital Marketing achieves the presence of various new different terms, for instance impacts on a page (happens when a customer sees a site page), advancement impression (happens when an individual points of view a notification on the site page), come to (different exceptional individuals see a notification), Click through (happens each time a site page visitor taps on an ad banner which drives them to objective site) and dynamic guest clicking rate (CTR) (is the amount of snaps your commercial gets isolated by the events your advancement is showed up (impressions) in advancement objections (http://adwords.google.com)). Associations must zero in on all such angles for advanced showcasing to measure the logical effect on savvy wearables in India.

REFERENCES

Brodie, R. J., Hollebeek, L. D., Jurić, B., & Ilić, A. (2011). Customer engagement: Conceptual domain, fundamental propositions, and implications for research. *Journal of Service Research, 14*(3), 252–271. doi:10.1177/1094670511411703

Goddard, M. (2015, September). TeleCommunication Systems Location Technologies. In *Proceedings of the 28th International Technical Meeting of the Satellite Division of The Institute of Navigation (ION GNSS+ 2015)* (pp. 1069-1075). Academic Press.

Hanna, R., Rohm, A., & Crittenden, V. L. (2011). We're all connected: The power of the social media ecosystem. *Business Horizons*, *54*(3), 265–273. doi:10.1016/j.bushor.2011.01.007

Koo, S. H. (2017). Consumer differences in the United States and India on wearable trackers. *Family and Consumer Sciences Research Journal*, *46*(1), 40–56. doi:10.1111/fcsr.12230

Kotler, P., & Lee, N. (2005). Best of breed: When it comes to gaining a market edge while supporting a social cause, "corporate social marketing" leads the pack. *Social Marketing Quarterly*, *11*(3-4), 91–103. doi:10.1080/15245000500414480

Rani, P., & Gupta, S. (2017). Factor Affecting the Students Buying Behavior of Two Wheelers. *Journal of Marketing Management*, *8*(1), 31.

Thomas, P. (1980). *Karl Marx and the anarchists*. Psychology Press.

Chapter 11
Institutionalization of Spatial Resources in Participatory Governance Systems

José G. Vargas-Hernández
https://orcid.org/0000-0003-0938-4197
Tecnológico Mario Molina Unidad Zapopan, Mexico

ABSTRACT

The study has the purpose to analyze the implications of the institutionalization process of spatial resources in the participatory governance system. It departs from the assumption that the institutional participatory governance policy as a political option has a chronic neglect despite the omnipresent decision-making authority, there is not binding authoritative allocation of values, public support, and the distribution of resources with a growing acceptance among the non-institutional space. The method employed is the analytic reflective thinking based on the theoretical and empirical review of the literature. It is concluded that the allocation of values and spatial resources from the institutional state power to society requires development in spatial form and new modes of participatory governance system in which actors and stakeholders through political actions allocate values and spatial resources to deal legitimately and effectively in the context of unity for the notion of common good for the community.

DOI: 10.4018/978-1-6684-4745-1.ch011

INTRODUCTION

The academic debate is challenging to determine the degree of institutionalization of participatory governance systems assessment and its impact in the varied programs and ongoing dynamic processes rooted in the complexity of the environment. This debate calls for a more systematic thinking about the impact on the contextual structure, adoption modalities, forms, design and rules, and the institutional participation nature of governance. Institutionalization of participatory governance systems overcomes the limitations of the general systems theory and institutional design.

Participatory governance is only a part of the governance theory that contributes to the creation of constructed and shaped institutional spaces by different sociopolitical actors and stakeholders (Fischer, 2006: 20). The sustainable spaces are the framework to develop the content of the institutional participatory governance aimed to facilitate the encounter of the different stakeholders to manifest and express their different interests. The individual approach tends to prevail over the collective perspective of governance of spaces. The public-civil partnership approach and the participatory governance framework developed and advocated by the independent socio intercultural scenes and spaces supported for the transference of democratic practices and knowledge in urban areas and institutions.

The theoretical and empirical framework of the systemic participatory governance approach addresses questions related to the design for the interactions between the structures of the social and political institutions with the potential social transformation. The different participatory governance arrangement approaches have also different perspectives considering the specific contextual backgrounds in socio economic and political systems with relative institutional frameworks leading to create democratic spaces for the functioning of states, civil society, communities, social and civil organizations, social movements, communities, and citizens following a political leadership.

The normative institutional basis is manifested in the form of conduct and behaviors that support and offers political opportunities to marginal actors mediated by civil society organizations willing to expand their political skills aimed to improve their public decision-making processes in new democratic spaces. Institutional development of participatory governance is attained through the enhancement of qualitative elements of practices and improvement of activities, investing in activities inherent to the spatial refurbishment and expansion currently limited to the users. Institutionalization of regional forms of cooperation structures is being studied under the rationale of a neo functionalist perspectives such as the multilevel-governance (Hooghe and Marks, 2003; Benz 2010) and the liberal intergovernmentalism perspective (Moravcsik, 1998).

INSTITUTIONALIZATION

The rationale for institutionalization of participatory governance provides an analytical framework for monitoring good governance taking the current situation as the starting point and considers the following stages. The public participatory governance organizational is related to the collective action institutionalization based on the structure and space purpose to guarantee formal long-term responsibility sharing and sustainability for public and civil sectors governance. Controlling the human nature environment needs to be institutionalized collective responsibility through participatory governance arrangements. However, the mismatches are framed in practice by the institutional ambiguity.

Institutionalization and proper monitoring of any participative governance model becomes essential for the long-term viability. Institutionalized participatory models of governance are often linked to institutions and regulatory frameworks that may be adequate to the specific matters. The model of participative governance set apart the institutions to map the relevant institutionalized interrelationships in the context of communities and their programmatic activities more dependent on sociopolitical changes. Institutionalization of participatory governance models requires a favorable context and many other factors to be implemented.

Organic public participation demonstrates working with induced iterative deliberations involving more actors and citizens in broader issues and concerns and promoting the institutionalization of more meaningful participatory governance. An institutionalized participation of citizens in public affairs and concerns is a framework for making more governable and provide possibilities to deal technically and politically all the matters.

The institutionalization of participatory governance and the public-civil partnership model is known as public participatory governance (Wampler and McNulty, 2011: 14). The institutionalization of committees for governance has several methodological challenges on data gathering to become viable in the long-term. Inclusive participatory governance has different forms, degree of institutionalization, methods, social relationships, and so forth. Advisory committees as a participatory governance methods become highly institutionalized for several years without any member changes in policy communities. Inactive advisory committees have not an impact in participatory governance.

Noninstitutionalized participatory governance is affected more by the political environments. Noninstitutionalized methods such as the public meetings are less effective than the institutionalized methods of participatory governance such as the advisory committees on the improvement of participatory governance. Less governance is driven by a neo-liberal perspective. Other versions for participatory democracy are concerned with the strengthening of local governance through citizen participation, and creating democratic spaces related to opportunities to develop social change.

The institutionalization of participatory governance framework is necessary for the space governed to increase the initiatives, contributions and ensure the dynamic creation of program contents of activities for the different actors involved. Institutionalization of participatory governance must be enacted among the involved actors and stakeholders (Buseth, 2017). Interest-based institutional participatory governance requires the institutionalization of consensual democracy, decentralization of the political system and social and political trust among all the actors and stakeholders (Denielsson et al., 2018).

Economic and social interests are the basis of the institutionalization inclusive processes of participatory governance. The economic interests may develop a privileged institutionalized relationship with local governments and with the participation or not of trade unions. These new democratic spaces are emerging for the creation of more inclusive practices from civil society organizations to become institutionalized mediating the state policies administration. Participatory governance practices may be institutionalized consultative within the structured civil society and third sector organizations involved and participating in political processes concerning economic, social, and environmental services, participatory budgeting, planning, management of resources and social services.

A decentralized political system enables institutionalization of arrangements for participatory governance depending on active cooperation among stakeholders and actor (Goldfrank, 2007). Institutionalized relationships of cooperation and conflict between firms and trade unions in a model of participatory governance arrangement practices in a model of unitary institutional and political vision. Socio-intercultural and institutional frameworks are required to be proposed for institutionalization processes of participatory governance project for ad-hoc community spaces (Tolj, 2005).

The institutionalization of participatory governance mechanisms crates more new democratic spaces for prospects beyond those of formal political institutions, to include engendering democracy into democratic structures (Cornwall, & Goetz, 2005). Decision making processes are based on membership in this model of indirectly governing the space as part of collective institutionalization of participative governance of common good (Ostrom, 2006). Public distrust of expertise led by the institutionalization of contra-expertise aimed to broaden the participatory arrangements in governance and decision-making processes on science and technology considering that the representation may be implicitly biased in terms of income, race, gender, etc.

Participatory technological assessment governance practices have also taken the form of consensus conferences and institutionalized in some countries considering the national contexts and normative implications. Public technology assessment in participatory governance has been institutionalized already in many countries. Institutionalization about the discourses of bioethics within expert committees and other institutions. A technocratic model of bioethics has been institutionalized by expert committees as a participatory form of governance to build trust and to fashion stable political compromises because discourses, emotions and sentiments that came relevant into governance and become prominent in many domains of life politics beyond the ethical expertise in government.

The participatory governance process has the risk of not resolving any problems but increase the scope of communication to maintain the status quo. However, participatory governance skills in communication, negotiations and leadership capabilities are crucial for the institutionalization of a community governed in accordance with the involved stakeholders and public-civil partnership.

The institutionalization of participative governance leads to possibilities of programmatic practices, situations, and initiatives. The institutionalization of these practices is the task of participatory governance, which may be reflected in the opening of new spaces, positions and possibilities for the citizens' action and active participation for the improvement of the individual and social quality of life. An action research initiative to explore the strengths of organic structured, induced, and meaningful participation practices and opportunities to enable and enhance participatory governance through the institutionalization of deliberative democracy.

In Policy analysis, the classification system of Durning (1993) offers types of participation in policy analysis. Institutionalization of participatory governance makes difficult for political actors to affect policy (Chubb & Peterson, 1985). In public meeting, the relationships between the social policy stakeholders and agencies are temporary and not well institutionalized (McComas, 2001).

Institutionalization of participatory governance in policy communities tends to be robust and may increase the mutual trust between stakeholders and agencies while the transaction costs tend to me limited. The institutionalized participatory governance has a robust positive effect on policy than non-institutional participatory governance given differences on transaction costs. The increase in the transaction costs has a limited effect on participatory governance on policy performance although institutionalized participatory methods have a positive effect on policy performance (Lee, 2016). Public meetings are a no institutionalized participatory governance vulnerable under the effects of internal and external low-transaction-cost policy conditions.

The institutionalization of a participatory makes a different system from others public venues allowing needs, demands and interests to be publicly debated, discussed, and negotiated. Knowing the roots of institutional participatory governance conflicts may avoid potential problems, may be able to channel demands and manage the interests in the institutionalized environment drawing into positive sum interactions. These processes generate coalitions, new ideas and public policies. Inclusive political institutions increase its engendering democracy with a gradual feminization turning into a growing number of women participating in public institutions, which does not necessarily result in major changes in institutionalization of participatory democracy.

The creation and institutionalization of participatory governance through regional and local links take a functional approach to determine the effect significance through economic motives that reinforce and encourage the trade and investment flows to increase productivity (Buseth, 2017). The institutionalization of participatory governance becomes significant in regional and local uneven development based on resilience (Wilson, 2013).

Participatory democracy is central to local politics and citizen committees for the development of a new form of transparent participatory managed by local democracy and nourished by the community and its social fabric, empowering citizens with initiatives and the institutionalization process. Autonomous and decentralized local governments may develop the institutionalization of public participation and participatory governance arrangements. A decentralization reform should be implemented towards the institutionalization of participatory democratic governance at the local level

The institutionalization of activities, allocation of public spaces and long-term contracts of hybrid institutions between civil society organizations networks and the administration of local authorities should enhance the participatory governance where they situated their practices to meeting the spatial needs of citizens and residents. The establishment of institutionalization increases the capabilities and capacities of participatory governance of local authorities, associations, and strategic alliances that increase the scope of responding and caring the citizen needs through different mechanisms of governance. The associations and the strategic alliances can govern the spaces where they implement their activities.

INSTITUTIONAL SPATIAL RESOURCES

Institutional participatory governance is determined by the actors, stakeholders, and representatives at the spatial collaborative decision-making level. Spatial governance of institutions can be reconfigured with other invited spaces for political engagements in institutional co-governance of illegitimate expressing dissents. Creating the vision of institutional participatory governance plays a crucial role in organizing and developing the different types, forms, and structures of institutions according to different models, typologies of spaces in the operating context focusing on different audience reach.

Civil society, nongovernmental and nonprofit organizations as political actor can question the institutional legitimacy and responsibility of the state and opening new organizational and institutional spaces for public and private sphere activities aimed to reshape the public and private spheres and influencing the policies of institutional participatory governance (Fischer, 2006). Some of these main tasks are the ones concerned with the allocation and use of funds, monitoring the institutional practices and activities, value orientation, distribution of responsibilities, institutional inequalities, human resources, spaces, technology, equipment, etc.

The spatial resources used by associations and organizations in participatory governance to advocate the reconstruction of spaces and development of a model of governance and public-civil partnership, that as users of spaces invest in the transformation into contemporary socio intercultural institutional governance. Socio-intercultural participatory governance implies a critical awareness and respect for other cultural values that reflect diversity in the public transformations of public policies, institutions, public spaces, and civic culture that enable initiative and projects.

One of the key stakeholders are the representatives of civil society organizations who are the controllers and users of spatial resources to be used in production distribution and consumption of social practices and activities, regional, local and community authorities and the neighborhood as the owners and representatives of the public spaces. Preservation of public spaces without being turned into private properties.

Participants in governing the space must develop the support for some programs for resources and capabilities development, funding sources reserved for institutional social, cultural, and political activities performed and supported by different councils, associations, and organizations (Petrić et al., 2015: 169 – 172). Different perceptions about the public issues create different spaces for participation, including spaces for prejudice as the main obstacle in establishing strategic alliances and interpectoral partnerships, mutual trust and understanding as the fundamentals for institutional participatory governance.

Local institutional participatory governance has considerable resilience around depoliticized and decentralized structures, which may widen the scope of participative inclusion involving individual, actors and stakeholders in spaces of decision-making processes. The institutional participatory governance model and public-civil partnerships in different economic and socio ecological contexts of local environments and based on historical backgrounds are being developed according to the local specificities and the way in which the use of the spatial, and temporal variables are relevant.

Urban morphology of space plays a relevant role in the concentration of traditional institutional governance in the in mediate vicinities, their backgrounds, and their histories. Participatory governance in urban spaces implemented by representatives of local authorities is considered a good model meanwhile the civil society organizations criticize that this model requires definition of priorities to demonstrate through transparency the willingness to cooperate.

A common cause such as the revitalization and restoration or urban spaces can be supported using public-civil partnerships and participatory governance compatible with the stakeholders´ expectations. Large urban spaces and areas spreading from city centers may be more concentrated in traditional institutions ranging from suburban shopping malls, cultural centers, and civil initiatives, although the participatory governance institutions may be more central in the urban area.

Aligned civil society organizations address the urgency of urban planning for common spaces with institutional models, infrastructure, and management arrangements to be used for local practices and activities. The use of space requires long term program planning and development of methods and formats in the institutional scheme to give voice to users and civil society organizations streaming up the management and ensuring communication subject to the hybrid governance structure that sustains uniqueness and the opposing logics of functioning between the public and civil sectors.

Public-private-civil partnership models require that all the stakeholders involved are well informed in active engagement with their communities, sharing responsibilities through participatory governance on the management of jurisdictional spaces. The public-civil partnership model involved in the governance of community resources, primarily space, may become a mean of involving citizens in participatory governance. Promotion of institutional participatory governance in local society and community may improve the active interests and positions in other areas supported and funded by organizations especially dedicated to design and develop a new spatial governing model y close collaboration with local and community public institutions and civil partners.

Hybrid institutional formal arrangements function as formal entities regulating the participatory governance models of spatial resources steaming from rules established by the involved agents, actors, stakeholders, and partners in finding solutions and implemented and controlled by the representatives. The orthodox model of policy sciences is being criticized regarding the policy spatial implementation where politics shapes stretching beyond the formal institutional government organizations. The participatory governance policy considered as a political option has a chronic neglect despite that assumes omnipresent decision making authority in the allocation of public support and the distribution of resources with a growing acceptance among the non-institutional space.

The spatial resources in infrastructure measure the status and position of actors in the institutionalized activities of participatory governance, mainly of civil society organizations. These actors have activities in initiating, interaction, planning, representation, inclusion and exclusion, confrontation, and advocating processes of policy change on the public spatial natural resources and the development of new forms of institutional participatory governance.

Inherent to new life-political issues in situation of institutional ambiguity, there is not binding authoritative allocation of values from the state institutional power to society, which requires to develop in adequate and spatial form, the new modes of governance in which actors and stakeholders may assume political actions and deal legitimately and effectively in the context of unity for the notion of common good for the community. Some spaces offer the opportunities for meaningful voices able to shape, shift and change the power relations. Spaces are imbued with power relations affecting the relationships of participants and reinforcing legitimation of the status quo. Institutional governance potential is dependent on the degree of restructuring of functional and spatial territories and constitute the basis for the autonomy of participatory governance.

Transversal cross-sectional analysis of participatory governance practices and public-civil partnerships complemented by socio intercultural spatial resources and infrastructures to determine and substantiate the nature, characteristics, role, and practices, assess the effects of participatory governance of involved actors and their interactions and processes on the development of programs. Also, this analysis of participatory governance must recognize the existing values of the involved actors in creating policies to enable changes on the development of participatory governance practices and public-civil partnerships and to improve their capacities to build trust for a more collaborative governance.

Organizations may occupy usable adequate spaces not used for services which may not be available for new users to practice common use of governance for the management of common goods. Changes of spaces requires also or internal management structures in the model of participatory governance connected to specific spaces. The development of a common space management model with the participation of all members involved but retaining the full autonomy is exceptional to the interested participating individual members. The establishment of public-private-civil partnerships as a structural form of participatory governance involves local authorities' representatives in management issues and making decision processes leading to investment into public spaces. A combination of several factors may influence the local authorities to manage the governance of public spaces.

There are some problems related to the inadequacy of the spatial factor such as the level of safety governed by participatory practices. Local participatory governance interrupts any major political infestation and controversies in the public sector with high level of cronyism in the decision making process, allocation of public resources, governance structure, participation space and non-institutional stakeholders' inclusiveness. Despite negative aspects of participatory governance practices and spatial design, civil society organizations and local authorities are recognized to have intensive and dynamic interactions, socially stimulating in community space engagement.

Local authorities and sectors may be generally aware, despite they still lack informed proficiency in institutional participatory governance, the existing and design of different public-civil partnership models and relevance of sharing responsibility in the usage and governance of territorial spaces under their jurisdiction which may require the needed knowledge and skills.

The participatory governance scheme is currently being decided upon within the institutional framework with the inclusion of the participative principles of the decision making processes for to take over the governing structure of local authorities in managing the territorial space. Local public administration representatives acknowledge the involvement of citizens have positive effects and consequences in the implementation of institutional participatory governance processes and programs functioning at the specific temporal and territorial spaces intended at local community and encouraging inclusiveness in the management processes. This is an important element of the model development of institutional participatory governance.

Polarization of interests among the stakeholders provoke spatial territorial, social and governance conflicts in regional and local spaces, which may be emblematic for the analysis of new democratic and participatory governance models rooted in local cultures of all involved. The relationship between participatory approaches and conflict in some regions is critical in spaces of engagement and real change created for participation (Cornwall and Coelho, 2004). The empowered participatory governance may be a permanent solution that relies in public resources (Fung and Wright 2003) considering that there are spatial, programmatic, and technical conditions for governance. The spaces are established as the point where actors can encounter and exchange.

Non-institutional participatory governance scene that meets the needs of all the involved stakeholders may be related to available, abandoned and adequately used temporal and territorial spatial public owned and natural resources as the most suitable for community development. The institutional participatory and collaborative governance model distributes responsibilities among the involved stakeholders in public-private-civil partnership between the representatives of local authorities, communities, and civil society organizations representatives as the users or temporal and territorial spaces.

The local administration authorities are concerned with the institutionalization of a participatory governance processes which may involve numerous decision making and arbitration processes, responsibilities for the orientation of spaces and financial support, etc. Local authority representatives are skeptical about the resolution of quality of the spaces depending on the financial capabilities rather than on the participative governance model of public-civil partnership. Local public authorities may be more manipulative engagement by having a ritual participation empowering the participant actors and stakeholders in institutional participatory governance through the new forms of institutionalization model to face struggles for power, which in fact may result in the lack of trust and respect among the involved stakeholders (Katunarić, 2004).

Local authorities and communities may design a model of participatory management, manage, and provide the necessary resources and capabilities for programs created to use the space where the civil society organizations together with local authorities and communities may be the owners of the space. Local public institutions and communities in their capacities of holding the ownership and manage the public spaces have become increasingly aware and recognize the participatory governance practices and activities. Local public authorities may entrust participatory governance of the space to independent and autonomous actors and establish public-private-civil partnerships, or an alliance of associations as owners and managers of the space, to support the creation and development of institutional participatory governance.

The dimensions of the regional institutionalization processes of participative governance are always in permanent exchange status. Participative governance at the regional level fosters the justification of policies, politics, institutionalization of citizenship and mobilization towards self-governance structural spaces, as in cross-border regions. Governing the space governance to work may require a program that responds to spatial needs of citizens in the wider community to focus and determine attitudes towards the public-private-civil partnerships.

Regional governance relies on the interconnection of symbolic cognitive, political-economic, and institutional dimensions linked in analytical framework of horizontal and vertical participatory governance. The symbolic-cognitive dimension derives from the regional cultural homogeneity context that depends on ethnic, linguistic, and historical proximity of local spaces (Gualini, 2003, p. 43).

The regional identity-building favors the institutionalization of participatory governance communities in established cultural identity –building farmed as the politics of identity (Jessop, 2000), the inventing communities (Anderson, 1991) and artificial constructions (Terlouw, 2012, 709). Organizations chosen and credentialed to represent identities of participants in broader public processes of participatory governance, addressing resource control and economic inequality in the emergence of potential spaces of democratic engagement. Local and community associations and social movements participating in formal governance and institutionalized structures, have positive outcomes. The participatory governance model designed and developed in one region may also be applicable to other regions and spatial territorial locations.

Territorial governance is functionally oriented that may offer conditions and channels for institutionalized participation of local population. (Bora 2005, p. 15; Bora, Hausendorfer, 2006, 2005). Large territorial spaces foster the connections between communities, governments, civil society organizations, business organizations, individual citizens, and other actor leading to creation of common and institutional participatory governance. However, some territorial spaces are functional entities lacking citizenship participation and participatory governance, assuming the provision of further legitimation towards the people affected by these policies and politics.

A qualitative analysis of institutionalized regional territories, organizational structure and cultural thickness are assumed to be some processes and mechanisms in causalities and conditions for participatory governance, which is highly actor-centered and difficult to operationalize (King et al. 1994, p.4). National policies may measure the institutional participation in governance to provide development in infrastructure at regional, local and community levels despite the lack of spaces for the incentive in participatory governance.

The institutionalization of multi-modal economic corridor creates new regional interdependence patterns among the regions (Colyvas and Jonsson, 2011) and regional economic links (Parnini 2010) Potential engagement spaces for economic issues involve citizens in issues of resource and capabilities mobilization and allocation processes monitoring use of budget at local government.

The institutionalization on agricultural agglomeration labor productivity (Lukban Rosetea, & Eleria, 2020) requires the application of measurements. The institutionalization participatory governance on green agricultural agglomeration must be consistent with anticipated effects on productivity, corridor development and construction attributable to initiatives of local government.

A strategic alliance between associations shares a common space must assume the required development of activities and participative tasks of governance. The institutionalization of participatory governance networks links regional and local governments increasing the potential for sectorial growth. The institutionalization of governance networks is supported by the clustering efforts to increase productivity (Suphannachart, 2017; Stein et al, 2014; Brunner, 2013; Dorward, 2013; Devkota & Upadhyay, 2013; van den Ban, 2011).

The participatory governance model may consider the implementation of the platform and networking programs to facilitate the participation of all the involved actors and agents through the integration of different practices, activities, and programs to be implemented in different levels, spaces, and territorial locations. Civil society organizations support the establishment of participatory governance responding to the attempts and efforts for the everyone´s responsibility to resolve this issue through the rationale of a platform networking rationale as the management model in project development dealing with public spaces.

Development of joint institutional participatory governance facilitated by a platform networking to initiate an open public dialogue, to support and advocate adequate development conditions and activities, to refurbish temporal and territorial space in which to invest in resources, capabilities, and infrastructure. The contribution of networking to institutional development based on the existing economic and socioecological circumstances, a strategic approach should aim to improve the quality of practices of participatory institutions and the non-institutional sector, building a new institutional infrastructure intended for a more efficient participatory governance of resources, spaces, services, projects, etc.

The platform and network must promote and advocate participatory governance practices in designing public policies and creating the institutional structural conditions for the development of participatory democracy in public and private spaces for the involvement of civil society organizations, citizens and all actors and stakeholders in governance and decision making processes at all levels. This platform and network must also address issues related to crate. Develop and use of territorial public spaces for social interactions, exchanges, discussions of responsibilities and rights.

A network of institutions developed for participatory governance may corroborate the distribution of institutional specializations in numerous economic, social, cultural, legal, political, and other activities at different spaces and levels.

New forms of participatory governance-participatory in transnational and transborder spaces are emerging for the establishment of inclusive citizenship The institutionalized spaces and forms of different structures in functional-transborder regions established on administrative grounds supported by administrative governance and transnational legal mechanisms. Regional cross-border participative governance is favored by the cultural thickness and homogeneity in the institutionalization processes based on the interplay among the symbolic, territorial, institutional, and functional dimensions (Paasi, 1986 and 1996).

Institutionalized spaces of participative governance tend to create a technocratic transnational structure (Majone, 1998; Moravcsik, 2002; Radaelli, 1999), despite those others assume the lack of participative forms in governance (Kohler-Koch and Quitkatt, 2013). Transnational institutionalization forms of deliberative, participative, and collaborative governance may respond better and efficiently to functional differentiation of policies and services.

The participatory turn at supranational and regional territorial spaces at the multilevel polity are the result of negotiations and politics between the elites and most of the times excluding the local interest. Institutionalized and organizational exclusion in global supply chains and service delivery is a common issue and concern which can be solve through consultation and participative governance.

PARTICIPATORY GOVERNANCE SYSTEM

The systemic approach to institutional participatory governance can propose diverse alternatives for more permanent and interconnected processes to overcome the limitations of public participation and expand the potential to deliver meaningful policy making and political impact. Institutional participatory governance systems focus on citizen participation through an ecosystem of participatory processes.

Institutions of participative governance are part of the flexible and complex organizational system where responsibility must be linked to decision making authority and distributed through the structure among all the units. Institutions and organizations can be structured to remain in networking to manage the complexity of participatory governance to be implemented to keep a more dynamic environmental relationship as the basis for improving and learning the institutional system (Wampler and McNulty, 2011: 35).

Participatory governance is defined as the various conventional types of cooperation with associations in issues such as the allocation of space and funds for establishing programs. Participatory governance is a shared commitment acted upon institutional models with transparent communication systems among the actors (Denielsson et al., 2018:40). Institutional participatory governance positioned in a public and political spaces must increase the transparency and accountability in decision-making, policy formulation and planning of development, increasing the awareness and learning of the public participation, redefining the relationships among citizens, public servants and elected officials, institutions, local and regional authorities, and governments, etc., reinforcing local democracy (Latendresse, 2010, p. 17).

Participatory governance model in practice is one of the solutions to improving the quality and level of democracy of a socio intercultural system to implement the multilevel democracy within the public-policy framework open to participation as the policy principle and practical implementation at different levels of developmental stages. The conceptual taxonomy-style system of classification analyses and assess the participatory governance practices (Fiorino 1990; Laird 1993; Collin & Evans 2002; Rowe & Frewer 2000).

Public participation has been discussed and debated in democratic systems that had undergone political participatory and administrative changes affecting the participatory abilities of citizens leading to more efficient decision-making processes. Power is concentrated in modern institutions diffused in the global network society in the state, firms, corporate media circulating flows of wealth, images and information in a political system characterized by dematerialized geography and variable geometry (Streeck & Schmitter 1986). Participatory governance arrangements ensure a more responsive political system in participation and mobilization of marginal interests (Gustafson and Hertting, 2016).

The democratic values in any cultural system based on the values of freedom, parity, and equality, demands the creation and development of participatory governance processes supported by collaborative policy design and decision making. Trust and understanding in participatory governance have tangible functions leading to avoid the system inefficiency and collapse.

Governing a complex system requires more than simple customary management rationale. The cultural and institutional scene developed in the form of associations provides some temporary solutions for specific spaces defined by a minimum common denominator of a complex system of participatory governance. The institutional participatory governance system involves permanent interconnected participation spaces (Bussu 2020; Dean et al. 2019).

On the interest-based assumption of participatory governance, the role of citizens is to participate assuming responsibilities and representing their interests, the role of politicians is to make decisions of participatory arrangements and articulate their interests, and the role of civil servants is the implementation of participatory arrangement decisions (Denielsson et al., 2018:32).

The institutional forms of participatory governance activities are observed in the public sector as part of the public system in which governance process is established straightforward as top-down decision-making processes. In a vertical top-down representative democracy system, the interest-based participatory governance improves horizontal reforms and participatory governance arrangements among actors to get involved in decision-making and negotiation processes Participatory governance institutions are a new form to represent the interest mediation replacing the old clientelism and corporatism systems. The representative system operates with democratic values through hierarchical, vertical, and top-down. A top-down case of institutional participatory governance may be the decentralization reforms implemented by political elites and institutionalized participatory institutions.

Participatory approach is a flexible institutional design that has been perceived as a threat or a progressive move from representative functioning system acting between representative democracy and citizens (Klijn and Koppenjan, 2000). The deliberative systems perspective focuses on the deliberative and non-deliberative quality sites of the democratic system. Legal and regulation systems are giving rise to new forms of citizen's participatory governance in deliberating regulatory concerns, such as the use of internet to make available to everybody policy information and processes. Institutionalized participatory governance programs sustain the creation of participatory governance new publics inducing activities from civil society and government officials engaging each other in public spaces to exchange information.

Public participation in participatory governance is being widely discussed around the main argument of systematic democratic deficits of representative democracy in terms of deliberation and participation as shortcomings of representative policy process (Fischer, 2006: Norval, 2014; Nabatchi, 2010). Failure of participatory governance institutions is part of a learning process to fix the problems of the political system. Participatory governance is an innovative form to address the democratic deficits in a representative democracy system of institutions that incorporates the marginalized and poor groups of people and communities into a political system. These programs not always provide solutions to solve participation problems.

The conceptualization of innovation system (Van Est 1999) and formal political system and styles of government in historical dynamic dimension. An innovative participatory model of governance should consider identifying clear objectives and public participation that have an impact on making decision processes in an institutionalized overseeing committee and involvement of partisanship and public servants processes (Rabouin, 2009, p. 89).

Institutional participatory governance attempts to develop systemically and overcome inadequate inclusion of citizens and civil society in decision making processes, despite the criticism of deliberative democracy that the decision-making power is only kept for the dominant and hegemonic elites (Kadlec and Friedman 2007). Participatory institutions have the potential to fix poor performance of illiberal democratic systems (Baiocchi et al 2011; Smith 2009). Comprehensive and explicit inclusion policy and initiatives can be classified in accordance with the participatory practices complementing participation and governance features to influence the governability and the political system.

Non-institutional informal structures of governance are more traditional expression of participation in decision making of public issues in erratic forms of unsystematic governance and management. Principles of institutional participatory governance may lead to founding supported by hybrid institutional public-civil partnerships and processes of advocacy originated by the congestion of traditional institutional system framework that resists modernization. Creation and development of advocacy platforms for socio-cultural centers developed on a model of participatory and collaborative governance in a civil and public partnership to provide support to solve issues related to secure formal spaces for civil society organizations.

The development of democratic, informed, and transparent participatory governance models of public policy shaping and implementation of sustainable systems of governance to promote the cultural diversity expressions. Transparent systems of participatory governance shared with the inclusion of citizens and their heritage must encourage all the stakeholders involved in decision making to become more effective, open, and coherent participatory approaches.

National public policies contribute to building the participatory governance system, which can be achieved with the involvement of civil society playing a strong role as the vehicle to enhance the participation of people and demanding transparency and accountability (Firmin, 2017: 87). The local participatory governance system often may overcome excessive politization supported by local authorities (Obuljen Koržinek, Žuvela, Jelinčić and Polić, 2014).

Decentralized systems of local governments are accessible institutional structures to citizens sustained by deliberative and participative mechanisms. Decentralized and autonomous local governments with social and political horizontal trust may help to explore the possibility of achieving more public participation and become a more participatory governance system. There are several serious amendments to the orthodox conceptualization of government without questioning the unified political system.

Institutional pluralism is related to participatory governance in the context of policy systems. Social exclusion of individuals and groups have limited access mediated by governance systems to entitlements within the policy making and development processes. Participatory work institutionalized and sustained with ethnic or religious minorities involving their citizen participation engaged with governments in governance and policy making in the emerging problems.

The institutional participatory governance systems have not been able to overcome the glass ceiling limiting the spaces for balancing and stablishing non-institutional and institutional development with inclusive spaces for inspiration, dialogue, influence, actions, and participation. Institutional and political investment is a motive to formulate and implement a city policy for inclusion even if participation and governance remain as separated spheres in more individualist political systems.

Any participatory system with high transaction costs is inefficient in the implementation of the policy performance, contracting mechanisms and production arrangements such as contracting, partnerships, franchises, etc. (Tang & Mazmanian, 2010; Brown and Potoski, 2003; Reeves, 2008). Shrinking of spaces and budget cutting affect the internal reality for non-institutional participatory governance spaces requiring the external cooperation of governance actors that may contribute by bringing the valuable exchanges, experiences, and funds to modernize the regional and local participatory governance system.

The creation and development of institutions supporting participatory governance model is crucial for the designing and implementation of the sustainable development and the socio ecological systems. The emergent policy outcomes from participatory governance institutions are the improved education or sanitation systems.

CONCLUSION

The analysis of this study concludes that allocation of values and spatial resources from the institutional state power to society requires developing an adequate spatial form and new modes of participatory governance system in which actors and stakeholders through political actions, allocate spatial resources and values to deal legitimately and effectively in the context of unity for the notion of common good for the community.

The process of institutionalization must include the debates on social and political horizontal trust, autonomous and decentralized political system, consensual and representative democracy with participatory governance. The institutionalization of participatory governance should be concerned with sustainability issues and processes to ensure the desired outcomes. A sustainable participatory governance model to be implemented requires long term experiences to have an opportune moment follow the guidelines and recommendations to monitor the governing administration and the collaboration process for institutionalization.

Citizens have participated and engaged in numerous experiments, discussions and debates revolving around public participation in facing the problems of democracy to establish a new participatory governance model, structures, processes, and norms in a representative democratic system. Creating and developing democratization perspectives based on the participatory principle for the establishment of new institutional participatory governance models requires the reconfiguration of meanings and logical foundations based on trust and understanding, settings, models and procedures for the implementation and maintenance of democratic values of the social systems and society.

Institutions must be responsive to the reality of an evolving context of participatory governance framework to be institutionalized and sustained to ensure the communication and coordination of publica participation. Public institutions involved in cooperation through participatory governance with interested actors and stakeholders create new practices and activities to be applied in nearly all aspects such as urban, historical, economic, social, political, cultural, transportation, etc., in specific places.

A stable institutional participatory governance framework may provide long term sustainability by the involved stakeholders, actors, agents, and partners for the functioning of local communities by ensuring the space resources and basic funding. This may result in a balanced relationship between the oversight of public financing, the participative decision making and the independent programming. Creating the institutional strategic framework for the participatory governance scheme must be supported by the creation of advisory boards and financial planning and programming to ensure through various modes of funding obtained by the institution and organizations using the spaces for infrastructural stability during the core operation.

The quality use of institutional participatory governance model in regional and local spaces faces some critical problems despite that has become increasingly necessary for the socio interrelationships between the local public authorities and civil sector. Local administration in strategic development may adhere to forms of participative and consultation relying more on symbolic than on institutionalized practice. Ensuring transparent, comprehensive, egalitarian, and influential participative processes must be overseen by an independent party aimed to foster legitimacy and enhance public trust in the deliberative democracy system.

REFERENCES

Anderson, B. (1991). *Imagined communities. Reflections on the origin and spread of nationalism* (2nd ed.). Verso.

Baiocchi, G., & Heller, P. (2011). *Bootstrapping Democracy: Transforming Local Governance and Civil Society in Brazil*. Stanford University Press.

Bora, A. (2005). Licensing Plant GMOs – A Brief Overview over European regulatory conditions for the Deliberate Release of Genetically Modified Plants. In H. Hausendorf & A. Bora (Eds.), *Communicating Citizenship and Social Positioning in Decision-Making Procedures: The Case of Modern Biotechnology*. Series Discourse Approaches to Politics, Society and Culture.

Bora, A., & Hausendorf, H. (2005). Participatory science governance and the communicative construction of citizenship. Science and Public Policy.

Bora, A., & Hausendorfer, H. (2006). Participatory science governance revisited: Normative expectations versus empirical evidence. *Science & Public Policy*, *33*(7), 478–488. doi:10.3152/147154306781778740

Brown, T. L., & Potoski, M. (2003). Transaction costs and institutional explanations for government service production decisions. *Journal of Public Administration: Research and Theory*, *13*(4), 441–468. doi:10.1093/jopart/mug030

Brunner, H. W. (2013). What is economic corridor development and what can it achieve in Asia's subregions? SSRN *Electronic Journal*. doi:10.2139/ssrn.2306801

Buseth, J. T. (2017). The green economy in Tanzania: From global discourses to institutionalization. *Geoforum*, *86*, 42–52. doi:10.1016/j.geoforum.2017.08.015

Bussu, S., Lalani, M., Pattison, S., & Marshall, M. (2020). Engaging with Care: Ethical Issues in Participatory Research. In Qualitative Research (pp. 1–19). Academic Press.

Chubb, J. E., & Peterson, P. E. (1985). *The new direction in American politics*. Brookings Institution Press.

Collins, H. M., & Evans, R. (2002). The third wave of science studies: Studies of expertise and experience. *Social Studies of Science*, *32*(2), 235–296. doi:10.1177/0306312702032002003

Colyvas, J. A., & Jonsson, S. (2011). Ubiquity and legitimacy: Disentangling diffusion and institutionalization. *Sociological Theory*, *29*(1), 27–53. doi:10.1111/j.1467-9558.2010.01386.x

Cornwall, A., & Coelho, V. (2004). New democratic spaces? *IDS Bulletin*, *35*(2).

Cornwall, A., & Goetz, A. M. (2005). Democratizing democracy: Feminist perspectives. *Democratization*, *12*(5), 783–800. doi:10.1080/13510340500322181

Dean, R., Boswell, J., & Smith, G. (2019). Designing democratic innovations as deliberative systems: The ambitious case of NHS citizen. *Political Studies*, *68*(3), 689–709. Advance online publication. doi:10.1177/0032321719866002

Denielsson, M., Hertting, N., & Klijn, E. H. (2018). Institutionalizing Local Participatory Governance in Representative Democracy. In Local Participatory Governance and Representative Democracy. Routledge.

Devkota, S., & Upadhyay, M. (2013). Agricultural productivity and poverty reduction in Nepal. *Review of Development Economics*, *17*(4), 732–746. doi:10.1111/rode.12062

Dorward, A. (2013). Agricultural labour productivity, food prices and sustainable development impacts and indicators. *Food Policy*, *39*, 40–50. doi:10.1016/j.foodpol.2012.12.003

Durning, D. (1993). Participatory policy analysis in a social service agency: A case study. *Journal of Policy Analysis and Management*, *12*(2), 297–322. doi:10.2307/3325237

Fiorino, D. J. (1990). Citizen participation and environmental risk: A survey of institutional mechanisms. *Science, Technology & Human Values*, *15*(2), 226–243. doi:10.1177/016224399001500204

Firmin, A. (2017). Engaging civil society in cultural governance. In *Reshaping Cultural Policies. Advancing creativity for development*. Paris: UNESCO. Available online at: http://unesdoc.unesco.org/images/0026/002605/260592e. pdf

Fischer, F. (2006). Participatory Governance as Deliberative Empowerment the Cultural Politics of Discursive Space. *American Review of Public Administration, 36*(1), 19–40. doi:10.1177/0275074005282582

Fung, A., & Wright, E. O. (2003). *Deepening Democracy: Institutional Innovations in Empowered Participatory Governance*. Verso Books.

Goldfrank, B. (2007). The Politics of Deepening Local Democracy: Decentralization, Party Institutionalization and Participation. *Comparative Politics, 40*(1), 147–168.

Gualini, E. (2004). Regionalization as 'experimental regionalism': The rescaling of territorial policy-making in Germany. *International Journal of Urban and Regional Research, 28*(2), 329–353. doi:10.1111/j.0309-1317.2004.00522.x

Gustafson, P., & Hertting, N. (2016). Understanding Participatory Governance: An Analysis of Participants' Motives for Participation. *American Review of Public Administration, 47*(5), 538–549. doi:10.1177/0275074015626298

Hooghe, L., & Marks, G. (2003). Unravelling the Central State, but how? Types of Multi-Level Governance. *The American Political Science Review, 97*(2), 233–243.

Jessop, B. (2000). The Crisis of the National Spatio-temporal Fix and the Tendential Ecological Dominance of Globalizing Capitalism. *International Journal of Urban and Regional Research, 24*(2), 323–360. doi:10.1111/1468-2427.00251

Kadlec, A., & Friedman, W. (2007). Deliberative Democracy and the Problem of Power. *Journal of Public Deliberation, 3*(1). Available online at: http://www.publicdeliberation.net/jpd/vol3/iss1/art8

Katunarić, V. (2004). Toward the New Public Culture. In N. Švob-Đokić (Ed.), *Cultural Transitions in Southeastern Europe. Culture link Joint Publication Series No 6* (pp. 19–43). Institute for International Relations.

King, G. (1994). *Designing social inquiry. Scientific inference in qualitative research*. Princeton University Press. doi:10.1515/9781400821211

Kohler-Koch, B., & Quittkat, C. (2013). *De-Mystification of Participatory Democracy*. Oxford University Press. doi:10.1093/acprof:oso/9780199674596.001.0001

Laird, F. N. (1993). Participatory analysis, democracy and technological decision making. *Science, Technology & Human Values, 18*(3), 341–361. doi:10.1177/016224399301800305

Latendresse, A. (2010). *Le BP du Plateau-Mont-Royal: Évaluation d'une experience unique à Montréal.* Preliminary document presented to Plateau-Mont-Royal administration, March 2010. Report.

Lee, J. (2016). Designed to Succeed: Participatory Governance, Transaction Cost, and Policy Performance. *Korean Journal of Policy Studies, 31*(2), 1–22. doi:10.52372/kjps31201

Lukban Rosetea, M. A., & Eleria, N. L. (2020). *Examining the Significance of the Luzon W-Growth Corridor to Agricultural Agglomeration and Labor Productivity.* Millennium Journal of Humanities and Social Sciences. doi:10.47340/mjhss.v1i3.1.2020

Majone, G. (1998). Europe's Democratic Deficit: The Question of Standards. *European Law Journal, 4*(1), 5–28. doi:10.1111/1468-0386.00040

McComas, K. A. (2001). Public meetings about local waste management problems: Comparing participants to nonparticipants. *Environmental Management, 27*(1), 135–147. doi:10.1007002670010139 PMID:11083914

Moravcsik, A. (1998). The choice for Europe. Social purpose and state power from Messina to Maastricht. Cornell Univ. Press.

Moravcsik, A. (2002). In Defence of the 'Democratic Deficit': Reassessing Legitimacy in the European Union. *Journal of Common Market Studies, 40*(4), 603–624. doi:10.1111/1468-5965.00390

Nabatchi, T. (2010). Addressing the Citizenship and Democracy Deficits: The Potential of Deliberative Democracy for Public Administration. *American Review of Public Administration, 40*(4), 376–399. doi:10.1177/0275074009356467

Norval, A. J. (2014). Deliberative, Agonistic and Aversive Grammars of Democracy: The Question of Criteria. In S. Griggs, A. J. Norval, & H. Wagenaar (Eds.), *Practices of Freedom: Decentered Governance, Conflict and Democratic Participation.* Cambridge University Press. doi:10.1017/CBO9781107296954.003

Obuljen Koržinek, N., Žuvela, A., Jelinčić, D. A., & Polić, M. (2014). *Strategija razvoja kulture Grada Dubrovnika 2015 – 2025.* Grad Dubrovnik. Available online at: https://dura.hr/user_files/admin/strateski%20dokumenti/Kulturna%20strategija%20grada%20Dubrovnika.pdf

Ostrom, E. (2006). *Upravljanje zajedničkim dobrima. Evolucija institucija za kolektivno djelovanje.* Naklada Jesenski i Turk.

Paasi, A. (1986). The institutionalization of regions: A theoretical framework for understanding the emergence of regions and the constitution of regional identity. *Fennia - International. The Journal of Geography*, *164*(1), 105–146. https://fennia.journal.fi/article/view/9052

Paasi, A. (1996). *Territories, boundaries, and consciousness. In The changing geographies of the Finnish-Russian border*. J. Wiley & Sons.

Parnini, S. N. (2010). Institutionalizing linkages between ASEAN & Bangladesh: Challenges & prospects. *The International Journal of the Arts in Society*, *3*(13), 375–392.

Petrić, L., Petrić, M., Pavičić, I., Miše, M., Hameršak, M., & Pleše, I. (2015). Kultura i kulturna baština. In *Nacrt prijedloga Plana upravljanja povijesnom jezgrom Splita i plana upravljanja podrumima Dioklecijanove palače (II – Analiza stanja).* Split: Grad Split. Available online at: https://www.split.hr/Default.aspx?art=7774

Rabouin, L. (2009). *Démocratiser la ville: Le budget participatif: De Porto Alegre à Montréal.* Montreal: Lux Éditeur.

Radaelli, C. M. (1999). *Technocracy in the European Union.* Addison Wesley Longman.

Reeves, E. (2008). The practice of contracting in public private partnerships: Transaction costs and relational contracting in the Irish school's sector. *Public Administration*, *86*(4), 969–986. doi:10.1111/j.1467-9299.2008.00743.x

Rowe, G., & Frewer, L. J. (2004). Evaluating Public-Participation Exercises: A Research Agenda. *Science, Technology & Human Values*, *29*(4), 512–556. doi:10.1177/0162243903259197

Stein, Ch., Barron, J., & Moss, T. (2014). *Governance of the nexus: from buzz words to a strategic action perspective.* Nexus Network Think Piece Series, Paper 3.

Streeck, W., & Schmitter, P. C. (Eds.). (1986) *Private Interest Government Beyond Market and State.* Sage.

Suphannachart, W. (2017). What drives labour productivity in the ageing agriculture of Thailand? *Advances in Management and Applied Economics*, *7*(1), 89.

TangS. Y.MazmanianD. (2010). Understanding Collaborative Governance from the Structural Choice - Politics, IAD, and Transaction Cost Perspectives. https://ssrn.com/abstract=1516851 doi:10.2139/ssrn.1516851

Terlouw, K. (2012). From thick to thin regional identities? *GeoJournal*, *77*(5), 707–721. doi:10.100710708-011-9422-x

Tolj, S. (2005). *Razgovor sa Slavenom Toljem*. http://www.zarez.hr/clanci/razgovor-sa-slavenom-toljem

Van den Ban, A. (2011). Increasing labour productivity in agriculture and its implications. *Journal of Agricultural Education and Extension*, *17*(5), 401–409. doi:10.1080/1389224X.2011.596414

Van Est, R. (1999). *Winds of Change. A comparative study of the politics of wind energy innovation in California and Denmark*. International Books.

Wampler, B., & McNulty, S. L. (2011). *Does Participatory Governanace Matter? Exploring the Nature and Impact of Participatory Reforms*. Woodrow Wilson International Centre for Scholars.

Wilson, G. A. (2013). Community resilience, policy corridors and the policy challenge. *Land Use Policy*, *31*, 298–310. doi:10.1016/j.landusepol.2012.07.011

Chapter 12
Conceptual Institutional Elements of Participatory Governance

José G. Vargas-Hernández
https://orcid.org/0000-0003-0938-4197
Tecnológico Mario Molina Unidad Zapopan, Mexico

ABSTRACT

This study aims to analyze the conceptual elements of institutional participatory governance from an institutional perspective. It is assumed that the efforts to increase institutional participation in governance through the inclusion of minority groups may lead to fairer and responsive government. The analysis is also based on the assumption that participation models applied to institutions as legal and political instruments to foster regional mobilization and citizenship participation lead to the merging of the concepts of institutions, participation, and governance. The method employed is the analytic sustained on the reflection of the theoretical and empirical literature. It is concluded that the conceptual framework of institutional participation in governance is related to projects focusing on the domains of politics of life issues and concerns.

INTRODUCTION

To analyze participatory governance is necessary to study the essential preconditions of the institutional framework. Political philosophers, partisan and elected politicians, and democratic activists are promoting the concept of institutional participatory governance with the intention to cure the ills of representative

DOI: 10.4018/978-1-6684-4745-1.ch012

democracies. Organizational theories and practices emphasize the transference from stable institutional structures to more fluid networks structures, clusters and other organizational forms of association (Castells, 1996a).

Institution, participation, and governance require to be conceptualized for institutional development. The conceptual forms of participatory governance with regional institutional and legal governance can be differentiated based on organizational cultures and structures, such as agreements of cooperation and working protocols (Haselsberger, 2007, p.7). Regional spaces and spaces of regionalism are different concepts in relation to cultural spaces of institutional participatory governance (Jones and MacLeod, 2004). Application of institutionalized forms of cooperation can be explained by the territorial and cultural proximity between the cross-border regions framed by the favorable spatial integration processes of administrative cooperation and the model of citizenship participation model.

A stable organizational structure regarding the institutional design farmed by cooperation framework in cross-border regions and their cultural pre-conditions and thickness (Ferreira 2015). This institutional design should be a meeting point between institutions, governments, business, civic organizations, and citizens (Committee of the Regions 2015a, p. 38). Institutional isomorphism is a phenomenon pointing to the shape influencing the morphology.

The re-politicization processes of politics lead to an institutional discursive construction of design between the diverse actors and institutions related to political life domains and issues at stake. Institutionalization is a stumbling block for design, planning and implementation of shared governance models that requires the synchronization of several trans-policy frameworks and regulatory provisions between local and regional authorities and ownership and legal responsibility, etc.

The construction of an analytical framework after the conceptualization of organizational and cultural conditions of institutional participatory governance serves as the construct of an empirical case analysis given the different forms of re-scaling differentiated in territorial, functional, legal, and institutional conditions. Empirical research in participatory governance on life-political issues and concerns requires methodological and conceptual innovation to expand the notion and unit of analysis of politics across formal political institutions, identification of publics in relation to the state and the adoption or generation of the social phenomena such as the power, knowledge, institutions, and agency in the in the different spheres of social action such as economy, science, and politics. These processes are constituted in mutual shape of coproduction in empirical research.

The concept of institutional participatory governance has already spread across the nation states borders to include active and passive forms of citizenship participation removing the ceiling barriers and introducing inclusion and deliberation and avoiding antidemocratic tendencies (Kangas 2017). Research perspectives on models of inclusion are differently perceived framed by translation sociology, (Czarniawska, 2002) policy transfer (Dolowitz & Marsh, 2000) and institutional transplantation (De Jong et al., 2002), supported by cognitive resources and conditionality instead of authority.

Efforts to create policy movements invested by organizations and associations in straightforward progression for a plausible conceptualization model of participatory governance. The concept of participatory governance is linked to institutional arrangements, organizational culture, and structure to become the right arena to convey requirements and demands.

Participatory institutions of governance continue with the same people experimenting on the outcomes expected, whereby a small group of individuals conceptualized as elite capture, gain control of the main issues. Organizational structure must remain open to maintain flexibility and fluidity to enable adaptation to the changes in public, private and civil sectors under the conceptual framework of institutional permeability and hybridity. Public field in a specific issue at stake is the unit of analysis for researching in participatory governance through practices of conceptual language.

The transdisciplinary approaches underlie governance applied to institutional spaces and settings. The participatory governance methods used by some institutions in policy making processes have generally been beneficial (Langbein & Kerwin, 2000), although when increasing the transaction costs due to conflicts between the interests of the stakeholders they become inefficient.

INSTITUTIONAL FRAMEWORK

Institutions are the rules of the game that have effects on the expected outcomes and that change from institution to institution. Institutions are conceptualized as the humanly devised rules of the game in society which are shaping and constrained the individual choices and the human interactions (North, 1991, 3). Institutions are created, change, and have influence on human behavior in such a way that the empowerment have an impact on them. The concepts of institutions can be assessed based on the actions of political actors that takes power to re-politicize politics (Stavrakakis 2002:16).

Institutions enable actors and stakeholders to retain entitlements and opportunities. Those actors and agents with weak power or without power must strive more to invest their assets and build agency. However, they do not have the opportunities to make more effective economic, social, and political choices. Institutions create certainty by developing a structure to regulate formally and informally the economic, social, and political life. The nation-state is a government institution supported by the apex of authority and power conceived as political center.

The institutional analysis of the broader environment is being conducted in isolation and ring-fenced from the embedded context. Contextual practices and issues precipitated in structures technoscapes in the shape of innovation systems, political institutions systems and government styles, political judgment the socio-material environments of knowledge making. Institutional analysis and design should consider the broader environmental factors affecting their implementation. These factors can be the structural issues, expectations and rules concerning the formation of the state, the economic environment, the nature of civil society, among other factors. An analysis of institutional power demonstrates that rules emerge to support the power relations either through consent or coercion aimed to develop dominant ideologies in specific contexts (March and Olsen, 1989).

The new institutionalism (Ostrom 1990; Bates 1984; and North 1990), is a framework of analysis using tools to base on institutional rules that change from institution to institution to create incentives that induce desired behaviors to achieve specific outcomes. It must be considered the macro-structural areas such as the formation of the state, the configuration of civil society and the economic environment. State formation includes the role of federalism, legal tradition, decentralization, political parties, etc., in a broad macro-level perspective helping to stablish the participatory institutional parameters. Time dimension is essential in domains and fields of life politics enable to build the political institutions and generate institutional trust in contentious political decisions to be pro-active though institutional and discursive mechanisms, strategies, designs, and reforms.

Economic, social, and political organizations and institutions are undergoing a dynamic dysfunctionalities and discrepancies since de turn of the 21st century with the conceptual framework of participation in governance of the last century. Extant institutions reflect political, moral, and scientific order that may not be in place. Practices of governance related to economic, social, political, technological dynamics, and the micro-politics of meaning to shape the practices under scrutiny. The monarchy as an institution reproduces the logic of an archaic rule of filling the divine as the constituting element of transcendent radiance.

The formation of modernity is the ordering principle that traces the development dynamics of the Enlightenment thinking with the potential of human beings' rights to self-determine individual and social lives and the granted power for the creation of social institutions and constellations. The development of industrial society and the welfare state is conceptualized and analyzed by the modern sociology, political science, and policy analysis, with implications to facilitate the stability (Lenzer 1975; Dahrendorf 1988; Beck1992; Heilbron et al 1996).

Life of late modernity politics domains are shaped in unprecedented ways challenging the natural ordering of institutional arrangements produced by political communities and challenging institutional structures by a reconceptualization of politics. Post war Western political nation-state institutions embody the separation of science and politics. The long-established statist institutions have developed in the combination of freedom and reason. The separation of society and nature and the distinction of politics and technology are the institutional dynamic expressions of the last century, which are being questioned in the academic and no-academic circles with profound consequences.

The world has changed, and our institutions needs to change too. The growing speed of technological change requires new and revised institutions to address upcoming challenges. The social construction of technology focuses more on technological development and the nature of science leading to the formal political institutions' sovereignty (Latour & Woolgar 1979; Latour 1987; Callon *et al* 1992). Environmental and agroeconomic scientific, technological, and political knowledge may shape the formation of institutional development in a new framework for the phenomena of life of politics domains and issues.

The development of new public spaces, institutions and programs are created by opportunities, social reach and organizations involved in economic activity. The public fields subsume the recursive activities and practices as agencies and institutions in organizational bureaucratic terms related civil society and sectors such as the non-profit social service, citizens' groups and forth estate engaged in public activities and actions. Language, historic and cultural background are common elements of citizenship scrutinized by government and administrative institutions.

Public environmental fields and issues is related the formal political institutions, their regulatory nodes as centers of formal politics, including governments and new political issues, stepping away from traditional politics and taking the nation-state as self-evident organizing. The creation of political spaces in near and existing organizations and institutions facilitates the involvement and participation as forums for the involvement of participants in debates and controversies, engagement of political participation, etc.

Political science and policy analysis have facilitated the creation and development of political institutions of the nation state in domains of comparative politics and international relations (Dryzek et al. 1995; Goodin & Klingemann 1996; Wagner 1996). A policy subsystem is the set of actors steaming from private and public institutions involved in participating to deal with policy issues and problems (Sabatier & Jenkins-Smith, 1993:24).

Political sciences study the social science dynamics and acknowledges the political nature of acts holding public consequences including the enacted the formal institutions outside the exclusive centers of political power. Among the functions of institutions are included the political interests of the officials and politicians, the civil society configurations, resources available, institutional rules, local party system, interactions between the legislative and executive powers (Abers 2000; Baiaocchi 2005; Wampler 2007; Heller 2000).

The *substance* of politics is intertwined in the shape of formal political institutions by the orthodox political science delineated by governmental organizations and operations The concept of government is related to the definition of politics as the authoritative allocation of values for the whole society (Easton 1953) by and within other institutional systems besides the political system and the allocation of values for society as a whole (Van de Graaf & Grin 1999) which are implemented by governmental administrators.

The traditional topography of politics between the classical and modern institutions with functions centralized of decision making based on collective interest issues and elected representatives are related to dynamics of the political system, inputs, and outputs (Hajer 2000; Wagner 2000). Human freedom has been organized in transforming institutions such as the political parties, and democratic elected representatives incarnated on reason as the result of dialectic between science and state increasing the tendency towards the public problem solving making full use of science (Hawkesworth 1988:14)

Politics can be approached in terms of non-constitutional and constitutional institutions from the perspective of pre-discursive ontological reality concealing government and politics as a social phenomenon based upon a discursive articulation (Stavrakakis 2002). Other alternative approaches are the interpretivism epistemology based in a discursive construction of work powers of institutions. Power should be articulated between the interactions of political actors, ideologies and institutional design based on scientific facts, public philosophies, articulations of power, subjective representation between individuals and institutions in the socio-political field (Gottweis 2003:254). The organization of politics and the politics of organization must be defined in terms of policy actors, institutional legitimation to shape the implementation of policy analysis and making addressing the power dimensions.

Institutions and organizations of the diverse domains of life politics base their regulatory and political decisions mainly on values, emotions, and sentiments, more than arguments of facts. The domains and field of life politics are related to normative, moral, and value-based factors, sense of responsibility any manifestation of life, human nature, and non-human nature where the traditional governance mechanisms taking place may hamper policymaking and institutional experimentation. A normative analysis of democratic political community is not organized around the common good dismissing any attempt to cope any formal representation with a national institutional framework to legitimate international political decisions (Mouffe 1992; Beetham & Lord 1998; Jachtenfuchs 1995).

Citizenry, formal political institutions, and scientific expertise are in disruption to challenge the dominant perception of social and political order, the functional differentiation between the distribution roles of the state, society, and the market. The concept of the state as the political space gives way to the networks of political actors (Castells 1996b). The networks of interrelated institutions in diverse policy domains are the implementation of nurtured knowledge driven by the state incarnation of reason development aimed to yield socioeconomic growth (Grin 2005).

The orthodox concepts of politics and political space are criticized provoking institutional innovations including the notion of participation at the center of empirical critique refining the simplifications of the state. New institutions that meet public concerns at the local government level is a phenomenon of institutional innovation.

Questions about regulations may turn into issues to be broadly politically debated and examined in novel public spaces to demonstrate the multiplicity of institutional innovations for political decision making, assessment of benefit and risk notions in an environment of radical uncertainty and to investigate the different types of discourses in the political ethical sphere. Some newer innovations call out for institutions to manage the issues they create. The creation of new organizations and regulations can contribute to create more supportive institutions, structures, and processes to promote involvement of citizens in public participation.

We cannot take institutions for granted. Institutions become to be part of the problem and part of the solution at the operational context in which they can be progressively realigned. The sustainability of our planet and the pace of change wont' wait. Dislocation is the sudden rupture or change of events in unprecedented crisis of credibility and legitimacy of political institutions and knowledge institutes. Social mobilization approach including networking and institutional thickening can support the identification of opportunities for institutional change among the excluded groups.

The more we work together through institutions, the more likely the change is to turn into our favor. Some institutions are included in the politics field conceptually as standing political rule directed marking the land scape and rule-altering in which the new political spaces take shape, both as coexisting arrangements and may not be replaced by new political arrangements (Van Tatenhove et al. 2000; Loeber 2004).

The nature of public and private spheres is related to the institutions in which individuals participate and the type of institutional governance reforms required. Political learning spaces available used to be more based on traditional and patriarchal institutions such as the family, community, formal and informal associations, etc. Political communities are collectives of individuals that share common institutional settings, ideological identities, values, interests, practices, expectations, etc. (Beiner 1983:138).

Application of institutional rules for management and collective action is relevant to be used in common goods (Ostrom, 2006). Social accountability approaches based on speculative and descriptive information reflect the institutional biases (McGee and Kelbert 2013). Social accountability involving the legal, fiscal and policy forms, enable partners to hold institutions and policymaking. Plural and participative democratic institutions provide relevant spaces for mobilization about the diverse issues and concerns. Organizational leadership tend to mold institutions as new institutions tend to mold the leadership (Putnam 1993). Civil social organizations provide support and technical leadership to citizens in organizing and working in policymaking processes to activate the institutional venues.

A pragmatic democracy promotes the institutional adaptation and adoption of rules to address specific problems. Representative democracy may be related to government hierarchical political institutions which in turn stretches the notion of popular democratic control. Political elites in conjuncture to civil social organizations tend to redesign democratic delivery and policymaking institutions (Collier and Collier 1991).

Elected representatives and institutions of representative democracy have integrity as administrative system with deficient communication between politicians and citizens without any interest in representative democracy (Fung, 2015). Vertical top-down implementation of representative democracy is not entirely a normative discussion in which are involved the hierarchical political institutions (Pateman, 2012; Cornwall, 2008; Ansell and Gash, 2008; Sorensen and Torfing, 2005).

Social and political institutions framed by the deliberative theory interact to produce at the macro level nondeliberative outcomes moving away from the evaluation of efficacy into normative standards and abandoning the deliberative democracy (Owen and Smith 2015). Institutional deliberative democracy allows the exercise of voice by the citizens without linking their participation to a vote aimed to bind decisions requiring specific actions of elected politicians and government officials (Fishkin 1991).

Deliberative institutions tend to be more participatory and inclusive subject to the political arenas and democratic spaces. A comprehensive, inclusive, and explicit policy based on a unitary policy and strategy of various policy sectors and institutional and territorial scales should be methodologically consistent. The third wave of democracy is identified with decentralization in new and well stablished democracies that provided engagement for civil society activists, citizens and governmental officials and reformers for new institutional arrangements.

Institutional arrangements have legitimacy and agency as intrinsic qualities in communities with more inclusive and participating citizens in a community driven development program. More inclusive and democratic institutions in community driven development programs lead to changes in alternative institutional arrangements.

New institutional arrangements and formats give support to make more meaningful environmental changes. The politics of meaning discursively constructs the reality in cases of institutional ambiguity in which the participants must develop a shared political discourse to set the stage for making policies and resolving conflicts based on the institutions as the rules of the game (Gottweis 2003: 257).

The ruled life political issues dominated by rules and structures may become unruled as the result of institutional ambiguity manifested in dislocations in specific areas of governance, which in fact may be articulated unrests, protest, and resistance. The dislocation is the result of sudden dynamics of more pervasive, lasting perceptions of skepticism and alienation giving rise to institutional ambiguity (Jasanoff 2004a). The institutional ambiguity creates dislocations and disruptions of the new life-political issues, government practices and structures, political spaces, political institutions, etc.

Institutional ambiguity refers to situations of the existing rules and norms shaping politics and policymaking related to specific issues considered problematic and unacceptable, with the evidence based on indispensable clear rules by the involved parties to determine responsibility, levels of authority and accountability. The institutional ambiguity does not clarify the rules of the game in which perceived problems can be framed and handled subject to political deliberation.

Institutional ambiguity is a manifestation of how functional the rules of the game are. Society, science, and politics are organized under a questioned conception leading to situational institutional ambiguity in historical perspective bounded to occur on a dominant mode of ordering society and the involved institutional dynamics dislodgement in the reals of action in the dichotomy between nature and society and between politics and science. The concept of bio-power (Foucault, 1977) has permeated the new forms of institutional arrangements and their emergence in the realm of science and politics manifest in the interactions between the individual and the collective in the new politics of life. Consequently, the institutional arrangements are challenged to eradicate associated uncertainty in scientific and political communities to deal with nature as the resource and threat to human life and social order.

The political formative dimension helps to understand the problems of institutional ambiguity in governing in the form of in situ enactment. Institutional ambiguity is perceived by the actors in formal institutions and other non-state actors. The so called dislocate moments occurring regarding the phenomena of life, trigger the institutional ambiguity and brings forth new political spaces. The institutional ambiguity of situations without self-evidence of the components of organizationally and individual trust, unity, cohesion, stability, and cooperation among the collective organization (Weinstock 1989).

The object of negotiations subject to institutional ambiguity comprises problem definitions and solutions for the participants working on rules to legitimate decision making and securing the mutual trust to consolidate policy decision making and solutions of operational power aimed to joint governance (Shachar 2001). The institutional ambiguity brings along empirical questions the absence of routinized and stable norms, rules and policy actions which are agreed by actors and participants to give signification and make sense of the issues at stake, generate mutual understanding and trust among the participants and actors responsible to act in line with the systems.

Regional institutionalization process of citizenship based on a functional structure required to make decisions aimed to solve problems. Symbolic identity-building depends on cultural identity bottom-up or top-down creations, territories are under contestation, institutionalization is a consequence of regional identity formation and functionality linked to a superordinate system (Terlouw, 2012, p.709; Paasi, 1986, p.115 et seq.) The doxa notion of Bordieu (1977) refers to the habitual and naturalized aspects of traditional and culture, rooted in entrenched cultural institutions.

Some politicians from oppositional parties and activists of social movements have developed new institutionalization processes to return to the democratic rule by the incorporation of citizens into the public space of state intuitions.

The institutional functioning logic creates the frameworks to treat equally the users as partners that build and invest in the regional and local spaces. It is necessary to build strong, inclusive, and global institutions to manage this change or it will manage us, to understand how societies organize themselves, the ability to coordinate at the large scale, coordination of humans is done through institutions that put the ideas into motion and coordinate our actions.

The implementation of institutional changes in the public policy system may require the development of hybrid institutional arrangements. Participatory modes of citizens' engagement try to link liberal institutions to reshape existing ones because democracy seeks the institutions that can give a voice and an ear (Barber, 1984). The re-scaling processes are distinguished from the political mobilization, functional needs, and institutional restructuring (Keating, 2002) Territorial and institutional re-scaling gives the support to the degree of organizational structure.

Regionalization of the institutionalization of participative governance, there are considered the social, substantial, and procedural dimensions (Perkmann 2007a). The development regional re-scaling processes of governance building have the political mobilization, institutional restructuring, and functional elements of shifting cross-border territorial scales and organizational building and set-up.

The new institutions and innovations in public policies have transformative potential. Institutional innovation assessment should adopt an empirical approach and avoid the conceptual determinism to investigate the publics, objects and issues which are mutually transformed and constructed in participatory governance practices. The liberalization of old political institutions into the governance reforms tend to enhance the growth of diverse new institutional participative democratic governance spaces. Neofunctionalism integration through cooperation process among economic agents and political actors tend to transfer loyalty to newly created regional institutions (Haas, 1968; Wolf, 2005; Lindberg, 1963). Organizational dependency of funds proves the institutional cooperation between agencies that act designing and implementing strategies.

The institutional solutions for the formalization of relationships between the strategic alliances and local authorities via contract are different in the intention to institutionalize the practices. A silent contract celebrated between citizens and political institutions formally operating with the enactment of scientific and technological knowledge and expertise embedded in building blocks of social practices, norms, discourses, identities, conventions, institutions, instruments, etc. (Jasanoff 2004b:3). Local authorities systematically may perceive problems in the public-civil partnership processes instead than solutions, often blaming the strict institutional rules of the game.

The institutional formalization must reflect congruity with programmatic and self-governance autonomy as the first step towards a governing structure supported by a public-civil partnership. Institutional autonomy while being controlled the work by local authorities in terms of law and regulations compliance, quality management, investments approvals, etc., are procedures regulated by the relationships between the local authorities and the institutions. Most of these procedures do not exist in public-civil partnerships but require the participation of the local authorities in the governance of spaces and programs which are not necessarily the role of the local administration. Regional institutions with legal personality and autonomy are legal instruments to represent and advantage.

The concepts of politics and political actors in practice requires a non-nationalist, and centralist methodology (Beck 2003, 2004) which may benefit the unorthodox approach to participatory governance. Strategies of action may be designed and implemented aimed to redefine the role of public institutions and establish protocols between the different stakeholders to develop funded urban projects, and more specifically to confront some problems regarding the institutional networking, individuals and independent scenes, development of intersectoral collaboration.

Urban society is related to political systems by regulations and policies based on institutional legacies and the ways in which the cities react to opportunities and challenges from the external environment. The policy actions created through consensual and cooperative relationships between the urban society and political institutions should be more governable and effective.

INCLUSIVE PARTICIPATION

In political theory, the concept of participation is undetermined (Oakley & Marsden 1985: 18-19), ranging from taking part in elections in elite democratic theory (Dahl 1971) to communicating information about interests, preferences and needs to public authorities' pressure for them to respond based on theories on citizen activism (Verba et al 1995). The political theory of participatory democracy, as a normative construct, outlines the notions of participation debated within liberalism of John Rawls (1995) and communitarism of Barber, 1984 and Pateman, 2000 framed as participatory democracy, associative democracy, expansive democracy, deliberative democracy, strong democracy, and dialogic democracy (Schmidt, 2000, p.251).

Participation is a mechanism of voice and vote and political reflection (Wampler and McNulty, 2011; Bora 2005). Participation in active citizenship in the decision of basic policies requires the deployment of power (Barber 1984, p. 151). The level of participation, purpose and power of citizens is decided by the initial participants that are the owners of the ideas and are committed to new patterns of behavior relationships in the public and private spheres and practices with capacity and confidence to achieve collective goals. Democratic participation is widely used and practiced with different meanings by actors such as multilateral and international institutions, governments at all levels, non-governmental organizations, social and civil organizations, local communities, citizens, grassroots activists, etc.

The notion of participation is vital for the discussion of democratic governance, which has been revisited by the institutional approach of the traditional state and the new forms of political and social perspectives (Fischer, 2006). The basic assumption behind the efforts to increase institutional participation in governance is if the inclusion of minority groups leads to fairer and responsive government.

Inclusive participation has the potential for responsibility and accountability of governance actors making more justified policies (Papadopoulos, 2010). Cultural diversity is essential for the democratic participation (Obuljen and Smiers, 2006: 3). Dysfunctional democratic societies require the participatory approach to enhance the direct participation of civil and society. Creation and development of democratic spaces for institutional participation governance must be tempered by the constraints of inclusion and the reproduction of political culture. The participation practices of the involved issues in relevant cases may be typical for the institutional contexts and policy culture where they are taking place.

The complexity of reality lead to the need to rethink the concepts of participation and participatory governance. Public participation and participatory governance are concepts that are becoming intermingled. The public-civil partnership establishes practices which may contribute to inclusion of various actors, to empowering citizens and foster the community participation, aimed to further development in the context. The concepts of participatory modes and accountability regarding the auto responsive participatory actions in institutional governance. The assumption of the participation models applied to institutions as legal and political instrument to foster regional mobilization and citizenship participation merging the concepts of participation and governance. The conceptual framework of participation is related to projects focusing the domains of politics of life issues and concerns.

The empirical research of the manifestations of participation in life political domains requires a methodological approach based on the conceptions of life, politics, and science, contingent with the core theme of participatory governance and the politics of life, considered as the intertwining of conceptual and institutional social innovation. The concept of innovative politics and participation in manifested participatory governance to be investigated empirically.

International organizations and institutions attempt to prompt local authorities to apply a bottom-up collaborative approach between citizens and civil society despite the criticisms on participation as the tyranny of development processes related to the hegemonic agenda under constructed participation and coercion of local communities in developing countries (Cook and Kothari, 2001). This criticism refers to the practices of participatory development used more as rhetoric than content.

Opening the decision-making processes for active participation affirmed on the concepts of democratization between all the stakeholders involved in a community is the foundation of good participatory governance model of public spatial natural resources. The spatial resources socioeconomic conditions may be a matter for contestation between the political, institutional, and non-institutional actors, stakeholders and partners involved in the scene. The real of the political participation is challenged by an open conceptual. Institutional actors and agents involved in deliberation and decision-making processes, according to the classification within the institutional set-up.

The transformation of political participation concept tends to the institutional reification as the product of period and political conflicts (Hobsbawn 1977; Joll 1978; Manin 1997). Institutional transformation by transplantation of initiatives leads to isomorphic practices bringing inclusiveness which may turn out difficult between civil society and other private stakeholder (Vicari Haddock, 2004, p. 123). Strengthening good governance in civil society organizations seeks to expand the participation in the public sphere in new waves of democratization outside formal political institutions that offer minority movements the possibility to exert influence on the policy processes.

Open of political space is the conceptual transformation of politics that leaves the question of public participation in terms of the traditional concept of the constructed public in relation to the ability to govern attributed to the state as the exclusive political power domain, in terms of in and or exclusion process of formal political decision making and policy analysis. Activists moving further to a new stage of democratization and formal governance institutions to provide alternative spaces for participation and political opportunities.

The concept of public participation is used as community engagement processes become active through a period to include methods and tools of information, communication, participation, and consultation. Public participation in politics must be supported by the intertwining between conceptual and institutional innovations to develop new forms of institutional participatory governance. Decoupling the act of governing from the spatial territory is an innovative concept for a human political community.

The structural hierarchical and horizontal approaches between local authorities, communities and citizens are sources of tensions created by the lack of participation and power. Local governments can pluralize public sites and spaces with institutional policies for citizen engagements in different forms of participation and deliberation institutional participative governance. Here the concept of participation is related to sustainable development of communities, cities, and places to become more creative and inclusive (Hristova, Dragičević-Šešić and Duxbury, 2015: 3).

Institutionalization of participative and deliberative mechanisms of post national and multilevel governance fostered by the institutionalization of transnational participation and cooperation in a new administrative space.

GOVERNANCE

An interdisciplinary perspective to the concept of governance highlights an alternative solution to the governmental practice of nation-state, focus on economic transnationality of policy, institutions, and developments with the involvement of a variety of actors interacting in decision making processes with different institutions. Participatory governance practices emerge in new political spaces rooted in territorial conceptions under the assumption that the nation states are la unit of analysis (Beck 2004:142); leading to national styles of governance (Vogel & Kagan 2004), that have a strong influence on life political issues at stake (Ansell et al. 2005).

The elements co-determining the potential for governing rooted in the empirical conception of politics at the nation-state level are the sovereignty of political institutions, patterns of economic and social organization and the normative commitment in civil society in the forms of shared political identity and cultural adherence (Hajer 2003)

Rethinking the political space for participatory governance, formal state-initiated arrangements framed by a conceptual mainstream political thought and pragmatist policy-scientific oriented critique on the nature of government organization and politics in society. Stepping away from earlier concepts of politics, the research object is leading towards the new political spaces (Hajer 2000). On the other hand, according to Popescu, (2022), sustainable development and a healthy life in the new economy require to meet the balanced needs of the environmental, social, and corporate governance fields of organizations and institutions participating and being supported by the knowledge-based economy and the digitalized economy, acting in the spirit of sustainability and centering efforts on efficiency, productivity, profitability, and performance.

The concept of multilevel governance based on comparative public policy analysis and public administration deals with policy making in response to state centered approaches (Richardson 1996; Wallace & Wallace 2000; Hooghe & Marks 2001; Van Kersbergen & Van Waarden 2001). The heterogeneous inclusion forms are more identified through concepts of governance and participation of self-reflexive community actors and social and political scientists with inclusive practices. Different practices and initiatives in places can be complementary for the political and institutional inclusion strategies of fragmented initiatives.

The inclusion process is relevant for its functional to control resources of non-institutional actors that is necessary due to the complexity of public policies. From the political point of view, the inclusion of non-institutional actors leads to democratization processes.

The political concept of neo-republican in theoretical and empirical studies addresses practices of citizenship participatory governance arrangements (Dryzek 1990; Fung & Wright 2003; Fung 2004). The discursive exchanges are mechanisms by means of which actors become participants among them to address public issues, concerns and problems find meaningful dialogue and participatory governance arrangement to be able to produce and reproduce a set of practices, concepts and categories allocated to physical and social phenomena (Hajer 1995).

Then concepts of governance and participation oppose in a semantic continuum of inclusive and practices and initiatives. Practices are the entry point to empirical study and contextual analysis of political science, governance and manifestations of institutional participatory governance, concepts of state, public, citizenry, and so forth. The value of inputs used by civil society in economic, social, and political environments are critical to achieve effective outcomes may lead to an inherent weakness of the analytical concept of participatory governance as the vehicle for the decision and policy making legitimacy.

A case in point is the representation of civil society in the deliberative and participatory budget in some spaces of Brazil. The strategies of deliberation, advocacy and participation and their interrelationships are conceptually used and implemented in practice to achieve local governance.

The theoretical and conceptual approach of participatory governance emerged in the beginning of the 2000's. The concept of participatory governance is linked to institutional and administrative practices considering the needs of local citizens, economic, social, and nongovernmental organizations, and associations, linking the demands to the public arena with institutional participatory governance arrangements.

CONCLUSION

This analysis concludes that the conceptual framework of institutional participation in governance is related to projects focusing the domains of politics of life issues and concerns. The assumptions confirmed that the efforts to increase institutional participation in governance through the inclusion of minority groups lead to fairer and responsive government. The analysis also confirms the assumption that participation models applied to institutions as legal and political instruments to foster regional mobilization and citizenship participation lead to the merging of the concepts of institutions, participation, and governance.

A comprehensive policy of inclusion transversal to different institutional and territorial scales is based on unitary strategy deduced from institutional regulation of supervision, coordination and harmonization roles and a programmatic document of inclusive practices. The fragmented initiatives of inclusive strategies developed by institutions of public action aim to collective problems and territorial scales.

Participation in institutional development governance faces structural and transformative challenges. Citizen participation policies in governance and decision-making structures for the multilevel design, development and implementation should be promoted in public institutions of local public administration and among natural and legal persons.

The structural composition of governance units must reflect the balance of participation among the diverse interests of actor, stakeholders, and the motivation of the community. The different forms of actors and stakeholder's participation must be considered when setting expectations and planning, to be designed and implement to express, negotiate, and manifest their interest.

Institutional participative governance represents the concepts of an analytical framework. The concept of institutional participatory governance is interrelated with sustainable planning and development spaces in urban places. The implementation process of a concept of space may facilitate the improvement of institutional participative governance model opening new possibilities for action. The concept of participatory governance takes place in geographical contexts and expands from developed economic and democratic societies to be implemented in developing ones. Comparison of similar participatory institutions within and across countries and regions, may lead to analyze the different concepts, research agenda of cases, policy recommendations, and strategic implementation.

Institutional participatory governance enables a more decisive directions of independent initiatives, practices and activities of the community and local government toward raising awareness, visibility and attracting public finance for ultimately facilitating the implementation of concepts and practices in spatial participatory governance.

The concept of participatory governance facilitated through the platform includes actors, agents, stakeholders and representatives of local authorities and local communities who have interest in the process at the level of information, knowledge, and learning about specific features of management and governance processes. Actors involved in the organization that establish participatory governance of public resources should understand concepts.

Advocacy, fatigue, and uncertainty of the urban development strategy to implement the concept of participatory governance and the establishment of a private-public-civil partnership is valuable experience and knowledge useful to the management of public and natural resources, leading to the development of a multi-location and multi-level governance structures. The development of social entrepreneurship establishes organizational and institutional processes to provide services to enable to enhance participative governance in development within the concept of socio-interculturality.

The conceptual and theoretical-methodological approaches of participatory governance have an impact on the quality of democracy among citizens, civil society organizations, communities, state institutions and agencies. The new geo-political ordering of the new politics of life, the conceptualization of governance and life sets the new agenda for research. The new participatory governance arrangements should be sustained upon a conceptual framework assuming access to truth and unity in the new modes of regulation.

The new types of participatory governance practices go beyond the traditional conceptualization of politics practiced by the actors and participants in formal political institutions.

REFERENCES

Abers, R. (2000). *Inventing Local Democracy: Grassroots Politics in Brazil*. Lynne Rienner Publishers.

Ansell, C. K., & Gash, A. (2008). Collaborative governance in theory and practice. *Journal of Public Administration: Research and Theory*, *18*(4), 543–571. doi:10.1093/jopart/mum032

Baiocchi, G. (2005). *Militants and Citizens: The Politics of Participatory Democracy in Porto Alegre*. Stanford University Press. doi:10.1515/9781503625129

Barber, B. R. (1984). *Strong democracy. Participatory politics for a new age*. Univ. of California Press.

Bates, R. H. (1984). Markets and States in Tropical Africa: The Political Basis of Agricultural Policy. University of California Press.

Beck, U. (1992). *Risk Society*. Sage.

Beck, U. (2003) Toward a new critical theory with cosmopolitan intent. *Constellations, 10*(4), 453-68.

Beck, U., & Holzer, B. (2004). Wie global ist die Weltrisikogesellschaft? In Entgrenzung und Entscheidung: was ist neu an der Theorie reflexiver Modernisierung? Suhrkamp.

Beetham, D., & Lord, C. (1998). *Legitimacy and the EU*. Addison Wesley Longman Limited.

Beiner, R. (1983). *Political Judgment*. Methuen.

Bourdieu, P. (1977). *Outline of a Theory of Practice*. Cambridge Uni-versity Press. doi:10.1017/CBO9780511812507

Callon, M., Laredo, P., Rabeharisoa, V., Gonard, T., & Leray, T. (1992). The management and evaluation of technological programs and the dynamics of techno-economic networks: The case of AFME. *Research Policy*, *21*(3), 215–236. doi:10.1016/0048-7333(92)90017-X

Castells, M. (1996a). *The Rise of the Network Society*. Blackwell.

Castells, M. (1996b). The Information Age: Economy, Society and Culture.: Vol. I. *The Rise of the Network Society*. Blackwell Publishers.

Collier, R. B., & Collier, D. (1991). *Shaping the Political Arena: Critical Junctures, the Labor Movement, and Regime Dynamics in Latin America*. Princeton University Press.

Committee of the Regions. (2014). *EGTC Monitoring Report 2013*. Towards the New Cohesion Policy.

Cooke, B., & Kothari, U. (Eds.). (2001). Participation: The New Tyranny? Zed Books Ltd.

Cornwall, A. (2008). Unpacking 'Participation': Models, Meaning and Practices. *Community Development Journal: An International Forum, 43*(3), 269–283. doi:10.1093/cdj/bsn010

Czarniawska, B. (2002). *A tale of three cities. Or the glocalization of city management.* Oxford University Press. doi:10.1093/acprof:oso/9780199252718.001.0001

Dahl, R. (1971). *Polyarchy: Participation and Opposition.* Yale University Press.

Dahrendorf, R. (1988). *The modern social conflict.* Weidenfeld and Nicolson.

De Jong, M., Lalenis, K., & Mamadouh, V. (2002). *The theory and practice of institutional transplantation. Experiences with the transfer of policy institutions.* Kluwer Academic Publishers. doi:10.1007/978-94-011-0001-4

Dolowitz, D. P., & Marsh, D. (2000). Learning from Abroad: The Role of Policy Transfer in Contemporary Policymaking. *Governance: An International Journal of Policy, Administration and Institutions, 13*(1), 5–23. doi:10.1111/0952-1895.00121

Dryzek, J. S. (1990). *Discursive democracy: politics, policy, and political science.* Cambridge University Press. doi:10.1017/9781139173810

Dryzek, J. S., Farr, J., & Leonard, S. T. (Eds.). (1995). *Political science in history.* Cambridge University Press.

Easton, D. (1965). *A Framework for Political Analysis.* Prentice-Hall.

Fischer, F. (2006). Participatory Governance as Deliberative Empowerment. The Cultural politics of Discursive Space. *American Review of Public Administration, 36*(1), 19–40. doi:10.1177/0275074005282582

Fishkin, J. S. (1993). *Democracy and Deliberation: New Directions for Democratic Reform.* Yale University Press.

Foucault, M. (1977). *Discipline and Punish: The Birth of the Prison.* Random House.

Fung, A. (2004). *Empowered Participation: Reinventing Urban Democracy.* Princeton University Press.

Fung, A. (2015). Putting the Public Back into Governance: The Challenges of Citizen Participation and Its Future. *Public Administration Review, 75*(4), 513–522. doi:10.1111/puar.12361

Fung, A., & Wright, E. O. (2003). Thinking about Empowered Participatory Governance. In A. Fung & E. O. Wright (Eds.), *Deepening Democracy. Institutional Innovations in Empowered Participatory Governance*. Verso.

Goodin, R. E., & Klingemann, H. D. (Eds.). (1996). *A new handbook of political science*. Oxford University Press.

Gottweis, H. (2003). Theoretical strategies of post-structuralist policy analysis: towards an Analytics of Government. In M. A. Hajer & H. Wagenaar (Eds.), *Deliberative policy analysis: understanding governance in the network society* (pp. 247–265). Cambridge University Press. doi:10.1017/CBO9780511490934.011

Grin, F. (2005, August). Linguistic human rights as a source of policy guidelines: A critical assessment. *Journal of Sociolinguistics*, *9*(3), 448–460. doi:10.1111/j.1360-6441.2005.00300.x

Haas, E. B. (1968). *The uniting of Europe. Political, social, and economic forces 1950 - 1957*. Stanford Univ. Press.

Hajer, M. A. (1995). *The politics of environmental discourse. Ecological modernisation and the policy process*. Clarendon Press.

Hajer, M. A. (2000) *Politiek als vormgeving*. Universiteit van Amsterdam: inaugurele rede 16 juni 2000.

Haselsberger, B. (2007). European Territorial Co-Operation: Regions of the Future. Regional Studies, (267), 6-8.

Hawkesworth, M. E. (1988). *Theoretical issues in policy analysis*. SUNY Press.

Heilbron, J., Magnusson, L., & Wittrock, B. (Eds.). (1997). *The rise of the social sciences and the formation of modernity*. Kluwer.

Heller, P. (2000). Degrees of Democracy: Some Comparative Lessons from India. *World Politics*, *52*(4), 484–519. doi:10.1017/S0043887100020086

Hobsbawm, E. J. (1977). *The age of revolution*. Abacus.

Hooghe, L., & Marks, G. (2001). *Multi-level governance and European integration*. Rowman & Littlefield Publishers.

Hristova, S., Dragičević Šešić, M., & Duxbury, N. (2015). Introduction. In S. Hristova, M. Dragičević Šešić, & N. Duxbury (Eds.), *Culture and Sustainability in European Cities. Imagining Europolis* (pp. 1–13). Routledge. doi:10.4324/9781315772028

Jachtenfuchs, M. (1995). Theoretical Perspectives on European Governance. *European Law Journal, 1*(2), 115–133. doi:10.1111/j.1468-0386.1995.tb00010.x

Jasanoff, S. (2004a) *post-sovereign science and global nature*. Harvard University, Environmental Politics/ Colloquium Papers.

Jasanoff, S. (2004b). The idiom of co-production. In S. Jasanoff (Ed.), *States of Knowledge. The coproduction of science and social order* (pp. 1–13). Routledge. doi:10.4324/9780203413845-6

Joll, J. (1978). *Europe since 1870*. Penguin.

Kangas, A. (2017). *Removing Barriers. Participative and Collaborative Cultural Activities in Kuulto Action Research*. Centre for Cultural Policy Research Cupore.

Keating, M. (2002). Territorial Politics and the New Regionalism. In Development in West European Politics (Vol. 2, pp. 201–220). Academic Press.

Langbein, L. I., & Kerwin, C. M. (2000). Regulatory negotiation versus conventional rule making: Claims, counterclaims, and empirical evidence. *Journal of Public Administration: Research and Theory, 10*(3), 599–632. doi:10.1093/oxfordjournals.jpart.a024283

Latour, B. (1987). *Science in Action*. Harvard University Press.

Latour, B., & Woolgar. (1997). *De Berlijnse sleutel en andere lessen van een liefhebber van wetenschap en techniek*. Amsterdam: Van Gennep.

Lenzer, G. (Ed.). (1975). *Auguste Comte and positivism; the essential writings*. University of Chicago Press.

Lindberg, L. N. (1963). *The political dynamics of European economic integration*. Stanford Univ. Press.

Loeber, A. (2004). *Practical wisdom in the risk society: methods and practice of interpretive analysis on questions of sustainable development* (Thesis). University of Amsterdam.

Manin, B. (1997). *The principles of representative government*. Cambridge University Press. doi:10.1017/CBO9780511659935

March, J., & Olsen, J. (1989). *Rediscovering Institutions: The Organizational Basis of Politics*. The Free Press.

McGee & Kelbert. (2013). *Review of approaches to social accountability for Citizens' Engagement Programme*. Academic Press.

Mouffe, C. (1992). Democratic Citizenship and the Political Community. In C. Mouffe (Ed.), *Dimensions of Radical Democracy. Pluralism, Citizenship, Community* (pp. 225–239). Verso.

North, D. C. (1990). *Institutions, Institutional Change and Economic Performance*. Press Syndicate of the University of Cambridge. doi:10.1017/CBO9780511808678

North, D. C. (1991). *Institutions, Institutional Change and Economic Performance*. Press Syndicate of the University of Cambridge.

Oakley, P., & Marsden, D. (1985). *Approaches to participation in rural development*. International Labour Office.

Obuljen, N., & Smiers, J. (2006). Introduction. In UNESCO's Convention on the Protection and Promotion of the Diversity of Cultural Expressions: Making it Work. Zagreb: Institute for International Relations.

Ostrom, E. (1990). *Governing the Commons: The Evolution of Institutions for Collective Action Cambridge University Press*. Cambridge University Press. doi:10.1017/CBO9780511807763

Ostrom, E. (2006). *Upravljanje zajedničkim dobrima. Evolucija institucija za kolektivno djelovanje*. Naklada Jesenski i Turk.

Owen, D., & Smith, G. (2015, June). Survey Article: Deliberation, Democracy, and the Systemic Turn. *Journal of Political Philosophy*, *23*(2), 213–234. doi:10.1111/jopp.12054

Paasi, A. (1996). *Territories, boundaries, and consciousness. In The changing geographies of the Finnish-Russian border*. J. Wiley & Sons.

Papadopoulos, Y. (2010) Governance und Demokratie. In Governance - Regieren in komplexen Regelsystemen eine Einführung. Wiesbaden VS, Verl. für Sozialwissenschaften. doi:10.1007/978-3-531-92325-3_11

Pateman, C. (2000). *Participation and democratic theory*. Cambridge Univ. Press.

Pateman, C. (2012). Participatory Democracy Revised. *Perspectives on Politics*, *10*(1), 7–19. doi:10.1017/S1537592711004877

Perkmann, M. (2007a). Construction of new territorial scales: A framework and case study of the EUREGIO cross-border region. *Regional Studies*, *41*(2), 253–266. doi:10.1080/00343400600990517

Popescu, C. R. G. (2022). Environmental, Social, and Corporate Governance by Avoiding Management Bias and Tax Minimization: Reaching a General Consensus Regarding a Minimum Global Tax Rate. In C. Popescu (Ed.), *COVID-19 Pandemic Impact on New Economy Development and Societal Change* (pp. 94–132). IGI Global. doi:10.4018/978-1-6684-3374-4.ch006

Putnam, R. D. (1993). *Making Democracy Work: Civic Traditions in Modern Italy*. Princeton University Press.

Rawls, J. (1995). Political Liberalism: Reply to Habermas. *The Journal of Philosophy*, *92*(3), 132–180. doi:10.2307/2940843

Richardson, J. J. (1996). *European Union: Power and Policy making*. Routledge.

Sabatier, P. A., & Jenkins-Smith, H. C. (1993). Policy Change and Learning. An Advocacy Coalition Approach. Westview Press.

Schmidt, M. G. (2000). *Demokratietheorien. In Eine Einführung* (3rd ed.). VS Verlag für Sozialwissenschaften. doi:10.1007/978-3-531-90008-7

Shachar, A. (2001). *Multicultural Jurisdictions: Cultural Differences and Women's Rights*. Cambridge University Press. doi:10.1017/CBO9780511490330

Sorensen, E., & Torfin, J. (2005). The Democratic Anchorage of Governance Networks. *Scandinavian Political Studies*, *28*(3), 195–218. doi:10.1111/j.1467-9477.2005.00129.x

Stavrakakis, Y. (2002). *The Ethical and Political challenge of Constructionism in Risk Societies: Post-democratic Trends and Civil Society. Essex papers in politics and government. Subseries in ideology and discourse analysis. No. 19, May 2002*. Dept. of Government, University of Essex.

Terlouw, K. (2012). From thick to thin regional identities? *GeoJournal*, *77*(5), 707–721. doi:10.100710708-011-9422-x

Van de Graaf, H., & Grin, J. (1999). *Policy analysis and the 'reinvention of politics. The question of closure*. Paper prepared for presentation at the Symposium "Theory, Policy and Society", Leiden, The Netherlands.

Van Kersbergen, K., & van Waarden, F. (2001). Shifts in Governance: Problems and Legitimacy and Accountability. Background Report NWO strategie nota 2002-2005, Den Haag: NOW.

van Van Tatenhove, J., Arts, B., & Leroy, P. (Eds.). (2000). *Political Modernisation and the Environment: The Renewal of Environmental Policy Arrangements*. Kluwer Academic Publishers. doi:10.1007/978-94-015-9524-7

Verba, S., Schlozman, L. K., & Brady, H. A. (1995). *Voice and Equality –Civic Voluntarism in American Politics*. Harvard University Press. doi:10.2307/j.ctv1pnc1k7

Vicari Haddock, S. (2004). *La città contemporanea*. Il Mulino.

Vogel, D., & Kagan, R. (2004). *The Dynamics of Regulatory Change: How Globalization Affects National Regulation Policy*. University of California Press.

Wagner, P. (1996) Certainty and order, liberty, and contingency. The birth of social science as empirical political philosophy. In The rise of the social sciences and the formation of modernity. Kluwer.

Wagner, P. (2000). *Theorizing modernity*. Sage.

Wallace, H., & Wallace, W. (Eds.). (2000). *Policymaking in the European Union* (4th ed.). Oxford University Press.

Wampler, B. (2007). *Participatory Budgeting in Brazil: Contestation, Cooperation, and Accountability*. Pennsylvania State University Press.

Wampler, B., & Mcnulty, S. L. (2011). *Does participatory governance matter? Exploring the nature and impact of participatory reforms*. Woodrow Wilson International Center for Scholars, Comparative Urban Studies Project.

Wolf, D. (2005). Neo-Funktionalismus. In H. J. Bieling & M. Lerch (Eds.), *Theorien der europäischen Integration* (pp. 65–91). VS Verlag für Sozialwissenschaften. doi:10.1007/978-3-663-11642-4_3

Chapter 13
SMART Technologies:
New Normal Manufacturing Industry 2020

Muskaan Arora
Chitkara Business School, Chitkara University, India

Archana Goel
Chitkara Business School, Chitkara University, India

Asmita Sharma
Chitkara School of Planning and Architecture, Chitkara University, India

ABSTRACT

The manufacturing industry plays a paramount role in the world economy, accounting for almost 16% of the global GDP in 2018. Manufacturing has been identified as the key driver of dynamic growth and development of the country. The COVID-19 pandemic has caused immense devastation around the world. Due to the downturn in the manufacturing industry along with the factory blackout, the coronavirus epidemic reduced the global FDI by 5-15%. This chapter aims to throw light on measures taken by manufacturers to combat the impact of the COVID-19 havoc. It will discuss how internet of things and artificial intelligence will help manufacturing industry to recover effectively and efficiently post pandemic. It would suggest a framework to manufacturing industry on how it can come back in a new normal position post-COVID-19 scenario. Manufacturers, who acknowledge the new standard policies discussed in the present paper and operate on it, will get enough growth opportunities and can have long-term sustainable success in the future.

DOI: 10.4018/978-1-6684-4745-1.ch013

INTRODUCTION

Manufacturing Industry plays a paramount role in the world economy, accounting for almost 16% of the global GDP in 2018. Manufacturing has been identified as the key driver of dynamic growth and development of the country (Rele, 2020). The most important production sectors where India has established its expertise are steel industry, electronics, automotive, health sector, engineering industry, textiles, food processing industry and many more (Deshmukh, 2016). The government has taken a lot of initiatives across the world to develop this industry. The contribution by the retail sector towards India's GDP is about 10% due to which the Global Retail Development Index (GRDI), 2019 has ranked India at the number 2 position. One of the major initiatives taken in 2015 to promote the manufacturing industry includes 'Make in India' to expedite the production of goods in India. Its purpose was to lessen India's dependence on exporting countries by manufacturing products in its own country. The COVID-19 pandemic has caused immense devastation around the world. It has contributed to an extensive human loss around the globe. Due to the downturn in the manufacturing industry along with the factory blackout, the Coronavirus epidemic reduced the global FDI by 5 per cent -15 per cent (UNCTAD).

The imposed lockdown for maintaining social distancing drained the manufacturing sector. Many manufacturing companies across the globe, including India, have shown concerns for their raw material supply (Pratheeesh and Arumugasamy, 2020). Companies have declined their production operations and have also postponed the launch of new products following the pandemic outbreak. Sales of these products were disrupted due to supply disruption. Moreover, the Chinese suppliers have raised the prices of some components by almost 2%, and more than 15% for TV panels. Furthermore, the well-being of a worker has been a considerable problem too, and physical contact was hazardous. Large number of workers, particularly semi-skilled and unskilled workers, migrated to their homelands, after the announcement of lockdown by the Government authorities. They didn't want to re-join their work because of the fear that the government might impose lockdown again, without informing. Additionally, the slower pace of banking activities, reduced work schedules, crowded and busy lines of communication contributed to delayed cash transactions which raised lot of financial risks for the manufacturing industry. The significant disturbances caused by COVID-19 are incomprehensible. Therefore, Governments and manufacturers should be sensitized with this situation and respond rapidly. For both academicians and practitioners, these disturbances have tremendous consequences.

Today, everybody is hoping to resume a semblance of production activities, and leaders are planning to face the new standard, such as how digital transformation will provide the industry with a swift recovery. This paper aims to throw light on measures taken by manufacturers to combat the impact of COVID 19 havoc. It will discuss how Internet of things and artificial Intelligence will help manufacturing industry to recover effectively and efficiently post pandemic. It would suggest a framework to manufacturing industry on how it can come back in a new normal position post-COVID-19 scenario. Manufacturers, who acknowledge the new standard policies discussed in the present paper and operate on it, will get enough growth opportunities and can have long-term sustainable success in the future.

2020 PANDEMIC REPERCUSSIONS ON THE MANUFACTURING SECTOR

The recent lockdown in the country has put a lot of strain on all sectors, including the manufacturing industry, which has shown a decline of about 27.4% (*HIS/Market Monthly Data*). This can be compared to 'root beer game' effect in the Supply Chain Management, whereby a market incident can lead to a highly intensified reaction from the suppliers which further will lead to short term overproduction and average discount sales.

The recent pandemic has affected the manufacturing sector in many ways. Few of them are as follows:

Low or No Production

The government directives all around the globe, including India, announced the lockdown to control coronavirus. Thus, with very little labour and slow movement of Cargoes, production got halted in the manufacturing industry, thereby, decreasing the scale of operations, and affecting the production volumes (National Statistics Office, Government of India, 2020).

Slump in Demand

Even though manufacturing organisations step up their production in future, a drop in the demand would be a matter of concern. Finally, due to all of these disturbances, the end consumer usually begins deferring non-essential transactions and disconnects from consuming processes by delaying their demands (Reserve Bank of India, 2020).

Transportation Woes/Supply Chain Disruptions

The slowdown in manufacturing had lowered the demand for logistics services, which further brought down prices through warehouses and freight. Constraints on air travel and international flights worldwide have led to a slowdown in the flow of goods, putting an end to first and last-mile transport and intermodal movement of goods.

Increased Labour Demand-Supply Mismatch

As per the International Labour Organisation, 2.7 billion workers worldwide are affected by the COVID-19 pandemic due to lockdowns. With a significant dip in the market, Indian companies looked at layoffs, although temporarily.

Liquidity Crunch

The Indian economy was stressed by labour capital/liquidity crisis due to production slowdowns amid global lock-downs and ongoing payments for fixed costs. Cash flow pressures persisted even after the lockdown due to the decreased demand, resulting in reduced inventories, with MYMEs having the worst hit cash flow problems could see a rise in NPA levels due to non-repayment.

Increasing Fraud Risks in The Manufacturing Sector

During these turbulent times, both the supply chain and the distribution side of the manufacturing sectors were under pressure. All these challenges enhanced fraud risks in Sales and distribution, Sale of damaged and expired products, Artificial inflation of prices.

INDUSTRY PILLARS AND SMART FACTORY CONCEPT

Indeed, the covid epidemic has wreaked devastation on mankind and is still claiming lives. As a result, reducing casualties and developing plans that are in accordance with quickly changing worldwide dynamics should be our top priorities. "There is light at the end of every tunnel," as the proverb goes, and every crisis has its own set of possibilities. According to new data, India's manufacturing production has nearly halved. On the other hand, this illness outbreak has the potential to pave the way for India's long-awaited foray into manufacturing.

Industry 4.0, is already in full swing. It is a relatively new term that is still being defined. There are various definitions in the literature. "On the basis of new technologies, primarily ICT, Industry 4.0 delivers an ideal collaborative value (smarter services and processes) through smart collaboration of new and enlarged competencies and capacities in a supply network," according to the company (Felser et.al, 2015). Modern industrial companies are the result of two centuries of continual technological advancements, organizational structure changes, and managerial techniques. In reality, Industry 4.0 entails the use of technology advancements that are currently in use in standard manufacturing systems in such a way that a seamless integration, regulated, and efficient production flow, also known as Smart Manufacturing, is created. The continuous change is centred on a number of fundamental innovations that include not only machines but also sensors, workpieces, and IT systems that are connected across the value chain. Different parts may, in reality, interact using conventional Web- based protocols and conduct analysis of data to prevent and forecast errors, reorganize themselves, and respond to changes, resulting in astonishing results (Cepin et.al., 2017). All appreciation lies to the developments in technologies, like the Internet of Things (IoT). The term Machine Learning, robotics, digital technologies, 3D Printing, Artificial Intelligence and Robotics which could facilitate the world of manufacturing.

1. **3D printing service**- It is a process of manufacturing three dimensional solid things from a digital image. This latest manufacturing technology uses the virtual model to manufacture items by printing layers of materials. It offers cost-effectiveness with its emphasis on lean production. Across the aftermath of COVID-19, the Digital Manufacturing Network has grown in all types of industries, including aerospace, automotive, healthcare, defence, and others. With mega-projects on the horizon in India, it has enormous potential. HP has formed agreements with renowned industrial businesses such as Siemens and BASF in order to speed up the design and manufacture of 3D printed products on a large scale. The entire 3D printing community has banded together to combat the pandemic.
2. **Internet of Things (IoT):** In the digital transformation process, the IOT is equally crucial. The IoT, which is a major disruptor, is the introduction of critical IOT technologies in the industry. With the growth of IoT in consumer technology, the industrial sector has also begun to introduce this new sensor network and actuators for data processing, tracking, selection and process optimisation over the digital infrastructure. Indian companies have a lot of opportunity in this field, like many large companies. Indian Rail Network will roll out locomotives with tools such as remote diagnostics and constructive predictive maintenance, and these trains will be part of a broader ecosystem linked to the new technology.
3. **Digital Technologies**: With the rise of the digital era, Indian manufacturing firms have begun to incorporate digital technology in their manufacturing processes, which will help to improve productivity. It is projected that 65 per cent of manufacturing firms will have a high degree of digitalisation by the end of 2020. For its commercial vehicles, Ashok Leyland uses machine learning

techniques and its newly developed telematics unit to boost the efficiency of vehicles, drivers and so on.

4. **Artificial Intelligence (AI)**: To survive in the long run, manufacturing companies and factories must adopt automation. Artificial intelligence-driven robots contribute enormous value to the industrial process by automating activities, boosting production quality, and bringing machine-human interaction closer together.
5. **Robotics manufacturing** – Human employees work alongside robots. As a result, through precision, rapidity, and any material handling capacity, they can play a critical role in optimising assembling efficiency and enhancing production time. Human workers are empowered by robots because their deployment allows them to learn valuable skills and gain a competitive edge over their peers. Though stand-alone robotic workstations are already commonplace even in Indian companies, autonomous robots use improved senses, dexterity and intellect to optimise tasks or work human workers.

Comparison Between Today and Smart Factory

Academic models explaining the characteristics of Holonic Manufacturing Systems, such as versatility, modular, and decentralization decision-making and certain Smart Manufacturing System traits have been predicted (Leitao et. al., 2008; Borangiu et. al., 2009, Valckenaers, et. al., 2006). Industry 4.0 promises a new manufacturing paradigm characterised by increased socio-technical interaction. Each decentralised network is self-contained and capable of reacting to a wide range of events. The so-called Smart Industrial, the final feature of this new factory design, is the result of the digital and physical worlds meeting (Lee et. al., 2015). "In a world of rising complexity, a Smart Factory is a manufacturing solution that enables flexible and adaptable production processes to tackle problems that develop in a productive environment with changing conditions" (Radziwon et al., 2015). A Smart Factory can channel and filter data, regulate data overflow, and correct obsolete data, ensuring that the right person gets access to the right data at the right time. It should provide real-time data decision assistance to human employees in production operations, resulting in manufacturing process optimization (Erol et al. 2016; Davis, et al. 2012; Lucke et al. 2008). The Smart Factory's products, resources, and processes offer benefits in terms of reliability, speed, resources, and money as compared to traditional production systems. Manufacturing processes based on CPS are monitored and altered automatically, allowing them to respond to displayed in total time. The industrial revolution has given rise to the concept of "bottom-up" manufacturing value creation, which involves more than just new thinking and cost savings. Because of CPS's adaptability and network management capabilities, new and more prospective markets, such as improved customer-specific production processes, can emerge. Standalone manufacturing cells will be turned into seamless integration, computerized, and optimum production processes, increasing efficiency and altering connections among suppliers, consumers, and producers, as well as between humans and machines. A smart factory offers numerous benefits that a typical factory does not, including efficient resources use, machine adaptability to the human work cycle, and operational efficiencies.

Applications of Smart Technology and Industry 4.0

New paradigms in industry management and engineering are being created by Industry 4.0 and smart technology adoption. In fact, each application scenario refers to a problem or a challenge that a user experiences, as explained in the business context. Table 1 summarises the application scenarios.

Table 1. Applications of smart industry 4.0

Applications	Description
Value-Based Services	IT systems that collect, analyze, and process data from product use in order to provide personalized services and build client loyalty are critical in this situation.
Plug-and-Produce Adaptable Factories	This scenario primarily depicts a factory's capacity to adjust through physical conversion as a result of modularity, which is particularly appealing to businesses whose orders are influenced by products originality and changing demand.
Transparency and Flexibility of Supplied Products	Delivered goods gather data on their own for the sake of optimizing company operations, developing new business models, and dynamically adapting product features. This application scenario illustrates how goods are evolving to become more flexible in design.
Self-Organizing Adaptive Supply chain	More decentralized, agile, and autonomously interacting materials-handling modules and reliable distribution logistics, as well as the deployment of more flexible and faster industrial and logistical systems, are all part of this scenario.

Challenges in India For Development of Smart Factories

India's current infrastructure must be improved in order to enable manufacturers and potential enterprises looking to establish plants in the country. We need to be able to compete with China's facilities and amenities, which have been in place for many years. It entails developing roads and highways, as well as ensuring a consistent supply of power and electricity for manufacturers to maintain a steady flow of output. Post-pandemic 2020, the world of sophisticated technology will change the four building blocks of the industrial industry into the New Normal.

1. **Material:** The global supply chain for raw materials relies heavily on one source. It will be subject to significant disruption, with most countries/industry announcing either move to alternative, near-shore or domestic locations. It will create new opportunities for countries such as India to become a manufacturing hub. However, this necessitates a well-organised plan to produce the right quality products, achieve economies of scale, and finally reduce costs. Advanced Technology can help to achieve this plan by which the entire supply chain can be automated and managed remotely, at anytime, anywhere.
2. **Machines:** There is also an excellent sign for traditional factories or brownfields, as emerging technology platforms offer the opportunity to digitise non-digital assets and protect existing investments. Industry 4.0 ushers in a new era of highly intelligent and connected equipment, producing a totally digital supply chain. It helps transform traditional plants into smart factories by combining communications, IT, data, and physical aspects throughout the value chain.
3. **Manpower:** Skilled labour has always been an issue, but in today's society, when people's needs have altered to be safe and secure, it will become even more difficult. Remotely controlled robots linked to computer systems that use Machine Learning algorithms can run manufacturing plants with little human intervention. On-duty personnel's safety and protection are very critical, particularly in remote and hazardous places. Today, connected and wearable devices help employees manage and track their workers on a single dashboard in real-time. It helps to provide urgent support and relief to staff in emergencies.
4. **Methods:** People, procedures, and business operations will all be transformed completely. Remote monitoring, problem detection, and control of machines for maintenance and predictive on-demand maintenance activities are possible because to the combined power of computers and automation. It also enables product quality uniformity at a lower output cost.

GOVERNMENT MEASURE TO BOOST MANUFACTURING INDUSTRY

Indian central government, state industry departments are already examining proposals at different levels. This could be seen alongside with formation of new policies by Indian authorities to promote its manufacturing industry.

1. To promote mobile phone manufacturing in India, the government had declared three policies in March with incentives totalling Rs. 48,000 crore and the production-linked incentive (PLI) scheme has a significant share close to Rs. 41,000 crore with sops to be spread over three years.
2. Rs 1,70,000 crores funding by the government to the transportation industry, includes expenditure in bridges, highways, railway, ships, docks and aviation safety.
3. The government has announced to create 100 million manufacturing jobs by 2022 in the "Make in India" programme. Also, Rs 6,940 crores have been allocated for the coming eight years. Additionally, 100 per cent Foreign Direct Investment is permitted in this sector through the automatic route.
4. The drive to reduce corporation taxes has resulted in India to be one of the lowest corporate tax rates globally, which is at 15 per cent for a new upcoming manufacturing organisation in India. It clearly shows the goal of the Indian government to grow the manufacturing industry as a significant share of national GDP.
5. India has projected USD 1.5 trillion in spending to develop capability and increase its infrastructure over the next five years.
6. The goal of doubling the current port capacity of 1500 MT, which has itself doubled over the last five years, is a positive one as rising port freight, shipbuilding capacity and the usage of portland for renewable energy production would further drive the manufacturing agenda.
7. The qualifying suppliers of listed 53 essential bulk drugs will get financial benefits for their increased revenue over the base year (2019-20) over a term of 6 years.
8. Out of 53 listed bulk drugs, 26 are bulk-based ferment drugs, and 27 are bulk-based chemical synthesis drugs.
9. The bonus rate would be 20% (of incremental market value) for bulk-based fermentation drugs and 10% for bulk-based chemical synthesis drugs.
10. Jump in India's place from 77th to 63rd in the World Bank's Ease of Doing Business Index testifies to India's government capacity and effort.

CONCLUSION

The continuing pandemic of COVID-19 caused temporary closures at numerous production facilities around sectors, leaving the supply chain cycle across the globe badly affected. Now that factories have resumed activities, the main emphasis is on returning to the average rate of production. It is not a simple job, but the Smart Automation technologies of Industry 4.0 are emerging to the assistance of businesses, not just to help them regain full productivity quicker, but also to improve operating productivity. The present paper provides an overview about Industry 4.0 and key enabling technologies such as Internet of Things (IoT), Machine Learning, robotics, digital technologies, 3D Printing, Artificial Intelligence and Robotics for the realization of smart factories. In particular, a set of application scenarios has been presented in order to evaluate the impacts of such technologies in real industrial scenarios. Smart Factory would improve the quality of the product and its efficiency as producers do not have to think about downfall and the loss of sales that goes with it.

REFERENCES

Borangiu, T. (2009). A service-orientated arhitecture for holonic manufacturing control. In *Towards Intelligent Engineering and Information Technology* (pp. 489–503). Springer. doi:10.1007/978-3-642-03737-5_35

Cepin, M., & Bris, R. (2017). *Safety and Reliability. Theory and Applications*. CRC Press. doi:10.1201/9781315210469

Davis, J., Edgar, T., Porter, J., Bernaden, J., & Sarli, M. (2012). Smart manufacturing, manufacturing intelligence and demand-dynamic performance. *Computers & Chemical Engineering*, *47*(12), 145–156. doi:10.1016/j.compchemeng.2012.06.037

Deshmukh, S. G. (2016). Manufacturing Competitiveness: Research Opportunities. *International Journal of Global Business and Competitiveness*, *11*(1), 1–6.

Erol, S., Schumacher, A., & Sihn, W. (2016, January). Strategic guidance towards Industry 4.0–a three-stage process model. In *International conference on competitive manufacturing* (*Vol. 9*, No. 1, pp. 495-501). Academic Press.

Felser, W., Kirsch, A., Kletti, J., Wießler, J., & Meuser, D. (2015). *Industrie 4.0 kompakt*. NetSkill Solutions.

Lee, J. (2015). Smart factory systems. *Informatik-Spektrum*, *38*(3), 230–235. doi:10.100700287-015-0891-z

Leitao, P., & Restivo, F. J. (2008). Implementation of a holonic control system in a flexible manufacturing system. *IEEE Transactions on Systems, Man and Cybernetics. Part C, Applications and Reviews*, *38*(5), 699–709. doi:10.1109/TSMCC.2008.923881

Lucke, D., Constantinescu, C., & Westkämper, E. (2008). Smart factory-a step towards the next generation of manufacturing. In *Manufacturing systems and technologies for the new frontier* (pp. 115–118). Springer. doi:10.1007/978-1-84800-267-8_23

Pratheeesh, J. T., & Arumugasamy, G. (2020). Impact of Coronavirus in Indian economy and banking sector-an overview. *Studies in Indian Place Names*, *40*(18), 2090–2101.

Radziwon, A., Bilberg, A., Bogers, M., & Madsen, E. S. (2014). The smart factory: Exploring adaptive and flexible manufacturing solutions. *Procedia Engineering*, *69*, 1184–1190. doi:10.1016/j.proeng.2014.03.108

RBI. (2020). Monetary Policy Report. Reserve Bank of India.

Rele, S. (2020). Emerging outbreaks and epidemic threats: The practicality and limitations in the development and manufacturing of treatments for Coronavirus (COVID-19). *Polymorphism*, *4*, 45–52.

Statistics, E. (2020). *National Statistical Office*. Ministry of Statistics and Programme Implementation. Government of India.

Valckenaers, P., Cavalieri, S., Germain, B. S., Verstraete, P., Hadeli, Bandinelli, R., Terzi, S., & Van Brussel, H. (2006). A benchmarking service for the manufacturing control research community. *Journal of Intelligent Manufacturing*, *17*(6), 667–679. doi:10.100710845-006-0036-y

Chapter 14
Blue Economy:
An Emerging Business and Employment Prospect in the Indian Ocean

Ram Singh
https://orcid.org/0000-0002-6565-3091
Quantum University, India

Sachin Chauhan
https://orcid.org/0000-0002-0073-9134
Quantum University, India

Rohit Bansal
https://orcid.org/0000-0001-7072-5005
Vaish Engineering College, India

ABSTRACT

The Indian Ocean is fundamentally related to the diverse economies, safety, reliability, and availability of jobs of its littoral zones. Notwithstanding, the amelioration in the financial and feasible issues in the edge are especially hard and tough whereas the nations, with varied political frameworks, advancement status, and plans, are home to 33% of the total populace that is widely dependent on marine resources for food. The chapter investigates the momentum administration structure of marine assets of the executives in the Indian Ocean and digs into the difficulties occurring in the blue economy improvement and prescribes approaches to propel blue economy administration to notify pressures and guarantee practical advancement in the locale, and it additionally investigates the flow administration design for blue economy and its substantial potential existing in the Indian Ocean district, especially with regards to fisheries, ecological security, and environmental change impacts.

DOI: 10.4018/978-1-6684-4745-1.ch014

INTRODUCTION

Sea worlds are the single biggest biological systems that cover almost three-fourths of the globe's surface. In this way, it is relevant to argue that it gives a gigantic field to arising unpredictable and interconnected improvement issues, for example, environmental change, occupations, trade, and security (Bouchard, C., & Crumplin, W. 2010). As per the indication by gauges by means of the Global Ocean Commission, sea assets contribute at least five percent of the world's GDP, secure the positions of three billion individuals, and support the employments of 350 million. Considering the world's maritime divisions, the Indian Ocean is said to be the third biggest one that covers a space of 70 million sq km that excessively incorporates broad Exclusive Economic Zones [EEZ] of various nations and huge "high oceans". The financial and concerns for improvement in the Indian Ocean edge are specifically difficult as maximum area of littorals are agricultural nations. These nations are however home to 33 percent of the total populace that are broadly dependant on marine assets for work and food security. The absolute size of this populace is directly subjected to the Indian Ocean's assets to pressures from contamination, environmental corruption and misuse or overtly abuse of marine resources (Bunce, M., Brown, K., & Rosendo, S. 2010).

As the number of inhabitants in the area is subjected to increment altogether in the upcoming years, its effect on the security of food and the economy related to marine assets would turn out to be more considerable (Rogers, A. D. 2013), Furthermore, the locale and its assets and amenities face multifarious difficulties from environmental change effects like ocean level ascent, sea fermentation, and outrageous climate occasions the last mentioned, thus, prompting changes in the dissemination of amphibian species, local area structures because of relocation, and diminished financial efficiency. It is basic, along these lines, to build participation towards protection and reasonable utilization of the seas, oceans, and marine assets as laid out in Goal 14 of the Sustainable Development Goals (SDG) (Bunce, M., Brown, K., & Rosendo, S. 2010) genuine endeavours are expected to show the developing pressing factors on sea assets, to guarantee worldwide security of food and secure jobs for the future posterity. The idea of 'Blue Economy' pointed toward producing occupations and building strength against environmental change and its accompanying ecological difficulties motivates the utilization of oceans and seas for manageable turn of events and comprehensive development, in the Mauritius Declaration on Blue Economy of September 2015, the Indian Ocean Rim Association (IORA) perceived the requirement for earnest activity towards further developed administration constructions to protect the sea's assets for people in the future (Pressey, R. L. 2014).

BLUE ECONOMY & INDIAN OCEAN

The Indian Ocean is proposed to turn into a prevailing worldwide international and financial power in the 21st century. Surely, the district's commitment to worldwide GDP has essentially expanded in the course of the previous century: from a normal of 6 to 7 percent in the year 1980 to 10 percent or $ 78 trillion of every 2014 (See Figure 1), in any case, in light of Gross National Income, there are three IOR nations i.e., namely Australia, Singapore, and the United Arab Emirates include amongst the main 20 countries with most noteworthy per capita net public pay. Attributable to the restricted land asset base, a large number of the waterfront and island IORCs are reliant upon marine assets for financial freedoms (Clark, B. M. 2006). Along these lines, seeking after the objectives of the blue economy is supposed to be basic to the locale's flourishing and improvement.

Figure 1. Global GDP (US$) since 1960 and the contributed percentage of Indian Ocean nations [13]

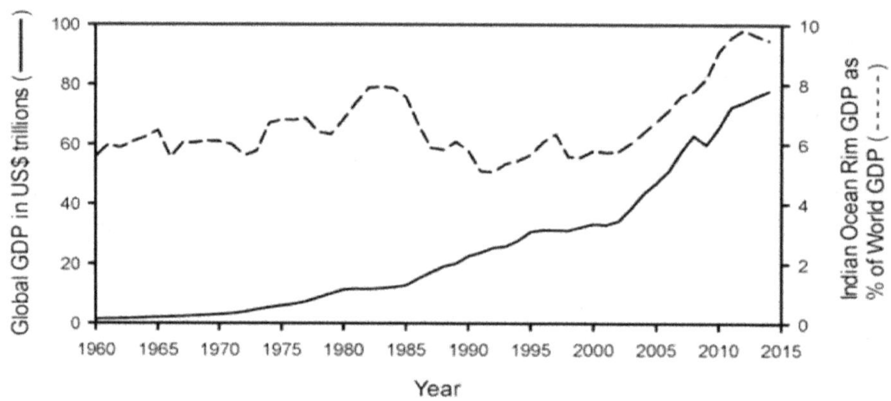

CONCEPTUAL FORMWORK OF BLUE ECONOMY

The 'Blue Economy' (BE) conceptualizes the seas as "shared advancement spaces". This is to say that the World Bank is characterised as the "manageable utilization of sea assets for financial development, further developed vocation and occupations, and sea biological system wellbeing". Frequently alluded to as "marine economy", "beach front economy", or "sea economy" in the writing, the idea is at an incipient stage and is still to be typified in a complete description according to a functional point of view (Smith, D. J. 2012). While the fundamental precepts and objectives of these standards might be comparable, there are contrasts in approaches and treatment regarding asset the board, development destinations, manageability, and social balance. For example, the expression "sea economy" alludes to the "decoupling of financial advancement from ecological corruption". Consequently, in such manner, "productivity and enhancement of normal marine assets inside biological cut-off points becomes principal". A "sea economy", in the interim, could be perceived through the information on the accompanying (Doyle, T. 2018).

1. A subdivision of the economy;
2. Dependent on the sea for contributions to fortify its creation cycle;
3. Industry based and furthermore topographical areas; and
4. These businesses/exercises are situated in beach front and non-seaside regions.

Apparently, the idea of "coastal economy" is bigger than "sea economy" which incorporates, grouping of exercises nearby the waterfront regions and amount of all exercises identifying with yield, work and wages in the seaside locale. In this way, (Colgan 2004) has characterized costal economy as "all monetary movement in the beach front district, and is subsequently the amount of work, wages, and yield in the area. A portion of the waterfront economy is the sea economy, yet the seaside economy fuses a more extensive arrangement of financial exercises". While, a marine economy is "on a level plane coordinated group ventures which incorporate areas implied for a typical market for the final results, utilizing normal innovation or workforce abilities, or require comparative regular assets". A subdivision of the seaside economy, the economy of marine incorporate business fish, marine transport, waterfront the travel industry and entertainment, sea life science and innovation, marine-related advancement and framework. In this regard, Australian Government, in its generated report named, 'Marine Nation 2025: Marine Science to Support Australia's Blue Economy' characterizes "Blue Economy" as "one in which our sea biological systems bring monetary and social advantages that are proficient, fair and economical" (Album, G. 2010). Whereas restricting the ideas around and points of BE, the Economist Intelligence Unit (2015) explained that the blue economy is almost equivalent to "greening of the sea economy," with advanced improvement suggestions by envisioning explicitly certain examples of creation and utilization of sea assets. According to this point of view, blue economy involves the transference of the old, "brown" the same old thing advancement model where seas are seen as a method with the expectation of complimentary asset extraction and waste unloading. This worldview doesn't acknowledge the expenses of the negative exteriorities to asset bookkeeping, neglecting the cognizant of the expenses of natural harm and biological lopsidedness by utilization. As far as concerns it's, the European Commission (2012) has characterized the scheme of blue economy as "all monetary exercises identified with the seas, oceans and coasts". The developing contest among the IOR nations over marine assets for their advancement features the requirement for improved provincial participation that permits them to bridle in a more feasible way. Reception of a complete meaning of BE is the initial move towards understanding and making a joint move to investigate the current capability of BE in the IOR area. Up until now, the idea of blue economy is as yet dependent upon various translations due to the inclusion of exercises, topographical areas and areas (Kelegama, S. 1998). From the accessible writing, a demonstrative rundown of areas and the exercises that comes under 'Blue Economy' is shown in Table 1. While a few investigations group various areas of blue economy into "conventional" and "arising" areas, there is not really any normal situation in this regard.

Table 1. Taxonomy of blue economy sectors and activities

Sector	Activity
Fishing	*Capture fishery, Aquaculture, seafood processing*
Marine Biotechnology	*Pharmaceuticals, Seaweed Harvesting, Marine Derived Bio-Products, Seaweed Products, Chemicals.*
Minerals	*Oil and gas, deep-sea mining*
Marine Renewable Energy	*Wave energy production, offshore wind energy production, tidal energy production*
Marine manufacturing	*Boat manufacturing, net manufacturing, sail making, boat and ship repair, aquaculture technology, water construction, marine industrial engineering, marine instrumentation.*
Shipping, Port & Maritime Logistics	*Ship owners & operators, ship management, ship building and repairing, shipping agents and brokers, liner and port agents, port companies, ship suppliers, container shipping services, stevedores, freight forwarders, safety & training custom clearance, roll-on roll-off operators.*
Marine Tourism & Leisure	*Sea angling from boats, sea angling from the shore, boating at sea, water skiing, surfing, sailing at sea, sail boarding, jet skiing, sea kayaking, scuba diving, bird watching in coastal areas, swimming in the sea, whale/dolphin watching, trips to the beach, seaside and islands, visiting coastal natural reserves.*
Marine Construction	*Marine Construction & Engineering*
Marine Commerce	*Marine financial services, ship finance & related services, charterers, media & publishing, marine insurance, marine legal services.*
Marine ICT	*Marine Engineering Consultancy, Hydro-Survey Consultancy, Project Management Consultancy, Submarine Telecom, Meteorological Consultancy, Environmental Consultancy, Geo-Informatics Services, Yacht Design, ICT Solutions.*
Education and research	*Education and training, R&D*

Source: Mohanty, Dash, Gupta and Gaur (2015).

BUSINESS AND EMPLOYMENT OPPORTUNITIES IN BLUE ECONOMY

The IORA Secretariat has recognized the accompanying six need columns in the blue economy as were suggested by the Council of Ministers meeting and amended by the Secretariat in discussion with Member States: Fisheries and Aquaculture, Renewable Ocean Energy, Seaports and Shipping, Offshore Hydrocarbons and Seabed Minerals, Marine Biotechnology, Research and Development, Tourism.

Fisheries and Aquaculture

Fisheries, which is an essential maritime asset frames the centre of the Blue Economy, as the most the fundamental assets of the Indian Ocean that give food to countless individuals and enormously add to the livelihoods of waterfront networks. It assumes a significant part in guaranteeing food security, neediness mitigation and furthermore has a substantial prospective for business openings. There has been a solid expansion in fish creation from 861,000 tons in 1950 to 11.5 million tons in the year 2010 and the world's all out interest for catch fish and fisheries items is relied upon to ascend from 50 million to 183 million tons in the year 2015, with hydroponics exercises anticipated to cover around 73 percent of this increment. Hydroponics that offers enormous possibility for arranging food and jobs, attempts to consolidate the worth of the normal investment in its turn of events, under the Blue Economy. Moreover, pertaining to the natural boundaries all through the pattern of creation, making maintainable, fair work, and offer high-esteem wares for send out. To satisfy the expanding public need for fish items, normal fisheries assets are being over-taken advantage of and undermined. Subsequently, the earnest need to discover a harmony between populace need and ecological wellbeing has given the driving force to the advancement of supportable fishing and hydroponics. All around oversaw fisheries are supposed to convey billions more in worth and a huge number of tons a few more fish every year, while hydroponics maintains the potential for proceeded with solid development to make available the food prerequisites of a developing world.

UNDERSTANDING OF RENEWABLE OCEAN ENERGY

The total populace is relied upon to increment to an expected 9 billion individuals in 2050, which is 1.5 occasions more noteworthy than the existing populace, expanding nations' requests on petroleum products. As of late there has been a breakdown in the cost of raw petroleum, however the chance of a possible standardization ought not to be dismissed and accordingly requires the proceeded with consideration of

IORA Member States to think about elective inexhaustible wellsprings of energy. Inexhaustible wellsprings of energy, for example, sun powered and wind are as of now being executed around the world. Be that as it may, extra motivating forces in sustainable power are firmly sought after two additional lessening the weight on petroleum products. The time is along these lines suitable to investigate the capability of sustainable power got from the sea. The sea proffers immense prospective for inexhaustible "blue energy" from various natural resources such as wave, flowing, warm, and biomass energy. In accordance with the aforementioned endeavours, it is to propose as such to unite the seaward oil and gas local area with the sustainable sea energy local area to embrace a whole investigation to Oil and Gas investigation. In such manner, the potential for fostering the gas industry as well as the seaward oil in the Indian Ocean area ought to likewise be thought about (Vliet, V. V. 2017).

SUBSTANTIAL SIGNIFICANCE OF SEAPORTS & SHIPPING

The seaport and sea transport or shipping areas are the most significantly required areas that come under the Blue Economy. Concerning this viewpoint, the Member States are showing more noteworthy interest in this area. Disregarding the consistent ascent of sea transport and delivery exchanges in the locale, lopsided conveyance of exchange subsists among the edge nations, where just a small bunch are providing benefits monetarily from sea trades and transportation. Some Member States lamentably are battling to stay up with the fast turn of events and intricacy of oceanic exchange as they face difficulties as far as blockage, new data innovation, and hardware, improvement of port framework, and expert administrations. In such manner, local participation is significant for opening the blockages to ports advancement and sea economy development in the Indian Ocean to upgrade blue development all the way through financial collaboration and the relations of exchange between the Member States (Barnwell, S. 2016).

IMPLICATIONS OF OFFSHORE HYDROCARBONS & SEABED MINERALS

Due to the diminishing inland mineral stores and expanding modern requests, much needed consideration is centred on the investigation of mineral and seabed mining. Furthermore, the seabed mineral resources address a fast pace in creating opportunity for monetary improvement in the Exclusive Economic Zones of beach front countries as well as the restrictions of public purview (Barnwell, S. 2016). The investigation of seabed in the Indian Ocean however maintains the substantial limitations in the commercialization of all such assets that lies in the way that Member States have restricted information on the assets. Moreover, the Exclusive Economic Zone (EEZ) has needed limit with respect to investigation, mining and preparing of these minerals.

RESEARCH & DEVELOPMENT IN BLUE BIOTECHNOLOGY

Blue Biotechnology is viewed as a space of an incredible inclination and potential because of the commitment towards the structure of an eco-feasible and developing society. A crucial perspective is identified with hydroponics, whereas new techniques will assist in: specific rearing of discrete species; expanding manageability of creation; and improving creature government assistance, remembering changes for food supply, preventive remedial measures, and utilization of zero-squander distribution frameworks. Hydroponics items will likewise be improved to acquire ideal wholesome properties for human wellbeing. One more essential space of marine biotechnology is identified with the improvement of environmentally friendly power items and cycles, for instance using marine green growth. Moreover, the marine climate is a to a great extent undiscovered wellspring of novel mixtures that could be possibly utilized as original medications, wellbeing, nutraceuticals, and individual consideration items; (Khan, R. 2021) Blue Biotechnology could be additionally engaged with resolving key natural issues, for example, in bio-detecting advances to permit in situ marine observing, in bioremediation and in creating savvy and non-harmful antifouling innovations. At long last, marine-determined particles would be of maximum utility as mechanical items or would be utilized in modern cycles as novel compounds, biopolymers, as well as biomaterials.

SCOPE OF DEVELOPMENT IN TOURISM INDUSTRY

Tourism industry is one of the fastest developing industries related to marine areas on the planet and is on the ascent in the IORA locale. Pertaining to this, the watching of whales and dolphins, the travel industry is probable to make financial, social, and ecological advantages, for example, comprehensive monetary development and occupation creation for seaside networks, while additionally uplifting the insurance of distinct species of marine and territories. The Indian Ocean area is common to numerous remarkable species of marine, including weak species, for example, the humpback dolphin of the Indian Ocean and the humpback whale of the Arabian Sea. Marine creatures like dolphins and whales are socially critical to numerous part of states. Being a threat to sea wellbeing and species of marine on the ascent, guarantee that the watching of dolphins and whales is moral, economical, non-obtrusive, and alright for the two vacationers and creatures. Perceiving such notion, the IORA Sustainable Whale and Dolphin Watching Tourism Network were set up in the year 2016 in order to uplift IORA part states to become world innovators in supportable practice (Roy, A. 2019). The motivation behind such Network is to give a provincial discussion to key partners to work with the trading of involvement, data, and mastery on whale and dolphin watching, as well as to energize joint effort.

SUBSTANTIAL POTENTIALS OF BLUE ECONOMY IN THE INDIAN OCEAN

'Blue Economy was for the first time expressed by Gunter Pauli in the year 2010 and then examined at the United Nations Conference on Sustainable Development, Rio+20 in 2012. Undoubtedly, BE has not only elevated as a compelling idea in the Indian Ocean district but also an amazing and challenged talk amongst the part conditions of the main provincial administration association, the Indian Ocean Rim Association's (IORA). In conceptualizing various IORA states have been unequivocally upholding for expanded participation and further developed administration of BE. Bangladesh, for one, has been at the cutting edge of local endeavours to advance BE; in 2014 it turned into the principal nation to have a significant gathering zeroed in on offering a Bay of Bengal organization for the Blue Economy. Furthermore, it was taken under trail by an IORA-coordinated gathering, so as to bring improvement in BE and a perfect backdrop for comprehensive Sustainable Development, in the year 2015. Such endeavours prompted an expanded spotlight on maintainable advancement in the Indian Ocean area as well as the development of the IORA Declaration on Enhancing Blue Economy Cooperation for Sustainability. In this way, BE acquired significance in India's key and improvement vision. In relation to this, Indian Prime Minister Narendra Modi expressed it as an apparatus for the country's turn of events, accentuating the assurance of joint marine spaces for 'Security and Growth for All in the Region' [30]. As far as his viewpoint is concerned, the previous leader of the Republic of Seychelles, James Alix Michel, advocated the idea according to the viewpoint of "Little Island Developing States (SIDS)" in his recently published book in 2016, 'Rethinking the Oceans: Towards the Blue Economy'.

Table 2. The national estimation of blue economy

Country	Size of Blue Economy			Indicative Employment	
	Year	Output (US$ Billion)	% of GDP	Year	No.
Australia	2004	17.00	3.6	-	-
Canada	2004	15.98	1.5	2006	1,71,365
France	2006	16.69	1.4	2009	4,59,358
New Zealand	2006	2.14	2.0	-	-
United Kingdom	2008	84.27	4.2	2006	5,48,674
United States	2009	138.0	1.2	2010	2,770,000
China	2010	239.09	4.0	2010	9,253,000
Ireland	2007	1.9	1.0	2007	17,000

Sources: Compiled by RIS from various sources

(Note: Data as per the size of blue economy in selected countries. The conception and methodology differs across the given sources, in which such numbers are indicative.)

The Indian Ocean locales insistently continue in giving a novel biological system and availability courses of the assets for the upcoming centuries. The development of innovation as well as the capacities has extended the chances in advance. Maintained and supportable development of the blue economy in the Indian Ocean wills definitely need purposeful endeavours by the government, the private area, and the more extensive local area, including the logical ones. As far as home grown utilization and exchange is concerned, there has been a huge ascent in the quantity of particular economic accords in the previous twenty years (World Trade Organization, 2011). However, the Indian Ocean nations linger behindhand the remainder of the entire globe, particularly contrasted with the United States and Europe had have a lot more arrangements set up (See Map 1). Without a non-provincial way to deal with reasonable monetary development, late upgrades and endeavours being sought after by IOR nations towards worldwide combination and expanded usefulness would be sabotaged (Satia, B. P. 2016).

Figure 2. Membership in preferential trade agreements as at 2010 (reproduced with permission WorldTrade Organisation, 2011)
Source: Llewellyn, English and Barnwell, 2016.

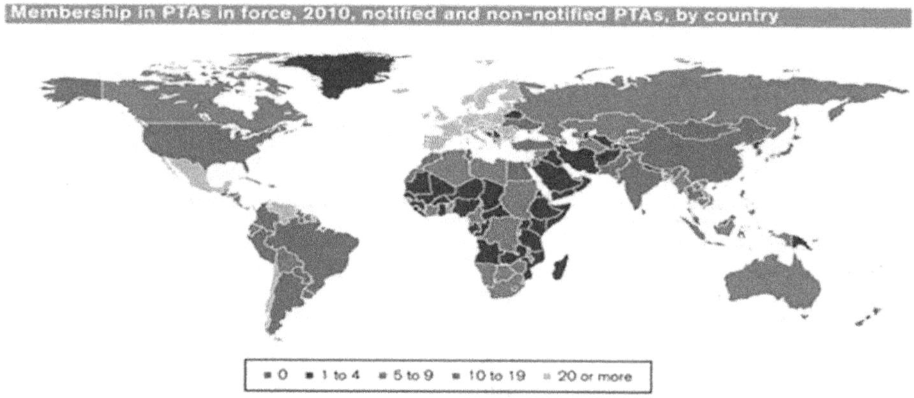

An expanded approach focal point of Indian Ocean littoral zones towards BE is definitely cause to notice the financial capability of the common marine assets and their capability to add to bigger advancement goals like destitution decrease, food security, and upgraded monetary freedoms. Be that as it may, this acknowledgment ought to be joined by attention to get monetary advancement from the marine assets while guaranteeing the preservation and practical administration of the marine environment. In this specific circumstance, an expanded political and monetary consideration regarding reasonable administration of marine assets is basic to cultivate better administration, safety and security for its huge assets. Steinberg experienced that the ocean is presently being perceived as an "asset rich however delicate space requiring judicious administration for reasonable turn of events" (Steinberg, P. E. 1999). It is basic, subsequently, to investigate existing law and strategy structures, especially for the security of food and reasonable administration, to understand the holes, and offer answers for the betterment in the administration of the district.

FISHERIES MANAGEMENT FOR SUSTAINING HUMAN POPULATION

Undoubtedly, fisheries are one of the most important means of sustaining human population for many ages. It also engages a healthy aquaculture that seems to be a critical element of global protein supply. In this viewpoint, The Indian Ocean's aquaculture is hindered in governance challenges that need a major overhaul. Whereas countries of IOR maintains their own specific laws, rules, regulations and policies that govern fisheries management and jurisdiction that come under them. In continuation with this, it is evidently true, that they are majorly not effective in alleviating illegal, unregulated and unreported (IUU) fishing (Jia, J. 2009). In not complying with domestic regulations and licenses it directly indicates towards the denial of economic profits from their proper owners, thereby intensifying domestic conflicts. Moreover, the challenges have a negative impact on the income of government, social distribution of benefits, accurateness in the given report and effective monitoring to maintain sustainability in fishing. Undeniably, the present status and architecture of fisheries management may bring negative impact in the capacity of fisheries so as to satisfy the growing demand of protein of the huge world population. "The IOR is home to both, business fishing and means exercises, while business fishing is to a great extent worked by unfamiliar fishing vessels from Europe and Asia in far off waters zeroed in on fish and comparable species, fishing in the area remains generally at the means level, including beach front networks getting to the assets for their nearby job". The worldwide yields from catch fisheries have settled as of late because of more notable consideration towards hydroponics. However, it stays a test to keep a supportable stock of fish. India Ocean fish, for instance, is a noteworthy donor, establishing a fourth of worldwide stockpile. Nonetheless, the heft of fish yields is cornered by unfamiliar vessels, obstructing the development of nearby fisheries. As outer gatherings keep on fishing activity in the Indian Ocean waters, it turns out to be more important to discover arrangements that go past provincial purviews (Techera, E. J. 2018). While critical divergence exists inside the part states as far as maintainable administration of the marine species and BE objectives, a local methodology would develop greater and less unpredictable development openings in the area. Be that as it may, this would definitely need a proof based approach upheld by nuanced information.

CURRENT STATUS OF BLUE ECONOMY GOVERNANCE AT NATIONAL LEVEL

The majority of the IORA part states initiated to plan their particular public strategies and enforced laws that independently pay heed to the issues relating to reasonable administration of distinct species depended on for their food, climate protection including area, marine, and change in environmental condition. Their execution, in any case, is changed. For example, South Africa's Constitution explicitly accommodates the option in order to get the regular assets and a climate helpful for human wellbeing that tends to feasible turn of events and biological honesty; natural protection, thusly, has a unified centre. The nation has ordered numerous arrangements and laws, for example, National Environmental Act 1998, Integrated

Coastal Management Act 2008, Disaster Management Act, Biodiversity Act 2004, and Environment Conservation Act 1989, pointed toward tending to reasonable advancement challenges, intergenerational value and the right to an ideal climate. In addition, fisheries have a different committed guideline the "Marine Living Resources Act 1998", covering dimensional arranging, permit grants for business fishing, and economical utilization of marine assets. In spite of this, there is as yet a shortage of deliberate activities that straightforwardly react to guaranteeing food security or tending to environmental change. Mozambique, in the interim, has presented important laws, for example, the Forestry and Wildlife Law, Fisheries Law and Local Organs Law, Environment Law 1997, and the National Adaption Program of Action, 2007 that spotlights on incorporated and feasible administration of the marine climate and activities to moderate the change in environment. Be that as it may, a feeble administration structure has brought about the abuse of the country's indigenous habitat, alongside helpless execution and delicate oversight instruments (Mishra, M. 2020). The greater part of the IORA part states, particularly the Small Island Developing States (SIDS), give a comparative representation. In this way, whereas attention is given to the dangers related to environmental change as well as natural debasement on the manageability of the restricted assets of marine living spaces, the absence of limit and helpless administration go about as blockages to execution.

Regional Level

Albeit the Indian Ocean littorals generally have come up short on a solid provincial system zeroed in on food security, supportable development and environment activity, there have been some important drives for a locale wide methodology to a great extent in the Indian Ocean Rim Association. Set up in 1997, IORA expects to accomplish "supported development and adjusted advancement of the area and of the part states and to make shared conviction for local co-activity". Its significant projects, for example, the Fisheries Support Unit (FSU) work to adjust the development in the area of fishing despite unlawful fishing and stocks exhaustion, just to restrict marine contamination. Consequently, IORA is most appropriate to give a structure to exercises identified with environmental change and the security of food. The 2013 Perth Communiqué of IORA is focused on "serene, useful and reasonable utilization of the sea and its assets" and supports feasible marine asset the board while combating illicit fishing through limit building. Since various countries are presently centred on the blue economy plan, limit building projects and studios for its progression have acquired force. There has been critical advancement as of late with the reception of the Jakarta Concord that again confirmed obligation to fisheries the executives through "science-based methodologies, advancing maintainable works on, building limit, tending to violations in the fisheries area and fortifying the FSU."Other than the endeavours drove by IORA, the Large Marine Ecosystems (LMEs) drives in the area have additionally made a critical commitment on the way to the preservation of the marine climate at the provincial level. The African LMEs under the condition of working have been in associations through various commissions, projects, and approaches for insurance in case of environmental change hazards (Vivekanandan, E., Hermes, R., & O'Brien, C. 2016). The Bay of Bengal LME drive is pointed toward further developing fisheries the executives and administration systems for improving the variation and flexibility of the marine environment. Moreover, the current provincial foundations in the Indian Ocean have set up associations to arrange exploration and the board exercises in the district. For example, the southwest Indian Ocean Fisheries Project (SWIOFP) and the UNEP WIO-Lab Project have worked together to make the 'Western Indian Ocean Sustainable Ecosystem Alliance' (WIOSEA), taking into consideration coordinated ways to deal with seas administration across huge scopes. While there have been some outstanding drives as of late, notwithstanding, local endeavours in the Indian Ocean have generally stayed disconnected, without a brought together law and strategy system. For example, while the Indian Ocean Commission (IOC) has fostered a Regional Climate Action Plan during 2016–2020, its execution was certainly scant because of its chief spotlight on territorial financial turn of events. Territorial arrangements like the African Convention on the Conservation of Nature and Natural Resources (ACCNNR), and the Nairobi Convention for the Protection, Management, and Development of the Marine and Coastal Environment of the Eastern African Region, just as the "Relationship for South East Asian Nations (ASEAN)", dynamically engaged in the space of biological system preservation and environmental change. Nonetheless, they could just assume a digressive part in working with local soundness in the Indian Ocean district as their extension reaches out past the area (van der Geest, C. 2017).

INTERNATIONAL LAW & FRAMEWORK

Different worldwide peaceful accords give a typical stage to law and strategy improvements in the Indian Ocean district. Most of the Indian Ocean States confirmed the vital worldwide ecological settlements and structure for seas administration that make commitments to ensure and save the marine climate. These remember the United Nations Framework Convention for Climate Change (UNFCCC), Convention on Biological Diversity (CBD), Convention on Migratory Species (CMS), Convention on International Trade in Endangered Species (CITES), United Nations Convention on the Law of the Sea (UNCLOS) and the Agreement on the Conservation and Management of Straddling Fish Stocks and Highly Migratory Fish

Stocks. Nonetheless, it is noticed that there was an absence of explicitness in rules in accomplishing the objectives set out by these arrangements (van der Geest, C. 2017). The UNEP Regional Seas Program covering almost 18 areas of the world and the South Asian Seas Program that incorporates India, Bangladesh, Sri Lanka, Pakistan, and the Maldives as individuals, centres on Integrated Coastal Zone Management, natural impacts and issues related to environmental change. Notwithstanding, their absence of spotlight on fisheries and their restrictions in acting past the limits of part states present execution challenges across the whole Indian Ocean. Among the drives in case of fisheries, the Food and Agriculture Organization (FAO) assumes the most conspicuous part in standard-setting, dispersal of information, and advancement of the rules that can be best practiced (Vivekanandan, E., Hermes, R., & O'Brien, C. 2016). In contrast to the Pacific Island area, where joint effort through local bodies seems to be normal, the Indian Ocean district shows that though there are various worldwide laws, tasks, and projects in activity, "they infrequently include every single applicable nation or address fisheries and food security on an entire of-locale premise".

CHALLENGES AND IMPLICATIONS IN DEVELOPMENT OF 'BE' GOVERNANCE

The Indian Ocean states remained associated with one another by authentic ties, most regularly bound together through the oceans. Nonetheless, their variety as far as populace, country size, normal assets, and social legacy makes powerful local collaboration troublesome. Whereas there has been some improvement following the foundation of IORA, Chellaney contends that the area is yet "far away from turning into a local area of normal qualities". The administration plans of the Indian Ocean involve a few holes which impede the execution of blue development in the required area. Moreover, anintricated administrative scene that includes disparate sovereign laws, provincial plans just as worldwide laws adds to extra difficulties. While the majority of the Indian Ocean nations have formed their own fisheries guidelines, they need legitimate principles, rules, and requirement systems inferable from restricted information and limit limitations. The IORCs are confronted with the normal squeezing difficulties of expanding urbanization, industrialization, and relocation, coming about in over-double-dealing of regular marine assets. The populaces of these nations are projected to encounter sensational development by 2050; by then, at that point, they will by and large host almost 50 percent of the globe's kin. Such blast will be powered by the fast international and geo-monetary ascent in the region of Africa. In doing so, it will just increase the difficulties in future. Nations such as Seychelles, for example, are as of now going through quick urbanization that is adding pressure to the restricted land and seaside assets. Consequently, close the existent holes in frail administration, absence of compelling approaches and requirement measures, and bigger security situations like illicit fishing, to develop economical improvement practices and blue development in the locale. In this specific situation, it is basic to guarantee fitting natural administration of the marine environment, upheld by powerful law and strategy. Food security, along with that of shell fishes, used to be a worldwide test that is now in danger because of environmental change. The Indian Ocean locale is wealthy in fish assets and is the most significant spaces of worldwide fishing. More than 800 million individuals in the area depend on fish for their requirement of protein. As far as agribusiness is concerned, the agribusiness areas of the Asian and African agrarian economies are probably going to experience the ill effects of the effects of environmental change, it is normal that their dependence on fish would increment. Simultaneously, fisheries are now being seriously influenced by marine contamination and unlawful fishing, subsequently weakening biological systems and contrarily influencing the number of inhabitants in different marine species. Environmental change is probably going to fuel the adverse consequences and lead to additional corruption of marine species. Environmental change sway like disintegration and immersion could cause loss of beach front living spaces like mangroves, in this manner influencing the propagation of species. Fermentation and ascend in ocean temperature annihilate the coral reefs which remain basic to different species of ocean. The effect of environmental change cannot be claimed exclusively to be calamitous for the marine species all alone, yet in addition to the networks that rely upon them when expanding their extra financial and ecological tensions. For the economies that address critical security of future concerns and deflect financial misery, this would be pivotal to keep fisheries and marine climate the board as a first concern. Nonetheless, the capacity to respond to the expanding effect of environmental change on the marine biological system would differ as per human and normal topography, limit, and current just as projected debasement. Whereas fisheries guideline and law by the side of the public level used to exist for quite a long time, there is an absence of intelligible provincial game plan in the Indian Ocean that covers either all the IORCs or guarantees the security of different species. Also, absence of administration component, helpless information, and assets propose that there are not very many foundations, money, and specialized assets accessible to manage the difficulties. Concerning this, it is argued that there is no single overall association that comes under all IORC in its enrolment. For example, the Southern Indian Ocean Fisheries Agreement (SIOFA) includes just eight nations, and further freedoms for enrolment are confined thinking about the association's limit in covering just the high oceans of the southern Indian Ocean. Comparative is the situation with the Indian Ocean Tuna Commission (IOTC) and the Southern Indian Ocean Fisheries Commission (SIOFC). Albeit the IOTC maintains a more extensive reach, it is simply restricted to tending to Tuna-like species, consequently leaving different others vulnerable in various topographical regions. Accordingly, a significant deficiency with these Regional Fisheries Management Organizations (RFMOs) is their sectoral way to deal with sea the board with a restricted spotlight on specific kinds of marine species. In addition, a general focal point of local deals towards the southern Indian Ocean disregards the administrative concerns related with non-profoundly transient, shared, and riding fisheries assets in the high oceans in the northern district of the Indian Ocean. Nations like Bangladesh and Myanmar that are not piece of these deals keep on fishing in important regions. Without a trace of a provincial system, exploration, observing and authorization estimates keep on being scattered and do not have a substantial coordinated information on the Indian Ocean environment that could cultivate compelling administration instruments. A significant justification for the absence of progress in fisheries and natural administration in the locale is the absence of examination, excepting a little collection of organic and actual logical information. Pursue research composed at dealing with the specialized information on the seabed, ocean segment just as the practices of those whose vocations are subject to the soundness of the sea. There is additionally an absence of examination that spotlights on the complicated engineering of administration needed to build a provincial BE. The Indian Ocean and other far reaching fishing spaces of our nation face certain challenges in doing common business. For example, overfishing/impractical fishing practices could prompt exhaustion of assets consequently eliminating occupation openings for networks of such explicit destinations.

Moreover, the difficulties that a blue economy would and right now confronting are contamination, loss of territory and biodiversity, privateers, wrongdoing, and environmental change separated from the wide international issues. As indicated by IPCC's (Intergovernmental Panel on Climate Change) report on environmental change, "India is the thirteenth weakest country to environmental change". Dakshina Kannada and Udupi regions of Karnataka have detailed 28 percent of their coasts dissolved because of ocean level ascent. In another occasion, Andhra Pradesh beach front regions have seen a decrease in fish get. Extra ocean level ascent of 1 meter, which is a logical effect of environmental change, would uproot 7.1 million individuals in India, which is a basic issue that should be provided consideration to have supportable financial development and improvement in the fisheries area. Sewage contamination keeps on being a significant issue for India, particularly in beach front regions, creating 4067 million liters of home-grown sewage daily; 80 percent being conveyed into the ocean and in this manner killing the fish and other marine items and subsequently diminishing the market potential. The issues relating to anglers in the worldwide waterlines particularly with our adjoining nations are additionally going about as a disincentive towards the fishing area.

Intensifying the issues is frail coordination on the current administration courses of action regulating Indian Ocean-wide checking and requirement of supportable turn of events and blue development plans like fisheries the executives. While the provincial courses of action, for example, IOTC and SIOFA are exceptional so as to combat IIU fishing, deficiency in coordinating in case of public, local, and worldwide level is endangering successful multilateral and exhaustive administration instruments for the Indian Ocean. Instruments and authorization systems could be utilized for supportable fishing. These ought to incorporate Monitoring, Control and Surveillance (MCS) frameworks that usually cover reconnaissance, checking, investigations, perceptions, misgiving, revealing, preliminary and discipline, and satellite-based Vessel Monitoring Systems (VMS) to screen continuous vessels fishing on high oceans. Whereas the components for authorization and innovative arrangements are accessible, the issue lies with conflicting and irregular utilization of such devices, absence of limit with respect to execution, an absence of clearness over which entertainer has implementation rights, and nonappearance of organized collaboration. The presence of huge quantities of entertainers with various degrees of abilities, regularizing standpoints, and key mentalities makes it hard for a nation to take on the situation as a vital participant in blue development in the Indian Ocean. All these have been noticed on account of catch and exchange, documentation and joint assessment plans. Thusly, to accomplish the blue economy destinations of diminishing non-reasonable fishing and satisfying objectives for more extensive manageable improvement in the Indian Ocean, the most significant is the productive utilization of present checking and authorization measures, alongside the responsibility of state and non-state entertainers to feasible turn of events and its maritime measurements.

SUGGESTING A SUSTAINABLE GOVERNANCE FRAMEWORK FOR INDIAN BLUE ECONOMY

The partners in the Indian Blue Economy would involve three significant things that are as follows:

1. Secure and Sustainable Economic Growth
2. Increased Policy Certainty
3. Greater Social License to Operate.

To guarantee financial development in the locale and achieve food security, oversee fisheries and confine ecological debasement, and fortify versatility to environmental change chances, this paper therefore makes the accompanying suggestions:

Major Amelioration in Governance Framework

Combination of logical administration and implementation in the Indian Ocean would certainly need another system consent to be arranged, that could assume a conspicuous and lawfully inserted part in the area of manageable seas administration. Since IORA is focused on the goal of "fortifying the blue economy," the structure could be formed under the support of IORA. Also, IORA is the main provincial discussion uniting most nations on the Indian Ocean edge through a yearly unfamiliar pastors' gathering. In any case, for IORA to satisfy the commission would expect it to altogether support its assets and devoted initiative by key nations like India, Australia, and South Africa. The imagined comprehensive multidimensional structure understanding ought to present an arrangement of administration that gives an overall system to sub-provincial and sectoral techniques covering marine regions, designation of fishing rights, battling contamination, environmental change moderation, and many other foundational issues. Apparently, it would support diminishing the administrative weight made by various deals and administration programs in various covering regions. As of now, the administration and preservation of fish stocks in IORCs are represented by the UNCLOS and United Nations Fish Stocks Agreement, as essentially all nations in the area are individuals from to some degree both of the two. In any case, accomplishing a harmony between responsibilities at worldwide scales as well as at the degree of individual biological systems for practical administration of fisheries would require provincial level collaboration and authorization components. Accordingly, the current administration systems of Fisheries Support Units of territorial associations, for example, the Indian Ocean Tuna Commission (IOTC), Southern Indian Ocean Fisheries Agreement (SIOFA), Southwest Indian Ocean Fisheries Commission (SWIOFC), and IORA ought to be reinforced. Such requirements to remember the increment for the quantity of marine species like sharks, clear cut guideline of participation, and extra explicitness on obligations of the distinctive state entertainers. Since IOTC individuals have set out on modernizing their system, they have a chance to plan best practices while gaining from the difficulties that other comparative associations have confronted. Illustrations can be taken out from Regional Fisheries Management Organizations (RFMOs), for example, the Western and Central Pacific Fisheries Commission and the Inter-American Tropical Tuna Commission that oversees all species in the marine biological system like fish, sharks, seabirds, and turtles influenced by fishing. In any case, the change would require renegotiation by associations, for example, the IOTC and SIOFA that would have the option to foster restricting approaches for the part nations. To keep up with impartiality and adequacy, the exchanges should join agricultural nation help.

EXTENSIVE, EFFECTIVE COLLABORATION

One more fundamental element for the accomplishment of the administration structure and to guarantee compelling results is through the inclusion of significant partners, along with the business area and nearby networks. Whereas governments are the overseers of the prescribed laws, guidelines, and settlements, fishing is carried out by the organizations and neighbourhood fisher folk. While the scholarly world including the business area's experiences are now covered under the IORA's "three sided structure," the opinions of the private area and neighbourhood networks should be remembered for amended deals, measures, or approaches. One stage could propose the applicable non-state partner bunches a spectator status in new and existing conversation discussions. However, this would certainly empower their dynamic commitments in moulding strategy advancement, limit building, and execution. The IOTC is a valid example. Additionally, this ought to incorporate mainstream researchers, as imagined economical natural practices should be deductively upheld. The logical clarification is fundamental to make support among private entertainers, persuade partners that further developing reasonable fish stocks is to their greatest advantage, and limit misfortunes for organizations and anglers.

Strengthening Monitoring and Mechanisms of Enforcement

Complete and powerful Monitoring, Control, and Surveillance (MCS) frameworks are basic for the objectives of lessening non-reasonable fishing rehearses and accomplishing more extensive supportable improvement in the Indian Ocean. Effective utilization of observing and implementation components would work on the responsibility of state and non-state entertainers to BE and its maritime measurements. Information regarding the Indian Ocean and its logical examination are typically restricted and ineffectively shared. Coordinated frameworks to distinguish and stop rebelliousness through free check and evaluating, extra information assortment, further developed information sharing, logical investigations concerning fishing exercises and ecological effects in the district, and the actuation of consistence by vessels are expected to screen and further develop participation and administration across the Indian Ocean. Be that as it may, accomplishing this would need setting uniform principles for the assortment and announcing of fishery-subordinate information. The Niue Treaty Subsidiary Agreement for the South Pacific Region gives an illustration on the best way to pool restricted assets, limit, and resources for sharing fisheries information and knowledge while reinforcing the capacity to recognize and uphold fisheries laws. More logical comprehension over information assortment can work on monetary proficiency and authorization frameworks, accordingly upgrading ability to adapt to changing marine environments.

ADOPTION OF SPECIFIC POLICIES FOR MARINE LIFE & RESOURCES

The significance of the seas to country is regularly revealed in the separate marine approaches of the littoral nations in a more extensive strategy and administrative system. While seas and the distinctions to earthbound frameworks are all around perceived, less consideration is paid to explicit marine-related issues like food security, fisheries guideline, contamination, and environmental change in this manner befuddling the strategy settings that might be applied. In this way, it seems to be helpful in the long haul to detail marine approaches independently in a sub-head in the more extensive administration structure. This would empower an attention on "marine" assets specifically while coordinating various features of marine approach where suitable. A more clear system to work would give more noteworthy sureness to the business, in this manner diminishing the consistence weight and expenses for government, controllers, and the enterprises.

CONCLUSION AND FINDINGS

There are various reciprocal and multilateral arrangements that at present day tie the Indian Ocean littoral nations. Notwithstanding, not exclusively these systems are restricted in centre, they have likewise neglected to remember all significant partners for the quarrel. The IORA, for instance, with 21 part states and various worldwide protection and financial forces, is the most exhaustive plan that accepts the whole district under one discussion. However, the momentum engineering needs intelligible administration apparatuses, which could hinder supportable blue improvement in the Indian Ocean, even if it is endeavoured to resolve issues like food security, biological system the executives, and biodiversity protection. The variety of the nations of the district as far as topography, governmental issues, economy, and culture till now have prevented the advancement of local establishments, union, and interpretation of blue improvement objectives into actuality. Accomplishing the blue economy objectives would surely require broad collaboration between the local area of seaside states and a scope of different partners that incorporate the private area, non-administrative associations, logical and nearby networks. It is significant to learn illustrations, consistence components, and administrative models from different provincial bodies like the Pacific and Caribbean people group. Adjusting the best preferable practices to the Indian Ocean setting would fill the momentum hole of a solid establishment of regionalism whereupon novel ways to deal with fisheries, environmental change, and food security can be easily created. Blue Economy is being seen as an all encompassing improvement worldview that spreads a development cycle that burdens the ideal and proficient usage of marine assets without compromising the manageability angles. Basically, blue economy worldview underscores upon most extreme and monetarily proficient usage of undertook advantage of marine assets or novel marine assets which remain as of now not utilized either for family usage or for business purposes. This methodology with regard to marine assets suits perfectly to the waterfront countries whose monetary prosperities rely upon the marine assets especially the Small Island Developing States (SIDSs) like Seychelles and Mauritius. Indeed, even the high level economies like the USA, Canada and Australia cogitate blue economy as the novel wellspring of financial development particularly after the monetary downturn ensuing the Subprime emergency in 2007. Overall, all seaside countries across the pay classifications currently see blue economy as a significant area of their economies which is reflected in the order of explicit enactments and projects for sea advancement. Numerous nations in the Indian Ocean area including India, Australia, Bangladesh, South Africa, Kenya, Mauritius and Seychelles see blue economy as a key monetary area for accomplishing financial development and other formative targets. Though there exists a type of agreement over the capability of blue economy (essentially as far as more extensive destinations) for social and financial turn of events, vulnerability beats its evaluation and observational approval. As of now, there is no such all around OK meaning of blue economy which not just makes trouble for estimation of its size and related markers yet additionally influences the approach making measure for sea asset improvement and the board. In view of accessible writing (Mohanty, Dash, Gupta and Gaur 2015) have endeavoured to explain those quarrelsome issues to a sensible degree, Blue economy comprehensively shelters living assets, for example, fisheries and oceanic plants and non-living assets like Polymetallic knobs, cobalt outside, uncommon earth metals and different minerals, oil and gas, port and transportation, beach front the travel industry, marine biotechnology, marine business, etc. Of those, catch fishery, oil and gas investigation, delivery, waterfront the travel industry and so forth are the conventional areas while multi-specie hydroponics, fish preparing, marine inferred bio-items, kelp items, journey the travel industry and innovative marine items are a portion of those arising areas of blue economy. Other than their present degree of commitment, there is tremendous potential existing in the previously said areas for expansion and modern applications. "There is a peril that highway struggle in the IOR in the coming years could be driven by rivalry less over political impact but rather more over scant assets (Chellaney, B. 2010)." Therefore, tending to local dependability and different stressors on assets because of environmental change impacts and natural debasement would critically require a bound together, comprehensive, multi-scalar, and incorporated provincial reaction to guarantee reasonable administration of marine assets. Central Marine Fisheries Research Institute (CMFRI) gauges have shown that, in India, for the year

2014, complete marine arrivals is 3.59 million tons, which is a 5 percent decay when contrasted with 3.78 million tons for the year 2013 (Nambudiri, 2015). To finish up, there is a lot of extension for development in the Indian fishery area like mechanical advancements, foundation projects, opening up promising circumstances for research and improvement by joint effort with set up scholarly establishments, powerful administration in handling issues like contamination, unlawful exchange, and ocean bed mining, and so forth

FUTURE SCOPE OF THE STUDY

It is in effect additionally accentuated to restoring lost linkages between scholastics, think tanks, government functionaries to work with worldwide exchange and sea exercises in the Indian Ocean district. Being one of the biggest and unmistakable makers of fish by catch and hydroponics on the planet, India, should find ways to reinforce its binds with different nations in global exchange and take a stab at outperforming China, and become the prominent supporter of the blue economy.

ABBREVIATIONS

Table 3.

ACCNNR: African Convention on the Conservation of Nature and Natural Resources	**SDG:** Sustainable Development Goals
ASEAN: Association for South East Asian Nations	**SIDS:** Small Island Developing States
BE: Blue Economy	**SIOFA:** Southern Indian Ocean Fisheries Agreement
CBD: Convention on Biological Diversity	**SWIOFP:** South West Indian Ocean Fisheries Project
CITES: Convention on International Trade in Endangered Species	**UNCLOS:** United Nations Convention on the Law of the Sea
CMFRI: Central Marine Fisheries Research Institute	**UNFCCC:** United Nations Framework Convention on Climate Change
CMS: Convention on Migratory Species	**WIOSEA:** Western Indian Ocean Sustainable Ecosystem Alliance
EEZ: Exclusive Economic Zones	**IORA:** Indian Ocean Rim Association
FSU: Fisheries Support Unit	**IOTC:** Indian Ocean Tuna Commission
GDP: Gross Domestic Product	**LMEs:** Large Marine Ecosystems
GOC: Global Ocean Commission	**RFMO:** Regional Fisheries Management Organizations
MCS: Monitoring, Control and Surveillance	

REFERENCES

Ban, N. C., Maxwell, S. M., Dunn, D. C., Hobday, A. J., Bax, N. J., Ardron, J., & Pressey, R. L. (2014). Better integration of sectoral planning and management approaches for the interlinked ecology of the open oceans. *Marine Policy*, *49*, 127–136. doi:10.1016/j.marpol.2013.11.024

Bijma, J., Pörtner, H. O., Yesson, C., & Rogers, A. D. (2013). Climate change and the oceans–What does the future hold? *Marine Pollution Bulletin*, *74*(2), 495–505. doi:10.1016/j.marpolbul.2013.07.022 PMID:23932473

Bouchard, C., & Crumplin, W. (2010). Neglected no longer: The Indian Ocean at the forefront of world geopolitics and global geostrategy. *Journal of the Indian Ocean Region*, *6*(1), 26–51. doi:10.1080/19480881.2010.489668

Bunce, M., Brown, K., & Rosendo, S. (2010). Policy misfits, climate change and cross-scale vulnerability in coastal Africa: How development projects undermine resilience. *Environmental Science & Policy*, *13*(6), 485–497. doi:10.1016/j.envsci.2010.06.003

Chellaney, B. (2010). Indian Ocean maritime security: Energy, environmental and climate challenges. *Journal of the Indian Ocean Region*, *6*(2), 155–168. doi:10.1080/19480881.2010.536662

Clark, B. M. (2006). Climate change: A looming challenge for fisheries management in southern Africa. *Marine Policy*, *30*(1), 84–95. doi:10.1016/j.marpol.2005.06.006

Clifton, J., Etienne, M., Barnes, D. K., Barnes, R. S., Suggett, D. J., & Smith, D. J. (2012). Marine conservation policy in Seychelles: Current constraints and prospects for improvement. *Marine Policy*, *36*(3), 823–831. doi:10.1016/j.marpol.2011.11.009

Doyle, T. (2018). Blue economy and the Indian Ocean rim. *Journal of the Indian Ocean Region*, *14*(1), 1–6. doi:10.1080/19480881.2018.1421450

Flothmann, S., von Kistowski, K., Dolan, E., Lee, E., Meere, F., & Album, G. (2010). Closing loopholes: Getting illegal fishing under control. *Science*, *328*(5983), 1235–1236. doi:10.1126cience.1190245 PMID:20488991

Global Ocean Commission. (2014). *From decline to recovery: A rescue package for the global ocean*. Global Ocean Commission.

Kelegama, S. (1998). Can Open Regionalism Work in the Indian Ocean Rim Association for Regional Co-operation? *ASEAN Economic Bulletin*, *15*(2), 153–167. doi:10.1355/AE15-2D

Larik, J. E., Daniëls, L., Oosterom, J., Ruiter, L. D., Smit, L., Vermeij, A., & Vliet, V. V. (2017). *Blue growth and sustainable development in Indian ocean governance*. The Hague Institute for Global Justice Policy Brief.

Llewellyn, L. E., English, S., & Barnwell, S. (2016). A roadmap to a sustainable Indian Ocean blue economy. *Journal of the Indian Ocean Region, 12*(1), 52–66. do i:10.1080/19480881.2016.1138713

Mehmood, Z. H., & Khan, R. (2021). Assessing Indian Ocean Economics: Perspective from Pakistan. [AJIS]. *Andalas Journal of International Studies, 10*(1), 1–15. doi:10.25077/ajis.10.1.1-15.2021

Roy, A. (2019). Blue economy in the Indian Ocean: Governance perspectives for sustainable development in the region. *ORF Occasional Paper, 181*.

Satia, B. P. (2016). An overview of the large marine ecosystem programs at work in Africa today. *Environmental Development, 17*, 11–19. doi:10.1016/j.envdev.2015.06.007

Steinberg, P. E. (1999). The maritime mystique: Sustainable development, capital mobility, and nostalgia in the world ocean. *Environment and Planning. D, Society & Space, 17*(4), 403–426. doi:10.1068/d170403

Subasinghe, R., Soto, D., & Jia, J. (2009). Global aquaculture and its role in sustainable development. *Reviews in Aquaculture, 1*(1), 2–9. doi:10.1111/j.1753-5131.2008.01002.x

Techera, E. J. (2018). Supporting blue economy agenda: Fisheries, food security and climate change in the Indian Ocean. *Journal of the Indian Ocean Region, 14*(1), 7–27. doi:10.1080/19480881.2017.1420579

Upadhyay, D. K., & Mishra, M. (2020). Blue economy: Emerging global trends and India's multilateral cooperation. *Maritime Affairs: Journal of the National Maritime Foundation of India, 16*(1), 30–45. doi:10.1080/09733159.2020.1785087

van der Geest, C. (2017). Redesigning Indian Ocean fisheries governance for 21st century sustainability. *Global Policy, 8*(2), 227–236. doi:10.1111/1758-5899.12447

Vivekanandan, E., Hermes, R., & O'Brien, C. (2016). Climate change effects in the Bay of Bengal large marine ecosystem. *Environmental Development, 17*, 46–56. doi:10.1016/j.envdev.2015.09.005

Compilation of References

Abers, R. (2000). *Inventing Local Democracy: Grassroots Politics in Brazil*. Lynne Rienner Publishers.

Abril, D. Y. O., Lopez, A. M. C., & Bravo, I. M. R. (2021). Empowerment of women in entrepreneurship and innovation. *Poblacion y Desarrollo*, *27*(52), 69–91. doi:10.18004/pdfce/2076-054x/2021.027.52.069

Achi, Z., Boulas, C., Buchanan, I., Forteza, J. H., & Zappei, L. (1998). *Conglomerates in emerging markets: Tigers or dinosaurs?* https://www.strategy-business.com/article/16137

Acs, Z., Arenius, P., Hay, M., & Minniti, M. (2005). Global Entrepreneurship Monitor 2004. Executive Report. Academic Press.

Adner, R., Oxley, J. E., & Silverman, B. S. (2013). Introduction: Collaboration and Competition in Business Ecosystems. In Collaboration and Competition in Business Ecosystems. Emerald Books.

Agarwal, S., & Lenka, U. (2017). *Does growth of ventures depend on competencies? Selected cases from India*. Academic Press.

Agarwal, S., & Lenka, U. (2016). An exploratory study on the development of women entrepreneurs: Indian cases. *Journal of Research in Marketing and Entrepreneurship*, *18*(2), 232–247. doi:10.1108/JRME-04-2015-0024

Aggarwal, A. (2019). Journey of Women Entrepreneurs for Two Decades: A Meta-Analytical Review. *Advancing Women in Leadership, 39*, 3-20. Available online at https://awl-ojs-tamu.tdl.org/awl/index.php/awl/article/view/343

Aghelie, A., Sorooshian, S., & Azizan, N. A. (2016). Research gap in sustainopreneurship. *Indian J. Sci. Technol., 9*. doi:10.17485/ijst/2016/v9i12/77648

Ajzen, I. (2002). Perceived Behavioral Control, Self-Efficacy, Locus of Control, and the Theory of Planned Behavior[1]. *Journal of Applied Social Psychology*, *32*(4), 665–683. doi:10.1111/j.1559-1816.2002.tb00236.x

Alam, S. S., Jani, M. F. M., & Omar, N. A. (2011). An empirical study of success factors of women entrepreneurs in southern region in Malaysia. *International Journal of Economics and Finance, 3*(2), 166.

Alrubaishi, D., McAdam, M., & Harrison, R. (2021). Culture, Islamic capital and the entrepreneurial behavior of family firms in Saudi Arabia. *International Journal of Entrepreneurial Behaviour & Research*, *27*(6), 1476–1501. doi:10.1108/IJEBR-09-2020-0575

Alsos, G. A., Isaksen, E. J., & Ljunggren, E. (2006). New venture financing and subsequent business growth in men–and women–Led businesses. *Entrepreneurship Theory and Practice*, *30*(5), 667–686. doi:10.1111/j.1540-6520.2006.00141.x

Alvord, S. H., Brown, L. D., & Letts, C. W. (2004). Social entrepreneurship and societal transformation. *The Journal of Applied Behavioral Science*, *40*(3), 260–282.

Anderson, B. (1991). *Imagined communities. Reflections on the origin and spread of nationalism* (2nd ed.). Verso.

Anderson, J. C., Kumar, N., & Narus, J. A. (2007). *Value merchants: Demonstrating and documenting superior value in business markets.* Harvard Business Press.

Anderson, J., Narus, J., & Van Rossum, W. (2006). Customer value propositions in business markets. *Harvard Business Review*, *84*(3), 91–99. PMID:16515158

Andersson, M., & Noseleit, F. (2011). Start-ups and employment dynamics within and across sectors. *Small Business Economics*, *36*(4), 483. doi:10.100711187-009-9252-0

Ansari, Z. N., & Kant, R. (2017). Exploring the framework development status for sustainability in supply chain management: a systematic literature synthesis and future research directions. *Business Strategy and the Environment*. doi:10.1002/bse.1945

Ansari, S., Munir, K., & Gregg, T. (2012). Impact at the "bottom of the pyramid": The role of social capital in capability development and community empowerment. *Journal of Management Studies*, (49), 813–842.

Ansell, C. K., & Gash, A. (2008). Collaborative governance in theory and practice. *Journal of Public Administration: Research and Theory*, *18*(4), 543–571. doi:10.1093/jopart/mum032

Aribaba, F. O., Oladele, R., Ahmodu, A. O., & Yusuff, S. A. (2019). Tax policies and entrepreneurship sustainability in Ondo State, Nigeria. *Journal of Global Entrepreneurship Research*, *9*(53), 1–13. doi:10.118640497-019-0168-0

Arranz, N., Ubierna, F., Arroyabe, M. F., Perez, C., & Fdez. de Arroyabe, J. C. (2017). The effect of curricular and extracurricular activities on university students' entrepreneurial intention and competences. *Studies in Higher Education*, *42*(11), 1979–2008. doi:10.1080/03075079.2015.1130030

Arruda, C., Nogueira, V. S., & Costa, V. (2013). The Brazilian entrepreneurial ecosystem of startups: An analysis of entrepreneurship determinants in Brazil as seen from the OECD pillars. *Journal of Entrepreneurship and Innovation Management*, *2*(3), 17–57.

Arum, R. (2000). Schools and communities: Ecological and institutional dimensions. *Annual Review of Sociology*, *26*(1), 395–418. doi:10.1146/annurev.soc.26.1.395

Asheim, B. T., Smith, H. L., & Oughton, C. (2011). Regional innovation systems: Theory, empirics, and policy. *Regional Studies*, *45*(7), 875–891. doi:10.1080/00343404.2011.596701

Atems, B., & Shand, G. (2018). An empirical analysis of the relationship between entrepreneurship and income inequality. *Small Business Economics*, *51*(4), 905–922. doi:10.100711187-017-9984-1

Audretsch, D. B., Cunningham, J. A., Kuratko, D. F., Lehmann, E. E., & Menter, M. (2019). Entrepreneurial ecosystems: Economic, technological, and societal impacts. *The Journal of Technology Transfer*, *44*(2), 313–325. doi:10.100710961-018-9690-4 PMID:30956392

Autio, E., & Fu, K. (2015). Economic and political institutions and entry into formal and informal entrepreneurship. *Asia Pacific Journal of Management*, *32*(1), 67–94. doi:10.100710490-014-9381-0

Autio, E., Keeley, R., Klofsten, M., Parker, G., & Hay, M. (2001). Entrepreneurial intent among students in Scandinavia and in the USA. *Enterprise and Innovation Management Studies*, *2*(2), 145–160. doi:10.1080/14632440110094632

Autio, E., Kenney, M., Mustar, P., Siegel, D., & Wright, M. (2014). Entrepreneurial innovation: The importance of context. *Research Policy*, *43*(7), 1097–1108. doi:10.1016/j.respol.2014.01.015

Autio, E., Nambisan, S., Thomas, L. D., & Wright, M. (2018). Digital affordances, spatial affordances, and the genesis of entrepreneurial ecosystems. *Strategic Entrepreneurship Journal*, *12*(1), 72–95. doi:10.1002ej.1266

Aykol, B., & Leonidou, L. C. (2015). Researching the Green Practices of Smaller Service Firms: A Theoretical, Methodological, and Empirical Assessment. *Journal of Small Business Management*, *53*(4), 1264–1288. doi:10.1111/jsbm.12118

Azmat, F., Ferdous, A. S., & Couchman, P. (2015). Understanding the dynamics between social entrepreneurship and inclusive growth in subsistence marketplaces. *Journal of Public Policy & Marketing*, (4), 252–271.

Bacq, S., Hartog, C., & Hoogendoorn, B. (2016). Beyond the moral portrayal of social entrepreneurs: An empirical approach to who they are and what drives them. *Journal of Business Ethics*, (133), 703–718.

Bae, T., Qian, S., Miao, C., & Fiet, J. (2014). The relationship between entrepreneurship education and entrepreneurial intentions: A meta-analytic review. *Entrepreneurship Theory and Practice*, *38*(2), 217–254. doi:10.1111/etap.12095

Bahena-Álvarez, I. L., Cordón-Pozo, E., & Delgado-Cruz, A. (2019). Social Entrepreneurship in the Conduct of Responsible Innovation: Analysis Cluster in Mexican SMEs. *Sustainability*, *11*(13), 3714. doi:10.3390u11133714

Baiocchi, G. (2005). *Militants and Citizens: The Politics of Participatory Democracy in Porto Alegre*. Stanford University Press. doi:10.1515/9781503625129

Baiocchi, G., & Heller, P. (2011). *Bootstrapping Democracy: Transforming Local Governance and Civil Society in Brazil*. Stanford University Press.

Bajdor, P., Pawełoszek, I., & Fidlerova, H. (2021). Analysis and Assessment of Sustainable Entrepreneurship Practices in Polish Small and Medium Enterprises. *Sustainability*, *13*(7), 3595. doi:10.3390u13073595

Ballantyne, D., Frow, P., Varey, R. J., & Payne, A. (2011). Value propositions as communication practice. *Industrial Marketing Management*, *40*(2), 202–210. doi:10.1016/j.indmarman.2010.06.032

Ballon, P. (2018). A structural equation model for female empowerment. *The Journal of Development Studies*, *54*(8), 1303–1320. doi:10.1080/00220388.2017.1414189

Banker, R. D., Mashruwala, R., & Tripathy, A. (2014). Does a differentiation strategy lead to more sustainable financial performance than a cost leadership strategy? *Management Decision*. Advance online publication. doi:10.1108/MD-05-2013-0282

Ban, N. C., Maxwell, S. M., Dunn, D. C., Hobday, A. J., Bax, N. J., Ardron, J., & Pressey, R. L. (2014). Better integration of sectoral planning and management approaches for the interlinked ecology of the open oceans. *Marine Policy*, *49*, 127–136. doi:10.1016/j.marpol.2013.11.024

Barber, B. R. (1984). *Strong democracy. Participatory politics for a new age*. Univ. of California Press.

Bartik, A. W., Bertrand, M., Cullen, Z., Glaeser, E. L., Luca, M., & Stanton, C. (2020). The impact of COVID-19 on small business outcomes and expectations. *Proceedings of the National Academy of Sciences of the United States of America*, *117*(30), 17656–17666. doi:10.1073/pnas.2006991117 PMID:32651281

Bates, R. H. (1984). Markets and States in Tropical Africa: The Political Basis of Agricultural Policy. University of California Press.

Battilana, J., Leca, B., & Boxenbaum, E. (2009). How actors change institutions: Towards a theory of institutional entrepreneurship. *The Academy of Management Annals*, (3), 65–107.

Battilana, J., Sengul, M., Pache, A. C., & Model, J. (2015). Harnessing productive tensions in hybrid organizations: The case of work integration social enterprises. *Academy of Management Journal*, (58), 1658–1685.

Beck, U. (2003) Toward a new critical theory with cosmopolitan intent. *Constellations, 10*(4), 453-68.

Beck, U., & Holzer, B. (2004). Wie global ist die Weltrisikogesellschaft? In Entgrenzung und Entscheidung: was ist neu an der Theorie reflexiver Modernisierung? Suhrkamp.

Beck, U. (1992). *Risk Society*. Sage.

Beetham, D., & Lord, C. (1998). *Legitimacy and the EU*. Addison Wesley Longman Limited.

Beiner, R. (1983). *Political Judgment*. Methuen.

Belitski, M., & Büyükbalci, P. (2021). Uncharted waters of the entrepreneurial ecosystems research: Comparing Greater Istanbul and Reading ecosystems. *Growth and Change*, *52*(2), 727–750. doi:10.1111/grow.12457

Belz, F. M., & Binder, J. K. (2017). Sustainable entrepreneurship: A convergent process model. *Bus. Strateg. Environ.*, *26*, 1–17. doi:10.1002/bse.1887

Bernardino, S., Santos, J. F., & Ribeiro, J. C. (2016). Social entrepreneurship: Does institutional environment make a difference? In L. Carvalho (Ed.), *Handbook of research on entrepreneurial success and its impact on regional development* (p. 26). IGI Global. doi:10.4018/978-1-4666-9567-2.ch022

Bijma, J., Pörtner, H. O., Yesson, C., & Rogers, A. D. (2013). Climate change and the oceans–What does the future hold? *Marine Pollution Bulletin*, *74*(2), 495–505. doi:10.1016/j.marpolbul.2013.07.022 PMID:23932473

Bird, B. (1988). Implementing entrepreneurial ideas: The case for intention. *Academy of Management Review*, *13*(3), 442–453. doi:10.5465/amr.1988.4306970

Bird, B. (1988). Implementing entrepreneurial ideas: The case for intentions. *Academy of Management Review*, *13*(3), 442–454.

Birden, M., Bastug, M., & Yazici, S. (2020). The Impact of Incubators on Entrepreneurial Process in Turkey: A Guide For Startups. *Journal of Business Economics and Finance*, *9*(2), 132–142. doi:10.17261/Pressacademia.2020.1219

Birley, S. (1989). Female entrepreneurs: Are they really different? *Journal of Small Business Management*, *27*, 32–37.

Bloom, P. N. (2009). Overcoming consumption constraints through social entrepreneurship. *Journal of Public Policy & Marketing*, (28), 128–134.

Boermans, M. A., & Willebrands, D. (2017). Entrepreneurship, risk perception and firm Performance. *International Journal of Entrepreneurship and Small Business*, *31*(4), 557–569. doi:10.1504/IJESB.2017.085426

Bonilla, C. A., Merigó, J. M., & Torres-Abad, C. (2015). Economics in Latin America: A bibliometric analysis. *Scientometrics*, *105*(2), 1239–1252. https://doi.org/10.1007/s11192-015-1747-7

Bora, A., & Hausendorf, H. (2005). Participatory science governance and the communicative construction of citizenship. Science and Public Policy.

Bora, A. (2005). Licensing Plant GMOs – A Brief Overview over European regulatory conditions for the Deliberate Release of Genetically Modified Plants. In H. Hausendorf & A. Bora (Eds.), *Communicating Citizenship and Social Positioning in Decision-Making Procedures: The Case of Modern Biotechnology*. Series Discourse Approaches to Politics, Society and Culture.

Bora, A., & Hausendorfer, H. (2006). Participatory science governance revisited: Normative expectations versus empirical evidence. *Science & Public Policy*, *33*(7), 478–488. doi:10.3152/147154306781778740

Borangiu, T. (2009). A service-orientated arhitecture for holonic manufacturing control. In *Towards Intelligent Engineering and Information Technology* (pp. 489–503). Springer. doi:10.1007/978-3-642-03737-5_35

Boschee, J. (1995). Social Entrepreneurship. *Across the Board*, *32*(3), 20–23.

Bouchard, C., & Crumplin, W. (2010). Neglected no longer: The Indian Ocean at the forefront of world geopolitics and global geostrategy. *Journal of the Indian Ocean Region*, *6*(1), 26–51. doi:10.1080/19480881.2010.489668

Bourdieu, P. (1977). *Outline of a Theory of Practice*. Cambridge Uni-versity Press. doi:10.1017/CBO9780511812507

Bowen, H. R. (1953). *The social responsibilities of the businessman*. Harper.

Bower, M., & Garda, R. A. (1986). The role of marketing in management. In V. P. Buell (Ed.), Handbook of Modern Marketing (pp. 1–3–1-15). New York: McGraw-Hill.

Boyack, K. W., & Klavans, R. (2010). Co-Citation Analysis, Bibliographic Coupling, and Direct Citation: Which Citation Approach Represents the Research Front Most Accurately? *Journal of the American Society for Information Science and Technology*, *12*(61), 2389–2404.

Brodie, R. J., Hollebeek, L. D., Jurić, B., & Ilić, A. (2011). Customer engagement: Conceptual domain, fundamental propositions, and implications for research. *Journal of Service Research*, *14*(3), 252–271. doi:10.1177/1094670511411703

Brown, T. L., & Potoski, M. (2003). Transaction costs and institutional explanations for government service production decisions. *Journal of Public Administration: Research and Theory*, *13*(4), 441–468. doi:10.1093/jopart/mug030

Brunner, H. W. (2013). What is economic corridor development and what can it achieve in Asia's subregions? SSRN *Electronic Journal*. doi:10.2139/ssrn.2306801

Brush, C. G. (1992). Research on Women Business Owners: Past Trends, a New Perspective and Future Directions. *Entrepreneurship Theory and Practice*, *16*(4), 4, 5–30. doi:10.1177/104225879201600401

Bunce, M., Brown, K., & Rosendo, S. (2010). Policy misfits, climate change and cross-scale vulnerability in coastal Africa: How development projects undermine resilience. *Environmental Science & Policy*, *13*(6), 485–497. doi:10.1016/j.envsci.2010.06.003

Buseth, J. T. (2017). The green economy in Tanzania: From global discourses to institutionalization. *Geoforum*, *86*, 42–52. doi:10.1016/j.geoforum.2017.08.015

Business Standard. (2013). *Exploiting institutional voids*. https://business-standard.com/article/management/exploiting-institutional-voids-110052400034_1.html

Bussu, S., Lalani, M., Pattison, S., & Marshall, M. (2020). Engaging with Care: Ethical Issues in Participatory Research. In Qualitative Research (pp. 1–19). Academic Press.

Buttle, F. (2009). *Customer relationship management: Concepts and technologies*. Routledge.

Callon, M., Laredo, P., Rabeharisoa, V., Gonard, T., & Leray, T. (1992). The management and evaluation of technological programs and the dynamics of techno-economic networks: The case of AFME. *Research Policy*, *21*(3), 215–236. doi:10.1016/0048-7333(92)90017-X

Cancino, C. A., Merigó, J. M., Torres, J. P., & Diaz, D. (2018). A bibliometric analysis of venture capital research. *Journal of Economics, Finance and Administrative Science*, *23*(45), 182–195. https://doi.org/10.1108/JEFAS-01-2018-0016

Cantele, S., Vernizzi, S., & Campedelli, B. (2020). Untangling the Origins of Sustainable Commitment: New Insights on the Small vs. Large Firms' Debate. *Sustainability*, *12*(2), 671. doi:10.3390u12020671

Cao, Z., & Shi, X. (2021). A systematic literature review of entrepreneurial ecosystems in advanced and emerging economies. *Small Business Economics*, *57*(1), 75–110. doi:10.100711187-020-00326-y

Capital. (n.d.). https://www.capital.com.tr/is-dunyasi/soylesiler/umit-beyin-2020-plani?sayfa=6

Capobianco-Uriarte, M. de las M., Casado-Belmonte, M. del P., Marín-Carrillo, G. M., & Terán-Yépez, E. (2019). A Bibliometric Analysis of International Competitiveness (1983–2017). *Sustain., 11*, 1877. doi:10.3390/su11071877

Carree, M., van Stel, A., Thurik, R., & Wennekers, S. (2002). Economic development and business ownership: An analysis using data of 23 OECD countries in the period 1976–1996. *Small Business Economics*, *19*(3), 271–290. doi:10.1023/A:1019604426387

Castells, M. (1996a). *The Rise of the Network Society*. Blackwell.

Castillo-Vergara, M., Alvarez-Marin, A., & Placencio-Hidalgo, D. (2018). A bibliometric analysis of creativity in the field of business economics. *Journal of Business Research*, *85*, 1–9. https://doi.org/10.1016/j.jbusres.2017.12.011

Cepin, M., & Bris, R. (2017). *Safety and Reliability. Theory and Applications*. CRC Press. doi:10.1201/9781315210469

Certo, S. T., & Miller, T. (2008). Social entrepreneurship: Key issues and concepts. *Business Horizons*, (51), 267–271.

Çeviker, E. (2021). *Strategic Actions in Response to Pro-market Reforms: A Study on Turkish Traffic Insurance Industry* (PhD thesis). İstanbul Bilgi University.

Chellaney, B. (2010). Indian Ocean maritime security: Energy, environmental and climate challenges. *Journal of the Indian Ocean Region, 6*(2), 155–168. doi:10.1080/19480881.2010.536662

Chesbrough, H., & Rosenbloom, R. S. (2002). The role of the business model in capturing value from innovation: Evidence from Xerox Corporation's technology spin-off companies. *Industrial and Corporate Change, 11*(3), 529–555. doi:10.1093/icc/11.3.529

Chubb, J. E., & Peterson, P. E. (1985). *The new direction in American politics*. Brookings Institution Press.

Civera, C., de Colle, S., & Casalegno, C. (2019). Stakeholder engagement through empowerment: The case of coffee farmers. *Journal of Business Ethics. European Review (Chichester, England), 28*(2), 156–174. doi:10.1111/beer.12208

Clark, B. M. (2006). Climate change: A looming challenge for fisheries management in southern Africa. *Marine Policy, 30*(1), 84–95. doi:10.1016/j.marpol.2005.06.006

Clifton, J., Etienne, M., Barnes, D. K., Barnes, R. S., Suggett, D. J., & Smith, D. J. (2012). Marine conservation policy in Seychelles: Current constraints and prospects for improvement. *Marine Policy, 36*(3), 823–831. doi:10.1016/j.marpol.2011.11.009

Cobo, M. J., López-Herrera, A. G., Herrera-Viedma, E., & Herrera, F. (2011). Science mapping software tools: Review, analysis, and cooperative study among tools. *Journal of the American Society for Information Science and Technology, 62*, 1382–1402. https://doi.org/10.1002/asi.21525

Cohen, B. (2006). Sustainable valley entrepreneurial ecosystems. *Business Strategy and the Environment, 15*(1), 1–14. doi:10.1002/bse.428

Cohen, B., & Winn, M. I. (2007). Market imperfections, opportunity and sustainable entrepreneurship. *Journal of Business Venturing, 22*, 29–49. https://doi.org/10.1016/j.jbusvent.2004.12.001

Collier, R. B., & Collier, D. (1991). *Shaping the Political Arena: Critical Junctures, the Labor Movement, and Regime Dynamics in Latin America*. Princeton University Press.

Collins, H. M., & Evans, R. (2002). The third wave of science studies: Studies of expertise and experience. *Social Studies of Science, 32*(2), 235–296. doi:10.1177/0306312702032002003

Colombo, M. G., Dagnino, G. B., Lehmann, E. E., & Salmador, M. (2019). The governance of entrepreneurial ecosystems. *Small Business Economics, 52*(2), 419–428. doi:10.100711187-017-9952-9

Colyvas, J. A., & Jonsson, S. (2011). Ubiquity and legitimacy: Disentangling diffusion and institutionalization. *Sociological Theory, 29*(1), 27–53. doi:10.1111/j.1467-9558.2010.01386.x

Committee of the Regions. (2014). *EGTC Monitoring Report 2013*. Towards the New Cohesion Policy.

Cooke, B., & Kothari, U. (Eds.). (2001). Participation: The New Tyranny? Zed Books Ltd.

Cornwall, A. (2008). Unpacking 'Participation': Models, Meaning and Practices. *Community Development Journal: An International Forum*, *43*(3), 269–283. doi:10.1093/cdj/bsn010

Cornwall, A., & Coelho, V. (2004). New democratic spaces? *IDS Bulletin*, *35*(2).

Cornwall, A., & Goetz, A. M. (2005). Democratizing democracy: Feminist perspectives. *Democratization*, *12*(5), 783–800. doi:10.1080/13510340500322181

Crals, E., & Vereeck, L. (2005). The affordability of sustainable entrepreneurship certification for SMEs. *International Journal of Sustainable Development and World Ecology*, *12*(2), 173–183. doi:10.1080/13504500509469628

Cuyper, L. D., Kucukkeles, B., & Reuben, R. (2020). *Discovering the real impact of COVID-19 on entrepreneurship*. World Economic Forum. https://www.weforum.org/agenda/2020/06/how-covid-19-will-change-entrepreneurial-business/

Czarniawska, B. (2002). *A tale of three cities. Or the glocalization of city management*. Oxford University Press. doi:10.1093/acprof:oso/9780199252718.001.0001

Dahl, R. (1971). *Polyarchy: Participation and Opposition*. Yale University Press.

Dahrendorf, R. (1988). *The modern social conflict*. Weidenfeld and Nicolson.

Dalal, K. (2011). Does economic empowerment protect women from intimate partner violence? *Journal of Injury & Violence Research*, *3*(1), 35–44. doi:10.5249/jivr.v3i1.76 PMID:21483213

Datta, P. B., & Gailey, R. (2012). Empowering women through social entrepreneurship: Case study of a women's cooperative in India. *Entrepreneurship Theory and Practice*, (36), 569–587.

Davidsson, P., Hunter, E., & Klofsten, M. (2006). Institutional forces: The invisible hand that shapes venture ideas? *International Small Business Journal*, *24*(2), 115–131. doi:10.1177/0266242606061834

Davis, J., Edgar, T., Porter, J., Bernaden, J., & Sarli, M. (2012). Smart manufacturing, manufacturing intelligence and demand-dynamic performance. *Computers & Chemical Engineering*, *47*(12), 145–156. doi:10.1016/j.compchemeng.2012.06.037

De Jong, M., Lalenis, K., & Mamadouh, V. (2002). *The theory and practice of institutional transplantation. Experiences with the transfer of policy institutions*. Kluwer Academic Publishers. doi:10.1007/978-94-011-0001-4

de la luz Fernandez-Alles, M., & Valle-Cabrera, R. (2006). Reconciling institutional theory with organizational theories: How neoinstitutionalism resolves five paradoxes. *Journal of Organizational Change Management, 19*(4), 503-517.

Dean, R., Boswell, J., & Smith, G. (2019). Designing democratic innovations as deliberative systems: The ambitious case of NHS citizen. *Political Studies*, *68*(3), 689–709. Advance online publication. doi:10.1177/0032321719866002

Dean, T. J., & McMullen, J. S. (2007). Toward a theory of sustainable entrepreneurship: Reducing environmental degradation through entrepreneurial action. *Journal of Business Venturing*, (22), 50–76.

Dees, G. (1998). *The meaning of social entrepreneurship*. http:// www.fuqua.duke.edu/centers/case/documents/dees_SE.pdf

Dees, J. G., Emerson, J., & Economy, P. (2001). Enterprising nonprofits: A toolkit for social entrepreneurs. Annual Review of Sociology, (36).

Denielsson, M., Hertting, N., & Klijn, E. H. (2018). Institutionalizing Local Participatory Governance in Representative Democracy. In Local Participatory Governance and Representative Democracy. Routledge.

Derimod. (n.d.). https://www.derimod.com.tr/hakkimizda

Desa. (n.d.). https://www.desa.com.tr/hakkimizda

Deshmukh, S. G. (2016). Manufacturing Competitiveness: Research Opportunities. *International Journal of Global Business and Competitiveness*, *11*(1), 1–6.

Devi, S. (2016). Social Entrepreneurship: Challenges in Way to rise. *International Journal of Research*, *4*(9), 191–197.

Devkota, S., & Upadhyay, M. (2013). Agricultural productivity and poverty reduction in Nepal. *Review of Development Economics*, *17*(4), 732–746. doi:10.1111/rode.12062

Dhahri, S., & Omri, A. (2018). Entrepreneurship contribution to the three pillars of sustainable development: What does the evidence really say? *World Development*, *106*, 64–77. doi:10.1016/j.worlddev.2018.01.008

DiMaggio, P., & Powell, W. (1983). The iron cage revisited: Institutional isomorphism and collective rationality in organizational fields. *American Sociological Review*, *48*(2), 147–160.

Dimitratos, P., & Plakoyiannaki, E. (2003). Theoretical foundations of an international entrepreneurial culture. *Journal of International Entrepreneurship*, *1*(2), 187–215. doi:10.1023/A:1023804318244

Djankov, S., La Porta, R., Lopez-de-Silanes, F., & Shleifer, A. (2002). The regulation of entry. *The Quarterly Journal of Economics*, *117*(1), 1–37. doi:10.1162/003355302753399436

Doğan, E. (2016). The role of national culture on entrepreneurship: An assessment on the entrepreneurial culture of Turkey. *Sosyal Bilimler Araştırma Dergisi*, *5*(1), 98–110.

Doherty, B., Haugh, H., & Lyon, F. (2014). Social enterprises as hybrid organizations: A review and research agenda. *International Journal of Management Reviews*, (16), 417–436.

Dolowitz, D. P., & Marsh, D. (2000). Learning from Abroad: The Role of Policy Transfer in Contemporary Policymaking. *Governance: An International Journal of Policy, Administration and Institutions*, *13*(1), 5–23. doi:10.1111/0952-1895.00121

Dorward, A. (2013). Agricultural labour productivity, food prices and sustainable development impacts and indicators. *Food Policy*, *39*, 40–50. doi:10.1016/j.foodpol.2012.12.003

Doyle, T. (2018). Blue economy and the Indian Ocean rim. *Journal of the Indian Ocean Region*, *14*(1), 1–6. doi:10.1080/19480881.2018.1421450

Dryzek, J. S. (1990). *Discursive democracy: politics, policy, and political science*. Cambridge University Press. doi:10.1017/9781139173810

Dryzek, J. S., Farr, J., & Leonard, S. T. (Eds.). (1995). *Political science in history*. Cambridge University Press.

Duflo, E. (2012). Women empowerment and economic development. *Journal of Economic Literature*, *50*(4), 1051–1079.

Durning, D. (1993). Participatory policy analysis in a social service agency: A case study. *Journal of Policy Analysis and Management*, *12*(2), 297–322. doi:10.2307/3325237

Easton, D. (1965). *A Framework for Political Analysis*. Prentice-Hall.

Ecco. (2022). *About Us*. https://group.ecco.com/en/about-us

Egerová, D., Eger, L., & Mičík, M. (2017). Does entrepreneurship education matter? Business students' perspectives. *Tertiary Education and Management*, *23*(4), 319–333. doi:10.1080/13583883.2017.1299205

Electrical Engineers Chambre (EMO). (2022). www.emo.org

Eller, F. J., Gielnik, M. M., Wimmer, H., Thölke, C., Holzapfel, S., Tegtmeier, S., & Halberstadt, J. (2020). Identifying business opportunities for sustainable development: Longitudinal and experimental evidence contributing to the field of sustainable entrepreneurship. *Business Strategy and the Environment*, *29*(3), 1387–1403. https://doi.org/10.1002/bse.2439

Erol, S., Schumacher, A., & Sihn, W. (2016, January). Strategic guidance towards Industry 4.0–a three-stage process model. In *International conference on competitive manufacturing* (*Vol. 9*, No. 1, pp. 495-501). Academic Press.

Euro NCAP. (2021, November 18). *Latest Safety Ratings*. Author.

Euro NCAP. (n.d.). https://www.euroncap.com/en/ratings-rewards/latest- safety- ratings/#?selectedMake=0&selectedMakeName=Select%20a%20make&selectedModel=0&selectedStar=&includeFullSafetyPackage=true&includeStandardSafetyPackage=true&selectedModelName=All&selectedProtocols=417

Fatoki, O. (2018). The impact of entrepreneurial resilience on the success of small and medium enterprises in South Africa. *Sustainability*, *10*, 2527–2539. https://doi.org/10.3390/su10072527

Fayolle, A., & Gailly, B. (2015). The impact of entrepreneurship education on entrepreneurial attitudes and intention: Hysteresis and persistence. *Journal of Small Business Management*, *53*(1), 75–93. doi:10.1111/jsbm.12065

Fayolle, A., Gailly, B., & Lassas-Clerc, N. (2006). Assessing the impact of entrepreneurship education programmes: A new methodology. *Journal of European Industrial Training, 30*(9), 701–720. doi:10.1108/03090590610715022

Felser, W., Kirsch, A., Kletti, J., Wießler, J., & Meuser, D. (2015). *Industrie 4.0 kompakt*. NetSkill Solutions.

Ferreira, J. J. M., Fernandes, C. I., Peris–Ortiz, M., & Ratten, V. (2017). Female entrepreneurship: A co–citation analysis. *International Journal of Entrepreneurship and Small Business, 31*(2), 325–340. doi:10.1504/IJESB.2017.10004863

Fifield, P. (2007). *Marketing Strategy Masterclass: Making Marketing Strategy Happen*. Butterworth-Heinemann.

Fiorino, D. J. (1990). Citizen participation and environmental risk: A survey of institutional mechanisms. *Science, Technology & Human Values, 15*(2), 226–243. doi:10.1177/016224399001500204

Firmin, A. (2017). Engaging civil society in cultural governance. In *Reshaping Cultural Policies. Advancing creativity for development*. Paris: UNESCO. Available online at: http://unesdoc.unesco.org/images/0026/002605/260592e. pdf

Fischer, F. (2006). Participatory Governance as Deliberative Empowerment the Cultural Politics of Discursive Space. *American Review of Public Administration, 36*(1), 19–40. doi:10.1177/0275074005282582

Fishkin, J. S. (1993). *Democracy and Deliberation: New Directions for Democratic Reform*. Yale University Press.

Flothmann, S., von Kistowski, K., Dolan, E., Lee, E., Meere, F., & Album, G. (2010). Closing loopholes: Getting illegal fishing under control. *Science, 328*(5983), 1235–1236. doi:10.1126cience.1190245 PMID:20488991

Fotache, G., & Bucsa, R.-C. (2020). Aspects regarding entrepreneurship education in Europe. *Economy Transdisciplinarity Cognition, 23*(2), 1–12.

Foucault, M. (1977). *Discipline and Punish: The Birth of the Prison*. Random House.

Fritsch, M. (1997). New firms and regional employment change. *Small Business Economics, 9*(5), 437–448. doi:10.1023/A:1007942918390

Frow, P., & Payne, A. (2012). *Diagnosing the value proposition*. Working paper, Discipline of Marketing, University of Sydney.

Frow, P. (2011). A. Payne A stakeholder perspective of the value proposition concept. *European Journal of Marketing, 45*(1–2), 223–240.

Fung, A. (2004). *Empowered Participation: Reinventing Urban Democracy*. Princeton University Press.

Fung, A. (2015). Putting the Public Back into Governance: The Challenges of Citizen Participation and Its Future. *Public Administration Review, 75*(4), 513–522. doi:10.1111/puar.12361

Fung, A., & Wright, E. O. (2003). *Deepening Democracy: Institutional Innovations in Empowered Participatory Governance*. Verso Books.

Fung, A., & Wright, E. O. (2003). Thinking about Empowered Participatory Governance. In A. Fung & E. O. Wright (Eds.), *Deepening Democracy. Institutional Innovations in Empowered Participatory Governance*. Verso.

Gao, C., Zuzul, T., Jones, G., & Khanna, T. (2017). Overcoming institutional voids: A reputation-based view of long run survival. *Strategic Management Journal, 38*(11), 2147–2167. https://doi.org/10.1002/smj.2649

Gao, Y., Gao, S., Zhou, Y., & Huang, K.-F. (2015). Picturing firms' institutional capital-based radical innovation under China's institutional voids. *Journal of Business Research, 68*(6), 1166–1175.

Gargi, B. (2019). Financial inclusion, women empowerment, and entrepreneurship: A special emphasis to India. *Malaysian E-commerce Journal, 3*(3), 18–21.

Gasbarro, F., Rizzi, F., & Frey, M. (2018). Sustainable institutional entrepreneurship in practice: Insights from SMEs in the clean energy sector in Tuscany (Italy). *International Journal of Entrepreneurial Behaviour & Research, 24*(2), 476–498. doi:10.1108/IJEBR-11-2015-0259

Gast, J., Gundolf, K., & Cesinger, B. (2017). Doing business in a green way: A systematic review of the ecological sustainability entrepreneurship literature and future research directions. *Journal of Cleaner Production, 147*, 44–56. https://doi.org/10.1016/j.jclepro.2017.01.065

Ghauri, P. N., Tasavori, M., & Zaefarian, R. (2014). Internationalisation of service firms through corporate social entrepreneurship and networking. *International Marketing Review*, (31), 576–600.

Global Entrepreneurship Monitor. (2020). https://www.gemconsortium.org/report/gem-2019-2020-global-report

Global Ocean Commission. (2014). *From decline to recovery: A rescue package for the global ocean*. Global Ocean Commission.

Global Partnership for Financial Inclusion (GPFI). (2021). *Why financial inclusion?* Global findex. https://gpfi.org/why-financial-inclusion

Goddard, M. (2015, September). TeleCommunication Systems Location Technologies. In *Proceedings of the 28th International Technical Meeting of the Satellite Division of The Institute of Navigation (ION GNSS+ 2015)* (pp. 1069-1075). Academic Press.

Gogo, A., Osta, A., McClafferty, H., & Rana, D. T. (2019). Cultivating a way of being and doing: Individual strategies for physician well-being and resilience. *Problems in Pediatric and Adolescent Health Care, 49*(12). doi:10.1016/j.cppeds.2019.100663

Golden Gate University. (2021, December). *Country research: Emerging markets*. https://ggu.libguides.com/country

Goldfrank, B. (2007). The Politics of Deepening Local Democracy: Decentralization, Party Institutionalization and Participation. *Comparative Politics*, *40*(1), 147–168.

Goodin, R. E., & Klingemann, H. D. (Eds.). (1996). *A new handbook of political science*. Oxford University Press.

Gorman, G., Hanlon, D., & King, W. (1997). Some Research Perspectives on Entrepreneurship Education, Enterprise Education and Education for Small Business Management: A Ten-Year Literature Review. *International Small Business Journal*, *15*(3), 56–77. doi:10.1177/0266242697153004

Gottweis, H. (2003). Theoretical strategies of post-structuralist policy analysis: towards an Analytics of Government. In M. A. Hajer & H. Wagenaar (Eds.), *Deliberative policy analysis: understanding governance in the network society* (pp. 247–265). Cambridge University Press. doi:10.1017/CBO9780511490934.011

Goyal, P., & Yadav, V. (2014). To be or not to be a woman entrepreneur in a developing country? *Psychosociological Issues in Human Resource Management*, *2*(2), 68–78.

Greene, W. (2017). *Econometric analysis* (8th ed.). Pearson.

Greenwald, H. P. (2008). *Organizations: Management without control*. Sage Publications.

Grin, F. (2005, August). Linguistic human rights as a source of policy guidelines: A critical assessment. *Journal of Sociolinguistics*, *9*(3), 448–460. doi:10.1111/j.1360-6441.2005.00300.x

Gualini, E. (2004). Regionalization as 'experimental regionalism': The rescaling of territorial policy-making in Germany. *International Journal of Urban and Regional Research*, *28*(2), 329–353. doi:10.1111/j.0309-1317.2004.00522.x

Guerrero, M., & Urbano, D. (2017). The dark side of entrepreneurial ecosystems in emerging economies: Exploring the case of Mexico. In Academy of Management Proceedings (Vol. 2017, No. 1, p. 12941). Academy of Management.

Gundry, L. K., Ben-Yoseph, M., & Posig, M. (2002). Contemporary perspectives on women's entrepreneurship: A review and strategic recommendations. *Journal of Enterprising Culture*, *10*(01), 67–86. doi:10.1142/S0218495802000141

Gustafson, P., & Hertting, N. (2016). Understanding Participatory Governance: An Analysis of Participants' Motives for Participation. *American Review of Public Administration*, *47*(5), 538–549. doi:10.1177/0275074015626298

Haas, E. B. (1968). *The uniting of Europe. Political, social, and economic forces 1950 - 1957*. Stanford Univ. Press.

Hackman, J. R., & Oldham, G. R. (1976). Motivation through the design of work: Test of a theory. *Organizational Behavior and Human Performance*, *16*(2), 250–279. doi:10.1016/0030-5073(76)90016-7

Hajer, M. A. (2000) *Politiek als vormgeving*. Universiteit van Amsterdam: inaugurele rede 16 juni 2000.

Hajer, M. A. (1995). *The politics of environmental discourse. Ecological modernisation and the policy process*. Clarendon Press.

Halberstadt, J., Niemand, T., Kraus, S., Rexhepi, G., Jones, P., & Kailer, N. (2021, April). Social entrepreneurship orientation: Drivers of success for start-ups and established industrial firms. *Industrial Marketing Management*, *94*, 137–149. Advance online publication. doi:10.1016/j.indmarman.2020.06.012

Hall, J., Daneke, G., & Lenox, M. (2010). Sustainable development and entrepreneurship: Past contributions and future directions. *Journal of Business Venturing*, *25*(5), 439–448.

Hall, J., & Wagner, M. (2012). Editorial: The Challenges and Opportunities of Sustainable Development for Entrepreneurship and Small Business. *Journal of Small Business and Entrepreneurship*, *25*(4), 409–416. doi:10.1080/08276331.2012.10593581

Hanna, R., Rohm, A., & Crittenden, V. L. (2011). We're all connected: The power of the social media ecosystem. *Business Horizons*, *54*(3), 265–273. doi:10.1016/j.bushor.2011.01.007

Haselsberger, B. (2007). European Territorial Co-Operation: Regions of the Future. Regional Studies, (267), 6-8.

Hawkesworth, M. E. (1988). *Theoretical issues in policy analysis*. SUNY Press.

Heilbron, J., Magnusson, L., & Wittrock, B. (Eds.). (1997). *The rise of the social sciences and the formation of modernity*. Kluwer.

Heller, P. (2000). Degrees of Democracy: Some Comparative Lessons from India. *World Politics*, *52*(4), 484–519. doi:10.1017/S0043887100020086

Henley, R., Marshall, R., Vetter, S., & Vetter, S. (2011). Integrating mental health services into humanitarian relief responses to social emergencies, disasters, and conflicts: A case study. *The Journal of Behavioral Health Services & Research*, *38*(1), 132–141.

Herman, E., & Stefanescu, D. (2017). Can higher education stimulate entrepreneurial intentions among engineering and business students? *Educational Studies*, *43*(3), 312–327. doi:10.1080/03055698.2016.1277134

Hinings, C. R., & Greenwood, R. (2015). Missing in action: The further contribution of Philip Selznick to contemporary institutional theory. *Research in the Sociology of Organizations*, *44*, 121–148. https://doi.org/10.1108/S0733-558X20150000044006

Hisrich, R. D., & Peters, M. P. (1998). *Entrepreneurship*. Prentice Hall.

Hobsbawm, E. J. (1977). *The age of revolution*. Abacus.

Hofstede Insights. (2022). https://www.hofstede-insights.com/product/compare-countries/

Hofstede, G. (1991). *Cultures and Organizations: Software of the Mind*. McGraw-Hill.

Hooghe, L., & Marks, G. (2001). *Multi-level governance and European integration*. Rowman & Littlefield Publishers.

Hooghe, L., & Marks, G. (2003). Unravelling the Central State, but how? Types of Multi-Level Governance. *The American Political Science Review*, *97*(2), 233–243.

Hopkins, C. (1923). *Scientific advertising*. Crown Publishers Inc.

Hörisch, J. (2018). 'Think big'or'small is beautiful'? An empirical analysis of characteristics and determinants of success of sustainable crowdfunding projects. *International Journal of Entrepreneurial Venturing*, *10*(1), 111–129. doi:10.1504/IJEV.2018.090982

Hotho, J., & Saka-Helmhout, A. (2017). In and between societies: Reconnecting comparative institutionalism and organizational theory. *Organization Studies*, *38*(5), 647–666.

Hotiç. (n.d.). *Markamız*. https://www.hotic.com.tr/pages/markamiz

Houston, F. S. (1986). The marketing concept: What it is and what it is not. *Journal of Marketing*, *50*(2), 81–87. doi:10.1177/002224298605000207

Hristova, S., Dragičević Šešić, M., & Duxbury, N. (2015). Introduction. In S. Hristova, M. Dragičević Šešić, & N. Duxbury (Eds.), *Culture and Sustainability in European Cities. Imagining Europolis* (pp. 1–13). Routledge. doi:10.4324/9781315772028

Hughes, K. D., Jennings, J. E., Brush, C. G., Carter, S., & Welter, F. (2012). Extending women's entrepreneurship research in new directions. *Entrepreneurship Theory and Practice*, *36*(3), 429–442. doi:10.1111/j.1540-6520.2012.00504.x

Iansiti, M., & Levien, R. (2004). *The keystone advantage: what the new dynamics of business ecosystems mean for strategy, innovation, and sustainability*. Harvard Business School Press.

İnci Deri. (n.d.). http://kurumsal.incideri.com/

Inclusive Internet Index. (2021). https://theinclusiveinternet.eiu.com/

International Monetary Fund (IMF). (2021). *Miles to go: The future of emerging markets*. https://www.imf.org/external/pubs/ft/fandd/2021/06/the-future-of-emerging-markets-duttagupta-and-pazarbasioglu.htm

ISCTE-IUL. (2014). *Plano Estratégico 2014-2017*. ISCTE-IUL.

Isenberg, D. (2014). What an entrepreneurship ecosystem actually is. *Harvard Business Review*, *5*(1), 7.

Isenberg, D. J. (2010). How to start an entrepreneurial revolution. *Harvard Business Review, 88*(6), 40–50.

Jabeen, F., Faisal, M., & Katsioloudes, M. (2017). Entrepreneurial mindset and the role of universities as strategic drivers of entrepreneurship: Evidence from the United Arab Emirates. *Journal of Small Business and Enterprise Development, 24*(1), 136–157. doi:10.1108/JSBED-07-2016-0117

Jachtenfuchs, M. (1995). Theoretical Perspectives on European Governance. *European Law Journal, 1*(2), 115–133. doi:10.1111/j.1468-0386.1995.tb00010.x

Jain-Chandra, S., Kochhar, K., Newiak, M., Zeinullayev, T., & Zhuang, L. (2017). Gender inequality around the world. In K. Kochhar, S. Jain-Chandra, & M. Newiak (Eds.), *Women, work, and economic growth: Leveling the playing field* (1st ed., pp. 13–27).

Jamal, Z., Alameddine, M., Diaconu, K., Lough, G., Witter, S., Ager, A., & Fouad, F. M. (2020). Health system resilience in the face of crisis: Analysing the challenges, strategies and capacities for UNRWA in Syria. *Health Policy and Planning, 35*, 26–35. https://doi.org/10.1093/heapol/czz129

Jasanoff, S. (2004a) *post-sovereign science and global nature*. Harvard University, Environmental Politics/ Colloquium Papers.

Jasanoff, S. (2004b). The idiom of co-production. In S. Jasanoff (Ed.), *States of Knowledge. The coproduction of science and social order* (pp. 1–13). Routledge. doi:10.4324/9780203413845-6

Jennings, J. E., & Brush, C. G. (2013). Research on women entrepreneurs: Challenges to (and from) the broader entrepreneurship literature? *The Academy of Management Annals, 7*(1), 663–715. doi:10.5465/19416520.2013.782190

Jennings, J. E., & McDougald, M. S. (2007). Work-Family Interface Experiences and Coping Strategies: Implications for Entrepreneurship Research and Practice. *Academy of Management Review, 32*(3), 747–760. doi:10.5465/amr.2007.25275510

Jessop, B. (2000). The Crisis of the National Spatio-temporal Fix and the Tendential Ecological Dominance of Globalizing Capitalism. *International Journal of Urban and Regional Research, 24*(2), 323–360. doi:10.1111/1468-2427.00251

Joll, J. (1978). *Europe since 1870*. Penguin.

Jones, G. R. (2013). *Organizational theory, design, and change* (7th ed.). Prentice Hall.

Jyoti, Verma, Gagandeep. (2020). A Holistic Approach of Quality in Higher Education System vis-a-vis Sustainable Development. *International Journal of Management, 11*, 10,433–440.

Kadlec, A., & Friedman, W. (2007). Deliberative Democracy and the Problem of Power. *Journal of Public Deliberation, 3*(1). Available online at: http://www. publicdeliberation.net/jpd/vol3/iss1/art8

Kambil, A., Ginsberg, A., & Bloch, M. (1996). Re-inventing value propositions. In *Information systems working paper series stern #IS-96-21*. University.

Kangas, A. (2017). *Removing Barriers. Participative and Collaborative Cultural Activities in Kuulto Action Research.* Centre for Cultural Policy Research Cupore.

Kara, A., Zhou, H., & Zhou, Y. (2021). Achieving the United Nations' sustainable development goals through financial inclusion: A systematic literature review of access to finance across the globe. *International Review of Financial Analysis, 77*, 12–23. https://doi.org/10.1016/j.irfa.2021.101833

Katunarić, V. (2004). Toward the New Public Culture. In N. Švob-Đokić (Ed.), *Cultural Transitions in Southeastern Europe. Culture link Joint Publication Series No 6* (pp. 19–43). Institute for International Relations.

Katz, J. (2003). The chronology and intellectual trajectory of American entrepreneurship education: 1876–1999. *Journal of Business Venturing, 18*(2), 283–300. doi:10.1016/S0883-9026(02)00098-8

Katz, J. A., & Gartner, W. B. (1988). Properties of emerging organizations. *Academy of Management Review, 13*(3), 429–441.

Keating, M. (2002). Territorial Politics and the New Regionalism. In Development in West European Politics (Vol. 2, pp. 201–220). Academic Press.

Kelegama, S. (1998). Can Open Regionalism Work in the Indian Ocean Rim Association for Regional Co-operation? *ASEAN Economic Bulletin, 15*(2), 153–167. doi:10.1355/AE15-2D

Kemal Tanca. (n.d.). https://www.kemaltanca.com.tr/hakkimizda-sc52ab

Kepenek, E. B., & Eser, Z. (2018). Impact of pre-incubators on entrepreneurial activities in Turkey: Problems, successes, and policy recommendations. In *Innovation and the Entrepreneurial University* (pp. 57–82). Springer. doi:10.1007/978-3-319-62649-9_4

Kerlin, J. A. (2006). *Social enterprise in the United States and Europe: Understanding and learning from the differences.* doi:10.1007/s11266-006-9016-2

Kessler, M. M. (1963). Bibliographic coupling between scientific articles. *American Documentation, 24*, 123–131.

Khanna, T., & Palepu, K. G. (2011). *Filling "institutional voids" in emerging markets.* https://www.hbs.edu/news/Pages/item.aspx?num=1524

Khanna, T., Palepu, K. G., & Sinha, J. (2005). *Strategies that fit emerging markets.* https://www.hbr.org/2005/06/strategies-that-fit-emerging-markets

Khanna, T., & Palepu, K. (1997). Why focused strategies. *Harvard Business Review, 75*(4), 41–51.

Khanna, T., & Palepu, K. (2000). The future of business groups in emerging markets: Long-run evidence from Chile. *Academy of Management Journal, 43*(3), 268–285.

King, G. (1994). *Designing social inquiry. Scientific inference in qualitative research.* Princeton University Press. doi:10.1515/9781400821211

Kirzner, I. M. (1973). *Competition and entrepreneurship*. University of Chicago Press.

Koe, W.-L., & Majid, I. A. (2014). Intention towards Sustainable Entrepreneurship: A Conceptual Framework. *The Journal of Technology Management and Technopreneurship, 1*(1).

Kohler-Koch, B., & Quittkat, C. (2013). *De-Mystification of Participatory Democracy*. Oxford University Press. doi:10.1093/acprof:oso/9780199674596.001.0001

Koo, S. H. (2017). Consumer differences in the United States and India on wearable trackers. *Family and Consumer Sciences Research Journal, 46*(1), 40–56. doi:10.1111/fcsr.12230

Korunka, C., Frank, H., Lueger, M., & Mugler, J. (2003). The Entrepreneurial Personality in the Context of Resources, Environment, and the Start- up Process -A Configurational Approach. *Entrepreneurship Theory and Practice, 28*(1), 23–42. doi:10.1111/1540-8520.00030

KOSGEB. (2022). https://en.kosgeb.gov.tr/site/tr/genel/destekler/6311/sme-finance-supports

Kostova, T., Roth, K., & Dacin, M. T. (2008). Institutional theory in the study of multinational corporations: A critique and new directions. *Academy of Management Review, 33*(4), 994–1006.

Kotler, P., & Lee, N. (2005). Best of breed: When it comes to gaining a market edge while supporting a social cause,"corporate social marketing" leads the pack. *Social Marketing Quarterly, 11*(3-4), 91–103. doi:10.1080/15245000500414480

Kraus, S., Burtscher, J., Vallaster, C., & Angerer, M. (2018). Sustainable entrepreneurship orientation: A reflection on status-quo research on factors facilitating responsible managerial practices. *Sustainability, 10*(2), 444. doi:10.3390u10020444

Krueger, N. F. Jr, Reilly, M. D., & Carsrud, A. L. (2000). Competing models of entrepreneurial intentions. *Journal of Business Venturing, 15*(5/6), 411–432.

Krueger, N. Jr, Reilly, M., & Carsrud, A. (2000). Competing models of entrepreneurial intentions. *Journal of Business Venturing, 15*(5-6), 411–432. doi:10.1016/S0883-9026(98)00033-0

Kumar, M. (2018). Institutional voids and Indian automotive industry: Challenges and reflection. In Emerging markets from a multidisciplinary perspective: Advances in theory and practice of emerging markets (1st ed., pp. 405–414). Springer. https://doi.org/10.1007/978-3-319-75013-2_30.

Lafley, A. G., & Martin, R. L. (2013). *Playing to win: How strategy really works*. Harvard Business Press.

Laird, F. N. (1993). Participatory analysis, democracy and technological decision making. *Science, Technology & Human Values, 18*(3), 341–361. doi:10.1177/016224399301800305

Langbein, L. I., & Kerwin, C. M. (2000). Regulatory negotiation versus conventional rule making: Claims, counterclaims, and empirical evidence. *Journal of Public Administration: Research and Theory, 10*(3), 599–632. doi:10.1093/oxfordjournals.jpart.a024283

Lanning, M. (2000). *An Introduction to the Market-Focused Philosophy, Framework and Methodology Called Delivering Profitable Value*. Available: http://www.exubrio.com/white-papers/DPVIntro- eXubrio.pdf

Lanning, M. (2003). *An introduction to the market-focused philosophy, framework and methodology called delivering profitable value*. Academic Press.

Lanning, M., & Michaels, E. (1988). *A business is a value delivery system*. McKinsey Staff Paper No. 41.

Lanning, M. (1998). *Delivering profitable value*. Perseus Publishing.

Lans, T., Blok, V., & Wesselink, R. (2014). Learning apart and together: Towards an integrated competence framework for sustainable entrepreneurship in higher education. *Journal of Cleaner Production, 62*(C), 37–47.

Larik, J. E., Daniëls, L., Oosterom, J., Ruiter, L. D., Smit, L., Vermeij, A., & Vliet, V. V. (2017). *Blue growth and sustainable development in Indian ocean governance*. The Hague Institute for Global Justice Policy Brief.

Latendresse, A. (2010). *Le BP du Plateau-Mont-Royal: Évaluation d'une experience unique à Montréal*. Preliminary document presented to Plateau-Mont-Royal administration, March 2010. Report.

Latour, B., & Woolgar. (1997). *De Berlijnse sleutel en andere lessen van een liefhebber van wetenschap en techniek*. Amsterdam: Van Gennep.

Latour, B. (1987). *Science in Action*. Harvard University Press.

Lee, J. (2015). Smart factory systems. *Informatik-Spektrum, 38*(3), 230–235. doi:10.100700287-015-0891-z

Lee, J. (2016). Designed to Succeed: Participatory Governance, Transaction Cost, and Policy Performance. *Korean Journal of Policy Studies, 31*(2), 1–22. doi:10.52372/kjps31201

Lee, S. H., & Wong, P. K. (2004). An exploratory study of technopreneurial intentions: A career anchor perspective. *Journal of Business Venturing, 19*(1), 7–28. doi:10.1016/S0883-9026(02)00112-X

Lehmann, E. E., & Seitz, N. (2017). Freedom and innovation: A country and state level analysis. *The Journal of Technology Transfer, 42*(5), 1009–1029. doi:10.100710961-016-9478-3

Leitao, P., & Restivo, F. J. (2008). Implementation of a holonic control system in a flexible manufacturing system. *IEEE Transactions on Systems, Man and Cybernetics. Part C, Applications and Reviews, 38*(5), 699–709. doi:10.1109/TSMCC.2008.923881

Lenka, U., & Agarwal, S. (2017). Role of women entrepreneurs and NGOs in promoting entrepreneurship: Case studies from Uttarakhand, India. *Journal of Asia Business Studies, 11*(4), 451–465. doi:10.1108/JABS-07-2015-0088

Lenzer, G. (Ed.). (1975). *Auguste Comte and positivism; the essential writings*. University of Chicago Press.

Levinsohn, D. (2013). Disembedded and beheaded? - a critical review of the emerging field of sustainability entrepreneurship. *International Journal of Entrepreneurship and Small Business*, *19*, 190–211. https://doi.org/10.1504/IJESB.2013.054963

Liao, H., Tang, M., Luo, L., Li, C., Chiclana, F., & Zeng, X. J. (2018). A bibliometric analysis and visualization of medical big data research. *Sustainability*, *10*(1), 1–18. https://doi.org/10.3390/su10010166

Lindberg, L. N. (1963). *The political dynamics of European economic integration*. Stanford Univ. Press.

Lindstrom, M. (2005). *Brand sense: Build powerful brands through touch, taste, smell, sight, and sound*. Free Press.

Llewellyn, L. E., English, S., & Barnwell, S. (2016). A roadmap to a sustainable Indian Ocean blue economy. *Journal of the Indian Ocean Region*, *12*(1), 52–66. doi:10.1080/19480881.2016.1138713

Loeber, A. (2004). *Practical wisdom in the risk society: methods and practice of interpretive analysis on questions of sustainable development* (Thesis). University of Amsterdam.

Love, J. H., & Roper, S. (2004). The organisation of innovation: Collaboration, cooperation and multifunctional groups in UK and German manufacturing. *Cambridge Journal of Economics*, *28*(3), 379–395.

Lucke, D., Constantinescu, C., & Westkämper, E. (2008). Smart factory-a step towards the next generation of manufacturing. In *Manufacturing systems and technologies for the new frontier* (pp. 115–118). Springer. doi:10.1007/978-1-84800-267-8_23

Lukban Rosetea, M. A., & Eleria, N. L. (2020). *Examining the Significance of the Luzon W-Growth Corridor to Agricultural Agglomeration and Labor Productivity*. Millennium Journal of Humanities and Social Sciences. doi:10.47340/mjhss.v1i3.1.2020

Lux, A. A., Macau, F. R., & Brown, K. A. (2020). Putting the entrepreneur back into entrepreneurial ecosystems. *International Journal of Entrepreneurial Behaviour & Research*, *26*(5), 1011–1041. doi:10.1108/IJEBR-01-2020-0031

Mack, E., & Mayer, H. (2016). The evolutionary dynamics of entrepreneurial ecosystems. *Urban Studies (Edinburgh, Scotland)*, *53*(10), 2118–2133. doi:10.1177/0042098015586547

Mair, J. (2005). Entrepreneurial behavior in a large traditional firm: Exploring key drivers. In T. Elfring (Ed.), *Corporate entrepreneurship and venturing* (pp. 49–72). Springer.

Majone, G. (1998). Europe's Democratic Deficit: The Question of Standards. *European Law Journal*, *4*(1), 5–28. doi:10.1111/1468-0386.00040

Malecki, E. J. (2018). Entrepreneurship and entrepreneurial ecosystems. *Geography Compass*, *12*(3), e12359. doi:10.1111/gec3.12359

Manimala, M. J., & Wasdani, K. P. (2015). Emerging Economies: muddling through to development. In M. Manimala & K. Wasdani (Eds.), *Entrepreneurial Ecosystem*. Springer. doi:10.1007/978-81-322-2086-2_1

Manin, B. (1997). *The principles of representative government*. Cambridge University Press. doi:10.1017/CBO9780511659935

March, J., & Olsen, J. (1989). *Rediscovering Institutions: The Organizational Basis of Politics*. The Free Press.

Maresch, D., Harms, R., Kailer, N., & Wimmer-Wurm, B. (2016). The impact of entrepreneurship education on the entrepreneurial intention of students in science and engineering versus business studies university programs. *Technological Forecasting and Social Change*, *104*, 172–179. doi:10.1016/j.techfore.2015.11.006

Martin, B., McNally, J., & Kay, M. (2013). Examining the formation of human capital in entrepreneurship: A meta-analysis of entrepreneurship education outcomes. *Journal of Business Venturing*, *28*(2), 211–224. doi:10.1016/j.jbusvent.2012.03.002

Martinez, V., & Bititci, U. S. (2006). Aligning value propositions in supply chains. *International Journal of Value Chain Management*, *1*(1), 6–18.

Masik, G., & Grabkowska, M. (2020). Practical dimension of urban and regional resilience concepts: A proposal of resilience strategy model. *Regional Studies on Development*, *24*(1), 30–34.

Mathew, R. V., & Panchanatham, N. (2011, July 1). An exploratory study on the work-life balance of women entrepreneurs in South India. *Asian Academy of Management Journal*, *16*(2), 77–105.

Mathew, V. (2009). Sustainable Entrepreneurship in Small-Scale Business: Application, Concepts and Cases. *ICFAI Journal of Entrepreneurship Development*, *6*(1), 41–61.

McComas, K. A. (2001). Public meetings about local waste management problems: Comparing participants to nonparticipants. *Environmental Management*, *27*(1), 135–147. doi:10.1007002670010139 PMID:11083914

McGee & Kelbert. (2013). *Review of approaches to social accountability for Citizens' Engagement Programme*. Academic Press.

McInerney. (2012). Social Enterprise in Mixed-Form Fields: Challenges and Prospects. In B. Gidron & Y. Hasenfeld (Eds.), *Social Enterprises: An Organizational Perspective* (pp. 162–184). Palgrave Macmillan.

McMullen, J. S. (2011). Delineating the domain of development entrepreneurship: A market-based approach to facilitating inclusive economic growth. *Entrepreneurship Theory and Practice*, (35), 185–215.

McWilliams, A., & Siegel, D. (2001). Corporate social responsibility: A theory of firm perspective. *Academy of Management Review*, *26*, 117–127.

Mehmood, Z. H., & Khan, R. (2021). Assessing Indian Ocean Economics: Perspective from Pakistan. [AJIS]. *Andalas Journal of International Studies*, *10*(1), 1–15. doi:10.25077/ajis.10.1.1-15.2021

Merigó, J. M., Pedrycz, W., Weber, R., & de la Sotta, C. (2018). Fifty years of Information Sciences: A bibliometric overview. *Information Sciences*, *432*, 245–268. https://doi.org/10.1016/j.ins.2017.11.054

Miller, D. (1983). The correlates of entrepreneurship in three types of firm. *Management Science*, *29*(7), 770–791. doi:10.1287/mnsc.29.7.770

Mohyuddin, A., Chaudhry, H., & Ambreen, M. (2012). Economic empowerment of women in the rural areas of Balochistan. *Pakistan Journal of Women's Studies, 19*(2), 239-257.

Moore, J. F. (1993). Predators and prey: A new ecology of competition. *Harvard Business Review*, *71*(3), 75–86. PMID:10126156

Moravcsik, A. (1998). The choice for Europe. Social purpose and state power from Messina to Maastricht. Cornell Univ. Press.

Moravcsik, A. (2002). In Defence of the 'Democratic Deficit': Reassessing Legitimacy in the European Union. *Journal of Common Market Studies*, *40*(4), 603–624. doi:10.1111/1468-5965.00390

Moriano, J. A., Gorgievski, M., Laguna, M., Stephan, U., & Zarafshani, K. (2012). A cross-cultural approach to understanding entrepreneurial intention. *Journal of Career Development*, *39*(2), 162–185. doi:10.1177/0894845310384481

Morris, M. H. (1998). *Entrepreneurial Intensity*. Quorum Publishing.

Mouffe, C. (1992). Democratic Citizenship and the Political Community. In C. Mouffe (Ed.), *Dimensions of Radical Democracy. Pluralism, Citizenship, Community* (pp. 225–239). Verso.

Muñoz, P., & Cohen, B. (2018). Sustainable entrepreneurship research: Taking stock and looking ahead. *Bus. Strateg. Environ.*, *27*, 300–322. doi:10.1002/bse.2000

Nabatchi, T. (2010). Addressing the Citizenship and Democracy Deficits: The Potential of Deliberative Democracy for Public Administration. *American Review of Public Administration*, *40*(4), 376–399. doi:10.1177/0275074009356467

Nabi, G., Walmsley, A., Liñán, F., Akhtar, I., & Neame, C. (2018). Does entrepreneurship education in the first year of higher education develop entrepreneurial intentions? The role of learning and inspiration. *Studies in Higher Education*, *43*(3), 452–467. doi:10.1080/03075079.2016.1177716

Nambisan, S., Siegel, D., & Kenney, M. (2018). On Open Innovation, Platforms, and Entrepreneurship. *Strategic Entrepreneurship Journal*, *12*(3), 354–368. doi:10.1002ej.1300

Nandakumar, M. K., Ghobadian, A., & O'Regan, N. (2011). Generic strategies and performance–evidence from manufacturing firms. *International Journal of Productivity and Performance Management*.

Neck, H. M., Meyer, G. D., Cohen, B., & Corbett, A. C. (2004). An entrepreneurial system view of new venture creation. *Journal of Small Business Management*, *42*(2), 190–208. doi:10.1111/j.1540-627X.2004.00105.x

Neneh, B. N. (2017, September 01). Family Support and Performance of Women-owned Enterprises: The Mediating Effect of Family-to-Work Enrichment. *The Journal of Entrepreneurship*, *26*(2), 196–219. doi:10.1177/0971355717716762

Newenham-Kahindi, A. (2015). Managing sustainable development through people: Implications for multinational enterprises in developing countries. *Personnel Review*, *44*(3), 388–407.

Ng, T., Sorensen, K., & Eby, L. (2006). Locus of control at work: A metaanalysis. *Journal of Organizational Behavior*, *27*(8), 1057–1087.

Nhemachena, C. (2017). *Motivations of sustainable entrepreneurship in Gauteng province, South Africa* (Doctoral dissertation).

Nicholls, A. (2008). *Social entrepreneurship: New models of sustainable social change*. Oxford University Press.

North, D. C. (1990). *Institutions, Institutional Change and Economic Performance*. Press Syndicate of the University of Cambridge. doi:10.1017/CBO9780511808678

North, D. C. (1991). Institutions. *The Journal of Economic Perspectives*, *5*(1), 97–112. doi:10.1257/jep.5.1.97

Norval, A. J. (2014). Deliberative, Agonistic and Aversive Grammars of Democracy: The Question of Criteria. In S. Griggs, A. J. Norval, & H. Wagenaar (Eds.), *Practices of Freedom: Decentered Governance, Conflict and Democratic Participation*. Cambridge University Press. doi:10.1017/CBO9781107296954.003

Nurul, A. F. (2018). *The role of self-leadership on student's entrepreneurial intention with self-efficacy as mediating variable: a study in Andalas University* (Doctoral dissertation). Universitas Andalas.

Nuwayhid, I., Zurayk, H., Yamout, R., & Cortas, C. S. (2011). Summer 2006 war on Lebanon: A lesson in community resilience. *Global Public Health: An International Journal for Research, Policy and Practice*, *6*(5), 505–519.

O'Neill, G. D., Jr., Hershauer, J. C., & Golden, J. S. (2006). The cultural context of sustainability entrepreneurship. *Greener Manag. Int.*, 33–46. doi:10.9774/GLEAF.3062.2006.au.00005

Oakley, P., & Marsden, D. (1985). *Approaches to participation in rural development*. International Labour Office.

Obeidat, A. M., Atef Wahiby, H., Alshammari, D. M., Alzu'bi, S. K., Hadrab, A. F., & Samarah, M. A. (2021). The moderate role of knowledge sharing on the effect of human capital in job empowerment. *Ilkogretim Online – Elementary Education, 20*(5), 163-172. doi:10.17051/ilkonline.2021.05.15

Obeidat, A. M., Abualoush, S. H., Irtaimeh, H. J., Khaddam, A. A., & Bataineh, K. A. (2018). The role of organizational culture in enhancing the human capital applied study on the social security corporation. *International Journal of Learning and Intellectual Capital, 15*(3), 258–276.

Obuljen Koržinek, N., Žuvela, A., Jelinčić, D. A., & Polić, M. (2014). *Strategija razvoja kulture Grada Dubrovnika 2015 – 2025*. Grad Dubrovnik. Available online at: https://dura.hr/user_files/admin/strateski%20dokumenti/Kulturna%20strategija%20grada%20Dubrovnika.pdf

Obuljen, N., & Smiers, J. (2006). Introduction. In UNESCO's Convention on the Protection and Promotion of the Diversity of Cultural Expressions: Making it Work. Zagreb: Institute for International Relations.

ODTU Technokent. (2022). http://odtuteknokent.com.tr/en/information/why-odtu-teknokent

OECD Country Report. (2021). https://data.oecd.org/turkey.htm

OECD. (2021a). https://data.oecd.org/tax/tax-on-corporate-profits.htm#indicator-chart

OECD. (2021b). https://data.oecd.org/tax/tax-wedge.htm#indicator-chart

OECD. (2021c). Key figures on immigration and emigration – Turkey. In *International Migration Outlook 2021*. OECD Publishing. doi:10.1787/7b896aa0-en

OECD. (2022). *Labour: Labour market statistics. Main Economic Indicators* (database). OECD.

OECD/Eurostat. (2018). *Oslo Manual 2018: Guidelines for Collecting, Reporting and Using Data on Innovation* (4th ed.). OECD Publishing. doi:10.1787/9789264304604-en

Ogilvy, D. (1947). *Correspondence to Rosser reeves from David Ogilvy. In 1 August 1947. Rosser Reeves Papers*. Wisconsin Historical Society.

Oliver, C. (1991). Strategic responses to institutional processes. *Academy of Management Review, 16*(1), 145–179.

Onsongo, E. (2019). Institutional entrepreneurship and social innovation at the base of the pyramid: The case of M-Pesa in Kenya. *Industry and Innovation, 26*(4), 369–390. https://doi.org/10.1080/13662716.2017.1409104

Oosterbeek, H., Van Praag, M., & Ijsselstein, A. (2010). The impact of entrepreneurship education on entrepreneurship skills and motivation. *European Economic Review, 54*(3), 442–454. doi:10.1016/j.euroecorev.2009.08.002

Osterwalder, A., & Pigneur, Y. (2010). *Business model generation*. Academic Press.

Ostrom, E. (1990). *Governing the Commons: The Evolution of Institutions for Collective Action Cambridge University Press*. Cambridge University Press. doi:10.1017/CBO9780511807763

Ostrom, E. (2006). *Upravljanje zajedničkim dobrima. Evolucija institucija za kolektivno djelovanje*. Naklada Jesenski i Turk.

Owen, D., & Smith, G. (2015, June). Survey Article: Deliberation, Democracy, and the Systemic Turn. *Journal of Political Philosophy*, *23*(2), 213–234. doi:10.1111/jopp.12054

Paasi, A. (1986). The institutionalization of regions: A theoretical framework for understanding the emergence of regions and the constitution of regional identity. *Fennia - International. The Journal of Geography*, *164*(1), 105–146. https://fennia.journal.fi/article/view/9052

Paasi, A. (1996). *Territories, boundaries, and consciousness. In The changing geographies of the Finnish-Russian border*. J. Wiley & Sons.

Pache, A., & Santos, F. (2013). Inside the hybrid organization: Selective coupling as a response to competing institutional logics. *Academy of Management Journal*, (56), 972–1001.

Palazzi, M., & Starcher, G. (2006). *Corporate Social Responsibility and Business Success*. Retrieved from http://centreonphilanthropy.com/files/kb_articles/1269270655EBBF%20Corporate%20Responsibility%20and%20Business%20Success.pdf

Papadopoulos, Y. (2010) Governance und Demokratie. In Governance - Regieren in komplexen Regelsystemen eine Einführung. Wiesbaden VS, Verl. für Sozialwissenschaften. doi:10.1007/978-3-531-92325-3_11

Park, C. (2017). A study on effect of entrepreneurship on entrepreneurial intention: Focusing on ICT majors. *Asia Pacific Journal of Innovation and Entrepreneurship*, *11*(2), 159–170. doi:10.1108/APJIE-08-2017-024

Park, J. H., & Ahn, T. U. (2016). A Study on the Influence of Young Entrepreneurs' Entrepreneurship and Entrepreneurial preparation upon the Entrepreneurial Performance: Centered on Mediated Effect of Entrepreneurial infra system using. *Asia-Pacific Journal of Business Venturing and Entrepreneurship*, *11*(1), 39–47. doi:10.16972/apjbve.11.1.201602.39

Parnini, S. N. (2010). Institutionalizing linkages between ASEAN & Bangladesh: Challenges & prospects. *The International Journal of the Arts in Society*, *3*(13), 375–392.

Parrish, B. D. (2010). Sustainability-driven entrepreneurship: Principles of organization design. *Journal of Business Venturing*, *25*(5), 510–523.

Pateman, C. (2000). *Participation and democratic theory*. Cambridge Univ. Press.

Pateman, C. (2012). Participatory Democracy Revised. *Perspectives on Politics*, *10*(1), 7–19. doi:10.1017/S1537592711004877

Payne, A., & Frow, P. (2005). A strategic framework for customer relationship management. *Journal of Marketing*, *69*(4), 167–176.

Payne, A., & Frow, P. (2014). Developing superior value propositions: A strategic marketing imperative. *Journal of Service Management*.

Pearson, R. M., Schlacheer, T. A., Jinks, K. I., Olds, A. D., Brown, C. J., & Connolly, R. M. (2021). Disturbance type determines how connectivity shapes ecosystem resilience. *Scientific Reports*, *11*(1), 1–8. https://doi.org/10.1038/s41598-021-80987-1

Peredo, A. M., & McLean, M. (2006). Social entrepreneurship: A critical review of the concept. *Journal of World Business*, *41*, 56–65.

Perkmann, M. (2007a). Construction of new territorial scales: A framework and case study of the EUREGIO cross-border region. *Regional Studies*, *41*(2), 253–266. doi:10.1080/00343400600990517

Petrić, L., Petrić, M., Pavičić, I., Miše, M., Hameršak, M., & Pleše, I. (2015). Kultura i kulturna baština. In *Nacrt prijedloga Plana upravljanja povijesnom jezgrom Splita i plana upravljanja podrumima Dioklecijanove palače (II – Analiza stanja)*. Split: Grad Split. Available online at: https://www.split.hr/Default.aspx?art=7774

Pittaway, L., & Cope, J. (2007). Entrepreneurship education: A systematic review of the evidence. *International Small Business Journal*, *25*(5), 479–510. doi:10.1177/0266242607080656

Popescu, C. R. G. (2022). Environmental, Social, and Corporate Governance by Avoiding Management Bias and Tax Minimization: Reaching a General Consensus Regarding a Minimum Global Tax Rate. In C. Popescu (Ed.), *COVID-19 Pandemic Impact on New Economy Development and Societal Change* (pp. 94–132). IGI Global. doi:10.4018/978-1-6684-3374-4.ch006

Porter, M. E. (1980). Competitive strategy. New York: Free Press.

Prabha, D. T., Panigrahi, S. K., Maisnam, C., Alyani, W. A., & Bino, E. (2019). The Female Entrepreneurs' attitude towards Entrepreneurship: How Entrepreneurial Orientation and Desirability Influence Intention of Entrepreneurial Students? *Delhi Business Review*, *20*(2), 11-24.

Pratheeesh, J. T., & Arumugasamy, G. (2020). Impact of Coronavirus in Indian economy and banking sector-an overview. *Studies in Indian Place Names*, *40*(18), 2090–2101.

Premand, P., Brodmann, S., Almeida, R., Grun, R., & Barouni, M. (2016). Entrepreneurship education and entry into self-employment among university graduates. *World Development*, *77*, 311–327. doi:10.1016/j.worlddev.2015.08.028

Provasnek, A. K., Schmid, E., Geissler, B., & Steiner, G. (2017). Sustainable corporate entrepreneurship: Performance and strategies toward innovation. *Business Strategy and the Environment*, *26*(4), 521–535.

Putnam, R. D. (1993). *Making Democracy Work: Civic Traditions in Modern Italy*. Princeton University Press.

Rabouin, L. (2009). *Démocratiser la ville: Le budget participatif: De Porto Alegre à Montréal*. Montreal: Lux Éditeur.

Radaelli, C. M. (1999). *Technocracy in the European Union*. Addison Wesley Longman.

Radziwon, A., Bilberg, A., Bogers, M., & Madsen, E. S. (2014). The smart factory: Exploring adaptive and flexible manufacturing solutions. *Procedia Engineering*, *69*, 1184–1190. doi:10.1016/j.proeng.2014.03.108

Rani, P., & Gupta, S. (2017). Factor Affecting the Students Buying Behavior of Two Wheelers. *Journal of Marketing Management*, *8*(1), 31.

Rao, S., Vlassoff, C., & Sarode, J. (2014). Economic development, women's social and economic empowerment and reproductive health in rural India. *Asian Population Studies*, *10*(1), 4–22.

Rawal, T. (2018). A study of Social Entrepreneurship in India. *International Research Journal of Engineering and Technology*, *5*(1), 829–837.

Rawls, J. (1995). Political Liberalism: Reply to Habermas. *The Journal of Philosophy*, *92*(3), 132–180. doi:10.2307/2940843

RBI. (2020). Monetary Policy Report. Reserve Bank of India.

Reeves, E. (2008). The practice of contracting in public private partnerships: Transaction costs and relational contracting in the Irish school's sector. *Public Administration*, *86*(4), 969–986. doi:10.1111/j.1467-9299.2008.00743.x

Reeves, R. (1961). *Reality in advertising*. Knopf.

Rele, S. (2020). Emerging outbreaks and epidemic threats: The practicality and limitations in the development and manufacturing of treatments for Coronavirus (COVID-19). *Polymorphism*, *4*, 45–52.

Republic of Turkey, Social Security Institution. (2022). http://www.sgk.gov.tr/wps/portal/sgk/tr/calisan/kayitdisi_istihdam/kayitdisi_istihdam_oranlari

Reyes-Rodríguez, J. F., Ulhøi, J. P., & Madsen, H. (2016). Corporate Environmental Sustainability in Danish SMEs: A Longitudinal Study of Motivators, Initiatives, and Strategic Effects. *Corporate Social Responsibility and Environmental Management*, *23*(4), 193–212. doi:10.1002/csr.1359

Richardson, J. J. (1996). *European Union: Power and Policy making*. Routledge.

Ries, A., & Trout, J. (1986). *Positioning: The battle for your mind*. McGraw-Hill.

Riess, H. (2021). Institutional resilience: The foundation for individual resilience, especially during COVID-19. *Global Advances in Health and Medicine: Improving Healthcare Outcomes Worldwide*, *10*, 1–3. https://doi.org/10.1177/21649561211006728

Rintamäki, T., Kuusela, H., & Mitronen, L. (2007). Identifying competitive customer value propositions in retailing. *Managing Service Quality*, *17*(6), 621–634.

Ronstadt, R. (1987). The educated entrepreneurs: A new era of entrepreneurial education is beginning. *American Journal of Small Business*, *11*(4), 37–53. doi:10.1177/104225878701100403

Rowe, G., & Frewer, L. J. (2004). Evaluating Public-Participation Exercises: A Research Agenda. *Science, Technology & Human Values, 29*(4), 512–556. doi:10.1177/0162243903259197

Roy, A. (2019). Blue economy in the Indian Ocean: Governance perspectives for sustainable development in the region. *ORF Occasional Paper, 181.*

Sabatier, P. A., & Jenkins-Smith, H. C. (1993). Policy Change and Learning. An Advocacy Coalition Approach. Westview Press.

Sagawa, S., & Segal, E. (2000). Common interest, common good: Creating value through business and social sector partnership. *California Management Review, 42*(2), 105–122.

Santhi, N., & Kumar, S. R. (2011). Entrepreneurship Challenges and Opportunities in India International. *Journal of Industrial Engineering and Management Science, 1*, 14–16.

Sarango-Lalangui, P., Santos, J. L. S., & Hormiga, E. (2018). The development of sustainable entrepreneurship research field. *Sustain., 10*(6), 2005. Advance online publication. doi:10.3390u10062005

Satia, B. P. (2016). An overview of the large marine ecosystem programs at work in Africa today. *Environmental Development, 17*, 11–19. doi:10.1016/j.envdev.2015.06.007

Sawaneh, K., & Badjie, F. (2021). Empowering women in the Agricultural Value Chain through Islamic blended products to attain the agenda 2030 in The Gambia. *European Journal of Islamic Finance, 17*, 1–11.

Schaefer, K., Corner, P. D., & Kearins, K. (2015). Social, environmental and sustainable entrepreneurship research. *Organization & Environment, 28*(4), 394–413.

Schaltegger, S., & Wagner, M. (2011). Sustainable entrepreneurship and sustainability innovation: Categories and interactions. *Bus. Strateg. Environ., 20*, 222–237. doi:10.1002/bse.682

Schaltegger, S., Synnestvedt, T., & Vei, E. S. (2001). *The Forgotten Link Between" Green" and Economic Success.* Center for Sustainability Management.

Schjoedt, L., & Shaver, K. G. (2007). Deciding on an entrepreneurial career: A test of the pull and push hypotheses using the panel study of entrepreneurial dynamics data. *Entrepreneurship Theory and Practice, 31*(5), 733–752. doi:10.1111/j.1540-6520.2007.00197.x

Schmidt, M. G. (2000). *Demokratietheorien. In Eine Einführung* (3rd ed.). VS Verlag für Sozialwissenschaften. doi:10.1007/978-3-531-90008-7

Schrammel, T. (2013). Bridging the institutional void: An analytical concept to develop valuable cluster services. *Management Revenue, 24*(2), 114-132. doi:10.1688/1861-9908_mrev_2013_02_Schrammel

Schwarz, E. J., Wdowiak, M. A., Almer-Jarz, D. A., & Breitenecker, R. J. (2009). The effects of attitudes and perceived environment conditions on students' entrepreneurial intent: An Austrian perspective. *Education + Training, 51*(4), 272–291. doi:10.1108/00400910910964566

Seelos, C., & Mair, J. (2005). Social entrepreneurship: Creating new business models to serve the poor. *Business Horizon*, (48), 241-246.

Segal, G., Borgia, D., & Schoenfeld, J. (2005). The motivation to become an entrepreneur. *International Journal of Entrepreneurial Behaviour & Research, 11*(1), 42–57. doi:10.1108/13552550510580834

Shachar, A. (2001). *Multicultural Jurisdictions: Cultural Differences and Women's Rights*. Cambridge University Press. doi:10.1017/CBO9780511490330

Shane, S. (2004). *Academic entrepreneurship: University spinoffs and wealth creation*. Edward Elgar Publishing. doi:10.4337/9781843769828

Shapero, A. (1981). Self-renewing economies. *Economic Development Commentary, 5*(Ap), 19-22.

Sharma, G., & Kulshreshtha, K. (2014). Challenges and Opportunities of Entrepreneurs in Emerging Economies. *International Journal of Public Administration and Management Research, 2*(3), 1–8.

Shaw, E., Wilson, J., & Pret, T. (2017). The process of embedding a small firm in its industrial context. *International Small Business Journal: Researching Entrepreneurship, 35*(3), 219-243. doi:10.1177/0266242616671170

Shepherd, D. A., & Patzelt, H. (2011). The new field of sustainable entrepreneurship: Studying entrepreneurial action linking "what is to be sustained" with "what is to be developed." *Entrepreneurship Theory and Practice, 35*, 137–163.

Shook, C. L., & Bratianu, C. (2010). Entrepreneurial intent in a transitional economy: An application of the theory of planned behavior to Romanian students. *The International Entrepreneurship and Management Journal, 6*(3), 231–247. doi:10.100711365-008-0091-2

Sieger, P., Fueglistaller, U., & Zellweger, T. (2014). *Student entrepreneurship across the globe: A look at intentions and activities. International Report of the GUESSS Project 2014*. Swiss Research Institute of Small Business and Entrepreneurship at the University of St. Gallen.

Simbar, M., Alizadeh, S., Hajifoghaha, M., & Dabiri, F. (2017). Comparison of social, economic, and familial empowerment in married women in three cities of Iran. *International Journal of Community Based Nursing and Midwifery, 5*(3), 248–255.

Singapore Management University (SMU). (2013). *Institutional voids: Black hole or opportunities?* https://ink.library.smu.edu.sg/pers/21

Singh, D., Pattnaik, C., Gaur, A. S., & Ketencioglu, E. (2018). Corporate expansion during pro-market reforms in emerging markets: The contingent value of group affiliation and diversification. *Journal of Business Research, 82*, 220–229.

Skålén, P., Gummerus, J., von Koskull, C., & Magnusson, P. R. (2015). Exploring value propositions and service innovation: A service-dominant logic study. *Journal of the Academy of Marketing Science, 43*(2), 137–158.

Small, H. (1973). Co-citation in the scientific literature: A new measure of the relationship between two documents. *Journal of the American Society for Information Science*, *24*(4), 265–269. https://doi.org/10.1002/asi.4630240406

Sorensen, E., & Torfin, J. (2005). The Democratic Anchorage of Governance Networks. *Scandinavian Political Studies*, *28*(3), 195–218. doi:10.1111/j.1467-9477.2005.00129.x

Souitaris, V., Zerbinati, S., & Al-Laham, A. (2007). Do entrepreneurship programmes raise entrepreneurial intention of science and engineering students? The effect of learning, inspiration and resources. *Journal of Business Venturing, 22*(4), 566.

Souitaris, V., Zerbinati, S., & Al-Laham, A. (2007). Do entrepreneurship programmes raise entrepreneurial intention of science and engineering students? The effect of learning, inspiration and resources. *Journal of Business Venturing*, *22*(4), 566–591. doi:10.1016/j.jbusvent.2006.05.002

Stam, E. (2018). Measuring Entrepreneurial Ecosystems. In A. O'Connor, E. Stam, F. Sussan, & D. Audretsch (Eds.), Entrepreneurial Ecosystems. International Studies in Entrepreneurship (Vol. 38). Springer. https://doi.org/10.1007/978-3-319-63531-6_9.

Stam, E. (2015). Entrepreneurial ecosystems and regional policy: A sympathetic critique. *European Planning Studies*, *23*(9), 1759–1769.

Starch, D. (1914). *Advertising: Its principles, practice, and technique*. Scott, Foresman.

Statistics Portugal. (2018). *Estatísticas das Empresas – 2016*. National Statistics.

Statistics, E. (2020). *National Statistical Office*. Ministry of Statistics and Programme Implementation. Government of India.

Stavrakakis, Y. (2002). *The Ethical and Political challenge of Constructionism in Risk Societies: Post-democratic Trends and Civil Society. Essex papers in politics and government. Subseries in ideology and discourse analysis. No. 19, May 2002*. Dept. of Government, University of Essex.

Stein, Ch., Barron, J., & Moss, T. (2014). *Governance of the nexus: from buzz words to a strategic action perspective*. Nexus Network Think Piece Series, Paper 3.

Steinberg, P. E. (1999). The maritime mystique: Sustainable development, capital mobility, and nostalgia in the world ocean. *Environment and Planning. D, Society & Space*, *17*(4), 403–426. doi:10.1068/d170403

Stephan, U., Zbierowski, P., Perez-Luno, A., & Klausen, A. (2021). *Entrepreneurship during the COVID-19 pandemic: A global study of entrepreneurs challenges, resilience, and well-being*. King's Business School. https://www.kcl.ac.uk/business/assets/pdf/research-papers/global-report-entrepreneurship-during-the-covid-19-pandemic-a-global-study-of-entrepreneurs'-challenges-resilience-and-well-being.pdf

Sternberg, R. (2009). *Regional dimensions of entrepreneurship*. Now Publishers Inc. doi:10.1561/0300000024

Stevenson, H. H., & Jarrillo-Mossi, J. C. (1986). Preserving entrepreneurship as companies grow. *The Journal of Business Strategy*, *7*(1), 10–23. doi:10.1108/eb039138

Streeck, W., & Schmitter, P. C. (Eds.). (1986) *Private Interest Government Beyond Market and State.* Sage.

Subasinghe, R., Soto, D., & Jia, J. (2009). Global aquaculture and its role in sustainable development. *Reviews in Aquaculture*, *1*(1), 2–9. doi:10.1111/j.1753-5131.2008.01002.x

Suddaby, R. (2013). Institutional theory. In E. Kessler (Ed.), *Encyclopedia of management theory* (pp. 379–384). Sage.

Suddaby, R. (2015). Can institutional theory be critical? *Journal of Management Inquiry*, *24*(1), 93–95.

Suddaby, R., & Greenwood, R. (2001). Colonizing knowledge: Commodification as a dynamic of jurisdictional expansion in professional service firms. *Human Relations*, *54*(7), 933–953.

Suphannachart, W. (2017). What drives labour productivity in the ageing agriculture of Thailand? *Advances in Management and Applied Economics*, *7*(1), 89.

Szerb, L., Lafuente, E., Krisztina Horvath, K., & Páger, B. (2019). The relevance of quantity and quality entrepreneurship for regional performance: The moderating role of the entrepreneurial ecosystem. *Regional Studies*, *53*(9), 1308–1320. doi:10.1080/00343404.2018.1510481

Tambunan, T. (2009). Women entrepreneurship in Asian developing countries: Their development and main constraints. *Journal of Development and Agricultural Economics, 1*(2), 27-40.

TangS. Y.MazmanianD. (2010). Understanding Collaborative Governance from the Structural Choice - Politics, IAD, and Transaction Cost Perspectives. https://ssrn.com/abstract=1516851 doi:10.2139/ssrn.1516851

Tech Startup School. (2015a). *Entrepreneurship ecosystem and its elements: Business accelerator.* https://techstartupschool.com/news/entrepreneurship-ecosystem-and-its-elements.html

Tech Startup School. (2015b). *Entrepreneurship ecosystem nine elements.* https://techstartupschool.com/news/img/

Techera, E. J. (2018). Supporting blue economy agenda: Fisheries, food security and climate change in the Indian Ocean. *Journal of the Indian Ocean Region*, *14*(1), 7–27. doi:10.1080/19480881.2017.1420579

Tehseen, S., & Ramayah, T. (2015). Entrepreneurial competencies and SMEs business success: The contingent role of external integration. *Mediterranean Journal of Social Sciences*, *6*(1), 50–61. doi:10.5901/mjss.2015.v6n1p50

Terlouw, K. (2012). From thick to thin regional identities? *GeoJournal*, *77*(5), 707–721. doi:10.100710708-011-9422-x

Testa, F., Gusmerottia, N. M., Corsini, F., Passetti, E., & Iraldo, F. (2016). Factors Affecting Environmental Management by Small and Micro Firms: The Importance of Entrepreneurs' Attitudes and Environmental Investment. *Corporate Social Responsibility and Environmental Management*, *23*(6), 373–385. doi:10.1002/csr.1382

The Scientific And Technological Research Council of Turkey (TUBITAK). (n.d.). https://www.tubitak.gov.tr/en/funds/industry/national-support-programmes

Theodoraki, C., Messeghem, K., & Rice, M. P. (2018). A social capital approach to the development of sustainable entrepreneurial ecosystems: An explorative study. *Small Business Economics*, *51*(1), 153–170.

Thomas, P. (1980). *Karl Marx and the anarchists*. Psychology Press.

Thompson, J. (2002). The world of the social entrepreneur. *International Journal of Public Sector Management*, (15), 412–431.

Thompson, N., Kiefer, K., & York, J. G. (2011). Distinctions not dichotomies: Exploring social, sustainable, and environmental entrepreneurship. In G. T. Lumpkin & J. A. Katz (Eds.), *Social and sustainable entrepreneurship: 201-230*. Emerald.

Tiba, S., & Frikha, M. (2020). Sustainability challenge in the agenda of African countries: Evidence from simultaneous equation models. *Journal of the Knowledge Economy*, *11*, 1270–1294. https://doi.org/10.1007/s13132-019-00605-4

Tilson, D., Lyytinen, K., & Sørensen, C. (2010). Research commentary—Digital infrastructures: The missing IS research agenda. *Information Systems Research*, *21*(4), 748–759.

Tolj, S. (2005). *Razgovor sa Slavenom Toljem*. http://www.zarez.hr/clanci/razgovor-sa-slavenom-toljem

Treacy, M., & Wiersema, F. (1995). *The discipline of market leaders*. Addison-Wesley.

Unanoğlu, M. (2019). *Girişimcilik, stratejik farkındalık ve inovasyon*. Seçkin Yayınevi.

Upadhyay, D. K., & Mishra, M. (2020). Blue economy: Emerging global trends and India's multilateral cooperation. *Maritime Affairs: Journal of the National Maritime Foundation of India*, *16*(1), 30–45. doi:10.1080/09733159.2020.1785087

Urban, G. L., & Hauser, J. R. (1980). *Design and marketing of new products*. Prentice-Hall.

Urbaniec, M. (2018). Sustainable entrepreneurship: Innovation-related activities in European enterprises. *Polish Journal of Environmental Studies*, *27*, 1773–1779. https://doi.org/10.15244/pjoes/78155

Urbano, D., & Aparicio, S. (2016). Technological forecasting & social change entrepreneurship capital types and economic growth: International evidence. *Technological Forecasting and Social Change*, *102*, 34–44. doi:10.1016/j.techfore.2015.02.018

V, V., & T.J, K. (1998). A Scale to Assess Entrepreneurial Motivation. *Journal of Entrepreneurship, 7*(2), 183-198.

Valckenaers, P., Cavalieri, S., Germain, B. S., Verstraete, P., Hadeli, Bandinelli, R., Terzi, S., & Van Brussel, H. (2006). A benchmarking service for the manufacturing control research community. *Journal of Intelligent Manufacturing, 17*(6), 667–679. doi:10.100710845-006-0036-y

Valente, M. (2018). *Organizing for sustainability*. https://www.organizingforsustainability.com

Van de Graaf, H., & Grin, J. (1999). *Policy analysis and the 'reinvention of politics. The question of closure*. Paper prepared for presentation at the Symposium "Theory, Policy and Society", Leiden, The Netherlands.

Van den Ban, A. (2011). Increasing labour productivity in agriculture and its implications. *Journal of Agricultural Education and Extension, 17*(5), 401–409. doi:10.1080/1389224X.2011.596414

van der Geest, C. (2017). Redesigning Indian Ocean fisheries governance for 21st century sustainability. *Global Policy, 8*(2), 227–236. doi:10.1111/1758-5899.12447

van der Sluis, J., Van Praag, M., & Vijverberg, W. (2008). Education and entrepreneurship selection and performance: A review of the empirical literature. *Journal of Economic Surveys, 22*(5), 795–841. doi:10.1111/j.1467-6419.2008.00550.x

van Dijk, P. (2018). *Dealing with institutional voids in emerging markets: A small and medium sized enterprise perspective* [Master's Thesis]. Radboud Universiteit Nijmegen Digital Archive. https://theses.ubn.ru.nl/bitstream/handle/123456789/6823/Dijk%2C_Philip_van_1.pdf?sequence=1

Van Eck, N. J., & Waltman, L. (2010). Software survey: VOSviewer, a computer program for bibliometric mapping. *Scientometrics, 84*(2), 523–538.

Van Est, R. (1999). *Winds of Change. A comparative study of the politics of wind energy innovation in California and Denmark*. International Books.

Van Kersbergen, K., & van Waarden, F. (2001). Shifts in Governance: Problems and Legitimacy and Accountability. Background Report NWO strategie nota 2002-2005, Den Haag: NOW.

Van Praag, C. M., & Versloot, P. H. (2007). What is the value of entrepreneurship? A review of recent research. *Small Business Economics, 29*(4), 351–382. doi:10.100711187-007-9074-x

van Van Tatenhove, J., Arts, B., & Leroy, P. (Eds.). (2000). *Political Modernisation and the Environment: The Renewal of Environmental Policy Arrangements*. Kluwer Academic Publishers. doi:10.1007/978-94-015-9524-7

Vargo, S. L. (2020). From promise to perspective: Reconsidering value propositions from a service-dominant logic orientation. *Industrial Marketing Management, 87*, 309–311.

Venugopalan, M., Bastian, B. L., & Viswanathan, P. K. (2021). The role of multi-actor engagement for women's empowerment and entrepreneurship in Kerala, India. *Administrative Sciences, 11*(1), 31. https://doi.org/10.3390/admsci11010031

Verba, S., Schlozman, L. K., & Brady, H. A. (1995). *Voice and Equality –Civic Voluntarism in American Politics*. Harvard University Press. doi:10.2307/j.ctv1pnc1k7

Verma, J., Sood, K., & Grima, S. (2021). Factors affecting Indian parents' adoption of online learning applications for their children. *Review of International Geographical Education Online*, *11*(9), 1328–1338.

Vicari Haddock, S. (2004). *La città contemporanea*. Il Mulino.

Vivekanandan, E., Hermes, R., & O'Brien, C. (2016). Climate change effects in the Bay of Bengal large marine ecosystem. *Environmental Development*, *17*, 46–56. doi:10.1016/j.envdev.2015.09.005

Vogel, D., & Kagan, R. (2004). *The Dynamics of Regulatory Change: How Globalization Affects National Regulation Policy*. University of California Press.

Volvo. (2021, November 18). *A heritage of safety innovations*. Retrieved from Volvo Cars: https://www.volvocars.com/intl/v/car-safety/safety-heritage

Waddock, S. A. (1988). Building successful partnerships. *Sloan Management Review*, *29*(4), 17–23.

Wagner, P. (1996) Certainty and order, liberty, and contingency. The birth of social science as empirical political philosophy. In The rise of the social sciences and the formation of modernity. Kluwer.

Wagner, P. (2000). *Theorizing modernity*. Sage.

Wahga, A. I., Blundel, R., & Schaefer, A. (2018). Understanding the drivers of sustainable entrepreneurial practices in Pakistan's leather industry: A multi-level approach. *International Journal of Entrepreneurial Behaviour & Research*, *24*(2), 382–407. doi:10.1108/IJEBR-11-2015-0263

Wallace, H., & Wallace, W. (Eds.). (2000). *Policymaking in the European Union* (4th ed.). Oxford University Press.

Wampler, B. (2007). *Participatory Budgeting in Brazil: Contestation, Cooperation, and Accountability*. Pennsylvania State University Press.

Wampler, B., & McNulty, S. L. (2011). *Does Participatory Governanace Matter? Exploring the Nature and Impact of Participatory Reforms*. Woodrow Wilson International Centre for Scholars.

Wampler, B., & Mcnulty, S. L. (2011). *Does participatory governance matter? Exploring the nature and impact of participatory reforms*. Woodrow Wilson International Center for Scholars, Comparative Urban Studies Project.

Wang, C.-H. (2014). A longitudinal study of innovation competence and quality management on firm performance. *Innovation (North Sydney, N.S.W.)*, *16*(3), 392–403.

Webster, F. E. (2002). *Market-driven management: How to define, develop and deliver customer value* (2nd ed.). John Wiley & Sons.

Weick, K. (1995). Definition of theory. In N. Nicholson (Ed.), *Blackwell dictionary of organizational behavior* (pp. 565–567). Blackwell.

White, L., & Kitimbo, A. (2018). Institutions and the location strategies of South African firms in Africa. *The Internationalization of African Firms, 61*(1), 61-73. doi:10.1002/tie.21965

Wilson, G. A. (2013). Community resilience, policy corridors and the policy challenge. *Land Use Policy, 31*, 298–310. doi:10.1016/j.landusepol.2012.07.011

WIPO. (2021a). https://www.wipo.int/global_innovation_index/en/

WIPO. (2021b). https://gpseducation.oecd.org/CountryProfile?plotter=h5&primaryCountry=TUR&treshold=5&topic=PI

Wolf, D. (2005). Neo-Funktionalismus. In H. J. Bieling & M. Lerch (Eds.), *Theorien der europäischen Integration* (pp. 65–91). VS Verlag für Sozialwissenschaften. doi:10.1007/978-3-663-11642-4_3

World Bank Enterprise Survey. (2019). https://www.enterprisesurveys.org/en/data/exploreeconomies/2019/turkey#firm-characteristics

World Economic Forum. (2014). *Entrepreneurial ecosystems around the globe and early-stage company growth dynamics: the entrepreneur's perspective*. Author.

Yoon, B. S. (2004). Determinants of entrepreneurial intentions: Individual characteristics and environmental factors. *Korean Academic and Industrial Society of Business Administration, 17*(2), 89–110.

York, J. G., O'Neil, I., & Sarasvathy, S. D. (2016). Exploring environmental entrepreneurship: Identity coupling, venture goals, and stakeholder incentives. *Journal of Management Studies*, (53), 695–737.

Zachary, R., & Mishra, C. (2011). The future of entrepreneurship research: Calling all researchers. *Entrepreneurship Research Journal, 1*(1), 1–15. doi:10.2202/2157-5665.1016

Zahra, S. A., Gedajlovic, E., Neubaum, D. O., & Shulman, J. M. (2009). A typology of social entrepreneurs: Motives, search processes and ethical challenges. *Journal of Business Venturing*, (24), 519–532.

Zahra, S. A., & Wright, M. (2016). Understanding the social role of entrepreneurship. *Journal of Management Studies*, (53), 610–629.

Zeithaml, C. P., & Rice, G. H. (1987). Entrepreneurship/Small business education in American universities. *Journal of Small Business Management, 25*(1), 44–50.

Zellweger, T., Sieger, P., & Halter, F. (2011). Should I stay or should I go? Career choice intentions of students with family business background. *Journal of Business Venturing, 26*(5), 521–536. doi:10.1016/j.jbusvent.2010.04.001

Zheng, C. (2012). Isomorph isomorphic influences and aspiration: Reference group choice in entry mode decisions. *Journal of International Business Research*, *11*(2), 129–141.

Zupic, I., & Čater, T. (2015). Bibliometric methods in management and organization. *Organizational Research Methods*, *18*(3), 429–472. https://doi.org/10.1177/1094428114562629

About the Contributors

Shivani Inder has done Ph.D. in finance. She is a certified Cost and Management Accountant (CMA). She has done M.B.A (finance) and M.F.C. She is currently working as Associate Professor at Chitkara Business School, Chitkara University, Punjab, India. Her domain areas are corporate finance, accounting, and entrepreneurship. She has more than ten years of teaching experience. She is associated with professional bodies and review for reputed journals.

Amandeep Singh has done BIT MBA PhD and he is also UGC-NET qualified. Currently, he is working as Professor Chitkara Business School, Chitkara University, Punjab, India. He is having more than 14 years of teaching experience. He has served as Dean / Principal in various reputed Universities and colleges. He has published 28 research papers in various journals and conferences. He has also chaired many National and International Conferences. He is on the editorial board for 3 International Journals. He was awarded as the Best Teacher in 2008.

Sandhir Sharma is Ph.D. in Strategic Management with nearly 22 years of experience in higher education and 5 years in Telecom industry. With more than 53 research papers to his credit published in various journals and conferences at national & international level, Dr. Sharma has developed his core expertise in the area of Strategy formulation. Currently, he is serving as Dean, Chitkara Business School & visiting faculty to Binus University, Indonesia, Kedge Business School, France and University of Applied Sciences, Osnabruck, Germany. He is widely travelled all across the globe and an active member of various management associations and University bodies. He is serving as consultant to various SME organizations in the area of strategy formulation. He is Major Guide to 8 Ph.D. Scholars from Academia and Industry. As of now, eight of his students have already completed their Ph.D. successfully in the fields of Neuromarketing| Consumers| Foods| Organic Foods, Work Engagement, Brands |Brands Personality| Brand love, Television |Broadcasting| Digital Television and Green Marketing| Consumer Behaviour. He has filed 14 patents in the fields of Health sciences, life sciences, social sciences, technology, and industrial products.

* * *

Raina Ahuja is a working professional in online learning industry with great passion for education. A technically sound professional with expertise in ed-tech domain whilst providing consultancy and designing customised solutions.

Muskaan Arora is an Assistant Professor in the Chitkara Business School at the Chitkara University.

Shradhha Awasthi is an experienced Associate Professor with a demonstrated history of working in the higher education industry. Skilled in Curriculum Development, Faculty Development, E-Learning, Teaching, and Education. Strong education professional with a Master of Business Administration (MBA) focused in Human Resources Management/Personnel Administration, General from Uttar Pradesh Technical University.

Rohit Bansal is working as Assistant Professor in Department of Management Studies in Vaish College of Engineering, Rohtak. He obtained Ph.D. in Management from Maharshi Dayanand University, Rohtak. With a rich experience of 13 years, he has achieved growth through robust and proactive academic initiatives. He has authored & edited 14 books with renowned publishers. In addition, he has published 105 research papers and chapters in Journals of repute as well as edited books. He has also presented papers in 35 conferences and seminars. His area of interest includes marketing management, organizational behaviour, digital marketing, services marketing, blockchain technology and human resource management. He is on Editorial Advisory Board as a member in 110 national and international peer reviewed journals. He is Managing Editor of International Journal of 360° Management Review & International Journal of Techno – Management Research. He Received "Excellence in Teaching Award" in Edge India Times Award organized by Edge India Publications Private Limited held on 15th November 2020 through virtual mode. He has acted as session chair in many conferences.

Devesh Bathla is an industry practitioner and a Business Analytics' Trainer to Working professionals and Management students who demand innovation & continuous improvement. Experienced in marketing analytics, consistently achieved business objectives, reduced marketing/operating costs, and improved productivity.

Xiaochang Chang is an independent researcher. Her research interests include FinTech, Chinese economy and business analytics.

Sachin Chauhan is working as Associate Professor, at Quantum School of Business, Quantum University Roorkee. He has a rich academic plus administrative experience of 14 years in different management institutions.

Nigel Chiweshe is a lecturer at the University of KwaZulu-natal. He is currently pursuing Doctoral studies specialising in Marketing with a focus on motivations for luxury brand consumption by deluxe aspirers. He also lectures Responsible & Sustainable Management Principles, Technology Management at the undergraduate level and Entrepreneurship Innovation and Venture Creation, at the Honours level and Contemporary Marketing at the Masters level. Through his engagement with the disciplines of management, marketing and entrepreneurship, Nigel has developed a keen interest in social enterprises, sustainability practices in SMMEs and luxury branding. He is currently involved in mentoring youth entrepreneurs, communities of practice in youth entrepreneurship, book editorship and research in social enterprises in the 4th Industrial Revolution.

Nuno Crespo holds a PhD in Economics and a Master degree in International Economics. He is the Director of the Master in Business Economics and Competition. In the most recent years, Nuno Crespo was Vice-Rector of ISCTE-IUL and assumed several other positions such as Director of the Department of Economics, Scientific Commission of the Department of Economics, and the coordination of courses (Master in Portuguese Economy and International Integration and Master in Health Services Management). Researcher at Business Research Unit (BRU-IUL), he has several publications in scientific journals such as World Economy, World Development, Economics Letters, Review of World Economics, Journal of Common Market Studies, Journal of Economic Surveys, Empirical Economics, Papers in Regional Science, Tourism Analysis, Journal of Economics and Social Measurement, Telecommunications Policy, Journal of Informetrics, Scientometrics, International Review of Applied Economics, International Journal of Social Economics. Publications of books and book chapters in his areas of expertise. He is Co-Editor-in-Chief of the Academy of Entrepreneurship Journal and member of the editorial board of several international scientific journals (European Journal of International Management, International Journal of Trade and Global Markets, International Journal of Knowledge and Learning, Sustainability, and Tourism Analysis, among others). Editor of the MPRA. Member of the International Economics Advisory Board of the Cambridge Scholars Publishing. Global Partner of the National Economic

Education Delegation (NEED). Board of the Portuguese Economists Association (Ordem dos Economistas). Member of the Advisory Council of A3ES.

Ankit Dhiraj is working in SOHMT, LPU as a research scholar and qualified JRF. Area of the specialization of tourism (Buddhist Tourism).

Archana Goel is an Assistant Professor at Chitkara University, Punjab Campus.

Sanjeev Kumar has pursued Ph.D. from Amity University Rajasthan Jaipur. He is currently associated with Lovely Professional University. His areas of interests are data analysis, LR in Hospitality area, Food and Beverages.

Kiran Mehta (PhD) is an educator, trainer, consultant, and researcher. She has almost twenty years of experience. She has published several research articles in a variety of international publications, including Emerald, Taylor & Francis, and Sage. She is the author of "Financial Services," a textbook published by CENGAGE. She has created study materials for a number of Indian institutes. Her areas of interest include climate finance, sustainable business, portfolio management, stock market efficiency, technology and education, entrepreneurship, and venture capital.

Beyza Oba is Professor of Organization Studies at İstanbul Bilgi University, Department of Business Administration. Her research interests include empirical studies on trust, governance, hegemony and innovation in different contexts. She has published in journals like Business History, Entrepreneurship and Regional Development, Journal of Technology Analysis and Strategic Management and Corporate Governance. She also has several journal articles in Turkish. Additionally, she has presented research papers in EIASM European Institute in Advanced Studies in Management), EGOS (European Group of Organization Studies) and British Academy of Management conferences.

Naisha Ramlal is an emerging researcher in the fields of management and entrepreneurship. Her research focus is on sustainability in Small, Medium and Micro Enterprises and large corporates.

Divya Rani is working in the Department of Economics, Pataliputra University Patna as a research scholar. She has interested in analysis of economic impact of tourism.

Asmita Sharma is an Assistant Professor at Chitkara University.

Renuka Sharma is a Professor (Finance) at Chitkara Business School at Chitkara University in Punjab. She has over 18 years of teaching and research experience (more than ten years post-doctoral and eight years before to obtaining her PhD). She has authored numerous research papers, a few of which have been published in international/national journals (Taylor & Francis, Emerald, Sage, Inderscience, etc.) and the rest have been presented at international/national conferences (IIM Bangalore, Shillong, Calcutta, Indore, and Kozhikode, among others), with numerous papers selected for Best Paper Awards. She also serves as a reviewer for numerous prestigious journals published by Emerald, Elsevier, and Inderscience, among others. Currently, she is guiding two PhD scholars and has successfully defended five others. She has been a consultant for several start-ups and MSMEs. She is the author of two textbooks for Cengage Pub. and Vikas Pub. Additionally, she has developed study materials for a variety of business-related courses for prominent Indian universities and institutions She has served as a resource person for several MDPs and FDPs related to research and finance. She is an entrepreneur too.

Nadia Simoes holds a PhD in Economics and a Master degree in Economics from ISEG (Universidade de Lisboa). Started to teach in the Economics Department of ISCTE - Instituto Universitário de Lisboa in 2002. Director of the Bachelor Degree in Economics (Iscte - Instituto Universitário de Lisboa). Former Director of the Master in Business Economics and Competition for nine editions of the programme. Researcher of the Economics Group of the Business Research Unit (BRU-IUL). She has published paper articles in several journals such as Economics Letters, Journal of Economic Surveys, Empirical Economics, Acta Oeconomica, International Review of Applied Economics, Telecommunications Policy, Panoeconomicus, International Journal of Social Economics, Economics Bulletin, among others. Associate Editor of the journal International Journal of Education Economics and Development (SCOPUS Q4) and Editor of the journal Cogent Economics & Finance (SCOPUS Q3). Member of the Editorial Board of the following journals: Entrepreneurship and Sustainability Issues (SCOPUS Q1); Journal of Entrepreneurship Education (SCOPUS Q2); Panoeconomicus (SCOPUS Q2); Journal of Entrepreneurship in Emerging Economies (SCOPUS Q2); Academy of Entrepreneurship Journal (SCOPUS Q3); the International Journal of Entrepreneurship (SCOPUS Q3); and Revista Galega de Economia (SCOPUS Q4). NEP Editor for the area of Education (nep-edu). Member of the Editorial Board of the European Training Foundation (European Union). She has participated in several research national and international research projects financed by public institutions (including two projects funded by FCT and a project funded by the Ministry of Employment). Expert for different national and international institutions such as the European Employment Observatory (European Commission), International Labour Organization, Cedefop, Eurofound, European Centre of Expertise, Portuguese Labour Ministry, and Portuguese Ministry of Education.

Jashandeep Singh (known as Jashan Kheiva) obtained his PhD from M.M. University, Haryana and MBA from RIMT, Punjab. He possesses 12 years of work experience in the field of academics, academic administration and research in premier institutions of Punjab and Haryana. He is specialized in the area of marketing, organizational behaviour and human values. He is IKGPTU's certified resource person in Human Values and Ethics. He has been trained at IIM Kozhikode, SPJIMR, IIM Ahmedabad, and IIM Rohtak, and attended several workshops and development programs at various institutions of repute. He has published numerous research papers and a book as well. He has also been appointed as an editorial board member and reviewer for numerous refereed journals. He has also served as a resource person at MGSIPA, Punjab and SEBI for imparting financial literacy among various sections of the society. He is a resource person of Value Ideas Investment and a freelance Personality development trainer too. He has filed nine patents so far. He has completed many Pro-Bono projects for the upliftment of the society. He has been a member of Nasha Mukt Abhiyan, Punjab (Punjab Govt run) team.

Ram Singh is an Associate Professor & Head of the Department of Commerce, Quantum School of Business, Quantum University Roorkee India. Dr. Singh has completed his Ph.D. degree in Commerce from HNB Garhwal Central University Srinagar Uttarakhand India. Currently, Dr. Singh is a member and secretary of Research Council of Quantum University, member of BOF/BOS (Commerce), a member of Editorial Board of numeral Journals, and Reviewer in various peer reviewed National and International Journals of Accounting, Finance & General Management. He has published 2 books and several research papers & articles in different SCOPUS/UGC listed/Peer-Reviewed journals. Besides this, he has also attended various FDPs, workshops, national & international webinars conducted by renowned institutions & organizations. He also presented papers in various national & International Seminars & Conferences and published more than a dozen articles/ Chapters in proceedings of seminars & Conferences.

Kyla L. Tennin is an industry practitioner and DM in Management and Organizational Leadership. She focuses on Change Management and mixed methods empirical research for continuous improvement, business transformation, and recovery during and after internal/external crises to institutions. She is a leader in various roles at investment forums where she works with Presidents of Nations, Heads of Banks, Prime Ministers, High Commissioners, and Chambers of Commerce and other business leaders to strategize and make business decisions to help businesses start-up, advance, and/or scale to improve economic development, promote social justice, and create jobs in various nations. Dr. Tennin is an MD track turned DM (doctor) with background in biology, biotechnology, and organic and biochemistry, has project management and lean six sigma certifications, a Master of Business Administration (MBA), and is a Ph.D. Fellow at the Global Peace Institute, headquartered in the United Kingdom. She contributed to the accreditation process at the University of Phoenix College of Doctoral Studies and completed additional studies (to launch and scale corporations) at Harvard, Stanford, Yale, University of Cape Town, and University of Glasgow to name a few. She has personally written approximately 18 books, 3 book chapters with colleagues, 3 patents, several other intellectual properties, and nearly 85 research reports, later conceptualized into products and services for global businesses. Dr. Tennin has presented research and posters in practitioner and academic conferences, workshops, and international webinars. She has professional experience in the financial services and investments, hospitality, restaurant, consumer products/beauty, and healthcare industries, with 95% of her experience spent in financial services and higher education. Dr. Tennin has 23 years of experience in higher education and 17 years owning her own global conglomerate corporation, *which she built while homeless, to recover*. Operating in 31 countries, with 24 locations, on 6 continents, and 2 world headquarters. She was awarded over 30 corporate awards, mentored entrepreneurs for 20 years with global organizations and world-renowned corporations and banks as sponsors, and currently owns a business academy where entrepreneurship, resilience, finance, pricing and tax strategy, research methodology and data analysis for consultants, digital transformation, and other courses are taught.

Murat Unanoğlu has 20 years of work experience covering business life and academia in entrepreneurship, strategy development and innovation. He is a graduate of ITÜ Mechanical Engineering and received an Executive MBA degree from Boğaziçi University and a PhD degree in Management from İstanbul Bilgi University. During his management consultancy career, he run and managed projects covering institutionalization and strategic planning for companies in different sectors. In order to support young artists, he initiated an e-commerce site www.myfirstartist.com, which operates in the field of art in Turkey, in 2013. He is the author of the book titled "Entrepreneurship, Strategic Awareness and Innovation". He has been teaching entrepreneurship course in the İstanbul Bilgi University MBA programs for the last five years. He still continues his academic studies as a full-time assistant professor doctor in the Department of Business Administration at IAU.

José G. Vargas-Hernández, M.B.A., Ph.D., Member of the National System of Researchers of Mexico and a research professor at Tecnológico Mario Molina

Unidad Zapopan formerly at University Center for Economic and Managerial Sciences, University of Guadalajara. Professor Vargas-Hernández has a Ph. D. in Public Administration and a Ph.D. in Organizational Economics. He has undertaken studies in Organisational Behaviour and has a Master of Business Administration, published four books and more than 200 papers in international journals and reviews (some translated to English, French, German, Portuguese, Farsi, Chinese, etc.) and more than 300 essays in national journals and reviews. He has obtained several international Awards and recognition.

Jyoti Verma is a faculty of BBA Fintech at Chitkara Business School, Chitkara University, Punjab, India. She has obtained a doctorate from Punjabi University, Patiala. She has qualified UGC NET in Management. Her areas of expertise are service quality, entrepreneurship, Blockchain and general management. She has versatile teaching and research experience along with publications in Scopus Indexed, UGC Care, and many refereed journals. She has also presented papers at international and national conferences. She has published 2 patents and is working on MOOC Courses as a Subject Matter Expert and Course Planner. She has prepared and delivered many E-Content programs on Research Methodology, which is comprised of video lectures, interactive script, learning objects repository, and textual content for the web learning platform of UGC-CEC (MHRD Projects). She is an Associate Editor (Finance & International Business) in Journal of Technology Management for Growing Economies, Chitkara University Publications. She is also appointed as a Reviewer in the International Journal of E-Business Research, IGI Global (Scopus Indexed Journal). She has reviewed many book chapters and research papers of Emerald, Wiley, IGI Global publishers. She successfully managed the accreditation process at Chitkara Business School and achieved NAAC A+ rating. Also successfully managed the accreditation process at Lovely Professional University and achieved ACBSP accreditation. She is very optimistic and believes in continuous learning and hard work. She has completed many online courses offered by IIM Bangalore, University of Illinois, Google Digital Unlocked, Coursera, and many more. She has attended many FDPs, webinars, seminars, symposiums, colloquiums at the national and international levels.

Poshan (Sam) Yu is a Lecturer in Accounting and Finance in the International Cooperative Education Program of Soochow University (China). He is also an External Professor of FinTech and Finance at SKEMA Business School (China), a Visiting Professor at Krirk University (Thailand) and a Visiting Researcher at the Australian Studies Centre of Shanghai University (China). Sam leads FasterCapital (Dubai, UAE) as a Regional Partner (China) and serves as a Startup Mentor for AIC RAISE (Coimbatore, India). His research interests include financial technology, regulatory technology, public-private partnerships, mergers and acquisitions, private equity, venture capital, start-ups, intellectual property, art finance, and China's "One Belt One Road" policy.

Index

G

I

J

L

M

P

R

S

www.ingramcontent.com/pod-product-compliance
Lightning Source LLC
LaVergne TN
LVHW061545290926
849162LV00004B/909